INTERNATIONAL TRADE AND MIGRATION IN THE APEC REGION

INTERNATIONAL TRADE AND MIGRATION IN THE APEC REGION

Edited by

P.J. Lloyd

& Lynne S. Williams

Melbourne
OXFORD UNIVERSITY PRESS
Oxford   Auckland   New York

OXFORD UNIVERSITY PRESS AUSTRALIA

Oxford   New York
Athens   Auckland   Bangkok   Bombay
Calcutta   Cape Town   Dar es Salaam   Delhi
Florence   Hong Kong   Istanbul   Karachi
Kuala Lumpur   Madras   Madrid   Melbourne
Mexico City   Nairobi   Paris   Port Moresby
Singapore   Taipei   Tokyo   Toronto

and associated companies in
Berlin Ibadan

OXFORD is a trade mark of Oxford University Press

National Library of Australia
Cataloguing-in-Publication data:

International trade and migration in the APEC region.

Bibliography.
Includes index.
ISBN 0 19 5537637.

1. Asia Pacific Economic Cooperation (Organization). 2. International trade. 3. Alien labor – Asia,
Southeastern. 4. Alien labor – Pacific Area. 5. Asia, Southeastern – Emigration and immigration.
6. Asia – Commerce. 7. Pacific Area – Emigration and immigration. 8. Pacific Area – Commerce.
I. Lloyd, P. J. (Peter John). II. Williams, Lynne S.

382.091823

Indexed by Russell Brooks
Text design by Heather Jones
Cover design by Heather Jones
Typeset by Superskill Graphics Pty Ltd
Printed by Oxford University Press Hong Kong
Published by Oxford University Press,
253 Normanby Road, South Melbourne, Australia

BUREAU OF IMMIGRATION,
MULTICULTURAL AND
POPULATION RESEARCH

Foreword

The Bureau of Immigration, Multicultural and Population Research has a strong tradition in international research. Its output includes comparisons of Australia with the United States, Canada and New Zealand; a major review of international labour movements, and their relevance for Australia; and several initiatives concerned with Asia–Pacific migration.

The Bureau has also been actively involved with international agencies. For example, it has published jointly with the International Labor Office (ILO) in Geneva, a study of discrimination, and was commissioned by the Secretary-General of the Organisation for Economic Co-operation and Development (OECD) in Paris to provide a possible research agenda for that organisation. Currently, the Bureau is taking a lead role in an initiative from the Canadian government and the Carnegie Peace Foundation in Washington to review the international effects of immigration on cities.

International Trade and Migration in the APEC Region, edited by Professor Peter Lloyd of The University of Melbourne, and Dr Lynne Williams of the Bureau, adds further to the Bureau's impressive record in studies of the international aspects of labour movement.

The origin of the idea for the volume stems from a paper (Does Trade Liberalisation Influence Migration? Some Evidence from OECD Countries) presented by Dr Anne Richards of the OECD to a conference in Madrid in 1993 entitled Migration and International Co-operation: Challenges for OECD Countries (Richards 1993). Dr Richards described some preliminary work which sought to identify correlations between trade liberalisation and the movement of people between countries. Her study emphasised that the substantial literature on international trade was insufficiently linked to the equally weighty volume of research on labour movement between nations.

The book organised by Professor Lloyd and Dr Williams goes some way towards filling this gap and is an excellent one. It covers very well the trade–labour relationships in a geographic region of great importance to Australian policy – the Asia–Pacific. The authors examine topics for the APEC region including patterns and links in trade and migration, and the consequences of regional trade liberalisation and people movement.

Preparation for the book included a now well-tried method in the Bureau's annals – meetings of the authors in conference to discuss and analyse each other's preliminary work. As on previous occasions, the results are testimony to this technique.

I wish to thank the authors and editors for their prompt and proficient efforts. Their study adds considerably to knowledge and perspective of a key aspect of growing trade liberalisation in Australia's region – the related expanding freedom of movement of people.

John Nieuwenhuysen
Director, Bureau of Immigration,
Multicultural and Population Research

Contents

List of tables

List of figures

Contributors

Mr Bijit Bora (Flinders University of South Australia)

Professor Wilfred Ethier (University of Pennsylvania)

Mr Will Foster

Dr Gary P. Freeman (University of Texas)

Professor Graeme Hugo (University of Adelaide)

Professor Peter Lloyd (University of Melbourne)

Dr Philip Martin (University of California Davis)

Dr Jongryn Mo (University of Texas)

Dr Ganesh Nana (Victoria University of Wellington)

Dr Jacques Poot (Victoria University of Wellington)

Dr Muhamed Quibria (Asian Development Bank)

Ms Tess Rod (Bureau of Immigration, Multicultural and Population Research)

Dr Chia Siow Yue (National University of Singapore)

Dr Ronald Skeldon (University of Hong Kong)

Professor Alan Taylor (Northwestern University)

Dr Lynne Williams (Bureau of Immigration, Multicultural and Population Research)

Acknowledgments

This book has been undertaken as a joint effort by Professor Peter Lloyd, Director, Asian Business Centre, The University of Melbourne and the Bureau of Immigration, Multicultural and Population Research as represented by Dr Lynne Williams, one of its Assistant Directors. Papers were written and presented at a conference held in July 1995 at the University of Melbourne.

There is a range of people we would like to thank for helping to bring this project to fruition. First and foremost, we are indebted to the authors for their excellent contributions, for their observance of both time and word deadlines, and for following our style guidelines. We would like to thank The University of Melbourne for making conference facilities available, and the University's (then)Vice-Chancellor, Professor David Penington, for opening the conference. We are also grateful to Sarah Carne and Jean-Luc Garlick, both of the Institute of Applied Economic and Social Research at the University, and Vicki Thompson, from the Bureau of Immigration, Multicultural and Population Research, for their help in organising the conference. The final manuscript benefited from incorporation of the insightful comments of Professor David Vines, Balliol College, Oxford.

Finally, we are indebted to Carol Corzo of the Bureau of Immigration, Multicultural and Population Research for her sterling efforts in pulling contributions from the various authors together into a consistent and presentable format.

The usual caveat that any remaining errors are our responsibility, rather than our employers', applies.

P.J. Lloyd and Lynne S. Williams
Editors

List of acronyms

ABS	Australian Bureau of Statistics
ANCERTA	Australia/New Zealand Closer Economic Relations Trade Agreement (also known as CER)
APEC	Asia Pacific Economic Co-operation
ASEAN	Association of South-East Asian Nations
BIMP-EAGA	Brunei–Indonesia–Malaysia–Philippines–East ASEAN Growth Area
BIMPR	Bureau of Immigration, Multicultural and Population Research
BOP	balance of payments
CAAIP	Committee to Advise on Australia's Immigration Policy
CER	Closer Economic Relations (agreement between Australia and New Zealand)
CGE	computable general equilibrium
CIF	cost insurance freight
CUSTA	Canada–United States Trade Agreement
DEET	Department of Employment, Education and Training (Australia)
EC	European Community
EU	European Union
FDI	foreign direct investment
FOB	free on board
GATS	General Agreement on Trade in Services
GATT	General Agreement on Tariffs and Trade
GDP	gross domestic product
GMS	Greater Mekong Sub-Region
GNP	gross national product
GSC	Greater South China
IIT	intra-industry trade
ILO	International Labor Office
IMF	International Monetary Fund
IMS-GT	Indonesia–Malaysia–Singapore Growth Triangle
INS	Immigration and Naturalisation Service

IRCA	Immigration Reform and Control Act
LDC	less developed country
LSIA	Longitudinal Survey of Immigrants to Australia
MDC	more developed country
MFA	multi-fibre arrangement
MNC	multinational corporation
NAFTA	North American Free Trade Agreement
NEP	new economic policy
NIC	newly industrialised country
NIE	newly industrialised economy
NPC	National Population Council
OECD	Organisation for Economic Co-operation and Development
PECC	Pacific Economic Co-operation Council
PPP	purchasing power parity
RCA	revealed comparative advantage
SAW	Special Agricultural Worker
SEZ	special economic zone
SME	small and medium enterprises
SREZ	sub-regional economic zone
TNC	transnational corporation
TRAD	Tumen River Area Development Program
TTTA	Trans-Tasman Travel Agreement
UNCTAD	United Nations Committee for Trade and Development
UNDP	United Nations Development Program
UNHCR	United Nations Human Rights Commission
USA	United States of America

Introduction

P.J. Lloyd and Lynne S. Williams

Context of study

Over the period of the 1980s and 1990s, world commodity trade has grown very rapidly by historical standards. The international movement of people for work has also grown at rates which are much higher than any observed since before the Great Depression. Simple observations inform us that the international movements of commodities and people are directly related. For example, the movement of people from one country to another is followed by remittances from the host country back to the source country; much temporary movement of business persons is associated with the production and international trade in goods and services by transnational corporations; and international trade in some services requires international movement of either service providers or customers. There are also likely to be indirect relationships between general equilibrium interactions at the country and world levels as the growth of international trade and output leads to changes in real incomes and factor prices.

The international movements of commodities and people, however, have almost always been regarded as separate phenomena. The links between these flows are a neglected aspect of the opening up of the national economies of the world. The basic objective of this book is to explore the nexus between the international movements of commodities and people.

The Asia–Pacific Region is an obvious region in which to explore this nexus. In the first place, the Asia–Pacific Region is the region of the world economy in which international commodity trade has grown most rapidly. This region has also experienced an acceleration in the movement of people within the region. Moreover, because of its outstanding growth rates of output and international trade, the Asia–Pacific Region has been attracting much attention from both the rich OECD countries and other developing countries alike. The region sees itself increasingly as a coherent economic region with growing linkages among its member countries. The Bogor Declaration of the Asia–Pacific Economic Co-operation (APEC) accepted in principle a goal of an Asia–Pacific economic community with 'free and open trade and investment' by the year 2010 for the industrialised countries and 2020 for the developing countries of the region. While the Bogor Declaration did not set a goal for the free movement of people, APEC is examining ways of facilitating the movement of people within the region for business purposes.

In this study, the Asia–Pacific Region has been defined as the set of countries which are members of the APEC organisation. There are currently eighteen member countries. Thus our definition includes the countries of East Asia excluding North Korea and the Pacific region of Russia, Vietnam, Laos and Cambodia, as well as the countries of South Asia and Latin America (other than Mexico). In addition to being members of APEC, these countries are those which followed economic policies that are generally outward looking and based on free markets.

The empirical study is confined in the main to the period since 1980. To provide a broader perspective, it has been useful for some authors to focus on the longer period since 1950 which has experienced almost uninterrupted expansion of international trade and migration flows.

Scope of the study

We have sought to identify and analyse the major links between the international movements of commodities on the one hand and of labour and people on the other in the Asia–Pacific Region. The papers fell into four parts.

Patterns of trade and migration

The first part of the book sets the scene for the detailed analyses of particular aspects of trade and migration flows in subsequent chapters. Patterns of trade and migration in the APEC region since 1980 are examined and analysed. In Chapter 1, 'Trade and Investment in the APEC Region: 1980 to 1993', Bora summarises the rapid changes occurring in the region. Overall, the data show that for the APEC region, this period has been one of rapid growth and change in trade patterns (both goods and services), and in sources of foreign direct investment within the region. Bora shows that the trading patterns of APEC as a whole are becoming increasingly outward looking. The GDP-to-trade ratio for APEC has increased steadily since 1980, and trade intensity indexes show that APEC has increased its trade with non-APEC countries. The newly industrialised economies (NIEs), countries which have traditionally been exporters of labour-intensive goods, have emerged as sources for capital and have moved to export technical, capital- and human capital-intensive products. ASEAN countries have in turn filled the gap in the production of labour-intensive products. Trade has also increased within the region, with marked increases in intra-industry trade and trade in services within APEC sub-regions.

In the companion chapter in the introductory part, 'Migration Intensification in the APEC Region: 1981 to 1994', Rod and Williams examine trends in both permanent and temporary movement in the APEC region over this period. While permanent migration to the four main receiving countries (USA, Canada, Australia and New Zealand) has fluctuated over the period under consideration, numbers have been increasing in the early 1990s. The biggest increases, however, have been in the movement of labour within the region for temporary periods. The chapter examines which countries import and/or export skilled and/or unskilled labour and shows how patterns within the region are changing. Evidence suggests that, despite disapproval from governments, temporary movement continues to be a source of people attempting to remain permanently, an outcome also observed in Europe as a result of guest worker schemes. A major change observed in the region is the increasing movement of unskilled workers between APEC countries.

Links between trade liberalisation and migration

The papers in this part look at an issue central to much of the debate about trade and migration: Are international trade in commodities and international movement of labour substitutes or complements? For example, in the public debate in the USA before Congressional approval of the North American Free Trade Agreement (NAFTA), one of the dominant themes of those pushing for the freeing of trade between Mexico and the USA and Canada was the belief that improved access for Mexico to markets in the USA and Canada would raise real incomes in Mexico. This was seen as reducing the incentives for migration from Mexico to the USA, in the long run at least, as well as being desirable in itself. Thus, in this case, it has been assumed that the relationship is one of substitutability between trade in commodities and the movement of labour.

The literature which has addressed this question has considered the indirect links between trade in goods and factors but has ignored direct links through input–output requirements and remittances of income. It treats the world economy as one economy and applies the methods of general equilibrium analysis to the world economy. This literature has been written almost exclusively by international trade economists who are more accustomed to analysing the general equilibrium interdependence among national economies.

Ethier in his chapter 'Theories About Trade Liberalisation and Migration: Substitutes or Complements?' notes that the question of whether the movement of goods and labour are substitutes or complements is ambiguous, as one may look at the quantities or the prices of goods and factors traded across national borders. The most common formulation of this question is to consider prices of goods and factors, and to begin with the liberalisation of international trade in goods and services which has been a dominant feature of the world economy in the period studied. The question then is: Does the liberalisation of international trade in goods and services, by means of reducing border barriers to such trade, reduce international differences in the real incomes of labour and capital factors, and thereby reduce the incentives for international migration of factors? Or does it increase these differences and incentives?

Ethier finds both substitutability and complementarity between trade in commodities and factors. When the cause of international trade in commodities is differences in factor endowments or consumer preferences or distortions, then they are generally substitutes. When the cause is international differences in technologies or production distortions, they are generally complements. When the cause is economies of scale or imperfectly competitive behaviour which gives rise to intra-industry trade, they are strongly complementary. The application of these theories to outcomes in the short term compared with the long term is discussed in more detail in the paper by Martin in Part III of this volume.

In 'Globalisation, Foreign Investment and Migration', Lloyd looks at the particular links which come about because of production activities across national borders with the multinational firm as the agent of production. Direct foreign investment has increased much more rapidly than trade in commodities. In some models with multinational firms, direct foreign investment substitutes for international trade in goods and services. This arises especially if international trade barriers and transport costs are high. However, in recent models in which the offshore production is destined for sale in third countries and uses intermediate and capital inputs supplied by the source country, direct foreign investment leads to increased quantities of trade in commodities. In these models, the liberalisation of international movements of capital, which has probably taken place at a faster rate than the liberalisation of trade in commodities, reinforce each other.

In addition, there are direct links between the international movement of capital and people. Multinational corporations fill shortages of executive and skilled labour in the host countries by moving or recruiting people across national borders, though such expatriate labour is small in relation to the workforce of these corporations and as a proportion of the host country workforce. Conversely, another form of direct link arises when the movement of permanent immigrants from countries with different cultures and languages has increased the diversity of the local population and thereby aided the development of exports of goods and services. There is evidence in Australia that immigrants from Asia have, with a substantial lag, helped the development of exports of new goods and services such as tourism to Asia.

In relation to indirect general equilibrium links between the international movement of capital and people, Lloyd uses a specific factor model rather than the Heckscher–Ohlin model which emphasises differences in factor endowments. He finds that an inflow of capital increases the incentive of foreign labour to migrate internationally to Australia and vice versa. In countries such as Australia, Canada and New Zealand, inflows of both capital and labour have complemented each other and exploited the abundant supply of a third primary factor: natural resources.

The set of direct links between trade and migration through worker remittances to their home countries is considered in Quibria's 'Migration, Remittances and Trade'. This has become very important for a number of developing countries in East (and South) Asia. These labour movements are temporary and have been destined for the oil-rich countries of West Asia and, starting in the late 1980s, for Japan and the other countries of East Asia which now have middle-level incomes.

Both the changes in source countries and the changes in destination countries show the sensitivity of these temporary labour movements to changes in per capita income levels. With rapid growth in countries such as Japan and Taiwan, labour shortages have emerged. Some of the imported labourers work in the production of non-tradeables such as construction, entertainment and domestic services. Others work in tradeable manufactures. In the latter case they may substitute for trade in goods and/or capital as the countries have the options of importing goods or moving offshore activities which are no longer competitive because of the rise in the relative price of labour. Malaysia is both a substantial host and destination country for temporary labour movements, receiving labour from the poorer neighbours of Indonesia, the Philippines and Bangladesh in particular, and sending labour to other richer countries in West and East Asia.

At the macroeconomic level, large remittances may lead to a real exchange rate appreciation which discourages international trade in other goods and services.

Regional trade liberalisation and migration

Because of the very rapid growth of regional trading arrangements around the world, including the Asia–Pacific Region, it was thought desirable to look at the nexus between the liberalisation of international trade and the movement of people at the regional level. NAFTA and the Closer Economic Relations Agreement between Australia and New Zealand (CER) are two interesting cases of regional trading arrangements from this point of view. The USA, Canada, Australia and New Zealand are the four countries which traditionally have accepted immigrants in large numbers who are permanent settlers and come from many source countries.

Martin looks at the NAFTA case in 'Effects of NAFTA on Labour Migration'. NAFTA is unusual in that it combines two high-income countries (Canada and the USA) with a country that has much lower per capita incomes (Mexico). NAFTA does not contain provisions for liberalising the movement of people, apart from provisions relating to the movement of business visitors and investors and professionals with a university degree. Martin focuses on Mexican immigration to the USA. The USA is the largest recipient of immigrants in the world and the flows from Mexico to the USA are the largest bilateral flows. This stems from the large disparity in income levels. The USA has sought to restrict legal flows of migrants from Mexico, with the result that most Mexican immigrants are illegal aliens, predominantly young male rural workers. But enforcement of these policies is difficult because of the presence of a land border between the two countries.

In this context, it was hoped that improved access to US markets for

Mexican exporters under NAFTA, including exporters of agricultural commodities, would raise real incomes in Mexico and reduce the number of Mexicans seeking entry into the USA. This process of development would be aided by foreign investment in Mexico, which would become a more attractive destination for foreign direct investors after the formation of NAFTA. This is another example of the substitute view of trade in commodities and the movement of people which derives from the Stolper–Samuelson effect of the changes in goods prices on factor prices and thereby on the incentives for factors to migrate.

Despite the predictions that NAFTA will raise real wages in Mexico, by up to 16 per cent perhaps, Martin predicts that the increase in incomes will initially increase the level of emigration to the USA and only later reduce it. This time profile of the migration pattern has been called the migration hump. This is an interesting variation on the (long-run) substitute view. He explains the hump by modifying the standard international trade model through introducing adjustment lags and imperfections in credit markets to finance migration as well as differences in technology, infrastructure and economies of scale that may give the USA a long-term comparative advantage in products that are produced in Mexico with a technology that is labour intensive but high cost. This raises questions as to how long the factors that produce the hump in the short run will persist and what will bring them to an end. These short-run effects may qualify the long-run outcomes predicted by Ethier in his chapter.

The case of Australia and New Zealand is very different. Per capita incomes are similar and residents of either country have been free to move and take up employment in the other country since the 1920s, that is long before the CER removed barriers to trade in goods and services. There is a long history of substantial movements in both directions, with the direction of net movement from New Zealand to Australia before CER showing emigration from the relatively more labour-abundant country. This is consistent with the substitute theory derived from the Heckscher–Ohlin model with the two factors, capital and labour, but there are wide annual fluctuations depending chiefly on current relative incomes and rates of unemployment.

The addition of free movement of goods and most services under the CER does not seem by itself to have affected the movement of people – partly because the effects on per capita income are small and partly because of the simultaneous liberalisation of trade vis-à-vis non-CER countries by both Australia and New Zealand.

Using a computable general equilibrium model, Nana and Poot in their chapter 'Trans-Tasman Migration and Closer Economic Relations' find that the movement to complete free trade vis-à-vis all countries by New Zealand and Australia would result in Australia becoming even more capital abundant relative to New Zealand, because free trade increases the return to capital more in Australia. Such trade liberalisation may encourage some movement of labour

from New Zealand to Australia, especially of professional workers, and movement of capital from Australia to New Zealand.

Chia in 'Sub-Regional Economic Zones in East Asia' examines this phenomenon. These are a uniquely East Asian phenomenon which began with the
establishment of the Indonesia–Malaysia–Singapore Growth Triangle (IMS-
GT) in 1990. They represent a different form of integration. There are no trade
preferences which apply to the sub-regional zones as a whole but the governments have acted to facilitate the movement of capital and the development of
infrastructure. They have helped Singapore, Hong Kong and Taiwan to overcome their growing labour shortages by moving activities to neighbouring labour-abundant areas of the sub-regional zones. The movement of capital and
commodities has substituted for the movement of cheap labour, though there is
some controlled movement of contract land labour and business persons. This
result flows directly from the application of the standard Heckscher–Ohlin
model.

In their chapter, 'Japan and the Asian NICs as New Countries of Destination', Freeman and Mo draw attention to an important aspect of the economies
in East Asia which have sustained rapid growth for one or two decades. Japan
and the Asian NICs have emerged as new countries of destination for international movements of labour. The demand for immigrant labour in these countries is a direct result of increasing demand for labour coupled with demographic
effects which have slowed down the rate of growth of the domestic labour
supplies. The switch from net emigration to net immigration is posing new
problems for the immigration policy of these new countries of destination. Their
policies appear to be converging. Freeman and Mo dub the emerging immigration policies a '3-S' strategy. They want *skilled* workers for *short-term* employment
in *specific* sectors. The selection of skilled workers is playing an important part in
the upgrading of the skills of the workforces in these countries and thereby
allowing them to continue with the upgrading of their export bundles and a high
rate of growth of the economies.

Trade liberalisation and migration: long-term consequences

This part views international migration as a multi-country phenomenon and
tries to identify the pattern among the countries collectively, and the global
pattern. It also examines the long-term effects of the relationships between trade
and migration.

The topic of convergence of real income (and other variables) among
countries has been examined in a number of empirical studies. To date, however,
the effects of emigration/immigration on convergence have not been considered.
In 'Growth and Convergence in the Asia–Pacific Region: the Role of Openness,

Trade and Migration', Taylor uses a structural as compared with the usual reduced form model to analyse the relationships between openness, trade and migration. Taylor finds that a complex pattern of convergence, with openness in finance and trade playing a major role. The key to high growth rates in the Asia–Pacific Region is relatively high investment rates, which in turn are caused by human capital complementarities, a low dependency rate and low distortions as reflected in commercial, financial and monetary policies. Neither financial depth nor natural resource endowments are found to affect growth to the same extent as high investment rates. While this book is concerned with investigating the links between growth, convergence and migration, Taylor finds that because of the historically low rates of migration (compared with the pre-First World War era) recent data provide no indication as to what might occur should migration between countries be totally unconstrained.

In 'The Impact of Immigration on Incomes in the Destination Country' Foster focuses on the effects of immigration on the four main receiving countries. However, Foster also considers the effects of both temporary movement and emigration, and discusses some of the more recent receiving countries such as Singapore. As is the case in the majority of analyses of the economic effects of immigration, Foster's analysis suggests that while any effects on income depend both on the characteristics of the country and the characteristics of the immigrants, such effects are likely to be small at the aggregate level. However, if a large, highly skilled immigrant intake is sustained over a long period then income per capita is likely to be significantly higher than it otherwise would be. How realistic such a policy might be is questionable, given that the rationale for immigration programs in the four main receiving countries is based on family reunion and humanitarian grounds, as well as having components which are skills focused.

A much-debated issue in the literature relates to the consequences of the movement of the more highly educated and skilled members of less developed countries (LDCs) to more developed countries (MDCs). The term 'brain drain' conjures up images of LDCs being further disadvantaged relative to MDCs as a result of such movement. Hugo, in 'Brain Drain and Student Movements', addresses this and several other issues related to the brain drain from the perspective of a geographer. While 'student migration' and 'brain drain' were almost synonymous in the twenty years immediately following the Second World War, this has not been the case in the period from 1975 to 1995. Hugo therefore expands the chapter to examine the extent to which the five major types of international movements are selective of the more skilled and educated groups. He looks in turn at refugees, permanent migration to MDCs, contract labour migration, illegal migration and student migration. He finds variations across these groups, with refugees, contract labour migrants and illegals generally having lower skill profiles than permanent migrants to MDCs (where visa category is important) and student migration (where experiences differ between the APEC countries).

Contrary to common perceptions that a brain drain has a negative effect on the source country, Hugo demonstrates that there are several examples where the reverse is the case. These include the situation of 'brain overflow', where excess supplies of skilled labour (relative to demand) exist in some APEC countries; the sending of remittances to the source country; eventual return migration; movements of expatriates to Asian nations; and immigrants acting as beach heads in their new country for production activities related to their source country and as a conduit for investment in their source country.

Because migration data are relatively rich for Australia, Hugo examines whether Australia has experienced a brain drain or a brain gain. He finds that while Australia has overall generally experienced a net gain in all skill categories, this gain has been greater in the unskilled occupations. He also finds that there is a net loss of skilled Australia-born people overseas. That is, despite the increased tendency for skilled workers to move overseas for several years before returning to their original country, over the fifteen years to 1995 Australia has experienced a small net loss of skilled personnel. Overall, then, what Hugo's paper shows is that there has been and will continue to be an increase in the movement of skilled workers in the APEC region, and that the negative connotations generally associated with brain drain are perhaps misplaced.

China historically has been a major participant in both world trade and particularly South-East Asian trade. Relationships with the 'outside world' have varied over the centuries. Given China's rich history and its dominance in terms of population numbers, the relationships between trade, migration and the more recent economic transformation of China are worthy of attention as a particular case study in this book.

Skeldon, in 'Trade and Migration: The Effects on Economic Transformation in China', traces the history of China as a trading nation. In terms of migration in the post-Second World War period, it was not until after 1978 that much occurred. This was due both to China's internal policies and the discriminatory policies of countries to the Chinese (e.g., the 'White Australia' policy in Australia). However, since 1978, following the reforms taken by the National People's Congress, trade with the rest of the world has increased rapidly. Migration has been an integral part of the development process in China leading to increased trade. Skeldon discusses the four main types of migration from China: student movements, legal migration, contract labourers, and illegal migration. He demonstrates that the return of Chinese students after studying around the world has played a critical part in the economic transformation of China. Skeldon argues that trade and increasing migration have been complementary. He notes that the migration of entrepreneurs leading to the setting up of a network of trading relations causes trade to increase. This is another addition to the complementarity of trade and migration flows, predicted by the long-run economic models described by Ethier. Even if China were to become more conservative in its trading behaviour, it is unlikely that migration would slow. However, it should also be recognised that in proportional terms, migration from China has been very small.

Insights from the study

The papers in this volume have certainly confirmed that there are both indirect and direct links between the movements of commodities and people across the borders of the countries in the Asia–Pacific Region. These deserve much more attention than they have received. We need to integrate the two flows in our understanding of the growth of the region and to model these interactions. It is not sufficient merely to examine trans-border flows of labour and people as responding to international differences in real incomes and family ties, since these differences in real incomes are themselves the endogenous result of integration of national economies and other major structural changes. Conversely, the growth of international trade is not independent of the growth in the movement of capital and people.

These relationships between international trade in commodities and the international movement of people are complex and they go both ways. That is, we have trade-related migration and migration-related trade in goods and services. To understand these links, we need to think of the world as a single economy which is becoming integrated through the liberalisation of flows of capital and labour and of goods and services across national borders.

We also need to view their effects on the whole world. At present, most of the literature focuses on the effects of inflows or outflows of people on the nation which is the source or destination of these flows. Much of the research on the nexus between international trade and international migration to date has been directed at the question of whether freeing international trade (or increasing capital or foreign aid) will ease the pressures for international migration, particularly of low-skill workers. This is important but only one of the many related questions. The international movement of labour is one set of flows which increase the efficiency of production in the world economy. With few exceptions, international movement of labour (and capital) involves the movement from an economy where the factor is less productive to one where it is more productive.

The flows of people and labour are today much more restricted than the flows of either goods and services or of capital but they are increasing quite rapidly, largely in response to changes in incomes and job opportunities which have been caused by the integration of the world economy. Changes in international migration are essentially following changes in the liberalisation of other factors or commodities as the extent of liberalisation of trans-border movements has been greatest for the movement of capital and second for the movement of goods and services. As well, technological improvement in transport and communication has increased the ease with which people can move around the world.

In examining changes in the movements of people in the APEC region, it is important to note that different countries adopt different definitions of migration. In the four main immigrant-receiving countries, migration implies a permanent move. Within Asia, however, migration has a more general interpretation, but predominantly applies to the temporary movement of workers. It is this latter movement which has increased most rapidly both within Asia and in the broader APEC region over the last decade.

In line with the increased movement of workers, it is likely that part of this movement will be illegal. Already countries like the USA and Canada have large numbers of illegal immigrants from Mexico. Based on the European experience, temporary workers often attempt to remain permanently, which may not be considered desirable by the host country. The USA has attempted to introduce a range of disincentives to illegal movements, without much success. However, it may be that countries within the Asian region can learn from these experiences that policies which favour selective short-run labour inflows are difficult to enforce and maintain if the incentives to migrate are strong.

Some of the relationships between the international movement of goods and services and of labour can only be understood if one also considers the international movement of capital. This applies, for example, to the movement of labour linked to the international production of multinational corporations or to the movement of labour associated with the movement of capital across national borders but within the sub-regional economic zones.

New patterns of international trade in goods and services and international migration of labour are emerging in the Asia–Pacific Region, largely as a result of the growing integration of these economies and the rapid increase in real incomes which it has produced. These new patterns will require new concepts and models. In this volume, the discussion of phenomena such as the migration transition, migration hump, the sub-regional economic zones and the 3-S and 3-D strategies are all products of the current decade. They reflect new developments in the pattern of international movements of commodities or factors which stem from rapid but uneven growth in the region. As the pattern of the demand for migration changes, the new destination countries in particular will have to devise new policies with these shifts in demand. Even APEC, the grouping of countries which defines the region of this study, dates only from 1989.

The results of analyses of the links between the international movement of goods and services and of people (and capital) will be important to an understanding of integration and growth in the Asia–Pacific Region. The liberalisation of trans-border movements of goods and services and capital is proceeding on the multilateral front through the implementation of the Uruguay Round, and possibly APEC on the regional front through the expansion of regional trading arrangements and sub-regional zones, and on the national front through unilateral liberalisations of the movements of trade in goods and services and capital.

At the APEC multilateral level, the countries in APEC are a more diverse set than in any of the regional or sub-regional groupings in the Asia–Pacific Region which have liberalised trade in goods and services and capital to date. The liberalisation of trade in goods and services and capital which is proposed in the Bogor Declaration may, therefore, produce a different pattern of effects than has been observed before and the analysis of these effects will require the bringing together of links analysed in this volume for trade-related migration and migration-related trade.

The increased understanding of the nexus between international movements of goods and services and of factors has important implications too for national migration policies. Nations faced with pressure to accept more immigrants have many options to deal with excess demand for immigration apart from increasing the number of immigrants admitted. As we have noted at the subregional and regional and multilateral levels, they may reduce some of these pressures by investing in other countries or increasing the international trade in goods and services.

These results of study of the Asia–Pacific Region will also be important for the rest of the world as these effects will spill over into other regions. In particular, international migration is never purely an intra-regional phenomena. Migration patterns in one region are related to those of other regions in numerous ways. For example, with the USA being the largest destination for immigrants in the world, US policy towards immigration has a direct effect on flows to other countries, both in the Asia–Pacific Region and elsewhere. The choice of preferred destinations is changing all of the time, largely reflecting the attractiveness of alternative destinations as the ranking of nations in terms of per capita incomes, unemployment rates and other variables change with differential rates of economic growth and macroeconomic performance.

One general theme emerges from these insights. The interdependencies between international movements of goods and services and of factors and interdependencies among national economies mean that we must study the changing patterns of international migration and international trade as parts of a single global system.

PART I

Patterns of Trade and Migration

1

Trade and Investment in the APEC Region: 1980 to 1993*

Bijit Bora

I Introduction

In 1994 the Asia–Pacific Economic Co-operation (APEC) group admitted Chile as a member, bringing its total membership to eighteen, including developed countries such as Japan, USA, Canada, Australia, New Zealand; small developing countries such as Papua New Guinea; large developing countries such as China; the rapidly developing countries in the Association of South-East Asian Nations (ASEAN); the newly industrialising economies (NIEs) of Asia–Hong Kong, Singapore, Korea and Taiwan; and Mexico and Chile.[1]

Despite the well-documented expansion of trade in the region, APEC's diverse membership, and the fact that common borders on the Pacific do not necessarily confer a proximity advantage, there is some question as to whether or not APEC fits Krugman's (1991a) definition of a 'natural trading partner'. This definition is meant to characterise pairs or groups of countries that would have a high propensity to trade with each other in the absence of discriminatory trade barriers. Nevertheless, there is some agreement among economists that the level of integration within the APEC region, in terms of trade and investment patterns, is on the rise and that the depth of integration is raising issues such as the implications for migration and the desirability of a regional trading arrangement. Before these analytical and policy questions can be addressed, there is a need to establish the magnitude of trade expansion and chart the various types of international linkages in the APEC region. The purpose of this paper is to review the empirical evidence on trade and investment in the APEC region.[2]

Throughout the paper an emphasis is placed on the fact that there are already strong linkages between some countries within APEC. For example, Australia and New Zealand are deeply integrated. The recent increase in intra-East Asian trade and the depth of their integration with Japan has been the focus of considerable attention and is now common knowledge (Petri 1993). The task here is not to dispute or scrutinise these linkages, but to see how they fit into the broader regional definition of APEC. An important finding of the paper is that the strength of these sub-APEC linkages can complement each other in a significant manner without creating an inward-looking region.

14

The paper focuses on trade and investment developments since 1980 and covers trade in goods, services and foreign direct investment flows. This study, as with other studies emphasising a particular time period, has a selection bias. Nevertheless, 1980 is considered to be the trough in a recession, so it coincides with the end of the sample period (1993) which also marks the end of another recessionary period. Another important element of the sample size is that it was characterised by an unprecedented growth in international trade and the emergence of East Asia as a considerable regional entity in world trade.

The data analysis in the following sections is divided into three categories: the absolute expansion of trade and investment in the region, the changing composition of trade and investment linkages, the geographical bias in the patterns of linkages.

II The expansion of trade and investment

APEC's absolute trade and investment figures during the 1980s are impressive and provide ample evidence of increased integration in the region. Since 1980, world trade has expanded, in nominal terms, at an impressive annual average rate of 7.80 per cent, but the APEC rate was much higher at 12.14 per cent.[3] Trade in factor services was the fastest growing component of international transactions. APEC's annual growth rate in this category was 20.32 per cent, compared with the world average of 15.63 per cent. Non-factor services were the second fastest component, growing at an average of 10 per cent worldwide and 15.72 per cent in APEC. The value of trade is also significant: APEC's total merchandise trade increased from US$1238 billion in 1980 to US$2758 billion in 1993.

The nominal figures, though interesting, can be misleading given the rapid growth rates of East Asian economies. A more realistic picture of trade expansion emerges from calculating the ratio of international transactions to gross domestic product (GDP).[4] A constant index with rising nominal GDP would imply an expansion of trade. The index also allows us to determine whether the growth figures in international transactions are structural or whether they are simply the outcome of rapid GDP growth. This is an important distinction and one central to the argument that APEC members are increasingly integrated intra- and extra-regionally. This distinction should not, however, be confused with the usual interpretation of the ratio as an indication of 'openness' or a reduction of barriers to trade. There is already a growing literature on whether the index is an appropriate measure, or whether alternative welfare-based measures should be used. In this paper the index will only be interpreted as an expansion of trade by an APEC member and not as an indication of any reduction in barriers to trade nor an indication of the extent to which APEC's trading regime can be interpreted as 'liberal'. Table 1.1 contains estimates of the indexes for private foreign

Table 1.1 Openness measures for APEC members

	Merchandise trade				Non-factor services				Factor services				Foreign direct investment			
	1980	1985	1990	1993	1980	1985	1990	1993	1980	1985	1990	1993	1980	1985	1990	1993
Australia	26.2	27.6	26.3	29.1	6.51	6.6	7.6	7.7	3.2	4.9	7.1	6.0	1.4	2.3	2.4	1.1
Canada	48.2	48.0	43.7	51.0	6.8	6.5	7.6	8.3	4.9	6.2	6.6	6.0	1.5	1.4	2.2	2.3
Chile	36.8	40.8	50.8	44.3	10.2	10.6	13.9	12.0	5.9	15.0	8.5	5.6	0.7	0.8	1.9	2.9
China	15.4	16.2	21.9	40.5	1.5	1.4	2.1	3.0	0.4	0.5	1.1	6.1	.001	.005	.09	6.1
Hong Kong	153.5	179.1	229.7	240.5	23.0	26.0	29.4	30.0	4.0	5.1	3.3	2.8	0.9	0.7	0.4	0.3
Indonesia	44.2	35.8	45.4	47.9	4.8	6.8	8.0	5.6	4.4	5.8	5.6	5.7	0.23	0.3	1.0	1.4
Japan	23.7	21.7	16.9	13.3	4.8	4.1	4.2	3.4	2.2	3.0	7.9	6.3	0.2	0.5	0.2	0.3
Korea, Rep.	62.0	57.0	50.5	49.5	14.0	10.5	8.7	8.9	5.3	5.4	2.6	2.3	0.03	0.2	0.8	0.5
Malaysia	95.3	85.6	127.6	137.1	17.3	19.5	22.8	21.8	9.5	10.8	13.0	9.7	3.8	2.2	5.4	8.1
Mexico	17.6	18.9	23.8	23.0	5.8	5.9	8.7	7.6	4.6	7.1	5.8	4.0	1.0	1.1	1.1	1.4
New Zealand	46.6	50.0	39.8	43.1	11.7	14.5	13.2	14.5	3.8	8.3	6.8	5.0	1.2	2.3	2.3	…
Papua New Guinea	78.8	74.3	71.5	71.0	13.5	14.5	22.3	12.8	11.7	8.9	9.8	13.9	3.6	3.4	4.8	6.8
Philippines	41.6	31.7	46.1	53.9	8.8	10.0	11.2	14.3	6.0	11.1	9.3	9.5	0.3	0.3	1.2	1.4
Singapore	346.4	252	304.2	278	76.7	58.5	70.8	64.5	19.9	16.9	32.9	30.9	11.3	7.2	20.4	16.2
Taiwan	95.7	84.4	75.7	72.0	11.4	13.8	14.3	14.8	5.1	5.7	6.1	4.7	0.3	0.4	2.4	0.3
Thailand	45.7	39.7	61.1	66.1	9.5	9.7	14.6	14.1	4.7	7.4	6.0	4.7	0.5	0.4	3.1	1.5
USA	18.1	20.2	29.2	31.0	17.5	13.8	16.1	16.6	3.0	3.4	4.4	4.7	1.3	0.8	1.4	1.3
ANZ	28.6	30.2	28.0	29.7	7.1	7.6	8.3	8.5	3.2	5.3	7.1	6.1	1.4	2.3	2.4	1.53
North America	20.22	16.5	18.7	19.38	3.32	3.65	4.74	4.9	4.59	4.33	5.38	4.1	1.35	0.88	1.49	1.35
Latin America	20.05	20.7	26.7	25.6	6.42	6.3	9.3	8.17	4.85	7.78	6.11	4.3	1.03	1.05	1.17	1.47
ASEAN	51.44	44.1	63.02	69.52	8.38	10.0	12.8	13.6	5.55	7.8	7.47	6.6	0.71	0.62	2.34	2.57
NIE	112.6	102.7	100.1	100.9	20.16	18.1	17.5	17.37	6.25	6.5	5.8	5.49	1.12	0.89	1.73	1.35
APEC	24.72	21.34	23.84	23.20	4.47	4.41	5.54	5.4	3.9	4.2	6.0	5.8	1.0	1.07	1.6	1.14
European Union	43.55	48.44	43.55	37.6	11.3	12.2	11.6	12.0	8.8	12.2	13.3	13.9	0.14	0.22	0.28	0.31
World	34.2	29.9	30.9	28.3	7.6	6.9	7.6	8.0	5.6	6.3	8.0	7.8	.06	.06	.17	.09

Source: Author's calculations from IMF, World Bank and national data sources provided by the International Economic Data Bank.
Notes: 1992 figures are reported for Hong Kong and APEC because of lack of data.
Foreign investment data was not reported for New Zealand from 1991 to 1993.

direct investment and three categories in the current account: merchandise trade, factor services, and non-factor services.[5]

Merchandise trade

The most striking feature about the data is the cross-country variance in each of the indexes.[6] Hong Kong, Malaysia and Singapore have merchandise trade values up to ten times higher than the world rate. Other countries have considerably lower rates. Of these, Japan stands out with a 1993 value of 13.3, a decline from 23.7 in 1980. Mexico also has a low index but it has increased since 1980 from 17.6 to 23.0.[7] Anderson and Norheim (1993) discuss reasons why there is a negative correlation between country size and openness. This provides a partial explanation of the noticeable decline in Singapore and Taiwan's values, as it reflects their rapid growth in GDP. The sharp decline in the Japanese figures, however, is clearly outside the norm.[8] Furthermore, the USA's (also a large country) figure rose considerably, from a 1980 value of 18.1 to a 1993 value of 31.0.

A clear majority of countries had an increase in the index, but for the APEC region as a whole the index appears to have been stable with fluctuations in each of the individual country indexes offsetting each other. Most of the growth for the group came from the ASEAN countries and China. ASEAN's index rose from 51.44 to 69.52 while China's climbed sharply from 15.4 to 40.5. Noticeable increases were also posted by Latin America as a result of Mexico and Chile's program of liberalisation.

Non-factor services

The classification of international transactions between factor and non-factor services is derived from the balance of payments accounting system. Non-factor services include income earned from activities that do not rely on the cross-border movement of factors of production. Examples include transportation items like shipping or travel and other transport services. The principal hurdle facing economists who have studied services is that activities other than transport or travel are aggregated into the ubiquitous 'other' category which proved to be the fastest growing component.[9]

A recent study by UNCTAD (1994a) on the growth and composition of trade in services concluded that trade in commercial services expanded faster than merchandise trade in the 1980s, but that there was no such dramatic increase between 1970 and 1990.[10] The same study also reports that thirteen of APEC's members rank in the top forty service exporters in the world, and fourteen rank in the top forty importers category. The data in Table 1.1 support UNCTAD's conclusion about the rapid growth in services during the 1980s. Between 1980 and 1993 the difference between the share of non-factor services and merchandise trade in world GDP was 6.3 per cent, indicating clearly the rise in their importance. In absolute terms non-factor services grew annually at 10 per cent, while APEC's rate was 15.72 per cent.

Table 1.1 also provides information on the relative importance of trade in services to developing and developed members of APEC. With the exception of Malaysia, Thailand and Chile, most developing members have relatively low ratios. Given the size of the GDPs of developing countries, their level of exports and imports is small relative to the figures for developed countries. Hong Kong and Singapore are noticeable for their large figures and Japan, again, for its low figures. In 1993 Japan recorded an index of only 3.4, which is barely above China's figure of 3.0. Furthermore, Japan accounted for only 5.5 per cent of world exports of commercial services in 1990, despite its size and level of development.

Factor services

Factor services refers to income earned from the cross-border movement of capital and labour and includes: returns to tangible and non-tangible assets, royalties and fees, and wages paid to non-resident workers.[11] Unfortunately, due to limitations in the provision of data, it is difficult to distinguish between returns from private versus official foreign direct investment. Nevertheless, the data in this category when combined with the FDI data give a good picture of the extent of integration.

As the data indicate, between 1980 and 1993 every country recorded an increase in their factor services index, except Korea, whose index declined from 5.3 to 2.3. Japan can again be singled out in this category, not because of a low index, but because its performance is consistent with that of the USA and the APEC value. This can be explained, in a large part, by income earned from Japan's foreign direct investments. Japan emerged as the world's largest supplier of foreign capital in the late 1980s (UNCTAD 1994b).

Foreign direct investment

APEC's foreign direct investment (FDI) figures are at least as impressive as, if not more impressive than, its trade figures. A combination of technological innovation, financial deregulation and the appreciation of the Japanese yen in the mid-1990s led to a massive outflow of foreign direct capital from Japan. As a result, global flows of FDI exploded in the late 1980s and peaked in 1991. After a modest decline FDI flows have recovered in 1993. An interesting feature of this significant expansion is that it was entirely market driven. Most APEC members did not liberalise their foreign investment regimes until the late 1980s and early 1990s (Bora 1996a). There is evidence (World Bank 1994) that while some East Asian economies induced FDI into export industries, many of these countries, such as Indonesia, are leading the way in investment liberalisation in the 1990s. If this liberalisation trend continues, intra-APEC FDI will continue to grow rapidly.

A direct outcome of the increased integration of East Asia through foreign direct investment was that the NIEs emerged as source countries for capital. Most of their investments were targeted in labour-intensive sectors in the ASEAN and in China, reflecting a shift in their comparative advantage. Large increases in intra-Asian flows, and the fact that two members of the foreign investment triad, USA and Japan, are APEC members, makes APEC an important component of global foreign direct capital flows.[12]

The data in Table 1.1 reflect many of these developments. ASEAN's openness index for FDI more than tripled between 1980 and 1993. North America's index did not increase at all, while Latin America's index increased from 1.03 to 1.47 and the NIE rate grew to 1.35. The most promising FDI development in the region is China's emergence as an important host for FDI. Its index grew from a negligible amount to over 6 per cent. UNCTAD (1994b) reports that in the past ten years China has become the largest host developing country for FDI. Europe, for the first time, posted growth rates greater than APEC due to its importance as a host to Japanese and American investment. It also posted an increase in its index in 1993 despite the fact that total global flows declined in 1991.

III Composition of trade

The rapid expansion of trade and investment among APEC members is only part of the story. Equally important is the changing composition of international transactions. In this section the focus will be on two elements of the structure of merchandise trade and FDI: shifting comparative advantage and the increase in intra-industry trade. There is also a third element of the changing structure of trade and that is the increase in the importance of intra-firm trade, but lack of data prevents a detailed analysis of these changes.

Shifting comparative advantage
Many studies on East Asia's trade patterns have concluded that the rapid growth of international trade and GDP can be traced to policies such as human capital investment and technology (World Bank 1994). These changes in factor endowment have shifted comparative advantages in many economies and created a string of new exports and exporters within the region. East Asia and Latin America can no longer be considered exporters of low-cost, labour-intensive goods. The NIEs and Mexico have adopted new technologies and quality control procedures to gradually shift into more capital- and technology-intensive products.

Evidence of this structural change can be found in Table 1.2 which reports calculations of five different revealed comparative advantage (RCA) indexes for each APEC member.[13] The categories were selected with a view to escaping from the traditional two-sector factor endowment model. Much of what is happening in the region is dynamic and can only be captured by adopting a broader framework. Table 1.2 reports indexes indicating comparative advantage in mineral-, agriculture-, technology-, labour-, capital- and human capital-intensive activities.

The first point to note is the complementarity in the region. Some countries have extremely high indexes in some categories. For example, Australia, Brunei, Canada, Indonesia, Malaysia, New Zealand, Papua New Guinea and Thailand have maintained strong comparative advantages in mineral- and agricultural-intensive products. Japan has an extremely low index for these two categories but a high index for technology-, human capital- and capital-intensive products.

The second point to note is the movement in the values during the 1980s and early 1990s. Japan has clearly shifted its comparative advantage away from labour-intensive products. In 1980 its RCA in labour-intensive products was 1.18, but that fell to 0.51 in 1993. Similar if not more significant declines were also recorded by the NIEs. Hong Kong, Taiwan, Korea and Singapore recorded 1993 values that were up to 50 per cent lower than their 1980 values. This latter change is also indicated by the NIE labour-intensive index which fell from 4.26 to 1.77 over the same period.

The large drop in the NIE labour-intensive index coincided with an increase in technology- and capital-intensive indexes. Their aggregate index moved from below 1 to above 1 in both categories, with a larger increase recorded for technology-intensive activities. Japan, on the other hand, recorded slight declines in its values but is still a strong exporter of these products.

ASEAN's members have emerged as important exporters of labour-intensive products in what appears to be a 'ladder' story.[14] The NIEs vacated their position as an exporter of labour-intensive products only to be replaced by the ASEAN region. Between 1980 and 1993 the ASEAN labour-intensive index rose from 0.58 to 1.51. Part of this movement can be explained by intra-Asian flows, in particular the rise in NIE investment in the ASEAN (see Table 1.5) region. As factor costs increased in the NIEs, lower cost and lower skilled labour-intensive activities were diverted into the ASEAN region.

China has held its position as a clear net exporter of labour-intensive products. Its relatively high RCA in that category fell from 4.96 to 4.06 but remains the highest figure in the region. If its open door policy on investment and encouragement of exports continues, this figure will more than likely increase throughout the 1990s as China competes with ASEAN members for labour-intensive production.

In Latin America, Chile solidified its position as a primary and agricultural exporter with an increase in both indexes to well above 3. Mexico, on the other hand, despite its strength in the petroleum industry, recorded a small decline in the mineral index but at the same time has shifted into technology-, human capital- and capital-intensive products. Most of these exports are destined for the USA and consist of elaborately transformed manufactures from US affiliates.[15]

The Mexican index for human capital- and capital-intensive exports rose to above 1 and its technology-intensive index is 0.98.

Moving to a regional assessment makes the picture more complex. The APEC index, as reported in Table 1.2, reflects the exports of the group in total. As a result, it necessarily balances high values in a particular category for some members with low values for other members. According to the trade figures, APEC has a declining comparative advantage in technology, labour, human capital and capital exports.

In an attempt to gain a better indication of regional movements, descriptive statistics were examined for the eighteen APEC members in each category and year. An increase (decrease) in the mean combined with a decrease (increase) in the standard deviation would imply that APEC was strengthening (weakening) its comparative advantage in that category. The statistics are shown in the bottom of Table 1.2 and relate a slightly different story from that of the APEC RCAs. In mineral-intensive categories, APEC's mean is well above 1, but the distribution is considerably greater, with a standard deviation larger than the mean. This is due to the increase in the Australian, Bruneian and Chilean indexes. It also indicates that some countries are strengthening their comparative advantage in this category while others are complementing these strengths with a decrease in their index. The end result would indicate an increase in intra-APEC trade.

Very little can be said about agriculture since both statistics declined slightly, but the standard deviation still remains quite high. This would indicate that some APEC members such as Australia, Canada, Indonesia, New Zealand and Papua New Guinea have high exports, while other members have considerably lower indexes. A similar story can be told for technology-intensive exports. The mean increased on the strength of exports from NIEs, Mexico and Japan, but the standard deviation also increased.

The descriptive statistics in the other three categories give us a clearer picture of movements in the indexes since a decrease in the variance can be interpreted as a consolidation of strengths in a particular category. The standard deviations in each category declined, although the labour-intensive value is relatively high. For human capital- and capital-intensive products the decline in the standard deviation was combined with an increase in the mean, implying a growing regional strength in these exports.

Intra-industry trade

Intra-industry trade (IIT) is an important feature of trade and IIT indexes are sometimes interpreted as deepening integration since they reflect an increase in the division of labour, combined with a reduction in transactions costs. Earlier trade theories could not recognise intra-industry trade since products in the same category would be supplied by only the most efficient producer. However, trade theories developed in the 1980s allow intra-industry specialisation and predict

Table 1.2 Revealed comparative advantage indexes for APEC members

	Mineral intensive		Agricultural intensive		Technology intensive		Labour intensive		Human capital intensive		Capital intensive	
	1980	1993	1980	1993	1980	1993	1980	1993	1980	1993	1980	1993
Australia	0.98	3.53	3.05	2.43	0.49	0.41	0.23	0.18	0.32	0.30	0.41	0.36
Brunei	3.32	6.47	0.00	0.00	0.00	0.03	0.00	0.12	0.00	0.69	0.00	0.30
Canada	0.96	1.40	1.61	1.39	0.73	0.57	0.24	0.31	1.46	1.52	1.06	0.96
Chile	2.18	3.54	1.64	3.15	0.19	0.13	0.14	0.23	0.15	0.26	0.17	0.18
China	0.53	0.43	0.81	0.72	0.39	0.45	4.96	4.06	0.83	0.55	0.59	0.49
Hong Kong	0.06	0.19	0.14	0.24	0.44	0.85	6.69	3.28	1.37	0.75	0.86	0.81
Indonesia	2.52	2.63	1.46	2.27	0.01	0.14	0.11	1.47	0.01	0.32	0.02	0.22
Japan	0.09	0.17	0.17	0.09	1.37	1.44	1.18	0.51	2.74	1.58	1.99	1.50
Korea, Rep.	0.11	0.29	0.75	0.41	0.62	0.93	4.96	2.18	1.44	1.20	0.99	1.04
Malaysia	1.16	0.89	3.14	1.58	0.15	0.75	1.08	1.45	0.11	0.82	0.32	0.97
Mexico	1.97	1.40	0.89	0.71	0.66	0.98	0.46	0.74	0.30	1.20	0.50	1.07
New Zealand	0.19	0.58	5.04	5.31	0.26	0.28	0.48	0.32	0.38	0.39	0.32	0.32
Papua New Guinea	1.62	4.31	3.27	3.56	0.03	0.01	0.01	0.04	0.02	0.00	0.02	0.01
Philippines	0.74	0.55	2.97	1.42	0.10	0.39	2.26	2.94	0.12	0.19	0.13	0.40
Singapore	0.94	1.13	1.30	0.53	0.81	1.49	1.43	0.99	0.65	0.68	0.87	1.20
Taiwan	0.08	0.13	0.95	0.60	0.74	1.25	5.24	2.05	1.05	0.74	0.88	1.04
Thailand	0.55	0.38	3.91	2.12	0.05	0.62	1.36	1.71	0.18	0.62	0.23	0.67
USA	0.32	0.39	1.58	1.14	0.74	1.45	0.64	0.52	0.84	0.82	1.42	1.19
ASEAN	1.81	1.30	2.23	1.87	0.09	0.52	0.58	1.51	0.07	0.58	0.13	0.63
NIE	0.32	0.47	0.84	0.48	0.74	1.20	4.26	1.77	1.10	0.86	0.9	1.06
APEC	0.57	0.66	1.30	0.90	1.21	1.14	1.16	1.00	1.23	1.03	1.22	1.09
EEC	0.49	0.62	0.91	1.05	1.40	1.00	1.30	0.88	1.38	1.13	1.39	1.10
APEC mean	1.02	1.58	1.82	1.54	0.43	0.68	1.75	1.28	0.67	0.70	0.60	0.71
APEC std dev.	0.95	1.80	1.43	1.40	0.37	0.50	2.16	1.21	0.73	0.44	0.54	0.43

Source: Calculations by the International Economic Data Bank, Australian National University. Time series data is available from the author upon request.

that the level of intra-industry trade is a function of factor endowments, relative size, absolute size, and transactions costs such as transport costs (Helpman & Krugman 1985). Changes in these determinants will be reflected in a changing pattern of intra-industry trade.

Table 1.3 reports Grubel–Lloyd intra-industry trade indexes for each of the APEC member countries, and APEC as a group, for 1980 and 1993. It is divided into two parts reflecting indexes calculated for 1980 (shaded cells) and 1993.[16] The IIT indexes are directly related to the indexes in Table 1.2. Countries with an extremely high RCA index in one category and extremely low indexes in other categories are not likely to have high IIT indexes. Furthermore, countries with complementarities in their RCAs combined with geographic proximity advantages will also have high indexes. Canada and the USA, Australia and New Zealand are good examples. Geographical proximity appears to be a strong indicator of integration, as evidenced by the high values of IIT reported for trade between China, Taiwan and Hong Kong. As well, the NIEs have extremely high indexes for trade among South-East Asian economies.

Table 1.3 also indicates that the IIT values for member countries have increased between 1980 and 1993, suggesting a more integrated region. Only Hong Kong and Papua New Guinea recorded decreases in their index with APEC. Interestingly enough, the largest increases were recorded by ASEAN members and Mexico.

The intra-APEC index rose slightly from 94.57 in 1980 to 97.27 in 1993. However, APEC's index with the rest of the world increased during the same period to 61.54 from 41.49. This jump in the index is quite significant since it is further evidence of APEC's continuing trend towards being an open region.

Foreign direct investment and services

There has been a number of changes in the composition of services and foreign direct investment. The sectoral distribution of inward FDI for the largest developed and developing host economies is skewed heavily in favour of the tertiary sector. In 1990 the tertiary sector hosted 48.4 per cent of the inward stock of FDI in developed economies and 29.5 per cent in developing economies. In 1980 the figures were 38.1 and 22.7 respectively (Bora 1996a).

The 1994 World Investment Report (UNCTAD 1994b) concluded that the FDI outlook is optimistic for APEC members and East Asia in particular. High growth rates are a significant factor in the explanation of FDI flows and the locational decisions of multinationals. Another important indicator is trade. Currently, most of the investments in the East Asia region are in intermediate goods production. For example, the local sales propensities of US affiliates in Asia are quite low compared to those of affiliates in developed countries (Bora 1992). Continued growth rates and rising per capita incomes will cause multinationals to refocus their investments towards market access as opposed to produc-

Table 1.3   Intra-industry trade indexes for APEC countries: 1980 and 1993

	Aust.	Brn	Can.	Chile	China	HK	Indon.	Japan	Korea	Mal.	Mex.	NZ	PNG	Phil.	Sing.	Twn	Thld	USA	APEC	ROW	World
Australia	...	...	14.08	3.04	...	21.02	24.83	6.56	10.49	...	13.10	51.99	...	17.92	43.78	...	18.60	22.18	30.04	19.95	28.64
Brunei	1.17	...	0.03	...	...	2.06	...	0.46	0.01	...	...	0.11	...	0.18	3.12	...	0.04	1.87	2.23	75.81	21.48
Canada	7.8	...	...	10.55	15.07	17.46	7.99	8.39	17.94	8.05	23.66	12.72	0.21	24.43	29.25	13.56	15.64	61.57	61.43	43.18	63.13
Chile	0.05	...	2.41	...	0.37	2.34	1.15	0.64	0.22	0.31	7.43	1.54	...	1.06	2.25	0.19	0.16	13.00	8.74	23.56	16.97
China	1.14	...	0.74	0.26	...	24.39	10.79	18.51	28.39	...	5.47	3.85	...	20.12	35.42	...	20.42	13.29	27.00	24.96	27.08
Hong Kong	17.41	...	13.75	0.05	28.81	...	23.38	10.88	24.65	37.51	12.67	11.82	0.59	46.31	45.19	36.23	34.93	36.55	39.21	69.01	76.32
Indonesia	3.62	...	2.26	...	...	6.77	...	6.94	11.06	25.26	0.94	7.54	1.04	13.82	...	15.27	19.15	12.05	20.93	18.74	24.42
Japan	4.76	...	6.22	2.49	6.78	11.42	0.72	...	37.97	24.37	7.58	6.42	0.07	27.23	31.39	31.52	23.89	28.21	27.89	26.45	27.99
Korea, Rep.	4.44	...	6.03	0.01	...	8.62	3.59	32.21	...	18.83	5.65	4.73	0.11	13.25	45.60	49.57	14.93	35.39	49.45	26.63	44.47
Malaysia	7.65	2.55	18.22	0.24	1.20	27.13	6.14	3.83	1.21	...	18.68	7.98	...	38.26	56.38	...	35.31	38.20	52.59	35.04	51.48
Mexico	4.22	...	14.48	3.34	...	5.01	0.04	4.16	1.14	0.31	...	0.62	...	3.84	23.88	...	12.34	63.66	64.77	40.59	65.21
New Zealand	31.29	...	7.27	...	4.14	10.58	0.15	3.64	1.14	7.98	0.14	...	0.61	4.57	25.49	5.92	12.42	19.02	33.78	21.04	32.61
Papua New Guinea	3.92	...	0.34	...	...	0.94	7.69	1.13	...	0.78	...	0.75	...	2.33	5.46	...	0.12	2.35	1.89	1.74	1.96
Philippines	7.72	0.07	7.19	...	0.64	35.81	0.26	8.17	2.92	17.63	0.14	1.61	0.41	...	31.30	32.12	38.95	33.38	42.20	24.04	41.77
Singapore	21.69	...	9.34	0.04	5.45	27.19	8.68	8.02	18.35	22.46	1.43	3.24	0.46	28.11	...	61.64	44.92	44.64	67.09	47.33	67.70
Taiwan	6.47	...	5.26	0.18	...	11.17	2.83	20.44	21.58	5.96	5.21	2.57	2.01	8.62	24.25	...	31.39	31.45	51.38	34.20	49.76
Thailand	9.90	...	1.99	...	9.09	25.86	1.54	5.81	17.50	10.64	0.64	4.32	0.11	5.16	24.23	9.08	...	29.68	42.40	28.57	41.16
USA	11.16	0.15	54.39	5.53	4.40	23.86	1.68	24.18	19.89	36.78	27.90	10.06	2.26	29.35	43.39	17.62	15.03	...	63.58	57.88	68.18
APEC	23.91	0.46	53.87	8.23	20.65	37.77	8.35	19.46	33.20	24.82	27.90	18.85	3.14	27.24	53.68	32.82	20.71	48.88	...	61.54	89.01
ROW	15.08	...	29.74	31.80	21.61	30.37	38.04	14.23	14.63	13.48	21.04	12.33	1.36	12.49	34.06	2.01	8.71	2.26	61.54	...	88.98
World	21.57	0.47	52.66	11.21	22.13	39.87	14.33	17.76	28.83	30.12	28.62	16.59	3.23	24.47	52.41	29.05	18.11	45.56	89.01	91.19	...

Source: International Economic Data Bank, Australian National University.

tion opportunities. Similar conclusions can also be made about US investments in Mexico.

The composition of trade in services varies significantly between developed and developing countries. Developed countries have a revealed comparative advantage in the exports of commercial services as evidenced by the fact that they account for 87 per cent of world exports in that category (UNCTAD 1994a).

IV Geographical bias in trade and investment

The trade issue in the APEC region that has captured most of the academic and policy interest is not the shifting composition of trade, but the question of whether or not an East Asia trading bloc will emerge. A related question is whether or not the bloc will be established intentionally. There is a similar question on the implementation of the APEC leader's Bogor Declaration to eliminate barriers to trade in goods, investment and services by the year 2020. Will APEC eliminate barriers to members only? Or will the reduction in barriers be offered unconditionally? In this section the extent of the bias in trade and investment within the APEC group is examined. The analysis is meant to contribute to the growing debate on the direction of APEC without being involved in the specifics. Elek (1996) provides a good overview of the issues in APEC and the data in this section complement his analysis.

Trade in goods

There are a number of indexes that can be used to measure the extent of bias in the international relationship between countries and regions. These range from simple bilateral shares to the trade entropy index. Petri (1993, p. 23) provides a good overview of the use of different deflators of the bilateral trade.

This paper has adopted the intensity index approach, which can be calculated for exports, imports and total trade.[17] A value greater than 1 implies that intra-APEC exports (imports) are larger than APEC's share of world trade. Export and import intensity indexes for each APEC member have been calculated and the results reported in Table 1.4. They differ from previous studies such as Anderson and Norheim (1993), Drysdale and Garnaut (1993), and Petri (1993, 1995), which have focused on intra-regional intensities with narrower definitions of regions, such as East Asia and North America. The region used in this study is APEC.

Since APEC consists of a set of sub-regional groups, we can expect its intensity to reflect this diversity. That is, Asia's high intra-Asian index will be balanced against a lower Asia–North America index. The index will also reflect the fact that some countries such as Chile have extremely diversified economies so that their APEC and European trade shares are almost identical.

The first thing to note about the data in Table 1.4 is that the indexes are

Table 1.4 Trade intensities for APEC countries and selected regions

	Intra-regional export intensity						Intra-regional import intensity					
	1980	1985	1990	1992	1993	1994	1980	1985	1990	1992	1993	1994
Australia	1.95	1.6	1.77	1.79	1.63	1.66	1.89	1.68	1.69	1.64	1.51	1.53
Brunei	2.89	2.28	2.42	2.15	1.72	1.7	2.47	1.92	2.04	1.7	1.49	1.45
Canada	2.09	1.96	2.11	2.06	1.91	1.97	0.34	0.42	0.34	.5	0.59	0.66
Chile	0.95	1.05	1.1	1.08	1.08	1.07	1.3	0.84	0.93	1.04	0.96	0.93
China	1.71	1.65	1.88	1.86	1.55	1.64	2.01	1.74	1.82	1.67	1.41	1.46
Hong Kong	1.71	1.83	1.76	1.7	1.56	1.63	2.49	2.08	2.1	1.98	1.81	1.84
Indonesia	2.64	2.12	2.06	1.88	1.67	1.67	2.26	1.72	1.73	1.63	1.45	1.58
Japan	1.6	1.56	1.59	1.54	1.46	1.52	1.58	1.39	1.43	1.39	1.31	1.36
Korea, Rep.	1.81	1.6	1.73	1.67	1.5	1.49	2.0	1.63	1.72	1.64	1.45	1.5
Malaysia	2.16	1.85	1.9	1.87	1.69	1.72	2.23	1.94	1.93	1.88	1.75	1.77
Mexico	2.14	1.72	1.93	1.83	1.9	1.95	2.24	1.95	1.92	1.79	1.76	1.84
New Zealand	1.68	1.44	1.63	1.66	1.61	1.49	1.99	1.76	1.7	1.68	1.54	1.61
Papua New Guinea	1.85	1.26	1.86	2.06	1.9	1.92	2.89	2.35	2.37	2.2	2.08	2.16
Philippines	2.21	1.93	1.96	1.85	1.66	1.73	2.05	1.94	1.79	1.72	1.66	1.75
Singapore	1.93	1.68	1.74	1.67	1.55	1.52	2.04	1.82	1.79	1.73	1.62	1.63
Taiwan	2.06	1.95	1.83	1.7	1.58		2.04	1.74	1.79	1.68	1.53	
Thailand	1.66	1.5	1.59	1.58	1.46	1.51	1.96	1.77	1.78	1.69	1.52	1.47
USA	1.23	1.08	1.25	1.22	1.11	1.15	1.37	1.42	1.42	1.38	1.27	1.35
ANZ	1.92	1.58	1.76	1.79	1.62	1.64	1.93	1.71	1.71	1.66	1.53	1.56
North America	1.58	1.54	1.64	1.59	1.48	1.54	1.72	1.69	1.68	1.63	1.51	1.59
Latin America	1.87	1.63	1.74	1.64	1.79	1.83	2.04	1.76	1.74	1.67	1.66	1.72
ASEAN	2.37	1.93	1.9	1.82	1.64	1.67	2.17	1.86	1.84	1.76	1.62	1.65
NIE	1.9	1.79	1.8	1.73	1.6	1.61	2.16	1.85	1.91	1.83	1.68	1.73
APEC	1.75	1.65	1.72	1.67	1.56	1.61	1.83	1.7	1.73	1.68	1.55	1.61
European Union	1.45	1.61	1.5	1.54	1.63	1.62	1.42	1.53	.44	1.5	1.53	1.55

Source: Calculations from the International Economic Data Bank, Australian National University.

greater than 1. Second, there is a clear negative trend in the index for most countries indicating that their intra-APEC trade intensities are actually declining. This conclusion is also supported by the APEC index which fell for exports from 1.75 to 1.61 and for imports from 1.93 to 1.56. This is interesting because it reflects the difference in the definition of a region which was discussed above. Given that the rise in intra-Asian shares represents declines in extra-Asian trade, some of the diversion may, in fact, be from APEC members.

Anderson and Norheim (1993) propose the use of another index, called the propensity to trade index, which overcomes some problems associated with the use of trade shares.[18] They argue that the propensity to trade index can capture the combined effects of bias and changes in the degree of openness.[19] Bora (1995) calculates this index for APEC and concludes that the decline in the intensity index for members seems to dominate the increase in openness resulting in a decline in the value of the propensity index for some countries. He also concludes that there is a strong contrast between Japan and the USA. The Japanese propensity for intra-regional trade fell from 0.38 to 0.18 and its extra-regional propensity fell to 0.07. The US index for intra-regional trade rose to 0.37 and for extra-regional trade rose to 0.18.

Foreign direct investment

The paucity of data on FDI has precluded the type of detailed analysis of bias that has been done for trade in goods. A recent study by Braga and Bannister (1994) used proposal data to examine FDI intensities for East Asia. This study makes use of a cross-country matrix of stocks of FDI to calculate intensity indexes for each APEC member's outward FDI and for the region.[20] The results of these calculations are given in Table 1.5.[21]

The table indicates there are very strong linkages between the sub-regions. Canadian and US investment in Mexico is extremely high, as is intra-NIE and NIE–ASEAN investment. This pattern of investment can be explained by a number of factors. First, as reported earlier, there is the high level of intra-triad FDI (Europe, Japan, USA). Second, there is the high degree of goods integration between the regions and the role played by multinationals in servicing existing markets, as opposed to creating new ones. Third, there is the 'ladders' story of shifting comparative advantage. The presence of NIE investments in ASEAN, for example, is concentrated in labour-intensive activities. In aggregate, these sub-linkages appear to have balanced each other. The intra-APEC index is below 1, reflecting the fact that European and other non-APEC investment are extremely important to the region.

Services

A recent study by Hargraves (1994) attempted to disaggregate the bias in services trade in the Asia–Pacific Region. He showed that the highest growth rates appeared among the triad members. Between 1986 and 1991, however,

Table 1.5 FDI intensities for APEC members: 1992

	Can.	USA	Mexico	Japan	China	Korea	HK	Taiwan	Sing.	Indon.	Mal.	Thld	Phil.	Aust.	NZ	NA	NIEs	ANZ	ASEAN	Asia APEC	Other APEC	APEC	EU	ROW
Canada	0.00	1.39	20.33	0.05	..	..	0.17	3.00	0.19	219.00	0.70	..	4.00	5.35	5.20	1.27	0.22	5.34	14.94	0.37	1.32	1.14	0.49	1.86
United States	4.38	0.00	90.67	0.38	..	6.50	1.13	11.50	3.44	60.00	2.90	..	9.50	7.25	5.20	0.47	1.89	7.06	9.53	0.74	0.54	0.57	1.09	3.81
Mexico	0.11	1.86	..	..	..	..	..	..	..	..	..	..	..	3.06	..	1.69	..	2.77	0.00	..	1.71	1.45	0.44	..
Japan	0.55	0.54	74.67	0.00	..	78.00	3.61	50.50	16.00	1212.00	17.80	..	28.17	12.35	7.00	0.59	9.23	11.85	98.06	3.05	0.71	1.05	0.05	3.49
PR China	0.13	1.08	..	0.26	0.00	..	29.52	..	0.63	..	4.00	..	..	..	..	0.99	23.43	..	2.35	3.11	0.98	1.30	0.06	2.81
Korea, Rep.	0.02	0.37	..	0.17	..	0.00	1.05	..	5.13	1-790.00	0.50	..	17.83	2.88	16.40	0.34	1.61	4.15	137.41	2.69	0.38	0.72	0.88	3.56
Hong Kong	0.23	0.08	..	0.24	1055.50	16.25	0.00	416.50	99.13	2595.00	121.50	..	22.50	9.31	..	0.09	23.66	8.43	250.59	10.43	0.18	1.70	0.02	..
Taiwan	..	0.97	..	0.13	..	9.75	4.64	0.00	43.81	888.00	30.60	..	162.83	1.85	..	0.88	10.71	1.68	155.65	4.47	0.89	1.59	0.00	2.14
Singapore	..	0.04	..	..	..	..	13.06	38.50	0.00	230.00	60.80	..	19.17	7.71	..	0.04	11.06	6.98	318.59	8.75	0.11	1.39	0.09	1.97
Indonesia	0.18	-0.05	..	..	11.50	..	..	777.00	478.63	0.00	49.50	..	..	5.63	..	0.05	87.73	5.09	35.76	11.36	0.01	1.69	0.03	..
Malaysia	0.03	0.07	..	..	..	..	0.27	710.50	417.13	521.00	0.00	..	1.33	15.56	..	0.07	77.31	14.09	46.59	10.29	0.22	1.71	..	..
Thailand	..	1.02	..	..	..	..	54.88	37.69	..	..	..	..	..	..	..	0.93	48.17	..	0.00	7.00	0.92	1.64	0.08	0.12
Philippines	..	0.57	..	..	49.00	..	3.89	3123.00	11.88	1491.00	1.80	..	0.00	..	..	0.52	54.84	..	97.18	8.56	0.51	1.70	0.01	..
Australia	0.02	0.32	..	..	27.50	1.00	0.28	5.00	34.31	1127.00	76.40	..	22.33	0.00	575.20	0.35	5.59	54.25	120.76	3.11	0.92	1.24	0.81	..
New Zealand	..	0.46	..	..	..	..	..	..	..	..	..	..	..	134.67	0.00	0.42	..	102.91	..	..	1.50	1.28	0.38	1.53
North America	0.52	0.13	84.00	0.35	..	6.00	1.05	10.50	3.13	74.00	2.70	..	9.00	7.06	4.52	0.55	1.72	6.89	10.00	0.71	0.61	0.63	1.03	3.63
NIEs	4.05	0.10	..	0.20	835.00	13.00	2.11	335.50	79.44	2172.00	187.80	..	24.67	8.69	0.60	0.11	20.66	7.92	263.00	9.77	0.19	1.61	0.06	0.48
ANZ	..	0.34	..	..	25.00	1.00	0.25	4.50	30.81	1013.00	68.70	..	20.00	11.48	517.00	0.35	5.02	59.17	108.53	2.80	0.98	1.25	0.77	0.15
ASEAN	4.01	0.25	..	..	17.50	..	2.35	1357.50	275.69	792.00	3.20	..	0.83	9.46	..	0.23	69.72	8.57	60.59	9.68	0.32	1.70	0.01	0.00
Asia APEC	0.49	0.49	64.00	0.02	101.50	68.25	3.47	110.50	28.75	1318.00	38.10	..	27.00	13.92	6.00	0.52	11.84	11.28	117.12	4.00	0.64	1.13	0.28	3.06
Non-Asia APEC	0.58	0.13	83.00	0.35	27.50	5.75	1.04	10.50	3.44	84.00	3.40	..	9.17	13.35	12.60	0.54	1.76	7.45	11.06	0.73	0.62	0.63	1.03	3.59
APEC	3.49	0.18	80.33	0.30	15.00	15.00	1.40	25.50	7.25	267.00	8.50	..	11.83	7.81	10.00	0.54	3.25	8.02	26.76	1.21	0.62	0.71	0.92	3.51
EU	0.83	0.64	14.33	0.10	3.00	0.50	1.28	1.00	16.38	11.00	7.10	..	0.67	9.63	7.60	0.67	3.53	9.43	5.41	0.63	0.76	0.74	0.95	3.14
ROW	1.00	1.00	1.00	1.00	1.00	1.00	1.00	1.00	1.00	1.00	1.00	..	1.00	1.00	1.00	1.00	1.00	1.00	1.00	1.00	1.00	1.00	1.00	1.00

... - Data is either zero, negligible, or unavailable.

Source: Industry Canada.

China emerged as the economy with the highest growth rate. Japanese trade with China grew by 22.1 per cent, while American trade with China grew by 11 per cent.

These figures are not altogether surprising since they parallel the movements in FDI that are highlighted in Table 1.5. Most of the service categories are related to FDI and merchandise trade. Given the integration in these categories between APEC members, a high bias in services trade would be expected.

V Conclusion

The proliferation of regional trading arrangements in the last decade has increased the awareness of policy-makers and academics to the possibility of trading blocs emerging within the Asia–Pacific Region. Concern about an increasing number of such blocs was reinforced when the APEC leaders delivered their Bogor Declaration on free trade and investment within the region. To evaluate various options it is important to distinguish between intentional and unintentional integration. This paper has attempted to chart the linkages and integration of the APEC region and set the stage for discussion of these kinds of policy issues as well as an analysis of the implications of integration. The study differs in one significant respect from other studies in that it focuses exclusively on APEC as the definition of a region as opposed to narrower regional definitions such as East Asia or North America.

Several conclusions can be drawn from the analysis. First, the APEC region has led the world in terms of outwardness. Its rate of growth in trade, for both goods and services has outstripped world totals and its trade to GDP ratio has increased steadily since 1980. Second, changes in factor endowments, technology and trade policy, especially in East Asia, have changed the composition of goods and foreign direct investment flows within APEC. The NIEs have emerged as sources for capital and exporters of technical-, capital- and human capital-intensive products. Their previous position as exporters of labour-intensive products has been filled by the ASEAN members.

These sectoral changes were also accompanied by changes in the composition of trade. There was a marked increase in intra-industry trade and trade in services within the sub-regions in APEC and among APEC members. These developments reflect the nexus of trade in goods, capital and services.

Third, the APEC region continues to link itself with the rest of the world. Using a trade intensity measure, this study showed that APEC has increased its trade with non-APEC members. It was argued that this result reflects the geographic and institutional composition of the region as reflected in the sub-regional linkages within APEC.

The implication of these results is that the APEC group can be characterised as dynamic and outward looking. International trade in goods, services and technology accompanied by foreign direct investment flows is having a significant impact on the goods and labour markets of APEC members. As APEC's economies respond to these changes with continued reductions in barriers to international transactions, there is no doubt that trade will continue to increase.

Notes

* Funding for this paper was received from the Asia Business Centre at the University of Melbourne, the Bureau of Immigration, Multiculturalism and Population Research, an Australian Research Council Grant and the South Pacific Forum. I am extremely grateful to Prue Phillips and the International Economic Data Bank at the Australian National University, Colin Hargraves and Industry Canada for assisting with the data requirements. Thanks also go to Laura Brewer, Phil Dupuis, Peter Lloyd and Richard Snape for providing comments on an earlier draft. The paper was written while I enjoyed the hospitality of the Centre for International Economic Studies at the University of Adelaide.

1 The aggregates used in this study are: ANZ–Australia and New Zealand; APEC–Singapore, Hong Kong, the Philippines, Taiwan, Singapore, Australia, New Zealand, Canada, USA, Chile, Mexico, Japan, Korea, Papua New Guinea, Malaysia, Thailand, Indonesia, Brunei; ASEAN–Indonesia, Thailand, Malaysia, the Philippines, Brunei; NIEs–Korea, Singapore, Hong Kong, Taiwan; Latin America–Chile and Mexico; North America–Canada and USA; Europe–England, France, Germany, Italy, Spain; ROW–world minus APEC members.

2 For a discussion of policy issues related to the Asia–Pacific Region see Pangestu (1996) and Bora (1996b).

3 Figures are obtained from the IMF and World Bank sources as provided by the International Economic Data Bank and are used in Table 1.

4 This index is sometimes referred to as the 'openness index' to indicate the extent to which a country trades with the rest of the world.

5 Definitions for each category are in UNCTAD (1994, p. 10).

6 There are a number of reasons why we would expect some variance in the absolute values of the various indexes. First, the degree of openness depends upon traditional determinants of trade, such as country size, proximity to markets, level of development and factor endowments. Second, government policy is also a strong determinant. During the 1980s the developing countries in East Asia, Mexico and Chile reversed their import-substitution policies and adopted more outward-oriented policies. The net result has been an increase in both imports and exports in these countries.

7 When interpreting these figures the reader should bear in mind the different categories. Most openness indexes refer to the sum of exports and imports of goods and services as opposed to solely merchandise trade. The figures referred to in this study were obtained from the World Bank.

8 Anderson and Norheim quote a GATT (1992) study which correlates the log of openness with respect to area, population and GDP as –0.48, –0.42 and –0.19.

9 The only available multilateral data set is provided by the International Monetary Fund, which is responsible for the vague classification of data on trade in services. However, a new reporting system has been put into place for 1994 which will provide more detailed data.

10 Commercial services includes shipment, other transportation travel, and other private goods, services and income.

11 It should clarified at the outset that this category (wages, salaries and other compensation) only includes remuneration for individuals working abroad for less than one year. Worker remittances and migrant transfers are also included.

12 The European Community is the third member of the triad.

13 Defined as the ratio of products in a given classification divided by the same ratio for the world. A list of three-digit commodity composition used for each classification is available from the author on request.

14 The ladder concept used by Pearson (1994) compares an economy's shift from one category to another as rungs on a ladder. The bottom of a ladder is meant to indicate lower sophistication of production, such as labour-intensive products, while the top of the ladder indicates sophisticated production, such as technology-intensive products.

15 A trade matrix for NAFTA members based on level of processing is included in Bora (1996b).

16 Theoretically, the index should be independent of the reporting country. In practice, however, reporting variations of the index depend upon which country is listed as the reporter. For example, the Australia and Canada bilateral index for 1980 as reported by Australia is 7.8, yet Canada reports the same index as 6.94. I have checked each pair of indexes and found the variance to be in the range of 10–15 per cent. In order to circumvent this problem, I have treated each country as they appear in the rows as the 1980 reporter and as the 1993 reporter in each column.

17 We shall define the intensity of trade between an APEC member and APEC as:

$$I_{ia} = \frac{x_{ia} / x_{iw}}{m_{wa} - x_{ia} / m_{ww} - x_{ia}}$$

I_{ij} is the intensity of exports (imports) to (from) i to a, w is the world and a is APEC.

18 The propensity to trade index is defined as:

$$P_{ij} = t_i \cdot I_{ij}^a$$

where I_{ij}^a is the average of the export and import intensity index defined in the previous footnote and ti is the openness of merchandise trade defined as the sum of exports and imports divided by GDP.

19 Marwah and Klein (1995) use univariate information theory to construct entropy measures of import and export market shares. They argue that imports and exports are flows of information that can be used as a measure of integration. In reality, however, despite the sophistication of their statistical measure the entropy indexes suffer from similar problems to those highlighted by Petri (1993).

20 The formula for investment is identical to the one used for goods, except country (region) i is the host country and country (region) j is the host.

21 A matrix of 1980 intensities is available from the author on request.

2

Migration Intensification in the APEC Region: 1981 to 1994

Tess Rod and Lynne S. Williams

I Overview

During the 1980s, global migratory movements of both a permanent and tempo-rary nature accelerated. This was largely due to buoyant economic conditions in the developed world and in the newly industrialising countries, to differences in the pattern of demographic change between countries, to the increasing globalisation of business enterprises, and to the relaxation of entry conditions in some of the major immigrant-receiving countries. At the same time, the esti-mated number of refugees nearly doubled from the previous decade (Segal 1993, p. 62). Throughout the 1980s and the early 1990s, these migratory movements were becoming more diverse and involved more countries (SOPEMI 1994, p. 13). The movements were also becoming increasingly intra- as well as inter-regional. This trend towards regionalisation of migration underscores the recent consolidation or emergence of regional economic groupings, such as the Asia–Pacific Economic Co-operation (APEC) (SOPEMI 1994, p. 13).

The increasingly large numbers of people involved in migratory movements since 1980 brought immigration into greater prominence as a politi-cal issue in the major receiving countries and in some sending countries. Con-cerns have been expressed in receiving countries about the impact of immigra-tion, both legal and illegal, on the economy, the environment and social cohesion. In sending countries, concerns centre on the living standards and working conditions of low-skilled immigrants in host countries (such as negative publicity about the 'slave-like' conditions of contract workers) and on the effect of the 'brain drain' on the source countries through the loss of highly skilled workers.

This chapter gives a brief overview of the recent trends in the pattern of international migration, focusing particularly on countries in the Asia–Pacific Region which are APEC members. It covers both permanent and temporary movements and the distribution of these by source and destination countries. Following analysis of permanent migration to the four major receiving countries, the chapter focuses on the labour market-related movement of people in the APEC region.

It should be noted at the outset that migration data for APEC countries vary considerably in quantity and quality. The most comprehensive and regular data collection occurs in the four major receiving countries. In the other APEC countries, immigration and emigration figures are usually estimates based on irregular collection of stock or flow data, and time-series data are rare. What is needed for the region is a continuous migration reporting system like the OECD has with SOPEMI, which is published annually. Yet even data from the USA, Canada, Australia and New Zealand are not directly comparable to each other. For example, the figures for the USA, Canada and Australia refer to immigrant admissions, whereas the figures for New Zealand show the number of resident visas issued during the year – although not all those who obtain a visa arrive in New Zealand within the same time period. Furthermore, entry categories and time periods used in official statistics differ in all four countries.

II Permanent migration in the APEC region

Four countries in the APEC region, the USA, Canada, Australia and New Zealand, share a long-established involvement in accepting permanent immigrants. These four countries also share a colonial past and had few, if any, controls over the entry of immigrants (except for non-Europeans) until after the First World War, when systematic immigration controls were imposed. This section focuses on these four countries.

As can be seen from Table 2.1, intake numbers in all four countries increased but also fluctuated throughout the 1980s and early 1990s. The most noticeable fluctuations occurred in Canada and Australia where the 'immigration tap' was turned on and off according to economic conditions. From 1989 the numbers increased considerably in both the USA and Canada due to deliberate policy initiatives. In the USA, more than half of the persons granted legal permanent residence between 1989 and 1991 were illegal immigrants adjusting their status under the legalising provisions of the Immigration Reform and Control Act (IRCA) of 1986. If these legalised immigrants (many of whom had been in the USA for a number of years) are excluded, then the numbers of new immigrants from 1989 onwards shows a steady, but less spectacular, increase (INS 1991, p. 37; INS 1993, p. 13).

In Canada, the increased intake coincided with the introduction of a five-year strategic plan in 1991 which projected progressive increases in immigration to 250 000 annually. The five-year plan was intended to remove some of the gross cyclical variations in intake levels, increase the number of immigrants selected primarily for economic reasons, and also demonstrate the Canadian government's commitment to a progressive, dynamic immigration program (CIC 1994b, p. 1). However, in late 1994 the intake level for 1995 was cut by 40 000 after concerns were expressed about the high intake and the continuing high proportions of family-sponsored immigrants (*The Economist* 1994a, p. 42).

Table 2.1   Immigration to permanent destination countries in the 1980s and early 1990s

Year	USA[1]	Canada[2]	Australia[3]	New Zealand[4]
1981	596 639	143 117	118 699	na
1982	594 131	128 618	93 177	11 373
1983	559 763	121 147	69 808	8965
1984	543 903	88 239	78 087	8332
1985	570 609	84 302	92 410	8467
1986	601 708	99 219	113 308	12 285
1987	601 516	152 098	143 490	14 419
1988	643 025	161 929	145 316	26 613
1989	1 090 924	192 001	121 227	20 811
1990	1 536 483	241 230	121 688	24 000
1991	1 827 167	230 718	107 391	10 313
1992	973 977	252 842	76 330	25 683
1993	904 292	254 321	69 768	29 353
1994	na	na	na	42 629

Notes
1   All aliens granted legal permanent resident status in the USA during the American fiscal year (the
     twelve months from 1 October to 30 September of the respective year).
2   All permanent immigrants to Canada during the calendar year.
3   All settler arrivals to Australia in the financial year from 1 July of the respective year to 30 June of the
     following year.
4   All persons approved for residency in New Zealand during the calendar year.
na   not available
Sources: BIR 1990; BIMPR 1995c; CIC 1994a; INS 1994; NZIS 1994, 1995 and personal communication.

The USA receives more immigrants per year than any other country, with
Canada, Australia and New Zealand following in rank order. Yet the order is
reversed when the annual intake per 10 000 of population (the immigration
rate) is considered. As Table 2.2 shows, in 1993 New Zealand had the highest
proportion with 125 settlers per 10 000, with the corresponding numbers for
Canada, Australia and the USA being 91, 39 and 35 per 10 000 respectively.
The ranking also alters when the proportions of overseas-born in the population
are examined. In this case, Australia comes first with the highest proportion of
overseas-born (22 per cent at the 1991 census), Canada next with 16 per cent,
followed by New Zealand with 15 per cent and finally the USA with 6 per cent
(Stahl et al. 1993, pp. 84, 93). This suggests that over time (at least over the last
generation), Australia had the highest immigration rate of the four countries.

    Historically, Europe was the major source of immigrants for all four coun-
tries, but in the 1980s Asia became the major source. Immigrants from Asia
accounted for about a third or more of all immigrants in these countries in the
early 1990s, compared with less that 10 per cent in the 1960s (Hugo 1991,

p. 124). Increased Asian immigration to these countries was triggered by the lowering of racial barriers and the introduction of non-discriminatory immigration policies in the 1960s; it was given added impetus by the resettlement of refugees following the Indochinese war, coupled with the economic buoyancy of these countries in the 1980s.

Migration policies in all four countries allow immigrants to enter under three broad categories: family reunification, supply of needed labour skills, and humanitarian considerations. Strong emphasis is given to family reunification which is the largest category of entry (except in New Zealand where demand for entry under this category is relatively low – see Table 2.2). The key criterion for entry through the family category is the nature of the kin relationship with a permanent resident in the receiving country. In the employment-related categories, on the other hand, immigrants are selected according to their degree of skill or expertise.

The third category of entry is humanitarian. Each country has an annual quota for persons qualifying as refugees under the Geneva Convention. In addition there are others who are granted entry for humanitarian reasons although they are not conventionally defined refugees. All four countries also have processes for granting permanent residence to persons who arrive in the country and request asylum. The numbers of onshore asylum-seekers rose during the 1980s in the USA, Canada and Australia, as a result of events occurring in neighbouring countries or regions. In the 1990s, asylum procedures in most receiving countries were thrown into crisis as each case had to be decided on its merits and asylum-seekers had the right of appeal, causing considerable congestion and delay in the refugee determination process. Many asylum-seekers are regarded as 'economic' refugees, who use requests for asylum as a means of bypassing legal immigration selection. Asylum cases can drag on for years, offering asylum-seekers the opportunity to find work and melt into the community – the majority staying on in the receiving countries, sometimes illegally.

In addition to immigrants entering under the three broad categories, there are others who arrive each year to settle as permanent residents, legally or illegally. For example, in the USA, additional legal entrants not covered in the three main categories include Amerasians born in Vietnam and IRCA adjustments, and in Australia they include New Zealand citizens. The numbers entering under these supplementary categories tend to be relatively small. More significant are the numbers who enter illegally. The USA has the largest number of illegal entrants with an estimated 200 000 successfully entering the country every year from over a million attempted illegal border crossings (*The Economist* 1995, p. 35). Its permeable land border with Mexico has made it a readily accessible destination for low-skilled workers from Mexico and Central America seeking jobs and better living conditions. So much so that the stock of undocumented immigrants in the country has been estimated to be in the vicinity of 2.5 million, with Mexicans accounting for about 80 per cent (SOPEMI 1994,

Table 2.2 Comparison of permanent immigration destinations

	USA	Canada	Australia	New Zealand
Immigrant intake 1993	904 292	254 321	69 768	29 353
Population 1993[1]	257 million	28 million	17.8 million	3.4 million
Immigration rate: intake per 10 000 population	35	91	39	125
Top three source regions for immigrants in 1993[2]	Asia (including South Asia and Middle East) – 40%; North America (including Mexico and Central America) – 33%; Europe – 18%	Asia & Pacific – 54%; Europe – 19%; Africa and Middle East – 15%;	East Asia – 32%; Europe & former USSR – 29%; Oceania – 15%	North and South-East Asia – 46%; Europe – 23%; Middle East and Africa – 13%
Limits to intake	Annual limits based on visa usage in previous year-however, ceilings can be 'pierced'	Five-year plan with progressively increasing annual intake, but plan interrupted in 1994-intake reduction in 1995.	Intake figures for Migration Program and Humanitarian Program set annually.	Quotas for refugees but other immigration to NZ depends on demand and compliance with selection criteria.
Categories of permanent migration	• Family sponsored (4 preference levels) • Employment based (5 preference levels) • Refugees & asylees	• Family • Economic – Independent – Assisted relatives – Business immigrants • Refugees & asylees	• Family stream – Preferential – Concessional • Skill stream – Employer nomination – Business skills – Special talents – Independent • Humanitarian program • Other visaed	• General • Business investment • Family • Humanitarian • Refugee
Other legal migration	Exempt from numerical cap: refugees & asylees. Amerasians and parolees (Soviet Union & Indochina)	Exempt from numerical cap: successful claims in Canada to refugee status.	Non-visaed immigrants: New Zealand citizens	Non-visaed immigrants: Australian citizens & residents of Cook Islands. Niue and Tokelau whose inhabitants are NZ citizens

Table 2.2 Comparison of permanent immigration destinations (cont.)

	USA	Canada	Australia	New Zealand
Size of intake in 1993 by category	Family – 60%; Employment-based – 16%; Refugees & asylees – 14%; Others – 10%; Total – 904 292	Family – 43%; Economic – 41%; Refugees – 10%; Others – 6%; Total – 254 321	Family – 48%; Skill – 18%; Humanitarian – 16%; Others – 18%; Total – 69 768	General – 69%; Family – 16%; Business – 3%; Humanitarian – 16%; Others – 9%; Total[2] – 42 629
Illegal entrants and visa overstayers	Illegal entrants 1992 – 200 000 (Stock estimated at 2.5 million in 1989)	Not a significant problem since refugee alternative exists	Overstayers in 1994 – 69 000	Overstayers in 1990 – 20 000
Emigration	No regular emigration statistics maintained. An annual figure of 160 000 used for computing national population estimates. Most who left in the 1980s returning to Mexico, Europe and Asia. Large net migration gain.	No regular emigration statistics maintained. Intake figures adjusted to ensure net migration gain.	Emigration statistics maintained from passenger cards and published annually. In 1993–94, there were 27 300 permanent departures, mainly to New Zealand, UK, USA, Canada and Hong Kong. Maintains a net migration gain.	Emigration statistics maintained from passenger cards. In 1980s had net migration loss, mainly to Australia. This has been reversed since 1991.
Temporary migration in 1993[3]	Foreign governments – 102 173; International organisations – 72 834; Students – 290 809; Workers/trainees – 205 002; Others – 432 043; Total – 1 102 861	Student – 89 238; Employment – 185 028; Total – 274 266	Skill – 20 902; Social/cultural – 25 937; Working holidays – 29 706; International relations – 11 284; Others – 237; Overseas students – 41 499; Total – 129 565	Student – 12 000[4]; Work – 21 000[4]; Total – 33 000[4]

Notes
1   1993 population estimates from *The SBS World Guide 1994*, The Text Publishing Company, Melbourne.
2   1994 figures for New Zealand.
3   Entry for temporary residence, excluding short-term visitors or tourists.
4   1993 figures for New Zealand are approximate.
Sources: BIMPR 1995c; CIC 1994a, b; DIEA 1995a, b; DIEA 1994a, b; INS 1994; NZIS 1994, 1995; Shu et al. 1995.

p. 105). While there is some illegal entry into Canada and Australia (for instance, nearly 1000 Sino-Vietnamese boat people arrived on Australia's northern coastline in 1994), the numbers are far smaller. Much more sizeable are the numbers of people who overstay their visas. Many of these are short-term visitors or students who remain in the country after the expiration of their visas.

The migration experiences of these four countries in the 1980s gave rise to a number of public debates and policy concerns about the size and composition of the annual intake and their effect on unemployment, government outlays, urban infrastructure, population growth, the environment and social cohesion. In the late 1980s and early 1990s a number of legislative and policy initiatives were introduced which aimed at rebalancing immigration to focus on economic criteria for entry. The initiatives further aimed at improving the management and control of the annual intake, particularly in relation to undocumented entrants and visa overstayers.

All four countries have experienced a considerable permanent outflow of their resident population but most maintained a net migration gain throughout the last decade. Only New Zealand experienced a net migration loss in the 1980s, mainly to Australia (the Trans-Tasman Travel Agreement gives permanent residents of the two countries the right to travel freely between Australia and New Zealand). However, there was a reversal of this outflow in the early 1990s as New Zealand's economy improved and New Zealanders moved back home, frequently from Australia (Shu et al. 1995, p. 28).

Many of those departing permanently are former immigrants. Some may be migrating to another country (for example, former immigrants to Canada moving on to the USA), while others return to their country of origin. Immigrants from Hong Kong to Canada, Australia and New Zealand generally immigrate to find a safe haven as the reversion of Hong Kong to China approaches in 1997. Many leave spouse and children behind in their adopted country and return to Hong Kong to continue operating their businesses, leading them to be dubbed 'astronauts' who have 'parachute' children. But apart from the Hong Kong immigrants, most Asian immigrants in both Canada and Australia have a low rate of return migration – not surprising given that many who arrived in the 1980s were refugees or the relatives of refugees and had little incentive to return to their place of birth (Samuel 1993; Struik & Ward 1992). The same is also true of the USA where the proportion of former immigrants leaving the country is estimated at about one-third of settler arrivals, with about 28 per cent of those who left in the 1980s returning to Mexico, 22 per cent to Europe and 15 per cent to Asia (Stalker 1994, p. 170). This relatively low rate of return migration among Asian, particularly Indochinese, immigrants may change as relations with countries like Vietnam and Cambodia are normalised, trade connections re-established and as real incomes in Asian countries rise.

Permanent settlement is not the only type of population movement affecting the main countries of settlement. All have experienced a considerable increase in short-term visitors (especially tourists) and temporary entrants (including overseas students, specialists and business persons) in the last ten years, far exceeding the numbers of permanent entrants (see Table 2.2). These movements are discussed in the next section.

III Labour movements in the APEC region

The most compelling feature of population movements throughout the APEC region in the 1980s and 1990s is their economic nature. Furthermore, the permanent flows have not been as significant as the temporary movements, both legal and illegal, within the region and beyond. These temporary labour movements involve both skilled and unskilled workers, and include increasing numbers of women, particularly from the Philippines and Indonesia.

The change in the pace, nature and direction of labour movements in recent years reflects growing imbalances within and among countries in the region, as well as increasing interdependence and regionalisation of labour markets (Lim & Abella 1994, p. 209). The interdependence has its roots (to some degree) in the ethnic affinity and historical links between countries, but more prominent is the economic integration fostered by investment flows, trade, the globalisation of company operations and political relations (Lim & Abella 1994, pp. 209–10).

Historically, large-scale migration has been neither a rare nor a recent phenomenon in the Asia–Pacific Region (Pang 1993a, p. 4). More recently, the relaxation of immigration rules in the main destination countries in the late 1960s, the resettlement of over a million Indochinese refugees, and the opening up of newly wealthy, labour-scarce economies in both the Middle East and the newly industrialising economies of East Asia have encouraged the rapid expansion in the 1970s and 1980s of skilled and unskilled labour flows. Yet in historic terms, these movements of are relatively small compared to those earlier this century (Lim & Abella 1994, p. 210).

APEC member countries can be broadly differentiated in terms of their labour migration experience as primarily labour importing, labour exporting or importing certain types of labour and exporting others (Castles & Miller 1993, p. 155):

- Primarily *labour-importing* countries. This is the largest category comprising the four major receiving countries, as well as Brunei, Japan, Papua New Guinea, Singapore, and Taiwan;
- Primarily *labour-exporting* countries comprising Chile, China, Indonesia, Mexico and the Philippines; and
- Countries which *export some types* of labour but *import others* comprising Hong Kong, the Republic of Korea, Malaysia, and Thailand.

This classification emphasises the direction of major flows, but flows in the opposite direction may also be occurring simultaneously (see Table 2.3). It also

Table 2.3 Labour movements in the APEC region

Country	Type of migration	Main source or destination countries/regions	Number
Labour importing			
Australia	Skill-permanent	Europe, Northeast Asia	1993–94[1] – 12 794
	Skill-temporary	United States, United Kingdom, Japan	1993–94[1] – 20 902
	Undocumented	China, United Kingdom, Fiji	1994[2] – 69 000
Brunei	Skilled and unskilled for private sector employment	Unskilled–Malaysia, Philippines, Thailand, Indonesia	1990[2] – 34 000
Canada	Permanent-economic	Hong Kong, Taiwan, South Korea	1993[1] – 105 489
	Temporary-employment	Asia and Pacific, USA, Europe	1993[1] – 185 028
	Undocumented	na	na
Japan	Skilled workers	na	1991[1] – 113 599
	Unskilled workers:	Thailand, South Korea, Malaysia, Philippines, Iran	1992[1] – 37 375;
	students; trainees		1992[1] – 43 627
	Illegals/overstayers	East Asia	1992[2] – 300 000
New Zealand	Permanent-general	South Korea, Taiwan, China	1994 – 29 213
	Business	na	1994[1] – 1419
	Temporary workers	na	1994[1] – 21 000
	Undocumented	na	1990[2] – 20 000
Papua New Guinea	Skilled workers	na	na
Taiwan	Unskilled (legal and illegal)	Philippines, Thailand, China, Malaysia, Indonesia	1995[3] – 270 000
Singapore	Importer of skilled labour	Malaysia, China, Hong Kong	na
	Unskilled labour	India, Bangladesh, Indonesia, Thailand, Philippines	1990[2] – 200 000
	Also exporter of skilled workers	na	1990[2] – <100 000
United States	Employment-based immigrants	Asia, North America, Europe	1993[1] – 147 012
	Non-immigrants: Workers/trainees	United Kingdom, Mexico, India	1993[1] – 205 002
	Exchange visitors	United Kingdom, Germany, France	1993[1] – 197 545
	Intracompany transfers	Japan, United Kingdom	1993[1] – 82 781
	USA–Canada Free Trade workers	Canada	1993[1] – 17 038
	Illegal workers	Mexico, Central America, China	1989[2] – 2.5 million

Table 2.3 Labour movements in the APEC region (cont.)

Country	Type of migration	Main source or destination countries/regions	Number
Labour exporting			
Chile	Skilled workers	Settled in over 40 countries in voluntary exile since 1973	1973 onwards 200 000[4]
China	Permanent emigration for employment	USA	1993[1] – 12 136
	Skilled and unskilled contract workers (engineering and construction projects)	Indonesia, former Soviet Republics, Eastern Europe	1994[2] – 219 000
	Low-skilled, undocumented workers	Japan, South Korea, Hong Kong, Taiwan	na
	Illegal workers	USA	1992[1] – 100 000
Indonesia	Contract remittance workers	Middle East, South-East Asia	1993[2] – 950 000
	Illegal unskilled workers	Malaysia	1994[2] – 1 million
Mexico	Temporary workers	USA	1993[5] – 23 169
		Canada	1992[6] – 216 882
	Illegal unskilled workers	USA	200 000[7] annually
Philippines	Permanent immigrants in employment class	USA	1993[1] – 11 923
	Contract remittance workers (skilled and unskilled)	Middle East, East and South-East Asia	1993[1] – 689 200
	Illegal unskilled workers	Sabah, Japan, other Asian countries	na
Labour exporting/importing			
Hong Kong	Exporter of skilled labour	Canada, Australia, Asia	na
	Importer of skilled workers	Asia	1991[2] – >24 000
	Importer of unskilled workers	China (largely illegal), Philippines (domestics)	na
			1990[2] – >70 000
Republic of Korea	Exporter of skilled labour	USA, Canada, Asia	na
	Exporter of unskilled labour	Middle East	1990[1] – 34 632
	Importer of unskilled labour, largely illegal	China (Chinese-Koreans), Philippines, Nepal	1994[2] – 170 000

Table 2.3 Labour movements in the APEC region (cont.)

Country	Type of migration	Main source or destination countries/regions	Number
Malaysia	Exporter of legal and illegal skilled and unskilled workers	USA, Canada, Australia, Singapore, Taiwan, Japan	na[8] 1990[2] – 100 000 1991[9] – 30 000 1991[9] – 18 000
	Importer of: • skilled workers	Japan, Singapore, Korea, Taiwan	na

	• unskilled workers	Indonesia – legal
		               – illegal
		Philippines – legal
		               – illegal
			1994[2] – 544 939
			1994[2] – <1 million
			1994[2] – 15 000
			1994[2] – 500 00

Thailand	Exporter of contract remittance workers	Middle East, Brunei, Malaysia, Hong Kong, Singapore, Taiwan, Japan	1994[1] – 430 000
	Importer of: • skilled labour	na	na
	• unskilled labour (illegal)	China, Cambodia, Burma	na

Notes

na   not available
1   Figures show number of immigrants or emigrants in that year (annual flow data).
2   Figures show number in the country at the time of the count (stock data).
3   Number authorised by the government of Taiwan – as at May 1995 160 000 were currently employed.
4   Estimate of number who left Chile to go into exile abroad in 1970s and 1980s (PECC 1993, p. 67).
5   Temporary workers according to Table 41 (INS 1994).
6   Special temporary programs for seasonal agricultural workers from Mexico and the Caribbean (Stalker 1994, p. 180).
7   Estimate of number of successful border crossings each year (Stalker 1994, p. 174).
8   Permanent immigration numbers relatively small and numbers of undocumented immigrants unavailable (Pang 1993b, p. 55).
9   Estimates of illegal Malaysian workers in the country at time of count (Pang 1993b, p. 55).

Sources: Asian Migrant 1993; Baum 1995; BIMPR 1995c; CIC 1994a, b; DIEA 1994c; DIEA 1995c; Fairclough 1995; Furuya, K. 1995; INS 1994; Lim & Abella 1994; NZIS 1994, 1995; Pang 1993b; PECC 1993, 1994; Shu et al. 1995; Stalker 1994; Yukawa 1994.

reflects the fact that countries in the region are at different stages of demographic transition (some having labour shortages and others surplus labour) and have different levels of real income per capita and different economic growth rates.

Labour-importing countries

Temporary labour movements are significant in the four major receiving countries: the USA, Canada, Australia and New Zealand. Except for the USA where there are specific programs for temporary entry of low-skilled workers for agricultural and non-agricultural employment, employment-based temporary arrivals in Canada, Australia and New Zealand are generally more highly skilled. There are no restrictions in any of the four countries on the total number of temporary arrivals for any given year (which can include tourists, business visitors and students among others) – only the USA has annual quotas in certain categories of entry for temporary entrants with employment rights (INS 1994, pp. 95–6). Indeed, temporary arrivals are regarded as a boon to the economy, although there are regulations covering grounds of entry, length of stay, employment, accompaniment by family members and change in admission status. These highly skilled temporary entrants participate in an international labour market where the flows are often circular and there is an exchange of skills, knowledge and experience between countries.

Other labour-importing countries, such as Brunei, Japan, Taiwan and Singapore, have been forced by labour shortages associated with their prosperity and low birth rate to import labour – mainly unskilled temporary labour, although skilled labour is imported also in Brunei and Singapore. Papua New Guinea also imports labour but this is to meet skill, rather than labour, shortages.

Both Japan and Taiwan are concerned with racial and cultural homogeneity, and have been reluctant to open the door to foreign workers, although foreigners with skills in demand and representatives of multinational corporations have little difficulty in getting work permits. Japan, where the labour shortages were felt as early as the late 1970s, exploited trainees from developing countries or students of Japanese language who could be given low-skilled work under less salubrious conditions than those enjoyed by the local population (Castles & Miller 1993, p. 159). Unskilled foreign workers were not officially welcomed (except for Brazilians of Japanese ethnic origin and women who worked in the entertainment industry), but many arrived on visitors' visas, found jobs in manufacturing and services and stayed on in Japan illegally.

The two countries responded differently to the upsurge in illegal foreign workers. Japan sought to outsource more of its manufacturing to low-wage countries in Asia. The sudden appreciation of the yen in 1985 and continuing trade friction between Japan and its trading partners provided a further impetus for Japanese firms to shift their production bases overseas (Ito & Iguchi 1993, p. 7). It increased its direct foreign investment in ASEAN countries from US$935 million in 1985 to US$4684 million in 1989, but the proportion of investment in Asia declined in the early 1990s compared with North America and Europe (p. 8). Yet this strategy did not obviate the need for unskilled workers in Japan in construction, services and small manufacturing businesses. Business associations favoured recruitment of foreign workers from overseas, but this was opposed by trade unions and the government for fear of eroding the social cohesion of the country. This encouraged the employment of illegal and undocumented workers. By the early 1990s, the importation of cheap foreign labour for construction gangs and prostitution rackets had become a thriving business operated by criminal elements in Japan and East Asia, and the detention and deportation of illegal workers a costly exercise for the government (*The Economist*, 1994b, p. 25).

In contrast, Taiwan allows the importation of foreign workers. In 1991 it established foreign worker quotas for certain industries, while at the same time declaring an amnesty for illegal foreign workers (offering tax concessions and the right to return legally in the future) and introducing harsher penalties for employing illegal workers (Stalker 1994, p. 262). Nevertheless, there are many restrictions attached to the employment of foreign workers (including an employment limit of two years) which have not eliminated the problem of illegal migration (Baum 1995, p. 56).

Singapore, unlike Japan and Taiwan, has a population with one of the highest proportions of overseas-born in Asia. According to the 1990 census, there were 300 000 foreigners in the country – 10 per cent of the population (Stalker 1994, p. 255). It is estimated that around 200 000 of these were unskilled foreign workers. In the 1980s, following two decades of declining natural population growth, Singapore experienced labour shortages in a number of industries (Choo 1995). Singapore has always encouraged the inflow of skilled and professional foreign workers (Low 1994, p. 253). Their entry is circumscribed to prevent the displacement of skilled local workers, but these restrictions can be circumvented (PECC 1994, pp. 67–8).

However, unskilled foreign workers in Singapore are treated differently. As in Taiwan, unskilled foreign workers are imported when needed and repatriated when demand falls and are regarded as a buffer to even out fluctuations in the business cycle (Stalker 1994, p. 255). They are not allowed to settle permanently nor to bring their families. They cannot marry Singaporeans and have to rotate every few years. The numbers are strictly controlled by setting a maximum percentage limit of foreign workers in any firm (which varies depending on labour market conditions) and by imposing a higher levy on employers for each unskilled immigrant worker to counter any cost advantage in employing cheaper foreign labour, to encourage businesses to train and use local workers, and to promote technological development.

Although the traditional source of unskilled workers in Singapore was Malaysia, the expansion of the Malaysian economy made recruitment more difficult and labour was then recruited from such non-traditional source countries as India, Bangladesh, Indonesia, and Thailand (Pang 1993b, p. 49). While most of the men are employed in manufacturing and construction, one of the largest categories is female domestic servants. Singapore has one of the highest ratios of households with domestic servants in the world, most of whom come from the Philippines (Stalker 1994, p. 256).

Labour-exporting countries

The main labour-exporting country is the Philippines. It has a long history as a country of emigrants, usually migrating to the USA, and is the largest official exporter of contract labour to the Middle East and Asia, as well as the source of illegal flows to countries in the East Asian region. The main characteristics of Filipino labour migration are the extensive government regional network for recruitment and provision of services to contract workers and their families, the dependence of the domestic economy on remittances (in 1991 remittances through official channels increased to US$1.5 billion from US$1.2 billion in 1990), and the increasing proportion of female migrants leaving to work as domestic servants, as well as doctors, nurses, clerks and sales assistants (*Asian Migrant* 1993, p. 11).

The next largest labour exporter is Indonesia. Like the Philippines, Indonesia has a large labour surplus, but it entered the ranks of labour-exporting countries much later. As a consequence Indonesian workers had not been exposed to a culture of emigration, nor did they have extensive information networks to assist them (Pang 1993b, p. 59). However, the training of skilled labour for export and generation of a steady and substantial stream of remittances has become an important factor in Indonesian economic and manpower planning. In the 1980s, Indonesia was sending workers mainly to other Moslem countries – the majority went to the Middle East, although Malaysia and Singapore were also destinations for a sizeable number (Pang 1993b, p. 59). However, the legal flows of Indonesian contract workers are small compared with the numbers working abroad illegally, mostly in Malaysia. The flows to the Middle East from both the Philippines and Indonesia were interrupted in the early 1990s by the Gulf War but have resumed, although not at the same intensity. This is partly due to the opening up of other destinations closer to home, but there has also been considerable negative publicity about the treatment of workers, especially female workers, in these countries. There are stories of employers exploiting women through withholding their passports, refusing to pay them, and sexually abusing them (Stalker 1994, pp. 244–5).

China has long been a major labour exporter to many countries. Under the communist regime, flows were restricted to officially sanctioned engineering and construction work projects which were the only legal means by which low-skilled Chinese workers could work abroad. However, in addition to these legal flows, there are growing unofficial flows of mainly low-skilled labour to neighbouring countries, such as Japan, Korea, Hong Kong and Taiwan where workers and students are employed illegally in factories and domestic duties. As well, around 100 000 Chinese citizens are believed to have entered the USA illegally in 1992, with many smuggled in on boats (Lim & Abella 1994, p. 215).

The other major labour-exporting country in the APEC region is Mexico. The broad wage differences between Mexico and the USA encourage large northward migration flows of mostly undocumented workers. These migrants are no longer predominantly agricultural workers, and most of them find work in other sectors of the economy (PECC 1993, p. 34). While in the past, most workers went to the USA with the intention of staying only for short periods, recent indications from the numbers applying for citizenship (many who regular-ised their status under IRCA provisions are only now becoming eligible for citizenship) suggest that many are making a long-term commitment to stay. This may eventually lead to new legal flows under family reunification preferences (*The Economist* 1995, p. 35). Mexico is also the conduit of transmigration from other parts of Central and South America, most of it headed for the USA.

Labour-exporting/importing countries

The labour flows to and from Hong Kong, Korea, Malaysia and Thailand are quite complex and have been changing rapidly with the changing fortunes of these countries. All four countries allow the temporary entry of foreign workers but the permitted numbers do not meet the demand, so the larger flows are illegal (see Table 2.3).

Throughout the 1980s, illegal immigrants from China continued to enter Hong Kong and find work in the colony, despite a stringent policy of immediate repatriation and stiff penalties for employers. In the 1990s, the ready availability of cheap foreign labour from mainland China, rather than replacing scarce labour, has been displacing more expensive local workers who are then forced to look for work elsewhere in the region (Thornton 1995, p. 59). China also became a major source of unskilled illegal workers in Korea. In the 1970s, Korea was a large labour exporter. Labour exports declined in the 1980s, partly as a result of declining oil revenues in the Middle East which reduced spending on infrastructure, and partly as a result of the rising wages of Korean workers which led Korean firms to find other sources of unskilled labour for their Middle East projects (Pang 1993b, p. 45). Although Korea does not permit entry of unskilled foreign labour, strong export-led growth stimulated considerable illegal flows. In contrast, Thailand is still a major exporter of labour, particularly to countries in East Asia where wages are higher, but it replaces them with legal and illegal workers from China, Cambodia and Burma (Hiebert 1995, p. 56).

Malaysia was the traditional source of unskilled labour for Singapore and other Asian countries, but during Malaysia's recession in the mid-1980s, over 200 000 skilled construction workers left to work elsewhere in Asia and did not return. The gap was filled by Indonesians and some Bangladeshis – the majority of Indonesians arrived illegally from across the Strait of Malacca (Hiebert 1995,

p. 55). The Malaysian state which attracted the most illegal immigrants was Sabah, which was estimated to have around half a million in the early 1990s, most of whom had entered as refugees from southern Philippines, but with a sizeable number from Indonesia (Pang 1993b, p. 52).

IV Future migration trends in the APEC region

Despite international efforts to deregulate capital flows, encourage foreign direct investment and lower barriers to trade, people flows continue to be tightly controlled. There is no discernible downward trend in the numbers of potential permanent immigrants seeking a new home. Family migration appears likely to remain the major category of intake in the four main receiving countries.

Temporary labour movement in the region will continue to outstrip permanent flows. Permanent destination countries are unlikely to increase their intakes substantially in the next decade, leaving temporary movement as the main avenue of entry to countries in the region. The skilled flow will grow, encouraged by the increasing mobility of skilled professionals and globalisation of multinational firms, but also by the policies of sending countries to increase the skill level of their overseas workers to maximise the returns. The transfer of skills, knowledge and experience from these circular labour flows will continue to benefit all participants.

Expansion of tertiary education in the Philippines, Korea, Mexico and Chile means that their skilled labour will become integrated into the global labour pool (Low 1994). If, however, economic growth is not maintained, and the skilled workforce is not fully utilised in the home country, work will be sought elsewhere and the pressure will build for temporary migration to become permanent. This could lead to problems similar to those occurring already with unskilled labour flows. Countries in the APEC region are beginning to experience what Europe discovered in the previous two decades, namely that operating a guest worker system does not guarantee a clear distinction between temporary and permanent migration. Some permanent settlement is occurring despite tough enforcement strategies. Maintaining the integrity of the guest worker system is especially difficult where ethnic and cultural differences between immigrants and the local population are minimal.

Unskilled labour migration, both legal and illegal, will not diminish as long as differences remain in the pace of development and the demographic and economic growth between countries in the region (Pang 1993b, p. 13). Neither trade flows nor foreign direct investment seem likely to reduce the gap between sending and receiving countries in the foreseeable future (Stalker 1994, p. 162). Competition between labour-exporting countries is likely to intensify, with China poised to overtake the Philippines as the major labour exporter in the region in the next decade. Labour-surplus countries will continue to send people to find work in countries where the more menial production and service jobs are no longer undertaken by locals. Concerns about living and working conditions of unskilled foreign workers will persist in the short to medium term – the experience of the last decade has shown that there are always new sources of unskilled workers willing to accept the poor conditions.

PART II

Links Between Trade Liberalisation and Migration

3

Theories About Trade Liberalisation and Migration: Substitutes or Complements?

*Wilfred J. Ethier**

This paper discusses what the theory of international trade has to say about the relation between international trade in commodities and human migration. The literature is enormous, so I constrain myself in several ways. First, I discuss only whether trade and migration are complements or substitutes, ignoring other aspects of their relationship. Though this area has been well mined, some new results emerge. Second, I address *factor* migration in general, ignoring distinct features of *labour* migration. I have addressed these before,[1] and also they are less relevant to the substitute–complement question than to other issues. Third, I ignore models which assume some *direct* link between trade and migration, for example, models in which trade generates knowledge required for direct investment, or in which labour migration generates host-country demand for source-country products and lowers transaction costs for trade between the two countries.[2] Fourth, I minimise analytical detail, offering a basically intuitive discussion in terms of simple, familiar models. But first some preliminaries.

I Why do we care?

Interest in substitution between trade in goods and the migration of factors – especially the migration of labour – centres on trade and migration policy. Such concerns are best indicated by examples. Mexican migration into the USA was a major consideration during the NAFTA negotiations (and also in the unilateral opening of the Mexican economy). Western European trade initiatives with Central and Eastern Europe are prompted significantly by fears of large-scale migration from the latter to the former. The guest-worker systems prominent in Western Europe during the 1960s were initiated partly to employ migrants for the provision of non-traded services, and partly to prevent the displacement of labour-intensive production of tradeables by imports – a substitution of migration for trade in each case.

Examples are not limited to labour. Various countries (for example, Canada with its National Policy) have tried to stimulate an inflow of capital by imposing barriers against the import of goods.[3]

These examples illustrate two critical features. First, implications for migration become important in trade relations only when the nations involved differ considerably in economic structure – North American integration had little concern with migration until Mexico joined Canada and the USA. The most important international commercial process since the Second World War, the progressive multilateral liberalisation of the exchange of manufactured goods among the industrial nations, has involved a large group of countries differing only modestly in economic structure. Concerns about migration have not been central to this process. But possible integration within APEC is another matter indeed. Here we have a large group of countries with much sharper differences in levels of development, incomes per capita, and relative factor endowments. Thus migration could turn out to be much more important to policy-makers than typically has been the case in the past.

The second important point is that, in all cases, the concerns of policy-makers have been based squarely on the presumption that trade and migration are substitutes. But is this so?

Our examples also suggest what motivates concern about the link between trade and migration. Concern for the social implications of a large influx of foreigners with alien characteristics is a common thread, as is the fear that migrant workers might displace native workers or bid down the wages they receive. Another important consideration is policy feasibility. Officials in the USA became seriously interested in the consequences of trade policy for migration only when they became convinced that immigration policy was ineffective and could not be made effective. Many Europeans believe that the attempts of the EU to complete the internal market will reduce its ability to implement immigration policy. The use of migrant labour to lower costs in labour-intensive sectors became more appealing as international commitments constrained the use of trade policy.

Finally, these examples suggest that substitution between different factors may be as important in practice as substitution between factors and trade. Investment in Mexico and in Eastern Europe is widely thought an alternative to emigration.

What is substitutability?

Broadly, trade and migration are complements if they tend to 'go together'. But they might do this in different ways, related but distinct. Which concept is the most useful depends on why one is interested in the relation between trade and migration. I distinguish three concepts.[4]

(i) *Quantity substitutability.* Trade substitutes for migration if an exogenous increase in the volume of trade produces a decrease in the volume of migration. This concept is natural if concern with migration centres on its social implications.

(ii) *Price substitutability*. Trade substitutes for migration if a convergence of commodity prices across countries (due, say, to trade liberalisation) produces a similar convergence of factor prices. This is the concept to use when concerned about the effects of international transactions on the rewards of domestic factors.

(iii) *Equilibrium substitutability*. Trade substitutes for migration if free trade without migration produces the same international equilibrium (except for the location of production) as would free migration without trade. This concept comes to mind if concern focuses on policy feasibility.

With the quantity and price concepts, one can also reverse the roles of goods and factors in the above definitions. We normally expect symmetry – trade substitutes for migration if, and only if, migration substitutes for trade – but this need not be the case. Equilibrium substitutability is, however, inherently symmetrical.

II Comparative-advantage trade

The influence of trade on factor mobility is intimately related to the reasons for trade itself. The 'traditional' explanation of international trade concerns comparative advantage, so let's begin there.

Comparative-advantage assumes away imperfect competition and all externalities, whether of production or of consumption. The proximate cause of trade is an international difference in the relative commodity prices that would hold in autarky. If commodity trade is allowed, countries will tend to export goods that would be relatively cheap in autarky and import those that would be relatively dear – a statement that can be made more definitive under certain unrealistic circumstances, such as the existence of only two goods or only one factor. The approach is easily extended to encompass factor trade, but let's assume for now that goods are tradeable and factors are immobile internationally.

More important to comparative advantage than positive predictions are its normative implications. Such trade renders the global economy efficient (conditional on the immobility of factors), and guarantees that no individual economy will lose from trade, compared to autarky, in that gainers in any country always gain at least the wherewithal to compensate the losers in that country.

The discrepancies in autarky relative prices can themselves be the result of one or more of three 'natural' causes, namely international differences in:

(i)   relative factor endowments;
(ii)   technology; and
(iii)   preferences.

In addition, autarky price differences can be due to any of an assortment of:

(iv)   'unnatural' causes, such as market distortions (but not imperfect competition, which comparative advantage rules out) or national tax policies.

Factor endowments

The Heckscher–Ohlin approach to trade theory, isolating the effects of international differences in relative factor endowments, has received the most attention over the years. It is also the approach within which the substitutability of trade and migration has been most extensively studied. Ohlin (1933) discussed such substitution at length, as did Meade (1955). The seminal paper of Mundell (1957) described the substitution in purest form.

Suppose that two countries are identical in every respect, except relative factor endowments. Suppose also that preferences in each country are homothetic, as well as identical, and suppose for simplicity there are but two goods – A and B – and two factors – capital (K) and labour (L).

In autarky, international differences in endowments produce international differences in factor rewards which in turn induce differences in relative commodity prices, so providing the basis for trade. If instead factors are allowed to migrate, that migration would produce internationally identical factor rewards. This implies equal costs and equal commodity prices across countries, and the disappearance of the basis for trade. Migration is a complete substitute for trade in both the quantity and the price sense.

The above assumes both factors can migrate. But suppose instead that only one – say, labour – can do so. Then wages will be equalised between countries, though rents need not be, and differences in relative commodity prices can persist. Thus labour mobility alone does not eliminate the basis for trade. But it 'almost' does so. If the two hypothetical goods are also traded, then international competition requires that rents be equalised across countries – otherwise the country with the higher rent, having the same wage, would not be competitive in either commodity market. This equalises commodity prices across countries, so no actual trade need occur. The international mobility of one factor together with the *potential* to trade both goods substitutes for both international mobility of the second factor and the *actual* trade of goods.

Now let's turn to whether trade can substitute for migration. Let w denote the vector of the two factor rewards and $c = c(w)$ the vector of unit cost functions of the two goods. Suppose the two countries engage in free trade, with an equilibrium price vector p. Suppose $p = c(w)$. Define the diversification cone $K(w)$ as the set of all non-negative linear combinations of non-negative multiples of the techniques which minimise unit costs in the respective sectors at factor rewards w. If both countries' endowments lie within $K(w)$, each produces both goods and experiences factor rewards w. If either country has an endowment outside $K(w)$ then factor–price equalisation is impossible, either because at least one country specialises production in one good or because a factor-intensity reversal[5] lies between the two countries.

This, the celebrated *factor–price equalisation* theorem, is illustrated in Figure 3.1, where E and E^* denote endowments of the two countries, and C and C^* the factor content of the commodity bundles consumed by the home and foreign countries respectively.[6] Essentially, free trade in goods will equalise factor rewards if relative endowments are 'sufficiently' similar. The degree of similarity which will prove sufficient depends on demand, first because the relevant diversification cone depends on world equilibrium prices, and second because, given factor endowments, world demand concentrated sufficiently on the capital-intensive good, for example, can always cause the capital-abundant country to specialise in the production of that good.

If the two countries' endowments are sufficiently similar,[7] trade is a perfect substitute for migration in the quantity, price and equilibrium senses. But what if this is not the case?

The answer is straightforward if the technology has no factor-intensity reversals. In that case, relative factor rewards are monotonically related to relative commodity costs, which, if both goods are produced, equal relative commodity prices. Then trade in goods draws prices closer together and thereby, at least until one country is driven to specialise, causes relative commodity costs to become more equal, so causing factor rewards to become more nearly equal also. Trade is a *partial* substitute for migration in both the quantity and price senses.

Factor-intensity reversals add ambiguity. If two countries are separated by one (or any odd number of) reversals, a partial convergence of relative commodity costs causes relative factor rewards in the two countries to move in the *same* direction. Whether they move closer together or further apart depends upon details of the technology. Thus factor-intensity reversals illustrate the possibility that, although migration substitutes perfectly for trade, the latter may be partially *complementary* to the former!

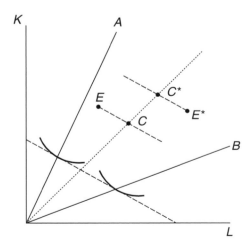

Figure 3.1   Factor–price equalisation

In sum, a variety of relations between trade and migration is possible, even with comparative-advantage trade driven solely by differences in relative factor endowments.[8] But the bottom line is clearly a strong presumption of substitutability, with the substitution being perfect and symmetric if endowments are sufficiently similar.

Preferences

Now suppose, in the model of the previous subsection, that the two countries have identical relative factor endowments but different preferences. The situation is much as above, but simpler. Migration, by causing factor rewards to become equal internationally, must again eliminate the basis for trade. In Figure 3.1, C and C^* now depict the *endowments* of the two countries and E and E^* the factor contents of their consumption bundles. The figure thus shows factor–price equalisation, with trade being a perfect substitute for factor mobility. If preferences in the two countries differ enough, one or both countries will specialise, so trade would be only a partial substitute. But trade must always be at least a partial substitute, because, with equal relative endowments, the two countries cannot be separated by a factor-intensity reversal, regardless of whether the technology possesses one.

Technology

There is a strong presumption that trade and migration are substitutes, with trade driven solely by differences in relative factor endowments or in preferences. But, with trade due to causes *other than* endowment and preference differences, there is a presumption that trade and migration will be complements.[9]

To investigate this, let's return to the previous model, but suppose that the home and foreign economies have identical endowments and identical, homothetic preferences, so that their autarky equilibria are unique and there is no basis for either trade or migration. Now let's perturb this boring situation by a uniform 10 per cent shift towards the origin of all A industry isoquants in the home country and all B industry isoquants in the foreign country. Such 'Hicks-neutral' technical changes imply that, at unchanged factor prices, all production techniques are also unchanged, but the cost of A production at home and B production abroad each falls by 10 per cent. In Figure 3.2, c shows the monotonic relation, before the technical changes, in each country, between the wage–rental ratio w and the cost of B production relative to A production, on the assumption that A is relatively capital intensive. With the technical changes, this curve shifts up 10 per cent to c^H at home and down to c^F abroad.

The technical changes establish a basis for international exchange. Consider first trade. The technical changes raise[10] the home autarky relative price of B in terms of A and lower it abroad. Thus the home country has a comparative advantage in A (the capital-intensive good) and the foreign country in B (the labour-intensive good).

Trade will establish a common price ratio, illustrated by p' in Figure 3.2. This requires that relative factor rewards be w_H at home and w_F abroad. Thus free trade enforces a basis for migration. If the migration is allowed, capital will move from the foreign country, and labour will flow in the opposite direction. This will shift production in each country towards its exportable good, thereby *expanding trade* still more.

Now suppose that, in response to the technical change, migration occurs instead of trade.[11] This will establish common factor rewards, illustrated by w' in Figure 3.2. This results in relative commodity prices of c_H' and c_F' respectively, giving a comparative advantage to the home country in A and the foreign country in B. Thus free migration enforces a basis for commodity trade. If the trade is allowed, the increased production by each country of its comparative-advantage good lowers the wage-rental ratio at home while raising it abroad, so inducing more migration. The resulting home capital inflow and/or labour out-flow shifts production in each country towards its comparative-advantage good, thereby expanding trade still more.

Clearly, migration alone establishes an equilibrium quite different from that established by trade alone. An equilibrium established with both trade and migration is represented by w' and p' in Figure 3.2. Since $c_H' > p' > c_F'$, the home economy produces only A and the foreign economy only B – the world is taking maximum advantage of the international productivity differences. Indeed, p' is the same as the common autarky relative price prior to the technical changes, but now everyone consumes exactly 10 per cent more of each good. (Note that each country exports the good, making relatively intensive use of its relatively abundant – after migration – factor.)

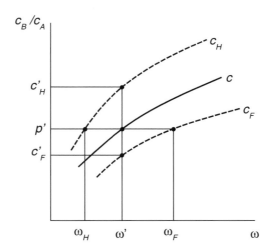

Figure 3.2   Effects of technology differences on trade and factor flows

In summary: an increase in trade stimulates migration, and an increase in migration stimulates trade; a convergence of commodity prices, through trade, supports a divergence of factor rewards, and a convergence of factor rewards, through migration, supports a divergence of commodity prices; the international equilibrium with trade alone is distinct from that with migration alone, and both are distinct from that with trade and migration together. The two types of international exchange are totally complementary.[12]

'Unnatural' causes of autarky price differences

The diversity of the taxes and other distortions included in this category render general conclusions impossible.[13] But the basic logic underlying the previous analysis of differences in technology is relevant here also and establishes a presumption that trade and migration are complements. Suppose that the home and foreign economies – otherwise identical – differ with respect to some tax policy or other distortion that causes the autarky relative price of A in terms of B to be lower at home than abroad. If trade commences, the home economy shifts resources towards the A sector, driving up the relative reward of the factor employed intensively there, while the reverse takes place abroad. If migration is then allowed, this will *increase* the volume of trade because each country will become relatively more abundant in the factor employed intensively by its export sector.

This logic is powerful and establishes a *presumption* of complementarity. But it cannot establish more than that because we cannot rule out the possibility that the distortion (unspecified, after all), in addition to causing international differences in autarky relative prices, might negate steps in the above logical chain. A class of distortions will in fact have this property.

Let's consider separately the production and consumption distortions, starting with the former.[14] Suppose, once again, that the home and foreign economies are identical, except that at home a production distortion causes the marginal rate of transformation of B for A to be less than the price of A in terms of B. This discrepancy might be due to a trade association, a production tax on A, a subsidy to B production, etc.

Autarky is shown in Figure 3.3. The two countries share the same transformation curve and indifference map. The foreign autarky equilibrium is shown by F and the home equilibrium by H. Since the distortion is to production, home relative prices equal the marginal rate of substitution of home consumers. Thus the home economy has a comparative advantage in B and the foreign economy a comparative advantage in A – there is a basis for trade. Note that the difference in home and foreign autarky relative prices is less than the home distortion. Since factor rewards relate to the marginal rate of transformation in the usual way, the home wage-rental ratio is greater in autarky than that abroad, if A is the relatively capital-intensive good – there is a basis for migration.

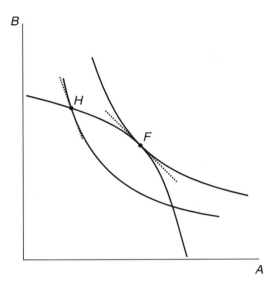

Figure 3.3   A production distortion and the marginal rate of transformation

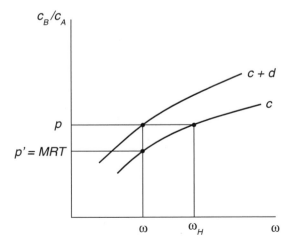

Figure 3.4   An example of factor migration increasing trade

Suppose there is free trade but no migration. Trade will establish a common price ratio, illustrated by p in Figure 3.4. In the figure, c shows the relation between relative commodity costs and relative factor rewards, as before, and $c + d$ adds to this the amount of the production distortion. Thus relative factor rewards must be w_H at home and w abroad. Free trade in goods *enhances* the basis for migration. If the migration is allowed, capital will move from the home country, and labour will flow in the opposite direction. This will shift production in each country towards its exportable good, *expanding trade* still more.

Now suppose that, instead of trade, migration occurs. This establishes common factor rewards, illustrated by w in Figure 3.4, and results in relative commodity prices of p abroad and p' at home, giving the home country an enhanced comparative advantage in B and the foreign country in A. The difference in commodity prices between the two countries has increased to the full extent of the distortion. Thus migration enhances the basis for trade. If the trade is allowed, increased production by each country of its comparative-advantage good raises the wage-rental ratio at home and lowers it abroad, inducing more migration. The resulting home capital outflow and/or labour inflow shifts production in each country towards its comparative-advantage good, expanding trade still more.

Clearly, migration alone establishes an equilibrium quite different from that of trade alone. An equilibrium established with *both* trade *and* migration is represented by w and by a relative price between p and p' inclusive. At least one country must specialise. (Note that each country exports the good making relatively intensive use of its relatively abundant – after migration – factor.)

So, the result is the same as with trade due to technology differences: an increase in trade stimulates migration, and an increase in migration stimulates trade; a convergence of commodity prices, through trade, supports a divergence of factor rewards, and a convergence of factor rewards, through migration, supports a divergence of commodity prices; the international equilibrium with trade alone is distinct from that with migration alone, and both are distinct from that with trade and migration together. The two types of international exchange are totally complementary.

Since a production distortion produces the same relation between trade and migration as do technology differences, one might conjecture that a consumption distortion would produce the same relation as do preference differences. This is indeed the case. Suppose that the situation depicted in Figure 3.3 is due not to a production distortion but rather to a home consumption distortion (between relative commodity prices and the marginal rates of substitution of domestic consumers). Then home autarky relative prices equal the marginal rate of transformation, and the home economy now has a comparative advantage in A rather than in B, but the home wage–rental ratio is still greater in autarky than abroad.

Trade will now drive factor rewards together across countries, and migration will drive commodity prices together. In Figure 3.4, the curve *c* now relates factor rewards to commodity prices (with production diversification) in both countries. The discussion of international exchange due solely to differences in preferences can now be repeated virtually unchanged.

To sum up, the following conclusion seems warranted by our discussion, concerning comparative-advantage trade.

There is a strong presumption that international differences in factor endowments or in consumption patterns – whether due to differences in preferences or to consumption distortions – render trade and migration substitutes. There is a strong presumption that international differences in production methods – whether due to differences in technology or to production distortions – render trade and migration complements.

Theoretical results like these should motivate empirical research, but here also conclusions have been ambiguous. The empirical literature[15] is beyond the scope of this paper, but my general impression is that the data weakly indicate trade and migration to be quantity complements and, even more weakly, indicate them to be price substitutes.

III Economies of scale and imperfect competition

Comparative advantage is an inclusive grab-bag, assuming only perfect competition and no externalities. Imperfect competition is accordingly a possible independent basis for trade. So are economies of scale because, if external to the firm they are externalities, and if internal they rule out perfectly competitive equilibria. Thus comparative advantage, economies of scale and imperfect competition almost exhaust all possible reasons to trade.[16]

Countries conduct comparative-advantage trade to exploit differences. With economies of scale, countries trade to concentrate on fewer tasks and to perform them better.[17] With imperfect competition, countries trade to expose their firms to more competition, and thereby force them to act more efficiently.

Economies of scale

Let's consider first economies of scale. To return to our 2×2×2 model, let's suppose that the two countries are identical in every way, that good *B* is produced with constant returns to scale, but that *A* production is characterised by increasing returns. In practice these occur in great variety, so a classification of the more important attributes is useful.
- *Internal vs. external* (to the firm). Internal economies require consideration of imperfect competition, so let's start with external economies and assume perfect competition.
- *National vs. international.* Economies of scale may depend on the scale of operations within a nation (e.g., large plant size) or on the scale of opera-

tions globally (e.g., division of labour and free trade in intermediate goods).[18] Either type might be either internal or external to the firm.

- *Aggregative vs. disaggregative.* Increasing returns to scale may be a property of manufacturing generally or of individual manufactured goods. The former can be modelled with A, a single homogeneous good possessing scale economies, but the latter require a large number n of distinct goods, each by itself characterised by increasing returns to scale.

These three considerations generate eight types of scale economies, each relevant to the world in which we live. Let's consider first national, aggregative, increasing returns external to the firm.[19]

National, aggregative, increasing returns to scale external to the firm

The two identical economies will possess identical autarky equilibria so there is no comparative-advantage basis for either trade or migration. Autarky behaviour, with internationally identical prices, will also constitute an equilibrium with free trade and/or free migration. Such an equilibrium may or may not be stable,[20] but it will definitely not be interesting. So consider the other possibilities. As before, commodity A is capital intensive.

Suppose, first, there is free trade but no migration. If the common preferences for the two goods are appropriately symmetric, relative to the degree of scale economies, there will be an international trade equilibrium with one country (call it the home economy) specialised in A and one in B. With internationally identical endowments and technology, such an equilibrium implies a lower wage–rental ratio at home than abroad. Thus trade generates a basis for migration, and such migration (capital moving to the home economy and labour to the foreign economy), if allowed, will expand the basis for trade. Trade complements migration.

Sufficiently pronounced preference for B will allow[21] a trade equilibrium with one country specialised in B production and one (call it home) diversified. Since the two countries have identical endowments and A is relatively capital intensive, the home country must be using a more labour-intensive technique in B production than does the foreign country. Thus, once again, there is a lower wage–rental ratio at home than abroad, and trade complements migration.

Sufficiently pronounced preference for A will allow a trade equilibrium with one country specialised in A production and one (call it foreign) diversified. Since the two countries have identical endowments and A is relatively capital intensive, the foreign country must be using a more capital-intensive technique in A production than does the home country. Thus, yet again, there is a lower wage–rental ratio at home than abroad, and trade complements migration. But now there is a deeper significance to this. A trade-only equilibrium here might well leave the foreign economy worse off than in autarky: its A sector must compete on equal terms with a larger – and therefore more productive – home A sector, implying generally lower factor rewards. Migration removes this possibility and could therefore be vital in rendering trade acceptable to the diversified economy (or in eliminating international conflict over which country is to assume this role). This is a totally new dimension to complementarity.

Now let's consider migration without trade. Equal factor rewards imply that the price of B is the same in both countries. If the equilibrium is distinct from autarky, one country (call it home) will have a larger A sector. With factor rewards – and therefore production techniques – being identical, the home economy must have a larger capital–labour ratio than the foreign economy and, with a larger A sector, a lower relative price of A. If trade is allowed, the home economy will export A, and this will induce additional migration. Migration is complementary to trade.

Thus trade and migration are, once again, thorough complements. What is new here is the possibility (not the certainty) that migration might be necessary for trade to be acceptable at all!

National, disaggregative, increasing returns to scale external to the firm

Now suppose that instead of one A sector, there are n differentiated A sectors with identical production functions, each perfectly competitive and each possessing external increasing returns to scale.[22] Much of the above logic applies here as well; for example, if the scale economies are sufficiently pronounced, trade-only equilibria with one or both countries completely specialised in A and/ or B will still exist, and such trade will generate a basis for migration. But there are two critical differences.

The first is the presence of *intra-industry* trade within the A sector. The two identical countries will possess a trade-only equilibrium in which they produce identical quantities of B and have equal-sized A sectors, with each country producing n/2 of the distinct varieties. Thus the countries will be self-sufficient in B and exchange only A varieties. Such trade does not produce a disparity in factor rewards and so will not generate a basis for migration. But intra-industry trade and migration will be complementary in the sense that (exogenous) endowment similarities will be associated with A production in both countries and therefore with intra-industry trade. In the same sense, the model restores a substitutability between migration and the *inter-industry* trade of B for all types of A.

The second critical difference is that disaggregative scale economies vitiate the possibility that migration could be necessary for trade to be acceptable. If a trade-only equilibrium requires a country to operate a small A sector, that result can be accomplished by producing only a small number of varieties, each at a large scale, and does not require the country to operate at an inefficient, small scale.

International external economies of scale

Now suppose that the economies of scale in A production depend upon a global division of labour within the A sector – a division of labour that can be realised if intermediate goods can be exchanged. Thus the economies of scale depend upon the global size of the A industry, independently of its distribution between the two countries, whenever goods can be freely traded.[23] Suppose that the scale economies are aggregative.[24] This situation produces an interesting blend of the relationships derived so far.

First, with the degree of scale economies being, in the presence of trade, independent of the allocation of A production between countries, trade will be consistent with the analysis in Section III above. That is, *inter-industry* trade induced by international differences in endowments or preferences, or by consumption distortions, will substitute for migration, and trade induced by technology differences or production distortions will complement migration.

Next, if the two countries share the world A sector and allow trade, then *intra-industry* trade within the A sector will emerge to exploit the international scale economies. As in the discussion of disaggregated scale economies, this can be expected to expand if endowments become more similar – intra-industry trade complements migration (the 'complementarity theorem').

Finally, let's consider free migration without trade. The absence of trade prevents the development of a single, integrated, world A industry, so the economies of scale will be national. The earlier discussion of national, aggregative, increasing returns to scale external to the firm applies here as well. Migration complements trade, even though, as we have just seen, trade substitutes for migration.

Thus far I have discussed the various forms of external scale economies. The basic effect of internal economies is to add imperfect competition.

Imperfect competition

Let's distinguish between monopolistic competition and oligopoly.

Monopolistic competition

First, let's return to the discussion of national, disaggregative, external scale economies and modify our assumptions in two ways. Suppose that the scale economies are internal to the individual firm, rather than external to it, and that the firms engage in monopolistic competition. Also, let's replace the assumption that the number of varieties n is exogenous with the assumption of free entry and exit, so n adjusts to ensure that firms in the A sector earn a normal rate of profit.

Such models highlighting differentiated consumer goods and monopolistic competition are central to a large literature.[25] It is not difficult to see, though, that our conclusions about the relation between trade and migration continue to hold. That is, migration and inter-industry trade are substitutes, while migration and intra-industry trade are complements.

Next, let's return to international economies of scale. These are based upon the division of labour. But if the division of labour is limited by the extent of the market, indivisibilities must be important, and these imply internal returns to scale. Thus it is reasonable to flesh out the model by adding the assumptions that, within the world A sector, intermediate goods are produced under internal increasing returns to scale by monopolistically competitive firms.[26] Free entry and exit determine both the number of such firms and the degree of the division of labour. Once again, though, when it comes to the relation between trade and migration, our earlier conclusions are unaffected by these modifications.

In these disaggregated models, the basic results are really driven by scale economies, not by features of imperfect competition. But the reverse is true when we come to oligopoly.

Oligopoly

Now let's return again to the basic $2 \times 2 \times 2$ model where the countries are identical in every way, and suppose that the A sector in each country is oligopolistic, with a common, small, exogenously determined number n of identical firms. To highlight the role of oligopoly, suppose that the common technology is characterised by constant returns to scale. Autarky equilibrium in each country can be depicted by point H in Figure 3.3.

Now suppose free trade without migration. The sole impact of this is that each A firm experiences an increase in the number of its rivals from $n - 1$ to $2n - 1$. This shifts the common equilibrium from H in Figure 3.3 to some point between H and F inclusive. A Cournot–Nash equilibrium would be strictly between these two points. Each country produces more A and less B, and the distorting effect of the imperfect competition is ameliorated. With both countries being self-sufficient in both goods, no trade need occur – it's the exposure to more competition that matters, not the actual exchange of goods. If trade does take place, it will be strictly intra-industry. The reallocation of resources towards the capital-intensive sector causes wages to rise and rents to fall, but they remain equal across countries, so the ability to trade goods does not induce a desire for migration.

If, instead, free migration is possible but not trade, nothing will happen. With autarky factor rewards equal across countries and all factor markets perfectly competitive, there is no basis for migration. Free migration cannot bring about the same outcome as free trade.

The above discussion focused narrowly on oligopoly as a basis for international exchange by assuming away scale economies and international dissimilarities (thereby excluding comparative advantage). Now let's consider international *differences* in the degree of imperfect competition. Assume that, while the home A industry still contains n firms, the foreign industry now contains $n^* > n$. Home autarky equilibrium is at H in Figure 3.3, with foreign equilibrium somewhere between H and F. Note that the relative price of A in terms of B is lower abroad than at home, but, with the foreign economy producing more of the capital-intensive good, the wage–rental ratio is higher. Thus there is a basis for migration.

Now suppose free trade without migration, and consider a symmetric, Cournot–Nash equilibrium. With all $n + n^*$ firms producing the same amount and $n^* > n$, the foreign economy exports A in exchange for B.[27] In each country, the relative price of A falls, the wage rises and the rent falls, but capital remains relatively cheap abroad. Thus trade cannot remove the basis for migration.

Next, suppose that migration is unfettered, but trade is disallowed. Migration will equalise factor rewards, and thus production techniques, across countries. In equilibrium, the two countries will still have identical *relative* factor endowments, but $n^*/(n + n^*)$ of the world endowment of each factor will reside in the foreign economy – the foreign economy will now be exactly like the home economy, but at n^*/n of the scale. Thus commodity prices are equal across countries: migration is a substitute for trade in the price sense. But this does not eliminate the basis for trade, since the latter would still expose A firms to increased competition. Also, the free-migration equilibrium must be distinct from the free-trade equilibrium.

So now suppose both trade and migration. This will differ from the free-migration equilibrium in the same way that free trade differed from autarky when $n = n^*$. In each country the relative price of A falls and resources are reallocated from B to A. Again, no trade need take place – it is the exposure to more competition that counts. But actual migration is necessary to sustain this equilibrium.

Note also that capital mobility does not substitute for labour mobility: both are necessary to attain this equilibrium. Suppose that there is free trade and free migration of labour but that capital is not mobile. The two countries are constrained to have equal capital stocks, as in autarky. Then, if both countries produce both goods, they must have equal factor prices and, therefore, employ the same techniques. But with $n^* > n$ and $K^* = K$, the foreign economy must have an excess demand for capital, and/or the home economy an excess demand for labour. Equilibrium requires[28] that capital rents differ across countries, and this requires that the foreign economy specialises in A, and/or the home economy in B.

To sum up, the following conclusions seem warranted.

There is a strong presumption that intra-industry trade and trade due to aggregative economies of scale or to international differences in the degree of imperfect competition are strongly complementary to migration. There is also a strong presumption that inter-industry trade due to disaggregative economies of scale or to monopolistic competition relates to migration in the same ways as does comparative-advantage trade.

IV The central puzzle

Markusen's statement (1983, p. 355) that 'trade in goods and factors are substitutes may be a rather special result which is generally true only for the Heckscher–Ohlin basis for trade' may be a bit too strong, but it does capture the essence of the relation between the two types of international exchange. This essence is that complementarity comes up all over the place once we move beyond factor endowment differences and demand conditions as reasons for international exchange.

Economists have been trying for almost half a century to implement empirically a factor-endowments model of trade but have yet to succeed. Indeed, the repeated failures have been a powerful force – perhaps the most powerful force – in stimulating new theoretical approaches. In addition, the 'new trade theory' of the last fifteen years or so has strongly emphasised just those features that render trade and migration complements. And much of this theory has had a pronounced policy motivation. These observations lead to the central puzzle: *if empirical work has been unable to establish the factor-endowments basis of trade, and if theoretical work has increasingly emphasised the relevance of a context in which trade and migration are complementary, why is it that serious policy debate almost always starts from the presumption that trade and migration are strong substitutes?*

Several possible explanations come to mind.

- *Ignorance and stupidity.* Their importance should never be discounted, but further discussion won't get us very far.
- *The failure to implement empirically a factor-endowments model reflects the difficulty of empirical research, not the irrelevance of factor-endowment differences.* I personally give much weight to this possibility: factor-endowment differences matter a great deal for trade, I believe.
- *The relation between trade liberalisation and migration is likely to be a sensitive policy issue when relative factor endowments differ significantly between countries.* This point came out in Section I's examples. Regardless of how important factor-endowment differences may be overall, migration is likely to matter when endowment differences are large, because then factor-reward differences are also likely to be large. This is also when trade and migration are most likely to be substitutes.
- *Precisely because of the complementarity between trade and migration, trade that is complementary is most likely to be important when countries are similar, and this is when migration is unlikely to be an important issue.* This is especially true with regard to the various types of intra-industry trade, which, as seen above, are complementary to migration.
- *In practice, trade liberalisation tends to be accompanied by other elements of economic reform.* That is, a decision to liberalise trade is usually accompanied by a decision to reduce distortions and increase competition, both associated with complementarity.

These explanations leave untouched the trade that is due to national, aggregative, external economies of scale. As seen above, this is strongly complementary to migration, and also raises the intriguing possibility that migration might be necessary to induce some countries to trade. But I am suspicious of the present practical relevance of this; I suspect international spill-overs are just too important, and, indeed, are a good part of what trade liberalisation is all about.

The central impression I get from all this is that circumstances in which trade and migration are most likely to affect trade policy are largely the circumstances under which they are most likely to be substitutes. If accurate, this impression would be very important for APEC, because the huge diversity between member states implies that all the potential reasons for international exchange are present.

Notes

* I am grateful to Peter Lloyd, Graeme Woodridge and other conference participants for many useful comments and suggestions, and to the Tinbergen Institute, Rotterdam, for its support.
1 See Ethier (1986).
2 For the latter, see Gould (1994).
3 But when Canada became critical of foreign direct investment in the 1960s, trade liberalisation was not considered as a possible remedy.
4 For more detail, see Wong (1986b).
5 A technology has a factor-intensity reversal at $w = w^*$ if the sector that employs relatively more capital per worker when the wage–rental ratio is slightly above that of w^* employs relatively less when it is slightly below it (so that both sectors employ the same ratio when $w = w^*$). Two countries are separated by such a reversal if one country is endowed with more capital per worker than is employed by the two sectors when $w = w^*$, and the other country is endowed with less.
6 The figure shows the two countries consuming factors in identical proportions because of identical and homothetic preferences, but the factor–price equalisation theorem does not require this.
7 In the sense of both lying within a common diversification cone consistent with equilibrium world prices.
8 Higher dimensions can furnish additional relations. For example, with more factors than goods, results analogous to those in the text emerge once the number of international markets (goods plus freely mobile factors) equals the number of factors. Thus these results describe the relations between international exchanges of goods and some subset of factors, on the one hand, and the remaining factors, on the other. This involves factor–factor substitution, referred to in the examples early in this paper. See Ethier (1984) and Ethier and Svensson (1986).
9 The seminal contribution is Markusen (1983).
10 Whether by more or less than 10 per cent depends on preferences.
11 I assume that home factors are identical in the production process to their foreign counterparts: migrating factors do not bring the source country technology with

them. An alternative assumption would be that, in production, factors are distinguished, Armington-style, by their country of origin.

12   But note that, if one country were more efficient than the other in both sectors, all factors would migrate to the former country, thereby eliminating trade – an extreme case of substitutability!

13   For domestic distortions and trade, see Bhagwati (1971).

14   See Markusen (1983) for production distortions.

15   See Wong (1988) for indications of complementarity in US international exchanges.

16   Almost, but not quite. There remain consumption externalities and production externalities that do not work through economies of scale. These are potentially important for the relation between trade, migration and environmental issues, but have received little attention as bases for trade, so I shall not consider them.

17   See Melvin (1969) and Markusen and Melvin (1981).

18   See Ethier (1979).

19   Trade in a one-factor version of such a model is analysed in Ethier (1982a). Trade and migration are addressed in Markusen (1983) and in Chapter 5 of Wong (1994).

20   See Chapter 5 of Wong (1994) for stability.

21   The various types of equilibria need not be mutually exclusive: more than one may be consistent with the same basic data. Indeed, with the countries identical, multiple equilibria can always be achieved simply by reversing the roles of the two countries.

22   See Ethier (1987) for a discussion of international trade in such a context.

23   For the dependence of international returns to scale on intra-industry trade, see Ethier (1979); for the 'complementarity theorem', discussed presently, see Ethier (1982b); for an introduction to the relation between international capital movements and international economies of scale, see Chapter 5 of Wong (1994).

24   Extension of the following discussion to disaggregative scale economies is straightforward.

25   Basic contributions include Krugman (1979), Lancaster (1979) and Helpman (1981). See Helpman and Krugman (1985) for an overview.

26   See Ethier (1982b).

27   Note that each country exports the good that is relatively cheap in autarky. But there is no causal relationship – this is not comparative-advantage trade. If the foreign factor endowments were made a sufficiently large multiple of the home endowments, then A would be relatively expensive in autarky in the foreign country, but it would still export A if $n^* > n$.

28   This case was discussed by Markusen (1983).

4

Globalisation, Foreign Investment and Migration

P. J. Lloyd*

'Globalisation' is a much-used but imprecise word. It alludes to the links in production activities across national borders. This chapter explores the links between the elements of the triangle of international flows: commodities, capital and labour. The literature on globalisation emphasises the role of capital flows in the form of direct foreign investments and their links to the growth of international trade in commodities, but it pays little attention to the international migration of people. My concern is to relate these movements of capital and commodities across national borders to the movement of people.

Section I discusses the nature of globalisation. The direct implications of globalisation and foreign direct investment for commodity trade are examined in Section II and those for the international movement of people in Section III. The indirect effects of foreign direct investment and immigration on factor prices, and thereby on each other, are considered in Section IV. Section V considers some links between the international movement of people and international flows of capital and commodity trade in which the movement of people precedes the movement of the capital.

I What is globalisation?

National economies have plainly become more interdependent over the last twenty years in the sense that cross-national flows are a larger part of markets for goods, services and factors. It is useful to refer to this process as 'internationalisation'.

Globalisation is not synonymous with internationalisation. Analysts who use the term 'globalisation' have in mind something more specific but there is little agreement on what this is. The focus is on production. In more recent years the focus has moved to the firm – as the unit which carries out production – and to 'global firms'.

In this usage, globalisation refers to the activities of *multinational firms* or enterprises. 'Multinational enterprises are firms that control and manage activities in at least two countries' (Bureau of Industry Economics 1993, p. 1). In this definition, control and management of the firms are requirements of multinationality. In Australia, as in the USA and some other countries, the minimum level of ownership to be classified as a direct investor is 10 per cent of the ordinary shares or voting stock.

The parents and affiliates of a multinational normally act jointly to maximise the interests of the group. Hence, their activities are integrated in a decision-making sense.

I shall use the term 'globalisation' in the sense of the integrated production activities of multinational firms. This convention is more precise and focuses on a set of important decisions by multinational firms. This definition of globalisation encompasses most of the activities usually regarded as a part of globalisation, including sourcing, multidomestic strategies and complex integration.

By definition, a multinational firm which controls production in more than one country is a *multi-plant* firm. Some authors refer to this form of production as 'international production'. 'International production refers to a firm controlling productive assets in more than one country' (UNCTAD 1994b, p. 118). A multi-plant multinational firm must also be a *direct foreign investor*. Foreign direct investments may, however, be financed by borrowing in the local markets of the host country and consequently there is not always a link between an increase in multinational production and the international movement of capital.

The international commodity trade strategy of the multinational firm

Since globalisation centres on the multinational firm, we need a model or models of the world economy which explicitly include multinationals as agents of production. From the 1970s, economists began to model the behaviour of the multinational. Markusen (1995) provides a timely and excellent survey of these developments.

The starting point of the economic models is the observation that a home country firm can increase the sales of its products in markets of a second country in three distinct ways:

- exporting from the home country;
- establishing a foreign affiliate in the domestic market of the other country; and
- licensing, franchising or employing other non-equity arrangements with firms already establishing in the domestic market of the other country.

In analysing these choices, it is usually assumed that foreign firms are at an inherent disadvantage in a domestic market because of barriers due to language and customs and local networks. Hence, foreign direct investment does not occur unless there are compensating advantages associated with the foreign investor.

In a well-known analysis, Dunning (1981) suggests that three conditions are necessary for a firm to choose foreign direct investment. These are known as the ownership advantage, the location advantage and the internalisation advantage.

The ownership advantage is exercised over other competitors and derives from ownership of a product or production process, such as a patent or blueprint or trade secret. The location advantage makes it more profitable to locate the production activity in the foreign market rather than the home market for export. This advantage could be due to tariffs or other trade barriers that protect the domestic market, natural protection from international transport costs, or the need to be close to customers. The internalisation advantage makes it more profitable to produce within the firm than to license or franchise a producer already established in the domestic market. If all three advantages hold, the choice will be direct foreign investment.

In these models multinationals arise endogenously as part of the solution to an equilibrium for the global (multi-country) market. They are, therefore, genuine models of the globalisation process. They can be applied to industries that produce homogeneous or differentiated final outputs.

What drives these models is the existence of economies of multi-plant operation. These are due to the 'public goods' characteristic of assets which are firm-specific and non-rivalrous across plants. Firm-specific assets such as product patents, processes and know-how can be used at no extra cost in more than one plant and therefore in more than one country. They give rise to firm-level fixed costs. There may also be plant-specific fixed costs which give rise to economies of scale. Furthermore, the preference for internal rather than arm's-length transfer of technology across countries may be explained by the same public goods characteristic of knowledge capital that explains multi-plant production. This can be seen, for example, in the non-excludability property – which makes knowledge capital easily transferable to potential competitors – or in reputation effects (see Markusen 1995). The endogenous equilibrium in the global industry is one with imperfect competition.

Whether multinational firms or national firms emerge in these models depends on the levels of international transport costs and tariffs relative to the plant level of economies of scale. Analytical and simulation results confirm that multinationals (multi-plant firms) are more likely to be supported in equilibrium when firm-level scale economies and tariff/transport costs are important relative to plant-level economies of scale.

Such models are a distinct improvement over earlier models of foreign investment.[1] They can explain the foreign investment and multi-plant activities of multinationals and the pattern of international trade. The multinational is a firm with distinctive characteristics in the models. Multinationals reduce the costs of production in the host country, because of the transfer at zero cost within the multinational of firm-specific assets, and therefore benefit the host country economy. They may give rise to two-way or intra-industry international trade in the outputs of the industry, especially as the two countries converge in terms of their technologies, relative factor endowments and size. They may also give rise to two-way investment flows between two countries.

II Links between foreign direct investment and commodity trade

In models with multinational firms, foreign direct investment replaces international trade in goods. This follows from the choice of supplying a foreign market by exporting from the home country or by foreign direct investment. This effect is especially strong if the countries are similar in terms of size, endowments and technologies (see Markusen 1995).

UNCTAD (1993, Table II.6) calculates that the world sales of foreign affiliates exceed the value of world exports of goods from the early 1990s: '. . . the sales of foreign affiliates have surpassed exports as the principal vehicle to deliver goods and services to foreign markets.' (UNCTAD 1993, p. 131). This led them to suggest that the integration of world markets has taken place more from the increased movement of capital than the increased movement of commodities.

However, these analyses of the displacement of foreign commodity trade by foreign direct investment derive from models with only two countries – the home country and the foreign country. When one recognises that there are third countries in the world, there is an additional option to the three methods of supplying a market which were noted in the previous section. A parent firm may now choose to export from the home base, or to set up a foreign plant in the country, or, thirdly, to export from an affiliate in another third country. All these choices are part of global strategies for a global firm.

With the third option, the effects of liberalisation of commodity trade combined with liberalisation of capital movements may encourage firms to enter markets which they did not previously supply. They would simply set up in a third country which has lower costs due, say, to cheaper materials or lower labour costs. In such instances, the simultaneous reduction in barriers to the international movements of capital and commodities may reinforce each other. Commodity exports lead to foreign direct investments, which in turn lead to more exports. There will be a positive association between the increase in international commodity trade and the increase in foreign direct investment.

Similarly, in models with vertically integrated production, the strategies of multinational firms lead to increased international trade through outsourcing of intermediate and capital inputs, frequently from foreign affiliates. This holds whether they supply markets by exporting or direct investment. The development of an international specialisation within multinationals may increase national specialisation and international trade in commodities.

Sometimes foreign direct investment occurs because of locationally immobile natural resources and many of the outputs of the foreign direct investor are exported. In these instances, too, foreign direct investment clearly creates additional commodity export trade.

In these situations, unlike the traditional Heckscher–Ohlin model under the conditions which yield factor price equalisation, international trade in commodities and factors are complements not substitutes.

Empirical evidence to document the links between foreign direct investments and international commodity trade is difficult to obtain as international
trade statistics do not record whether an export is made by a national or a
multinational firm. Cantwell (1994, p. 316) concludes that 'The relationship
between international trade and international production is an essentially
complementary one . . . the empirical evidence suggests that as a rule the trade-
creating effect tends to outweigh the trade-replacing effect.' In a similar survey of
the aggregated and firm-level empirical studies for East Asia and the Pacific,
Petri (1995) also concludes that commodity trade and foreign direct investment
are complementary and reinforce each other.

These associations can explain what has been called *foreign-investment-
related trade* (see Borrmann and Jungnickel 1992 and Asian Development Bank
1992). This term refers to the establishment of foreign plants for exporting,
especially in East Asia, and it recognises a specific form of complementarity
between foreign direct investment by multinationals and commodity exports.
One example of this is the Flying Geese pattern of international production
observed in East Asia.[2]

Finally, these models predict that if border barriers continue to fall in most
countries then foreign direct investment will eventually fall too, other things
being equal, because the locational advantage in setting up additional plants in
foreign countries which is due to border policies will be eliminated. (There will,
however, still be locational advantages due to differences in national endowments of labour and other immobile factors.)

III Links between foreign direct investment and the movement of people

International production has direct implications for the international movement
of people. International production involves a package of technology, capital,
and executive and skilled labour inputs.

Host-country labour markets are unable to supply all labour requirements of
the foreign investors for a number of reasons. Foreign investments may create a
demand for new skills or occupations. The incentives to move staff internationally are greater when the skill composition of staff differs greatly in the source
and host countries because of differences in average per capita incomes and
associated differences in expenditures on education and in other human capital-
formation policies. Differences in language, culture and management practices
between the host and source country may also encourage the use of imported
labour in order to facilitate communications between the parent and its foreign
affiliates. In addition, the firm-specific assets are often embodied in employees of
the firm and can only be transferred through the movement of personnel, at least
initially, or the multinational may prefer to move personnel in sensitive areas
with access to this firm-specific know-how and technology in order to prevent
the dispersion of this knowledge to competitors.

Shortages of particular skills in the labour markets of the host countries may be filled by the development of the skills of local workers, or by the temporary movement of expatriate workers or, thirdly, by the admittance of permanent immigrants. Few countries have allowed the permanent entry of skilled workers for the purpose of employment in foreign affiliate companies. Consequently, some labour is transferred from the parent company in the home country or other foreign affiliates.

The employees of a foreign investor in a host country may be divided into three categories: nationals of the host country, nationals of the home country and nationals of third countries. The sum of the home-country nationals and third-country nationals may be called expatriate labour. Data on the employment patterns and practices of multinationals is sparse. Comprehensive data is available only for the USA and Japan which do regular surveys of the multinational firm population.

Expatriate employment in Asia–Pacific countries

The number of expatriates working in foreign-affiliate operations is small in absolute terms and as a proportion of the host-country workforce. For multinationals located in the USA and Japan, home-country nationals accounted for only 3 and 0.4 per cent respectively of total employees in their foreign affiliates in 1989 (UNCTAD 1994b, p. 238). Within the manufacturing sectors of some East Asian countries, however, the percentages are higher because of the higher levels of foreign ownership in this sector. This is especially true of Singapore and Malaysia: multinationals account for 59 per cent of total manufacturing employment in Singapore and 49 per cent in Malaysia (PECC 1994, p. 62). By definition, these expatriates are not permanent immigrants.

The percentage of expatriate staff is higher in key management positions or in technical and engineering jobs where they execute more sophisticated or specialised tasks than in skilled work (see UNCTAD 1994b, Table V.5 for illustrative data from Thailand). Reliance on expatriate managers is greater in developing countries than in developed host countries. From a sample of large US multinationals, Tung (1988) found that in European affiliates 40 per cent of the positions at senior management level were expatriates (33 per cent were from the USA and 7 per cent from third countries), compared to 53 per cent in Latin America (44 per cent home-country nationals and 9 per cent third-country nationals). Japanese multinationals on average have higher proportions of expatriate staff than do US multinationals. For a sample of large Japanese multinationals, Tung (1988) found the proportions to be 77 per cent in Europe and 83 per cent in Latin American affiliates.

An UNCTAD survey conducted in 1991–92 also showed that the proportion of expatriates declines with the age of the foreign investment (UNCTAD 1994b, p. 238).

Moreover, the proportion of staff employed by multinationals who are from the multinationals' home country has been declining around the world. The policies of many companies are increasingly oriented at all levels towards what has become known as 'localisation', the training and use of local staff. Expatriate labour is usually high-cost and has other disadvantages in some countries such as lack of knowledge of the host-country language and culture. Many host-country governments have been promoting the localisation of labour. For example, five ASEAN countries (Singapore, Indonesia, Thailand, the Philippines and Malaysia) have laws and regulations tightly restricting the employment of high-skilled foreign workers and require multinationals to train local staff in specified occupations (see PECC 1994, Table 5.5).

At the management level, the development of international production has led to another trend towards the development of a team of international managers within the company. 'International experience within the corporate system becomes more important than being a national of the parent company, and opens the possibility to nationals from other countries to reach top management positions in the TNCs' (UNCTAD 1994b, p. 239).

Although the movement of people associated directly with international production is small as a proportion of the employment in the host countries, it poses a number of policy issues. The main instruments of regulation for these flows are visa and work permit requirements, and the recognition of professional and skilled qualifications.

The main issue here is the effectiveness of these restrictions as a means of transferring skills and know-how to local workers. Unfortunately, as PECC (1994, p. 67) noted, 'Little research has been conducted to explore the role of expatriates as instruments of technology transfer.'

There are some developments at the regional and multilateral levels to ease restrictions on temporary immigration associated with international production. For example, the Canada–US Free Trade Agreement of 1988 contains provisions relating to temporary movement of business people and these were extended to Mexico under the North American Free Trade Agreement of 1992. The member countries have not forgone the right to restrict entry from other member countries but they have agreed to permit this entry temporarily without labour market tests. The General Agreement on Trade in Services (GATS), which is a part of the Uruguay Round, seeks to eliminate those restrictions on the international movement of people associated with the international delivery of services.

Australia as a case study

Compared to most countries in the world, and perhaps even to all, Australia has an immigration policy which is relatively open.[3] While the emphasis in Australian policy is on permanent settlement, a large number of temporary residents are admitted for work. This section relates these temporary inward movements of people to the levels of inward foreign direct investment.

Consider first the pattern of foreign direct investment. For some years the Australian Bureau of Statistics (ABS) published occasional statistics on employment, wages and salaries, value-adding and other aspects of production in foreign-controlled enterprises in the manufacturing and mining sectors. These were obtained by matching the data from annual censuses of manufacturing and mining establishments with the data on foreign ownership and control from the ABS surveys of shareholdings. Manufacturing is of special interest because of the growth of integrated international production in this sector. The last study for this sector provides data for 1986–87. This shows that in that year foreign ownership accounted for 30.9 per cent of the value added and 23.8 per cent of the employment in the manufacturing sector (ABS 1990a). (This includes both direct foreign ownership in foreign-controlled enterprises and other equity interests.) Foreign ownership is even more important in the mining sector, accounting for over 40 per cent of the value added in the mid-1980s (ABS (1990b).

Unlike the USA and Japan, Australia does not conduct an annual or benchmark survey of the production activities of multinationals operating inside its national borders. Australia has no statistics of expatriate employment in foreign-controlled enterprises.

Limited information can be gleaned from Australian immigration statistics. In Australia there are no visa classes specifically for the employees of foreign direct investors. Expatriates employed by foreign affiliates operating in Australia would normally be employed under a 'temporary resident' visa, although those coming for short visits may be issued with other types of visas such as the 'business visitor' visa. Australia's Temporary Resident Program comprises twenty-six visa categories which can be divided into three broad groups: skilled, social/cultural and international relations. Temporary residents may stay for up to two years initially, depending on the visa category. Temporary residents are allowed entry to work only when an Australian resident is not available for the job.

Within this program, the chief categories which cover expatriate workers employed by foreign direct investors are the 'independent executive' (for those who wish to establish new businesses using their own capital), 'executive' (for those who intend to establish a branch of an overseas company in Australia or who have been appointed top managers or senior managers joining establishing companies in Australia) and 'specialist' (for those with professional and technical skills) categories. There are sub-categories of the 'skilled temporary resident' category. (Foreign direct investors may also employ expatriates under other temporary resident categories, such as 'working holiday makers', but the numbers are small, there are restrictions on work duration and these workers are largely unskilled.) Most applicants for skilled temporary resident visas require sponsorship and normally the prospective employer is expected to act as the sponsor. Stahl et al. (1993, p. 48) believe that the majority of temporary resident immigration in Australia is 'directly related to foreign direct investment'.

Stock estimates of temporary residents can be made from statistics of arrivals and departures. As at 23 July 1993, there were 100 'independent executive', 3986 'executive' and 6572 'specialist' temporary residents in Australia. These numbers are equivalent to 0.24 per cent of the Australian total employment at that time, though one should note that the numbers of temporary residents were depressed in the early 1990s by the recession in the Australian economy. Thus Australia follows the pattern in other Asia–Pacific countries in that the flows of people associated directly with foreign direct investment provide a small part of the labour employed in these enterprises.[4]

There have been studies of Japanese temporary residents in particular. Japanese account for 40 per cent of the 'executive' and 19 per cent of the 'specialist' temporary residents. Many of these are in the tourist industry where they are employed as tour guides, travel agents, salespersons, cooks and other service workers. In Queensland 70 per cent of the lodged applications covering Japanese temporary residents were sponsored by organisations directly associated with tourist activities. A study of Japanese temporary residents in the tourist industry in Cairns, the main location within Queensland for these workers, found that 'Japanese-owned firms exhibited a markedly higher tendency to employ Japanese temporary residents than did those with Australian ownership' (Bell & Carr 1994, p. xvi).

These temporary resident expatriate workers have undoubtedly assisted the development of service exports to Japan, which is the country of source of the foreign direct investments in this case, though these labour market arrangements seem also to have resulted in the transfer of rents to the Japanese investors.

In Australia as in other countries, an important aspect of the presence of expatriate workers employed by foreign multinationals is the transfer of labour market skills to Australian-resident employees. In their review, Brooks, Murphy and Williams (1994, p. 17) concluded 'In general, these studies showed that significant skill transfer occurred from the temporary residents to the local workers.' But there are no quantitative estimates of the extent of skills transfer. The absence of post-entry labour market requirements and the persistence of labour market shortages filled by temporary resident workers over the years suggest that no effective measures have been taken to localise these positions.

IV General equilibrium links between the international movement of capital and labour

Significant flows of labour or foreign direct investment perturb the whole economy and have numerous indirect effects on the prices and employment of factors, the rate of technological change, competition, exports and other variables in the host economy. This section concentrates on the effects of factor inflows on factor prices as these prices largely determine the incentives for international migration of factors and the pattern of commodity trade.

To analyse these indirect effects, one requires a computable general equilibrium model. Little has been done to translate the effects of international labour flows into computable general equilibrium models and almost nothing has been

done on foreign direct investments. (McDougall 1993 offers a preliminary specification of the modelling of foreign direct investment in the Australian Salter
model.) The obvious model to consider in this context is that of Markusen,
discussed in Section I. This model has a labour factor employed in both industries and one additional factor, called land, used in the sector which does not
produce the differentiated products; there is, however, no specific factor in the
industry in which multinationals operate.

The model used here is the specific factor model. This belongs to the earlier
generation of models in which there is no multinational firm and there are
constant returns to scale in all industries, but it does capture the effects of specific
capital. Consider the minimal version of the specific factor model in which there
are two industries or sectors, 1 and 2, and three factors – specific capital in sectors
1 and 2 and mobile labour. (Alternatively, the two specific factors might be
capital and land.) In this model, there is no unique mapping from world commodity prices to domestic factor prices and any change in endowments will
change equilibrium factor prices, given international prices for the produced
commodities.

Standard analysis of the model reveals that the increase in the stock of
specific capital in one sector must decrease the return to the specific capital in
both that sector and the other sector (the two specific capital factors are mutual
'natural enemies'), while raising the wages of labour (specific capital and labour
are 'natural friends') (see Jones 1971). The harmful effect on own factor price is
a general result which holds in constant returns to scale models as it stems from
the diminishing marginal productivity of the factor. The effect on the specific
capital in the other sector arises because the expansion of the output of the
industry in which the increased supply of the specific factor occurs requires a
transfer of labour inputs from the other industry which lowers the labour–capital
ratio and the marginal productivity of capital in that industry. The third effect
on real wages arises because the return to labour must increase in order to induce
the intra-sector movement of labour.

The model can be used to predict the magnitude of gains and losses to factor
incomes when there is a capital or labour inflow into the Australian economy.
Although Australia is a relatively small country, we have estimates of the
parameters of the model for it. Australia is also of interest because it is one of the
few countries that has been a net recipient of both capital and labour over a long
period.

Following the Australian tradition, I shall partition the economy into a
land-and-resource-rich non-urban sector called 'agriculture' (which comprises
the agricultural and mining industries) and 'manufacturing' (which comprises
the manufacturing and service industries). Only about 6 per cent of the total
employment is in the agriculture sector today but it still accounts for one-half of
merchandise exports. Let the agriculture and manufacturing sectors be called
sectors 1 and 2 respectively. Let K_1, K_2, and L be the factors capital specific to

sectors 1 and 2 and labour respectively and the prices of these factors r_1, r_2, and w respectively.

The effects of changes in the stocks of factors from inflows from other countries then depends on the three sets of parameter values – the matrix of factor shares, the proportions of labour employed in the two sectors, and the elasticities of substitution between sector-specific capital and labour in the two sectors (see Jones 1971). The matrix of primary factor shares is taken from Garrett (1992, p. 27), who aggregated the industries in the Australian input–output tables. 'Agriculture' is the relatively capital-intensive sector. The elasticities of substitution are assumed to be unity, which is consistent with constant factor shares. (An increase in the elasticities lowers the responsiveness of all factor prices to factor flows, other things being equal.)

With these parameter values, the 3×3 matrix showing the effect on each of the three factor prices of a 1 per cent increase in the stock of each of the factors is

$$\begin{bmatrix} \hat{r}_1/\hat{K}_1 & \hat{r}_1/\hat{L} & \hat{r}_1/\hat{K}_2 \\ \hat{w}/\hat{K}_1 & \hat{w}/\hat{L} & \hat{w}/\hat{K}_2 \\ \hat{r}_2/\hat{K}_1 & \hat{r}_2/\hat{L} & \hat{r}_2/\hat{K}_2 \end{bmatrix} = \begin{bmatrix} -0.01 & +0.13 & -0.12 \\ +0.02 & -0.38 & -0.35 \\ -0.04 & +0.66 & -0.62 \end{bmatrix} \quad (1)$$

The $^\wedge$ notation denotes proportional changes in the variables. Because product prices are assumed to be constant, the changes in factor prices occur in real factor prices. Thus, the -0.01 in the first row and column indicated that a 1 per cent increase in the stock of capital specific to the agriculture sector lowers the return to this factor by 0.01 per cent. The diagonal and corner effects are negative, as previously indicated.[5]

Comparing the columns, this model predicts that a 1 per cent increase in the endowment of labour has the largest effect on factor prices. A 1 per cent increase in the endowment of capital specific to the agriculture sector would cause a much smaller set of changes in real factor prices than a 1 per cent increase in the stock of capital specific to the manufacturing sector. This is a reflection of the smaller size of the agriculture sector in terms of employment.

Most capital and labour flows into Australia have gone to the manufacturing sector. A 1 per cent increase in the stock of capital in this sector raises the real wage by 0.35 per cent, while a 1 per cent increase in the stock of labour raises the real rate of return on capital in the manufacturing sector by 0.66 per cent. Hence, an inflow of foreign capital by itself increases the incentives of foreign labour to migrate internationally to Australia and vice versa.

A basic feature of the Australian economy is that it has been a large-scale recipient of both *capital and labour* for most of the last 150 years. (The same is true of Canada and New Zealand). Clarke and Smith (1994) have compiled long-term series of the inflows of capital and labour into Australia (and Canada).

These series range from 1820–70 to 1992. Over the period 1870–1992, Australia, for example, ran a current account surplus in only 28 of 122 years and the capital inflow averaged 3 per cent of GNP (peaking at 17.5 per cent in 1853). Over this period immigration has been similarly positive for all but a few years and has been sustained at an average rate of more than 0.5 per cent of the population. For Australia and Canada there is a very close relationship over time between the international movements of labour and of capital.

Economic historians have examined this relationship in Australia and Canada and posited that 'capital chases labour'.[6] This view has been justified partly on the effects of the immigrant labour in raising the marginal productivity of capital and partly on the net stimulation to aggregate demand from immigration which induces a transfer of capital. Clarke and Smith find the direction of causation ambiguous.

This is not surprising. It is equally true that a capital inflow raises the marginal productivity of capital and hence that 'labour chases capital'. From equation (1) above, the effect of an increase in the stock of one factor on a factor price depends on two quantities: the proportionate increase in the factor stock and the elasticity coefficient in the matrix. Thus, when the stock of capital specific to manufacturing increases, the effect on the real wage is $\hat{w} = 0.35\ \hat{K}_2$. And when the stock of labour increases, the effect on the real return to capital specific to the manufacturing sector is $\hat{r}_2 = 0.66\ \hat{L}$. Historically, the inflow of capital has increased the stock of capital more rapidly than have the inflows of labour. However, this is offset by the higher elasticity of the capital rental to changes in the stock of labour. The inflows of capital may have increased the incentives for labour to migrate to capital more than the migration of labour has increased the incentives for capital to flow to Australia. It is probably more correct to conclude that capital and labour have both flowed into Australia because of the abundance of natural resources and have complemented each other.

Other linkages between movements of capital, labour and commodities

Another link between capital and labour movements is provided by the simultaneous inflows of immigrants and capital through the promotion of immigration schemes which target overseas entrepreneurs with business talents and capital. Australia introduced a Business Migration program, modelled in part on those in Canada, in 1981. It required migrants under this program to transfer to Australia, for the purpose of engaging in a commercial enterprise of benefit to Australia, capital which varied from unspecified amounts to $500 000. More than half of the Business Migration migrants came from Asia, with Hong Kong the single most important source country. A sample survey of business migrants who arrived in the mid-1980s found that the average amount transferred was $840 000 and 64 per cent had set up businesses in Australia (M.S.J. Keys Young Planners

1990). This program was severely criticised by the auditor-general in his annual report to parliament and by the Parliamentary Joint Committee on Public Accounts in 1991 for the failure of many of these business people to set up businesses in Australia, for the use of agents and for the alleged entry into Australia under the scheme of criminals. It was replaced in 1992 by a Business Skills program which gives permanent residence to temporary residents who have established a business in Australia or allows business migrants to invest money in Australia. All Business Skills immigrants are now monitored.

V Links between immigration and commodity trade and foreign direct investment

There is a link between immigrants on the one hand and exports of commodities and foreign direct investment on the other – a link based on the use of the language and cultural skills of immigrants to develop new commodity exports or foreign direct investment. The Bureau of Immigration, Multicultural and Population Research recently commissioned two studies on the links between past immigration and exports. Dawkins, Kemp and Cabalu (1995) examined three service industries: professional services, technical services, and further and higher education services. Rod and Webster (1995) examined the food industry. Both studies have found significant links between past immigration and the growth of exports.

Both studies looked at a sample of firms in the industries and found successful exporters to East Asia have a strong tendency to employ more East Asians and utilise their East Asian skills to help their export effort. Dawkins, Kemp and Cabalu found that East Asian employment in 3.6 times higher in businesses that export to East Asia than among those that do not, and Rod and Webster found it to be 2.4 times higher. This suggests that the employment of East Asians increases the East Asian export orientation of firms.

Responses from the businesses in the service industries indicated that the most valuable skills of their East Asian employees were knowledge of East Asian business ethics and practices, extensive contacts with East Asian peoples, and specific cultural knowledge rather than their output-related skills. These factors are distinct from the changes in factor proportions which affect factor prices, and the changes in technology which shift comparative advantage and export patterns.

In both of the industry groups studied, there is also a shift in the orientation of outward foreign direct investment towards East Asia, but this has lagged behind the shift in the export orientation of outputs. These studies found that outward investment into East Asia was more likely in firms with higher levels of East Asian skills. Outflows of capital from Australia have been directed overwhelmingly to the USA, UK and New Zealand – all of which are English-speaking countries with which Australia has had strong cultural links – with only about 15 per cent going to East Asia. This preference has been attributed to the familiarity factor. East Asia has become more important as a destination of Australian outward foreign direct investment in the past two years. The *1995 Access Economics* survey of major projects underway and planned indicates that a further big shift in the orientation of outward investment towards East Asia is occurring. By value, almost 50 per cent of the Australian projects overseas is now being directed to East Asia.

It may be that the shift in immigration towards East Asia in the last twenty years, and especially since the mid-1980s, is having a lagged effect on the orientation of our exports and, more recently, on outward foreign direct investment. More research needs to be done on the cause of the shifts in patterns of trade and investment. One needs to separate the true influence of the immigration factor from the more rapid growth in markets in this region and other factors which are changing the comparative advantage of Australia and Asia. The patterns of trade and factor flows suggest that there are long lags between immigration and exporting to or investing in the countries of origin or other East Asian countries. In the long run, however, immigration may have a strong effect on the patterns of trade and direct foreign investment.

This paper has discussed relationships between the trio of international movements of commodities, capital and labour. There are relationships between all pairs and in both directions. Some may have long lags. Some relationships between the international movement of goods and labour can only be understood if one also considers the international movements of capital. The relationships between international movements of capital and labour are complex and work in both ways. Finally, the growth of multinationals and international production has added new links between the trio of international movements, changing the pattern of imports and exports of commodities and immigration.

Notes

*   I acknowledge the valuable comments received from Bijit Bora, Harry Clarke and Lynne Williams.

1   Some service industries have the feature that either the service provider or the consumer must move in order for production to occur; consequently, there is no international trade in the commodity itself. These services can be provided by foreign companies located in the country in which the service is provided. Indeed, the share of service industries in world foreign direct investment has been rising and is now about 50 per cent (UNCTAD 1994b, Table 1.7). These industries require new theories.

     Cantwell (1994, p. 316) argues that we also need to incorporate in these theories the existence of skills and learning which are location specific rather than firm specific. These have been developed in recent theories of endogenous growth.

2   By contrast, in Australia, sketchy firm-level data indicates that foreign-controlled manufacturing firms have resembled their locally owned counterparts, having generally been inward-oriented with a low propensity to export (see Bureau of Industry Economics 1993, Chapter 2.4). In this respect, they are unlike foreign-controlled firms in the East Asian countries which are export-oriented and export a higher proportion of their sales than do local firms (see Chia 1995, pp. 230–1). Australian affiliates of overseas parents have been multidomestics rather than global firms in the terminology of business strategy. This is not surprising, given the historically high average levels of protection for Australian manufacturers.

3   It is difficult to measure openness with respect to people flows because the restrictions have several dimensions. In the last decade Australia has received a number of permanent immigrants relative to the resident population which is matched only by Canada and New Zealand in some years. Australia does not discriminate in favour of any ethnic or religious group.

4   A number of writers have observed that the annual flow of 'skilled temporary' residents is roughly equal to that of skilled immigrants under the permanent immigration program. However, the comparison of the flows is misleading as the temporary resident must leave in a short time while the permanent settler mostly remains resident in Australia for the remainder of his/her working life. Bell and Carr (1994, p. 31) found that the stock of 'skilled temporary' residents as at 23 July was 1.2 times the flow but the stock of immigrant settlers admitted under the 'skilled' categories (allowing for some return to the country of origin and other departures from the labour force due to retirement and death) must be more than 10 times the annual flow. Consequently, the use of flow measures greatly exaggerates the relative importance of temporary residents as a source of skilled labour.

5   If all factors increase equiproportionately, there is no change in the real factor prices because of constant returns to scale. In equation (1) the row sums are zero.

6   There is another major strand in the history of Australian economic thought, stated explicitly in the 1929 Brigden Report, which argues that restrictions on the importation of manufactures raise the real wage of urban labourers and support a larger population and consequently higher rates of immigration. One should add that additions to the labour force via immigration partially offset the effect of protection on the rate of return to capital and may induce higher rates of capital inflow (see Vines 1995 on this aspect).

5

Migration, Remittances and Trade: With Special Reference to Asian Developing Economies

M. G. *Quibria*

I Introduction

The flow of international labour migration appears to have accelerated in the last three to four decades. According to one estimate, in the late 1980s, around 80 million people were living in foreign countries (Widgren 1987). With the dismemberment of the former Soviet Union and the political instability that exists in the former socialist countries of Eastern Europe, labour migration has increased further in recent years. Many diverse factors have contributed to the process of migration, including the demographic patterns in developing countries and the wide differentials in living standards between rich and poor countries. These are not likely to disappear in the near future. With rapid technological advances in transport and communication, the forces contributing to migration will be further reinforced as cross-border movement is facilitated.

While international migration is a phenomenon of global scope, Asia has seen large movements of labour between countries in the last three decades or so. International labour migration in Asia has followed two major geographical foci - namely, West Asia and East Asia. In West Asia, the oil-exporting economies of the Middle East were rendered prosperous, practically overnight, by the oil crisis that ensued in 1973 after the outbreak of the Middle East War. In East Asia, Japan and the newly industrialising economies (NIEs) became affluent by pursuing an outward-oriented strategy of development in the wake of the unprecedented growth in global trade that followed the Second World War. In this strategy, Japan, which took the lead in the 1950s and the 1960s, was followed by the NIEs in the 1970s and the 1980s.

The remaining Asian developing countries, however, have found themselves economically lagging behind the richer countries of the east and the west. To the extent that labour responds to differences in economic rewards, migration between countries ensued. Migration to the west began en masse after the oil shock of 1973 when West Asian countries started to accumulate large oil surpluses and embarked on an ambitious program of infrastructure building. However, migration to the east only began in the late 1980s when the prosperity of West Asia waned significantly due to falling oil prices, while the economic prosperity of East Asia, especially of the NIEs, showed no signs of decline. As a result, while the growth of migration from South and South-East Asian countries to West Asia has slowed down, that to East Asia has grown rapidly, despite strict immigration controls. This chapter focuses mainly on migration from South and South-East Asian economies. However, the conclusions apply, without significant modifications, to the general phenomenon of migration.

Section II discusses the various measurement and conceptual issues relating to labour migration and remittances. Section III provides a background to the present state of migration to West and East Asia and the flow of remittances accruing to various Asian developing countries. Section IV discusses briefly some important policy issues relating to migration and remittances. Section V provides some concluding remarks.

II Issues

Measurement issues

Migration

Available statistics on labour flows from human resource export bureaus are unreliable for a number of reasons. First, there is a substantial flow of labour handled by private agencies which do not necessarily report to the official bureaus. Second, many migrants travel out initially as tourists and subsequently divert their journey to the intended destinations. Third, a significant segment of Asian migration takes place without registration or visas, as is often the case with intra-ASEAN labour flows. Fourth, there is a substantial, but largely seasonal, flow of labour in the form of border crossing – for example, between Thailand and Malaysia or between Malaysia and Indonesia – which is not monitorable. Finally, official time-series data on labour migration need to be interpreted with extreme care as the numbers are highly sensitive to 'variations in procedures for the registration of migrants' – i.e., whether they have been registered at the labour bureaus, or at the points of exit or at the consulates of the receiving countries (Saith 1987). With respect to return migrants, Saith notes 'the position is even worse', as in most developing countries 'there is virtually no administrative system in place which can record the numbers of such workers on a regular basis'. An alternative source of data for labour outflows and inflows is the receiving countries. However, Saith also notes that no such comprehensive data are available in most receiving countries on an annual basis. Whatever internal census or survey data are available on an *ad hoc* basis can be used merely for cross-checking the plausibility of data derived from other sources.

Remittances

Estimating the volume of remittances is fraught with many difficulties. The *Balance of Payments Statistics Yearbook* of the International Monetary Fund (IMF BOP) is the principal source of data for estimating official remittances. However, as Russell and Teitelbaum (1992) note, there are a 'number of limitations' inherent in these data. These limitations (Russell & Teitelbaum 1992, p. 29), include:

- data in the relevant categories not being reported for all countries;
- countries recording and reporting remittances in different categories of the BOP statistics: e.g., some report 'worker remittances' in a separate line; others aggregate these receipts with 'other private transfers'; some include only cash transfers; others include the value of in-kind transfers;
- reporting requirements which differ between countries (e.g., reporting of remittance receipts below a certain amount may not be required);
- most importantly, the flow of only a portion of total remittances through official channels. It must be stressed that remittances are largely private transfers, and any number of factors may serve as disincentives to their reporting (e.g., exchange regulations, differentials between official and grey or black market exchange rates, etc.).

Russell and Teitelbaum note that there are three categories in the BOP's detailed current account statistics that are relevant for calculating the total flows of remittances – namely 'workers' remittances', 'migrant transfers', and 'labour income'. 'Workers' remittances' are defined as the value of transfers from workers abroad for more than a year; 'migrant transfers' indicate the flow of goods and changes in financial assets resulting from migration; and 'labour income' is factor income of migrants working in the foreign land for less than one year. It is difficult in practice to distinguish between the three categories of income. In the World Bank definition of remittances, as devised by Swamy (1981), all three categories have been lumped together. However, the effort to estimate remittances from IMF BOP data has remained limited. Therefore, the figures on global remittance flows and their changes on an annual basis are not readily available. A recent attempt at compiling global remittance flows was made by Russell and Teitelbaum (1992).

Conceptual issues

Migration remittances and economic welfare

The issue of labour migration and its impact on the welfare of the source country has been the subject of a good deal of theoretical analysis. The important conclusion that emerged from the literature is that emigration may lead to a decline in the welfare of the source country (see Kenen 1971 and Bhagwati & Rodriguez 1986). However, this conclusion hinges on the welfare function adopted for the purpose (Quibria 1990a). In addition, the bulk of the literature that deals with the welfare implication of migration is based on a simplifying assumption that labour migration is *unaccompanied* by remittances. But this assumption is at odds with observed reality: the empirical literature shows that remittances[1] are an important feature of labour migration.

Using a model of a small, open economy with two factors of production, producing two commodities (one traded and one non-traded), the relationships between migration, remittances and source-country gross national product (GNP) can be explored.

Under certain simplifying assumptions (spelt out elsewhere in Quibria 1988a, 1988b, 1993 and 1995) the following intuitively plausible inferences can be demonstrated:

*   emigration will lead to an increase in the aggregate GNP of the labour-exporting country if, and only if, remittances per migrant exceed the source-country wage rate;
*   emigration decreases the (nominal) returns to capital and increases the return to labour; and
*   emigration increases the price of the non-traded good in the source country.

Note that the last result holds irrespective of whether or not remittances exist. Remittances, however, tend to reinforce it. The basic intuition behind the result runs as follows: as the non-traded good is labour-intensive in production, labour migration, due to the operation of the Rybczynski effect, leads to a decline in (per worker) output. At the same time, labour migration leads to an increase in (per worker) income and demand. The decrease in supply, along with the increase in demand, leads to an increase in the price of non-traded goods. This result is in accord with the casual evidence from many developing labour-exporting countries of Asia, where the relative price of non-traded services has tended to increase following the exodus of labour due to overseas migration.[2] The price of the non-traded good relative to the traded good can alternatively be interpreted as the real exchange rate (see Neary 1988). The above result, therefore, implies that emigration leads to an increase in the real exchange rate and opens up the possibility of the 'Dutch disease' (Athukorala 1993).

As Quibria (1990a) has argued, the welfare function for non-emigrants can be defined either in per capita or in aggregate terms. Following Nerlove, Razin and Sadka (1982), we call the former the Millian welfare function and the latter, the Benthamite welfare function. This distinction is important because alternate welfare criteria often have conflicting theoretical and policy implications (Quibria 1990a, 1995). Again, using a simple model, the following results can be shown:

*   if the welfare function of the non-emigrant is represented by a Millian welfare function, the welfare of the society improves due to emigration; and
*   if the welfare function of the non-emigrant is represented by a Benthamite welfare function, the welfare of the society improves if there are sufficient remittances.

The above explores the impact of emigration on the national welfare of the source country.[3] An important point that emerges from this exercise is that, in addition to the welfare function, the presence of remittances can make a significant difference to whether the source country benefits from migration.

Trade, aid and remittances, and international migration

In an autarkic situation, different economies are characterised by different commodity and factor prices. A relevant policy question with regard to migration is whether trade in goods can narrow or eliminate the wage differentials that exist between countries, thereby reducing the incentives for labour migration. Or alternatively, whether such trade tends to widen the wage differentials, thereby creating further incentives for migration. In short, is trade in goods a substitute or complement to labour mobility? This issue has been discussed by, among others, Markusen (1983) and Wong (1986b), and the results have been elegantly summarised and extended by Ethier in this volume. Hence the short discussion on the issue that follows is essentially to motivate and introduce the policy discussion in Section IV.

The putative conclusion of standard trade theory is that trade and migration are substitutes. The Heckscher–Ohlin proposition in international trade theory states that in the absence of international factor mobility, each country exports the good which is intensive in its abundant factor. Trade between countries equalises not only commodity prices but factor prices across countries. Therefore, when free trade exists, it eliminates the incentives for factors to move across countries. However, if there is no trade between countries, but factors are allowed to move freely, then labour will move from the labour-abundant to the labour-scarce country, and capital will move from the capital-abundant to the capital-poor country. The factor price equalisation theorem predicts that commodity prices will be equalised across countries, assuming that the same technology prevails across countries. Thus, with either commodity trade and no labour mobility, or no commodity trade but perfect labour mobility, the outcome with respect to commodity and factor prices will be the same. So, free trade in commodities and free mobility of factors are perfect substitutes. The classic statement of this proposition is to be found in Mundell (1957).[4]

However, migration and trade may be complements, at least in the short run. Trade theory has identified a number of conditions and circumstances where such complementarity may exist (see Ethier for details). There are three such cases. First, if countries are identical in terms of relative endowments but differ in terms of technologies – i.e., one country is more productive than the other in the production of a particular commodity – then the post-trade factor price ratios between countries may diverge more widely as compared to the pre-trade situation. If factor mobility is allowed, capital and labour will move in the opposite direction and factor mobility and commodity trade will complement each other. Second, as Markusen (1983) has noted, the existence of external economies may also lead to complementarity between trade and factor mobility. If countries differ in absolute size but possess identical relative factor endowments, then the large country will export the good in the production of which it has external economies.

Third, Schiff (1994) has provided a further instance where migration and trade may be complements. He adopts the Heckscher–Ohlin framework but adds two additional features that affect migration – namely, migration costs and imperfect capital markets. He maintains that migration costs, along with the existence of imperfect capital markets, constitute a constraint on labour mobility. The costs of migration include transportation, living expenses until employment becomes available in the new country, and, for illegal migrants, additional payments to intermediaries for services and information. In this framework, trade liberalisation in a labour-abundant country, foreign aid and remittances help increase labour income and the workers' ability to incur the cost of migration and lead to greater outward migration. Schiff notes that trade liberalisation may result in higher migration also through transfer of income within the household, as the industries to flourish first are those that are intensive in the use of female labour. In Asia, Latin America and North Africa, the textile, garments, light electronics, and agricultural-processing sectors use women disproportionately compared with men. Savings by these women have been used to finance the migration of men.

III Magnitudes of migration and remittances

Migration from Asia to Europe and America has been a long-standing phenomenon. Migration from Asia – particularly the People's Republic of China and Japan – can be traced back to the late nineteenth century. Similarly, migration from South Asia to Europe – particularly to the United Kingdom – dates back to the early twentieth century but gained momentum in the early 1950s. However, the magnitude of migration to destinations outside Asia is now relatively modest compared with the volume of recent migration that has taken place within Asia.

Migration: levels and trends[5]
Migration to West Asia
The process of large migrations from South and South-East Asia to West Asia began in the aftermath of the first oil shock in 1973 when West Asian oil-exporting countries embarked on a massive program of infrastructure development. Given their small population base, low labour force participation ratio, as well as limited availability of skills, the West Asian countries had to rely heavily on imported labour for the implementation of this program. On the other hand, the South and South-East Asian countries have a large population base, a generally high labour force participation ratio, as well as a lower level of per

capita income. In South and South-East Asia, per capita income in 1990 varied from $210 to about $1400 and the national population size often exceeded 50 million and in some cases, even 100 million. The economic and demographic complementarities between the West Asian countries and the South and South-East Asian countries constituted a basis for a mutually advantageous exchange between them. Compared to the heydays of the Middle Eastern economic boom, there has, however, been a slowdown in labour import in recent years, partly due to the completion or near-completion of major infrastructure projects in West Asia as well as a decline in oil revenues due to the fall in oil prices. The process has suffered a further setback from the Gulf War, which seems to have sapped the residual dynamism of the West Asian economies.

While it is well known that there is large-scale migration from South and South-East Asian countries to West Asia, there is hardly any consensus on migrants' numbers or profile. As Shah (1993) indicates, the stock of South Asian workers in West Asia in 1985 easily exceeded 2 million while workers from South-East Asia would exceed 1 million. With regard to the composition of migrants, there have been significant changes over the years. Immediately after the 1973 Middle East War, India and Pakistan were the first among the non-Arab countries to send their labour to West Asia, followed by Bangladesh, the Philippines, the Republic of Korea and Thailand. As Shah notes, Indonesia, the Philippines, the Republic of Korea and Thailand constituted about 2 per cent of processed labour migrants in Asia in 1975, but their share increased rapidly over the 1970s to account for more than 50 per cent of all migrant workers in 1980. Despite fluctuations in their shares, these countries continued to account for more than 50 per cent of workers in 1989. In contrast, India and Pakistan, which had accounted for 97 per cent of the flow of migrant workers, contributed less than 30 per cent of that flow in 1989. Meanwhile, the share of Bangladesh and Sri Lanka went up significantly, from less than 1 per cent in 1975 to 22 per cent in 1989.

Migration to East Asia

Migration to East Asia, as noted earlier, started in the late 1980s. In the 1980s, while the world economy performed in a lacklustre fashion, the growth rate of Japan exceeded 4 per cent, and the growth rates of the NIEs varied between 6 and 10 per cent. Japan and the NIEs are now the major capital-surplus economies of the world, having posted large current account surpluses as well as accumulated enormous international reserves. There are two options for these countries with regard to managing their capital surpluses: one is to increase domestic investment and import foreign labour to meet the increasing demands resulting from such investment; and the other is to increase foreign investment and thereby reduce the demand for imported labour.

Japan has invested a large part of its surplus capital in Asian economies. The ASEAN economies, especially Indonesia, Malaysia and Thailand, are major recipients of Japanese investment. Low labour cost, a relatively good infrastructure and geographical proximity – all these factors have made these countries attractive to investment from Japan. The South Asian economies – despite the potentially large markets they offer – did not succeed in attracting any significant investment from Japan, partly because of various restrictions on trade and investment. The NIEs have recently become major investors in export-oriented, labour-intensive manufacturing in ASEAN and the People's Republic of China.

While it appears that the capital-surplus economies have extensively utilised the option of foreign investment, there are limits to this option. First, there are certain industries, including various service industries, which are labour-intensive and cannot be relocated outside the source country. Second, many of these countries need to expand, or at the very least maintain, their existing physical infrastructure facilities. Finally, there are certain industries that are strategically important from a country's economic, social and political perspectives. For these reasons, the capital-surplus economies may choose the option of importing foreign labour for employment in domestic industries. Indeed, it appears that Japan and the NIEs have been using a combination of both options.

Given the magnitude of capital surplus and the level of domestic investment, the domestic supply of labour has fallen short of demand in Japan and the NIEs, leading to a labour shortage that may be further exacerbated in the future. One can already discern a substantial flow of labour within this region, a significant part of which, as is well known, is illegal and not sanctioned by laws of the labour-importing countries. As in migration to West Asia, it is difficult to arrive at any precise number for the volume of migration to East Asia. The following provides a rough estimate of the magnitudes involved.

Japan's shortage of labour is most acute in construction, manufacturing and shipbuilding. To ease this shortage, the country has, in recent years, liberalised its immigration laws with respect to persons of Japanese descent, and allowed migration of 30 000–50 000 Brazilians and Peruvians. There has also been some relaxation with regard to the import of legal workers under certain admissible categories. The majority of legal migrant workers are female entertainers who are estimated at between 50 000 and 100 000. The number of illegal workers is difficult to estimate with any degree of precision. According to one estimate (Mori 1991, cited by Shah 1993), there were about 273 000 illegal workers in Japan in 1990. These illegal workers include women from the Philippines and Thailand who are mostly entertainers and men from Bangladesh, the People's Republic of China, the Republic of Korea and Pakistan who work in shipyards and industrial plants. However, despite a significant increase in migration, migrant workers constitute a small share of the labour force.

A significant proportion of the Singapore workforce, about 10–15 per cent, is made up of foreign workers. While historically Malaysia, especially Johore, constituted the most important source of this supply, there has been some diversification in recent years. These diversified sources include Bangladesh,

India, Indonesia, the Philippines and Thailand. The Filipinos are essentially concentrated in domestic service while the Thais are mostly construction workers. The majority of migrant workers are unskilled, although the share of skilled migrant workers is on the rise, perhaps due to a policy of active encouragement by the government.

While the Republic of Korea was an important source of migrant workers to West Asia during the 1970s and early 1980s, it has become less prominent in the 1990s. The total stock of Korean migrant workers to West Asia has fallen to less than 10 000 in the 1990s from about 150 000 in 1982, reflecting both increasing competition from the cheaper labour-exporting countries of South and South-East Asia, and improving economic conditions in the Republic of Korea. The Republic of Korea follows a restrictive migration policy that does not allow unskilled workers to enter the country. Most of the migrant workers in the Republic of Korea are therefore illegal; estimated at between 2000 and 25 000, they account for a small part of the total labour force. The illegal workers, who come from such countries as Bangladesh, Pakistan, the Philippines and Thailand, work as language teachers, maids and workers in construction and garment factories.

Hong Kong's labour force is now essentially comprised of migrants from the People's Republic of China. It is estimated, however, that the flow of migrants to Hong Kong has fallen from about 80 000 in 1976–81 to about 25 000 in 1981–86. This reduction is largely the result of the relocation of labour-intensive industries to the People's Republic of China. According to available estimates, about 3 million mainland Chinese workers were employed in 1992 in the Pearl River Delta area in business enterprises and industries owned by Hong Kong citizens. There has been some recent inflow of unskilled workers, although mostly illegal, to Hong Kong from the subcontinent.

Taipei, China (Taiwan) has grown at an average rate of 7 per cent in the last twenty-five years, while its population growth rate has now declined to about 1.1 per cent. This combination of fast growth in income and slow growth in population has led to a serious labour shortage. In addition, the country has recently embarked on a large infrastructure development program, leading to a further exacerbation of the shortage problem. Estimates of foreign workers vary between 20 000 and 300 000. According to Tsay (1992), who has undertaken the most systematic study in this regard, a realistic estimate would be around 40 000. Foreign workers come mainly from the People's Republic of China, Malaysia, the Philippines and Thailand, and are employed mostly in construction and service industries.

Malaysia is both a receiving and a sending country as far as migration is concerned. It is estimated that half of Sabah's population, about 70 000, is made up of migrants from Indonesia. Another 350 000 Indonesians work in Peninsular Malaysia. Besides Indonesians, Malaysia has a relatively large migrant population from Bangladesh and the Philippines.

Magnitude of remittances

The international financial flows that accrue from labour migration are substantial. According to an estimate by Russell and Teitelbaum (1992), the total value of official remittance flows worldwide was about $66 billion in 1989, a figure which exceeded the total value of official development assistance in 1988, which was estimated at $51 billion.

Some of the Asian developing countries, as noted earlier, being important source countries for labour migrants, have received considerable amounts of workers' remittances. Table 5.1 reports remittances for various developing economies, from 1972 to 1993, calculated on the basis of IMF BOP data. As noted earlier, these estimates suffer from a number of shortcomings. Data on all relevant categories are not reported in all countries and they are often lumped together with other related categories. Different countries have different reporting requirements: some countries do not report receipts on a particular category if it is below a certain amount. Subject to these limitations, the figures reported in Table 5.1 would provide a sense of magnitudes involved.

Table 5.2 expresses remittances as ratios of selected macroeconomic variables to highlight the importance of remittances in the economies of labour-sending economies. As the table shows, for South Asian countries, remittances constitute a major source of foreign exchange earnings. In Bangladesh, remittances were equivalent to about 44 per cent of total merchandise exports in 1993; in India, about 13 per cent in 1990; and in Pakistan, about 24 per cent in 1993. Remittances are, however, relatively less important for South-East Asian countries (except for the Philippines) because of their relatively high export earnings.

It may be noted that the remittance figures, derived from IMF BOP statistics, include remittances from official channels. It is widely believed that these figures underestimate in varying degrees the actual flows because there is a significant leakage from official channels. This leakage, which results in a substantial flow of funds through private channels, can be attributed to a number of reasons such as the lack of banking facilities in the work area and/or the place of origin of the migrant, unfamiliarity with banking procedures, and sometimes, overvalued exchange rates. However, it seems that the institution of various incentive schemes for workers' remittances, greater reliance on market forces for the determination of the exchange rate, and improvements in the banking facilities in the migrants' home countries have all helped to reduce the degree of leakage in remittances in recent years in labour-exporting countries.

IV Policies

The following discusses briefly some policy issues relating to migration, remittances, and the political economy of migration policy.

Table 5.1 Workers' remittances of selected Asian developing countries ($ million)

	1972	1973	1974	1975	1976	1977	1978	1979	1980	1981	1982	1983	1984	1985	1986	1987	1988	1989	1990	1991	1992	1993
PR. China	68	49	70	85	95	...	71	...	...	...	548	498	389	262	454	300	451	291	274	518	463	...
Korea, Rep.	20	25	24	32	46	100	103	97	100	35	47	108	132	265	349	418	498	603	597	340	229	605
Indonesia	–	–	–	–	–	–	–	–	–	0	0	10	53	61	71	86	99	167	166	130	229	346
Philippines	...	...	...	...	...	330	439	547	613	788	944	1043	717	805	855	1017	1252	1358	1460	1841	2530	2542
Thailand	...	...	...	5	12	34	89	169	348	443	519	753	838	809	737	784	836	821	774	966	1126	...
Bangladesh	...	0	0	15	18	78	115	152	286	387	341	589	501	502	576	748	764	758	779	769	912	1004
India	73	110	194	414	625	914	1094	1415	2715	2262	2587	2612	2255	2427	2184	2575	2209	2498	2263	...	...	...
Pakistan	129	155	172	263	18	888	1340	1544	2108	2126	2368	2777	2646	2573	2513	2277	1964	2142	2175	1664	1650	1602
Sri Lanka	–8	–2	–2	–1	4	17	23	68	139	210	222	256	275	233	282	304	326	333	369	393	482	551

Note: Total remittances include net labour income, migrants' transfers and workers' remittances.
...   data not available
—   data is either zero or insignificant
Source: Author's calculations based on International Monetary Fund, *Balance of Payments Statistics Yearbook*, Part 1, various issues.

Table 5.2   Relationship of remittances to selected economic indicators in selected Asian developing countries (percentages)

	Gross Domestic Product	Current Merchandise Exports	Merchandise Imports	Trade Balance	Current Account Balance
PR. China					
1980	...	...	..	...	...
1985	0.1	1.0	0.7	2.0	2.3
1990	0.1	0.5	0.6	3.0	2.3
1993	...	...	..	...	...
Korea, Rep.					
1980	0.2	0.6	0.5	2.3	1.9
1985	0.3	1.0	1.0	1394.7	29.9
1990	0.2	0.9	0.9	29.8	27.5
1993	0.2	0.7	0.8	32.5	157.6
Indonesia					
1980	–	–	–	–	–
1985	0.1	0.3	0.5	1.0	3.2
1990	0.2	0.6	0.8	3.1	5.6
1993	0.2	0.9	1.2	4.2	17.2
Philippines					
1980	1.9	10.6	7.9	31.6	32.0
1985	2.6	17.4	15.8	167.0	2300.0
1990	3.3	17.8	12.0	36.3	54.2
1993	4.7	22.3	14.4	40.9	77.3
Thailand					
1980	1.1	5.4	4.2	18.3	16.8
1985	2.2	11.5	9.6	60.7	52.6
1990	0.9	3.4	2.6	11.5	10.6
1993	...	...	...	...	...
Bangladesh					
1980	2.2	36.1	12.2	18.3	40.6
1985	4.0	50.2	22.0	39.0	109.7
1990	3.7	46.6	23.9	49.1	196.0
1993	4.2	44.1	28.2	78.3	508.9
India					
1980	1.6	32.7	19.5	48.1	152.1
1985	1.1	25.6	16.1	43.2	58.1
1990	0.7	12.4	9.7	43.9	32.2
1993	...	...	...	...	...
Pakistan					
1980	8.9	82.1	38.7	73.3	228.9
1985	8.7	97.2	43.8	79.7	238.2
1990	5.5	40.4	26.9	80.1	131.5
1993	3.3	23.7	17.2	62.8	54.6
Sri Lanka					
1980	3.5	13.1	7.5	17.7	21.2
1985	3.9	17.7	12.7	44.6	55.7
1990	4.6	19.9	15.9	78.1	123.7
1993	5.4	19.8	15.6	74.2	144.8

...   data not available
–   data on remittances is either zero or insignificant
Sources: International Monetary Fund, *International Financial Statistics Yearbook* (various issues); and International Monetary Fund, *Balance of Payments Statistics Yearbook* (various issues).

Migration

As indicated in Section II, under most usual economic circumstances, trade and migration tend to be substitutes. This has also been borne out by the experiences of East Asian outward-oriented economies. Many of these economies which pursued outward-oriented strategies of development have experienced a rapid increase in real wages and a shortage in labour supply. Economies which were once major suppliers of migrant workers have turned into net receiving countries. If, for political and social reasons, it is considered that the international movement of labour should be restricted, then it is important that the world trading environment should be kept as free as possible so that the poorer, labour-surplus economies can derive maximum benefit from the system. The conclusion of the Uruguay Round of multilateral trading agreements is an important step in this regard. However, there are areas where the threat of protectionism still exists insofar as poorer developing countries are concerned. The textile and garments trades, where the developing countries have a major stake, are largely dominated by a quota system in the form of the Multi-fibre Arrangement (MFA). While MFA is scheduled to be phased out by 2005, developing countries fear that MFA may be replaced by anti-dumping measures. Likewise, it is widely perceived in developing countries that the initiative to impose 'labour standards' is an indirect way of imposing import protectionism. 'Labour standards' are viewed both as an instrument to nullify the comparative advantage of the poorer countries in labour-intensive commodities and services as well as a means to protect the sunset industries in the industrialised countries. Finally, the emergence of various preferential trading blocs, to the extent that they are discriminatory and exclude the poorer developing countries, is considered a threat to the evolution of a freer world trade system. If the above issues are not satisfactorily resolved and a freer trading system established where poorer countries can gainfully participate and benefit, then the tide of migration will not ebb.

As noted earlier, trade can be a complement to labour mobility – in the sense that trade can widen, rather than narrow, the wage differentials between countries – and thereby generate greater incentives for labour migration. This complementarity can occur if the high-wage country has a productivity advantage over the low-wage country in some key industries. This productivity advantage can arise from many factors, including the existence of a superior infrastructure such as roads and highways, ports and telecommunications. If an important plank of the immigration policy is to contain migration, then foreign aid should be directed towards building such an infrastructure in poorer countries. Foreign direct investment can also play an important part in raising productivity and diffusing technology. However, to attract foreign investment, the developing countries themselves have to play an important role by fostering an environment conducive to it.

Remittances

Labour migration, in conjunction with remittances, can lead to the so-called 'Dutch disease' – i.e., the appreciation of the real exchange rate. The Dutch disease creates a condition of greater vulnerability to external shocks by stimulating imports and reducing the incentives to develop exports. The Dutch disease also leads to an over-emphasis on capital-intensive methods of production. To avert the deleterious consequences of the Dutch disease, a number of policies can be adopted, including the depreciation of the currency, and structural reforms in the production sector to achieve greater economic efficiency.

Political economy

Any economic policy, trade and migration policies included, generates winners and losers in society. Whether a particular policy in a democratic society gets adopted depends on the relative political strengths of the losers and winners. A liberal immigration policy improves the real returns to capital and land, and decreases the returns to labour. A liberal trade policy improves the welfare of the consumers but decreases the welfare of the workers working in the import-competing industries, either because the wage rate declines or because there is a loss of employment. Countries have followed different policies. Some have followed liberal trade policies but more strict immigration policies; other countries have followed more protectionist trade policies in particular sectors but more liberal migration policies. As well, some countries have often gone through several phases – for example, from a more liberal migration policy to a stricter one and vice versa. While a good deal has been written on the political economy of trade policy (see, for example, Baldwin 1984 and Quibria 1989a), much less has been written on the political economy of immigration policies and the interrelationship between trade and migration policies. Our understanding of the issues can be further enhanced by research into areas such as the nature of the political decision-making process, the key political-economic characteristics that enable an industry to obtain greater protection, and the reason that countries go through phases in immigration policies.

V Conclusion

The relationships between migration, remittances and trade are extremely complex. A review of the theoretical literature indicates that the relationships among them are not unilinear. For example, migration can both substitute and complement trade; remittances can both help and hurt the economy. Remittances can lead to an appreciation of the real exchange rate and to an erosion of trade competitiveness of the economy. At the same time, as this chapter has shown, remittances can make a significant difference in the welfare of the labour-sending countries. For example, while emigration can lead to a decline in the welfare (as defined by a Benthamite welfare function) of the labour-sending country, the result can be over-turned if migration is accompanied by sufficient remittances.

Though international trade theory has clarified many issues relating to the interlinkages among migration, remittances and trade, empirical studies have been greatly hampered by the lack of reliable data on migration and remittances. Researchers need to pay particular attention to improving the quality of data, by engaging in both the collection as well as the processing of data, to allow further advances in empirical research.

Notes

1   Remittances have been a principal source of foreign exchange in many Asian labour-exporting countries (Quibria 1986, Quibria and Thant 1988).

2   Indeed, there is a large literature that relates to service prices across countries. One strand of this literature relates service prices to factor endowments: the poorer countries with larger endowments of labour tend to have lower service prices (see, for example, Bhagwhati 1984 and Quibria 1990b). The present result provides a confirmation of the hypothesis in a different context.

3   Work has recently been initiated to generalise these results in the context of an arbitrary number of goods and services. See, for example, Wong (1986a) and Quibria (1988b).

4   For a rigorous demonstration of this result and the subsequent results, see Razin and Sadka (1993).

5   This section draws heavily on Quibria (1994). The discussion that follows relates largely to temporary migration of unskilled workers. However, the distinction between temporary and permanent migration is often arbitrary. Many migrants who are often admitted as temporary workers may end up as permanent migrants.

PART III

Regional Trade Liberalisation and Migration

6

Effects of NAFTA on Labour Migration

Philip Martin

Migration trends

The USA is the world's major country of immigration, and Mexico is the world's major country of emigration. As with US–Mexican trade in goods, there is an asymmetry in the two countries' migration patterns. The USA accepts immigrants from many nations, but virtually all Mexican emigrants head for the USA.

For most of the twentieth century, the major linkage between the two most populous countries in North America has been the migration of people from Mexico to the USA – the slogan 'go north' for economic opportunity is deeply embedded in rural Mexico. Today, 2–4 million of Mexico's 30 million workers rely on the US labour market for most of their annual earnings, and the US labour force of 130 million includes 3–5 million Mexican-born workers who have been in the USA fewer than ten years.

Mexico is the single largest source of immigrants bound for the USA. However, most Mexican immigrants are 'illegal aliens' for at least several years before they become legal US immigrants. For this reason, one must examine both apprehension and immigration data to determine Mexico–USA migration. There is often a lag of 3–5 years between a peak in apprehensions and a peak in legal Mexican immigration – for example, the 1991 legal immigration peak reflects the amnesty granted to primarily illegal Mexicans in 1987–88.

Over the period 1981–95, some 3 million legal Mexican immigrants have been recognised by the USA. This is equivalent to 20 per cent of Mexico's net population growth, and 25 per cent of total legal US immigration.

Under US immigration law, legal immigrants do not have to remain continuously living or employed in the USA – they can come and go freely. Many US immigrants who were Mexican nationals live at least part of the year in Mexico, and many Mexicans who are not legal US immigrants or visitors live and work at least part of each year in the USA.

Migration permits more Mexicans to find jobs in the USA than the North American Free Trade Agreement (NAFTA) was expected to create in Mexico, even under the best of circumstances. The best estimates of the number of additional Mexicans – legal and illegal – who find US jobs and settle each year – 150 000 to 200 000 – and the number who work at least seasonally in the USA – 1–3 million – dwarf even the most optimistic estimates of job gains in Mexico due to freer trade. For example, Hufbauer and Schott (1992) projected that up to 600 000 additional Mexican jobs might be created by NAFTA during the agreement's first ten years.

Mexico both exports and imports labour. According to press accounts, Mexico issues about 125 000 work permits to foreign workers each year, and there are thousands more unauthorised foreign workers in Mexico. Most Mexican work visas are issued to unskilled Central Americans employed at the bottom of the Mexican labour market picking coffee beans, doing unskilled construction work, or working for wealthy Mexicans as maids and gardeners. Poor conditions for some of these workers were spotlighted in the US press after Mexico's active participation in the anti-Proposition 187 campaign in California in autumn 1994, and President Zedillo has promised to improve conditions for migrant workers in Mexico.

There were reports in 1994 of 'thousands' of professional foreign workers in Mexico, including both legal non-immigrants and illegal 'dryback' Americans.[1] Unlike most other Western hemisphere visitors, who receive 30-day tourist visas to enter Mexico, the 2 million people from the USA who came to Mexico in 1993 were issued six-month tourist visas.

In 1994, an estimated 17 million US residents visited Mexico, and they accounted for about three-fourths of Mexico's $7.5 billion tourism revenues. US residents who live in Mexico can simply cross into the USA every six months and get a new tourist visa on their return to Mexico, thus retaining their legal status in Mexico.

NAFTA

On 1 January 1994 NAFTA came into effect, laying the basis for an eventual free-trade area encompassing 380 million people with a combined GDP of $7 trillion. The purpose of NAFTA is to reduce trade barriers and promote investment in the region, thereby stimulating economic and job growth throughout North America.

NAFTA brought together three very different countries. Canada and the USA have similar GDPs per capita, but their per capita GDP and population growth rates diverged since 1985, with Canada experiencing very slow economic growth and relatively fast population growth compared with the USA.

Mexico, in comparison to the USA, has had the same average real GNP growth rate of 1.1 per cent per year since 1985, but its population has grown at twice the US rate, widening the per capita income gap between the two countries (*The World Bank Atlas* 1994.)

Mexico's President Carlos Salinas de Gortari announced his support for a free-trade agreement (FTA) with the USA in May 1990. On 21 September 1990

President Salinas formally requested negotiations, and on 25 September 1990 President Bush notified Congress that the USA intended to negotiate a free-trade agreement with Mexico. On 17 and 18 May 1991 Congress failed to deny Bush the authority to negotiate an FTA with Mexico. Negotiations began on 12 June 1991, and the US Congress voted to approve NAFTA in November 1993.

NAFTA is based on four principles:
- the elimination of tariff and non-tariff barriers to trade between Canada, Mexico and the USA;
- equal treatment in each country for all goods and services produced in North America;
- a commitment not to erect new obstacles to trade after NAFTA is signed; and
- a commitment to extend to NAFTA partners any special trade preferences that any of the three countries make available to non-NAFTA countries.

More than fifty models were developed to project the global effects of NAFTA on the economies and labour markets of Canada, Mexico and the USA. Most emphasised that NAFTA would primarily affect the relationship between the USA and Mexico, because the USA and Canada are more similar economies and they have had a free-trade agreement since 1989.

The economic effects of NAFTA in the USA were projected to be small because the Mexican economy is small – Mexico's annual economic output is less than that of Los Angeles county – and because tariffs were low before NAFTA – the average US tariff on Mexican imports in 1991 was 4 per cent, and the average Mexican tariff on US imports was 10 per cent.

Most of the models projected that Mexico would be the agreement's major economic 'winner.' According to the US International Trade Commission (ITC), 'Trade between the three economies should rise, and this should increase the GDP of each country as firms are forced to compete harder and because costs of production may fall as firms produce for a larger market.'

The ITC estimated that Mexico's real GDP could rise by 0.1 to 11.4 per cent because of NAFTA, and the US and Canadian GDPs might rise by up to 0.5 per cent as a result of freer North American trade. All three economies were expected to experience job gains – the ITC projected a 7 per cent employment gain due to NAFTA in Mexico, and up to 1 per cent employment gains for the USA and Canada.

Real wages were projected to rise 0.7 to 16.2 per cent in Mexico because of NAFTA, but less than 0.5 per cent in the USA and Canada. Mexico has relatively low savings, so projections of NAFTA's economic effects were based on the expectation that foreign capital would flow to Mexico. Mexico could, in this development-with-foreign-investment scenario, run a trade deficit for years as foreign investors built up Mexico's productive capacity and infrastructure, much as the USA did in the late nineteenth century and South Korea did in the 1960s and 1970s.

Mexico in 1994 permitted the peso to become overvalued, making imports of both capital and consumer goods cheap. The overvalued peso could be maintained as long as foreigners believed that Mexico truly was the next economic 'tiger'. In effect, US and other foreign investors lent billions of dollars to Mexico, and Mexicans used these foreign savings to import US goods. It is in this manner that the US Treasury could assert, in January 1995, that $40 billion in US exports to Mexico supported about 800 000 US jobs.

Mexican President Salinas wanted to be one of the few recent Mexican presidents to leave office without devaluing the peso, so he resisted an 'orderly' devaluation during the summer of 1994. The Chiapas uprising on 1 January 1994 and several political assassinations prompted fears that, if Mexico devalued, foreign confidence in the country would evaporate, pushing Mexico into recession.

At the same time, the Mexican government apparently printed money to buoy the economy in advance of the August 1994 presidential elections.[2] When President Zedillo took office on 1 December 1994, and there were difficulties re-negotiating the 'pacto' between labour and management that sets wage guide-lines and thus influences real wages and inflation, devaluation became widely anticipated.

Savvy local investors saw that the $30 billion trade deficit would not be reduced in 1995, and they began to convert pesos to dollars at the rate of 3.45 pesos to $1.[3] The Mexican Central Bank almost ran out of reserves to support the peso at this rate, and the flight from the peso forced a devaluation on 20 December 1994.

The peso crisis and illegal migration

Mexico has had major devaluations at the end of each of the last four presiden-cies: in 1976, in 1982, again in 1986–87, and in 1994–95. However, data show that there is no immediate and consistent relationship between peso devalua-tions and illegal immigration to the USA, at least as measured by apprehensions.

For example, after the 1982–83 peso devaluation, it took about sixteen months for the US Border Patrol to notice a significant increase in illegal immigration. In 1987, apprehensions dropped despite a devaluation of the peso, largely because so many Mexicans were becoming legalised US immigrants under the 1986 Immigration Reform and Control Act (IRCA).

The drop in apprehensions in the mid-1980s despite the peso devaluation emphasises the importance of US policies in determining whether Mexicans respond to economic crisis by emigrating. In 1987–88, the USA offered an easy legalisation program to illegal alien farm workers, and over 800 000 Mexicans took advantage of it to become legal US immigrants. There was less need to risk apprehension when legalisation applications could be filed in Mexico and Mexicans could come to the border, assert that they qualified for legalisation but had no records to prove that they had worked illegally in US agriculture, and then obtain 90-day entry and work permits (Martin 1993). Smuggling fees dropped as Mexicans entered legally, while the fraudulent document industry boomed.

Most applicants for legalisation under the special agricultural worker (SAW) program submitted only letters from US labour contractors and farmers that asserted, for example, that 'Juan Gonzalez picked tomatoes for me for 92 days between May 1985 and May 1986'. By one estimate, over half of the 1 million aliens legalised around the USA under the SAW program were not eligible (Martin et al. 1995).

The economic background and US immigration responses to the first two peso devaluations may provide clues about responses to the 1994–95 devaluation. The 70 per cent peso devaluation of 1982–83 lowered real wages in urban areas and put Mexican farmers in a cost–price squeeze, but the fact that urban Mexican workers kept their jobs and saw their standard of living erode only gradually helps to explain the delayed illegal emigration response.

The 1986–87 peso devaluation, by contrast, occurred when the USA was offering amnesty to illegal immigrants, and the Immigration and Naturalization Service (INS) was educating employers about the sanctions that prohibited them from hiring illegal workers, rather than enforcing them. During the late 1980s, the USA also experienced rapid job growth, helping to attract Mexican workers.

The 1994–95 peso devaluation (the peso traded at 6.4 pesos to $1 at the end of September 1995) is occurring in a different climate in Mexico and the USA. Mexico is experiencing significant layoffs from formal sector jobs. The Mexican government reported that 750 000 Mexican workers lost their jobs in January–February 1995, and 10 per cent of the labour force was reported to be unemployed in September 1995. Real wages have fallen sharply.

These are official figures, and they reflect primarily separations from the 10 million urban jobs covered by the social security system. As more urban workers face unemployment without a safety net and as most of the relief programs are apparently designed to help rural people – Mexico plans to employ 500 000 workers temporarily to build and repair rural roads – poor farmers could be joined in their northward trek by unemployed factory workers. INS Commissioner Doris Meissner, for example, noted on 24 February 1995 that some of the Mexican aliens apprehended by INS agents said they had crossed the border because of plant closings or other job losses related to the peso devaluation.

The emigration potential in Mexico is significant. Village economic models predict a high migration elasticity with respect to devaluations. Taylor (1987), for example, finds that each 1 per cent devaluation of the peso increases emigration by 0.7 per cent, and other studies assert that there is a 1:1 relationship between devaluation and emigration.

It is sometimes argued that the peso devaluation will slow emigration because the value of the $3–5 billion in US remittances received in Mexico from workers in the USA will increase in value, and that higher smuggling fees, which are set in dollars, will deter attempts to emigrate illegally. However, those studying Mexican villages that have traditionally sent migrants to the USA report that 'bags are packed' for the northward trek (*Los Angeles Times*, 20 February 1995).

Despite the $46 million US border control effort launched as Operation Gatekeeper on 1 October 1994, the cost of being smuggled from Tijuana to Los Angeles, the destination of about 40 per cent of all unauthorised Mexican immigrants, has remained in the $200–400 range, representing less than one month's wages at the US minimum of $4.25 hourly.[4]

Operation Gatekeeper

In the USA, estimates of the number of illegal aliens have fallen while the recorded actual number of resident illegal aliens has increased. For example, estimates of 6–12 million illegal aliens were common in the late 1970s, even though it was later estimated that about 2.1 illegal aliens were included in the 1980 Census.

In 1985, Passel estimated that there were 3–5 million illegal aliens in the USA. In 1987–88 some 1.7 million long-term illegal aliens were legalised, representing about two-thirds of the illegal aliens in the USA since 1982. Also in 1987–88 another 1 million short-term illegal entrants, mostly Mexicans, were legalised. The number of illegal aliens was estimated to reach its modern-day low of 2.2 million in 1988. The number of illegal aliens then began to increase, reaching an estimated 3.4 million in October 1992, and 4 million at the end of 1994 (Warren 1994).

There are two broad strategies to combat illegal immigration. What might be called the 'island' strategy is reflected in the policies of the UK and Australia. Both emphasise strict entry controls, but neither has residence permits nor employer sanctions. The so-called 'continental' strategy, by contrast, acknowledges that land borders and large tourism sectors makes it impossible to prevent all illegal entries, but internal controls such as residence and employment permits can prevent aliens who entered legally from violating the terms of their entry.

The USA has traditionally relied on an island strategy, counting on the Border Patrol to deter illegal entry. In 1993, the Border Patrol in Texas shifted its focus from apprehending aliens to preventing their entry. The results were dramatic. Operation Hold-the-Line in El Paso flooded the border with agents to deter illegal entries, and the two types of illegal border crossers that caused the most problems – petty criminals and street vendors – were stopped, while daily commuter workers and long-distance migrants continued to cross.

In October 1994, the Border Patrol launched a similar strategy in California. Operation Gatekeeper in California used three lines of agents, fences and lights in a prevention-through-deterrence strategy south of San Diego. Each of the 170 000 aliens apprehended between 1 October 1994 and 31 March 1995 was fingerprinted and photographed, enabling the INS to determine that about 20 per cent of those apprehended were being caught for the second time.

These recidivism data show clearly that the Border Patrol has succeeded in pushing aliens to the east; aliens who were caught in the westernmost section of the border are being apprehended on their second and third entry attempts five to ten miles further east. Apprehensions in the westernmost section fell 50 per cent since October 1994 and, according to the INS, 'entries' fell by 40 per cent.

However, apprehensions in the entire twenty-four-mile sector were up 14 per cent to 512 000, and critics assert that this simply shows that controlling the border is like squeezing a balloon – concentrating efforts at one point simply transfers the aliens further east. Those who interview Mexicans attempting to cross, or Mexicans illegally in the USA, report that relatively few are discouraged by smugglers fees that have risen by $100 or more from the previous level of $200–$300.

Informal surveys of aliens in the USA suggest that about 70 per cent of them succeed in entering illegally on their first try. Surveys of aliens in Mexico find that, even though most of those planning to enter the USA illegally know about Gatekeeper, the INS operation is not deterring them from planning to attempt illegal entry. It has been estimated that one-half of all Mexicans have a relative in the USA, and one-third have been to the USA (Doug Massey, 17 March 1995), indicating that many Mexicans know what awaits them north of the border.

There is clearly some level of border enforcement that could minimise illegal Mexican entries. However, 5000 Border Patrol agents and an annual budget of $2.6 billion has not done the trick so far. For these reasons, many in the USA believe that effective long-term immigration controls will require computer systems and enforcement to prevent unauthorised aliens from obtaining jobs and benefits, and faster wage and job growth than in Mexico.

SouthPAW and Proposition 187

Many believe that the INS should devote more resources to interior enforcement to prevent unauthorised workers from obtaining US jobs. On 26 September 1995 the INS announced that Operation SouthPAW (PAW – Protecting America's Workers) had, in thirty-one days of co-ordinated inspections with Department of

Labor (DOL) investigators in June and September, removed 4000 unauthorised workers – almost 90 per cent Mexicans – from 300 US firms in Mississippi, Tennessee, Arkansas, Georgia, Alabama and Florida.

One-third of the illegal workers were found in Georgia, and one-quarter in Arkansas. Follow-up surveys by the INS found that local residents filled over half of the jobs from which illegal aliens were removed – these jobs paid $2–$15 per hour. Some employers were re-inspected, and ten were fined for continuing to employ illegal alien workers.

If the cost of the enforcement team was $100 per person per day, then the total cost of Operation SouthPAW would have been about $3 million, implying a cost of about $750 to open each job that paid an average $14 000.

Democrats and their union allies usually argue that unauthorised workers come to the USA to obtain jobs, and they urge more penalties on US employers who hire unauthorised workers. Republicans, on the other hand, often argue that unauthorised aliens come to the USA to obtain public benefits, and they often urge that the US welfare system be scaled back, and that more controls be put into place to prevent unauthorised aliens from getting benefits.

Proposition 187 in California put the spotlight on the access of aliens to public benefits. California voters on 8 November 1994 voted 59 to 41 per cent to approve Proposition 187, a measure that primarily creates a state-mandated screening system for persons seeking tax-supported benefits. In the language of Proposition 187, no person-citizen, legal immigrant or illegal immigrant – 'shall receive any public social services to which he or she may otherwise be entitled until the legal status of that person has been verified'.

Proposition 187 has five major sections. First, it bars illegal aliens from the state's public education systems – from kindergarten through to university – and requires public educational institutions to begin verifying the legal status of both students (effective 1 January 1995, but stayed by court order) and their parents (effective 1 January 1996).

Second, Proposition 187 requires all providers of publicly paid, non-emergency health care services to verify the legal status of persons seeking services in order to be reimbursed by the state of California. Persons seeking emergency care must also establish their legal status, but all persons, including unauthorised aliens, must be provided with emergency health services.

Third, Proposition 187 requires persons seeking cash assistance and other benefits to verify their legal status before receiving benefits. Unauthorised aliens are generally not eligible for such benefits, so this provision adds a state-run verification system on top of the current federal screening system.

Fourth, all service providers are required to report suspected illegal aliens to California's attorney-general and to the INS. This means that parents enrolling children in school, or clerks who determine whether someone is eligible for public benefits, are required to report persons requesting education or benefits if they suspect of that the applicants are unauthorised aliens. State and local police must determine the legal status of persons arrested, and also report suspected unauthorised aliens.

Fifth, the making, distribution and use of false documents to obtain public benefits or employment by concealing one's legal status is now a state felony, punishable by fines and prison terms. Proposition 187 does not affect, for example, teenagers who buy or use false documents to obtain alcohol. As of May 1995, this is the only section of Proposition 187 in effect.

Proposition 187 may mark the beginning of national efforts to reduce legal and illegal immigration, much as Proposition 13 in 1978 arguably laid the basis for the Reagan-era tax cuts of the early 1980s. On the other hand, Proposition 187 may turn out to be a largely symbolic expression of frustration with illegal immigration, much as was Proposition 63, which made English the state's 'official language' in 1986.

The migration hump

The increase in legal and illegal immigration from Mexico is a predictable consequence of the economic integration of North America symbolised by NAFTA. Immigration was downplayed in the USA during the NAFTA debate in order to avoid discussion of an issue that has no easy answer. Most government statements echoed US Attorney-General Janet Reno, who said, in urging Congress to approve NAFTA: 'We will not reduce the flow of illegal immigration until these immigrants can find decent jobs at decent wages in Mexico.' (San Diego Union-Tribune, 14 November 1993, p. 1)

In the long run, the economic growth and job creation accelerated by free-trade and investment policies promote what has been called stay-at-home development. But emigration pressures do not cease when an emigration country such as Mexico adopts growth-accelerating economic policies. Indeed, the US Commission for the Study of International Migration and Cooperative Economic Development (1990) concluded just the opposite: 'The economic development process itself tends in the short to medium term to stimulate migration.' In other words, the increased migration pressures that are now obvious in Mexico were widely predicted but ignored in the run-up to NAFTA.

The 'migration hump' is a term used to describe the temporary increase in immigration that is followed by declining migration. The important point is that the same economic policies that increase illegal emigration pressures in the short run reduce them in the longer run. Furthermore, if Mexico-to-USA migration is viewed over several decades rather than several years, then there should be less migration with the free-trade and investment policies formalised by NAFTA than without them.

The migration hump presents a trade-off for policy-makers. Suppose that economic integration adds 10–20 per cent to current immigration for ten years, but then sharply reduces economically motivated migration. Policy-makers who emphasise the short run may oppose economic integration on the grounds that unwanted immigration will increase, and those who take the long view may favour economic integration on the grounds that, in the long run, economic integration will accelerate stay-at-home growth.

Economists have not emphasised the migration hump, a major concern of policy-makers, because they tend to emphasise comparative statics – comparing before-and-after equilibrium points, thereby ignoring the process of adjustment to free trade. In neo-classical trade models, the prediction that free trade in goods offers a substitute for migration, or trade in people, is a long-run prediction. The migration hump, by contrast, is the result of a hypothesised short-run relationship between migration and economic adjustment to free trade.

Consider two countries with different factor endowments – a country in the North (Country N) is capital rich, and a country in the South (Country S) is capital poor but has an abundance of labour. Assume that the two countries share the same technologies (production functions), and that the same two factors of production – capital and labour – are used in each country to produce the two goods. If the two countries engage in free trade, each country will export (import) the good more intensive in the factor that is relatively more (less) abundant in that country. That is, Country N will import labour-intensive goods from Country S, while Country S will import capital-intensive goods from Country N.

Stolper and Samuelson considered the effect on factor prices (wages and the return on capital) of an import tariff that increases the domestic price of the import-competing good relative to that of the export good. Under the Heckscher–Ohlin assumptions, and the assumption that the basic trade pattern is not altered by the tariff, an import tariff increases the price of the relatively scarce factor relative to the prices of the other factor and of both goods. Thus, a tariff levied against labour-intensive imports in Country N will increase Country N wages relative to other factor and goods prices, compared with the free-trade case.

The Stolper–Samuelson model rules out international factor movements, including migration. If migration responds positively to international wage differentials, then protectionism in the North (Country N) should increase migration from the South, or the protection of capital-intensive industries in the South should spur emigration.

Even if trade in goods is restricted, labour will flow across borders to equalise wages, at which time economically motivated migration between the two countries will cease. According to this theory, 'labour mobility [can] fully compensate for the non-traded good' (Krauss 1976, p. 474).

In this admittedly simple scenario, trade liberalisation permits the capital-rich and labour-rich countries to specialise in producing the goods in which they have a comparative advantage, and to satisfy their demand for other goods through trade. A shift in production of labour-intensive goods to Country S and of capital-intensive goods to Country N will put upward pressure on Country S wages, discouraging emigration and bringing migrants back home.

The standard model can produce a migration hump by altering some underlying assumptions. The critical assumptions fall into five main categories:

1   The two countries share identical production technologies;
2   The two countries use the same factors of production (factor homogeneity);
3   Technologies exhibit constant returns to scale in production (there are no scale economies);
4   Adjustment to changes in international markets is instantaneous, an implicit assumption;
5   There is perfect competition, with full employment and complete markets.

Technology differences

One critical assumption of the standard model is that the two countries share the same technologies (production functions). In other words, if we observe tractors plowing fields in the USA and oxen pulling plows in Mexico, the reason is that Mexico has more labour, not that tractor technology is unavailable in Mexico. In the language of economics, differences in the labour and capital intensities of production between the two countries are due solely to differences in their factor endowments.

Without migration, this leads Country N to produce with a higher capital–labour ratio than Country S; the assumed higher price for labour in Country N encourages more use of relatively cheaper capital. Migration, by reducing wages in the North, encourages more labour intensity in production and also the production of goods that use more labour-intensive technologies (including the preservation of 'sunset industries').

Now suppose that the protected good is produced with a labour-intensive technology in the South, but with a highly efficient capital-intensive technology in the North. This is the case, for example, with grain production in the USA or Europe compared with low-input grain production on family farms in Mexico and North Africa.

If the North's high-tech production technology gives it a comparative advantage in producing a good such as grain, then, with free trade, it may be able to export more to the South, forcing the South to substitute away from what is, for the South, a labour-intensive production activity. Displacement of labour in the South's 'protected' sector may easily drive down wages and encourage South–North migration.

The identical technologies assumption in standard trade models has been questioned by Markusen (1983), who argues that, if the basis for trade is a difference in technologies across borders, migration and trade may be complements. A critique of this assumption is also implicit in Schiff's (1994) argument. Schiff (1994) notes that most import substitutes in LDCs are produced on small, labour-intensive farms, and that domestic production that competes with agricultural imports is often more labour intensive than other tradeable goods.

Productivity differences

Differences in factor productivity between countries are implicit in the standard trade model. The issue for the trade–migration linkage is why such differences exist. In many cases, they are due to the presence of complementary public inputs, as when public services, transportation, communication and education systems in the North make the same resource more productive there than in the South.

In some cases, Country S may have so little infrastructure that it may not have a comparative advantage even in the production of labour-intensive goods. Under such conditions, it may be more efficient to produce labour-intensive goods using third-world workers and a first-world infrastructure in Country N than to produce them with third-world workers and a third-world infrastructure in Country S, as allegedly occurred in Los Angeles in the 1980s when the Mexican shoe industry shrank, while a shoe industry that employed Mexican workers in Los Angeles expanded. Under such circumstances, trade liberalisation that expands the market for labour-intensive products may lead to more migration, not less.

This point is closely related to a long-standing debate in the trade literature concerning the definition of labour abundance, rooted in the Leontief Paradox. If labour supply is measured in efficiency units, and if workers are significantly more efficient in the North than in the South, then the North may be labour abundant. Migration, by converting southern workers into northern ones, can increase the amount of labour available in the North, measured in these efficiency units. The greater efficiency of labour in the North relative to the South may discourage the production of some labour-intensive goods in the South, and thus encourage South–North migration.

This was one of the initial results of NAFTA in labour-intensive agriculture. After Mexico reduced its barriers to imports, US exports of lettuce and grapes jumped sharply, as the US producers who dominate North American production learned that it was cheaper to produce such commodities for Mexico with Mexican workers in the USA because of better US infrastructure.

The assumptions of the basic trade models do not permit disparities in public infrastructure and labour quality between countries. The two countries are assumed to use the same factors of production. But capital (infrastructure) that is important in the production of goods in the North may not be available – or it may be of lower quality – in the South.

This means that a day of labour by a worker in Country N may be substantially more productive than a day of labour by the same worker in Country S. Because of differences in schooling and in experience with advanced technologies, Country N workers may not be comparable in terms of quality with Country S workers.

If infrastructure has important effects on productivity, then the development of public services and infrastructure is critical if countries in the South are to exploit their potential comparative advantage in labour-intensive production. Even if market integration stimulates North–South investment, countries in the South may not be able to depend on private investment to overcome their comparative disadvantage with regard to infrastructure and public services. As the decision by some US companies to 'return home' from Mexico illustrates, large wage differences often are not sufficient to overcome the infrastructure deficit and lure capital southward, even to produce labour-intensive goods.

Economies of scale

Assumption (3) is that the (identical) production functions in the two countries exhibit constant returns to scale. Standard trade theory denies the existence of economies of scale. If costs fall as production increases in migrant-intensive industries in the North, however, trade liberalisation may lead to more such activities in the North, along with more immigration to support them.

This means that if there are economies of scale in the production of certain labour-intensive commodities, the expansion of production in the USA lowers costs and encourages immigration to staff a growing industry. In general, when trade is due only to scale economies, migration and trade are complements (Markusen 1983; Markusen & Melvin 1981).

Slow adjustments

Comparative static models ignore the adjustment path, implicitly assuming that (a) adjustment is instantaneous, and (b) the process of adjustment will not affect the comparative-static outcome. However, the costs of adjusting to new market and policy environments can be significant, and the adjustment process takes time.

The adjustment process is complicated by the fact that, while the negative impacts of trade liberalisation (on protected sectors) often are immediate, the expansion of production and employment in sectors favoured by trade reforms takes time. Even if investors respond swiftly to the opportunities created by trade reforms, there may be a long lag between investment and the creation of new jobs, with pressures for emigration building during the interim. Since investment and job creation are, by their nature, intertemporal, the adjustment period offers a recipe for a migration hump in the wake of trade reforms.

An important aspect of the adjustment process that is likely to lead to more migration in the short run is the problem of factor specificity (e.g., see Schiff 1994). Differences in the attributes of factors demanded across sectors within migrant-sending countries can delay the adjustment process, leading to a temporary increase in unemployment.

This means that there are costs involved in moving factors from one sector to another. For example, many of the jobs created in export-oriented manufacturing are filled by young women, while many of those displaced in protected sectors such as government-owned heavy industry and agriculture are older men. Some factors, such as illiterate farmers who are displaced by freer trade, may not find jobs in the expanding manufacturing sector.

Unemployment (and correspondingly lower wages) can then promote more migration, at least in the short run. In the long run, migration pressures should decrease if workers become more mobile within Country S, perhaps as a result of improved information or retraining programs.

Imperfect markets

Standard trade models assume that all markets clear, that information is perfect, and that transactions costs are zero. In the real world, particularly in developing countries, these assumptions are unrealistic. Missing or incomplete markets, imperfect information and high transactions costs are real. Indeed, they are at the heart of what has become known as 'the new economics of labour migration' (hereafter NELM).

The NELM views migration in the context of household economic and family relationships. Country S households often face imperfect credit and risk markets (Stark 1991), and these imperfections can change in the way in which the connection between migration and development is conceptualised and modelled.

Schiff (1994) offers one reason – the costs of migration – to expect trade and migration to be complements in the short run. If the financial cost of migration – which may be considerable relative to Country S incomes[5] – constrains migration, then an initial increase in incomes as a result of trade liberalisation may encourage migration by enabling families to overcome this financial constraint. One mechanism through which the financial constraint limiting the ability to emigrate may come about is through intra-family transfers.

Migration risk adds another dimension to this argument. Even if, on average, the economic returns from migration are high, there is at least some risk of failure. Families that can afford to pay the cost of international migration may not have access to income insurance to protect themselves against the risk that a family member will fail to get a high-wage job abroad.

Diversification of family income, perhaps through local employment opportunities created by freer trade, may promote migration by making families more willing to bear the risks associated with migration. In the long run, once the pent-up demand to migrate is exhausted, migration pressures should subside as employment continues to expand in the South, exerting upward pressure on southern wages.

In economic sectors that are characterised by small-scale production activities, including most rural activities and many urban activities in LDCs, financial and risk constraints limit the extent to which many families can respond to the new market opportunities created by trade liberalisation. These constraints also limit the ability of small producers to shift their production out of once-protected activities.

For example, the vast majority of maize farmers in Mexico, who benefited from a high government-guaranteed price for their crop in the past, lack access to well-functioning rural credit and insurance markets, and they lack the resources locally to self-finance new production activities and insure themselves against income risks. International migration makes it possible to overcome these constraints, as suggested by Stark (1991).

Once family migrants are employed in the Country N labour market, they can send home remittances that finance local investments and act as a family income insurance policy. That is, in the short run, increasing international migration may be a prerequisite to adjusting to market reforms in economies without social safety nets.

In the long run, after families have made the transition to an open economy and social safety nets develop, migration is no longer needed to remedy missing markets. Indeed, as the productivity of family resources in the South increases, emigration pressures fall. However, the adjustment to new risks while the economy transforms itself produces a migration hump.

NAFTA's migration provisions

Migration played almost no role in the negotiation of the Canada–US Free Trade Agreement (CUSTA), and migration is still largely non-controversial on the northern border. On the 5500-mile Canada–USA border, about 8 per cent of the US Border Patrol's 4000 agents apprehended about 13 000 illegal aliens in 1994, or 1 per cent of all foreigners apprehended. Most were Canadians, but there are reports that, increasingly, smugglers are attempting to use the 'northern route' to smuggle, for example, Chinese into the USA.

NAFTA permits limited free migration for employment. Under Chapter 16 of NAFTA, four groups of persons can cross North American borders for business reasons:

- business visitors – persons engaged in international business activities who receive no wages in the country they are visiting;
- traders and investors – persons selling goods in another North American country, or persons with management roles in enterprises created with a person's funds;
- intra-company transfers – managers and executives with specialised knowledge who are transferred between branches of companies with operations in two or more North American companies; and

- professionals – persons with at least a Bachelor's degree seeking to engage in professional activities in another North American country, including accountants, doctors and nurses, scientists, and college teachers.

The only category that may become the subject of controversy is the professional category, since it arguably creates a common labour market for the 20 per cent of the labour force with a Bachelor's degree or more. A professional Canadian wanting to work in the USA simply shows a passport, credential, and offer of 'temporary' employment from a US employer, and then receives a TN work visa at the US border entry point. There is no numerical limit on how many professionals can cross the border between the USA and Canada, but the number of Mexican professionals who can enter the USA under NAFTA provisions is limited to 5500 per year until 2003.[6]

The number of Canadian professionals who have entered the USA since 1989 has risen sharply, from 2700 in 1989 to 17 000 in 1993 (these are crossings, not unique individuals, so that one person could be counted several times). There is no definition of 'temporary' in the NAFTA agreement, so Canadians could conceivably work for ten or more years, since there is no recording of or controls over length of stay under the NAFTA program.

Table 6.1   Canadian professionals admitted under CUSTA/NAFTA

	1989	1990	1991	1992	1993
Professionals	2677	5293	8344	12675	17038
Dependants	140	594	804	1283	2414

Note: These are crossings, not unique individuals, so one person could be recorded several times.
Source: Department of Labor, ILAB, 1995.

US nurses have complained of losing jobs to Canadians who have entered under NAFTA provisions, and the US Department of Labor (DOL) is considering removing nurses from the list of professionals who enjoy free entry. Canada has asked that spouses be permitted to work temporarily in the USA, an idea that the USA has so far opposed.

Policy options

There are three broad options to deal with the migration hump, and all are being considered in the USA. First, the USA could try to unilaterally develop better border and interior controls designed to deter Mexican and all other illegal immigrants from arriving and seeking jobs. Second, the USA could convert at least some illegal Mexican migrants with a unilateral or bilateral guest worker program. Third, the USA could induce Mexico to co-operate to reduce illegal immigration.

Border and interior controls

The Immigration Reform and Control Act (IRCA) of 1986 sought to reduce illegal immigration by wiping the slate clean with legalisation and using employer sanctions to close the labour market to additional illegal entrants. The Border Patrol was increased in size, and a computer system was implemented to enable states and cities to verify the legal status of applicants for welfare benefits.

While IRCA was being debated, there were warnings that, without a secure eligibility document, illegal aliens might continue to enter the USA and find employment. These warnings proved prophetic. The INS concentrated on educating employers rather than aggressively enforcing sanctions, while the fraudulent documents industry expanded into immigrant communities across the nation. Even when there was enforcement, employers often appealed INS fines, settling them for thirty cents in the dollar after involving their political representatives in disputes with the INS over what they claimed were 'paperwork' or technical violations.

IRCA imposed penalties on employers who knowingly hired illegal aliens, but it did not change the structure of industries that had become dependent on such workers. For this reason, fraudulent documents permitted pre-IRCA employment patterns to persist.

The USA has begun a catch-up enforcement effort. The Border Patrol has launched its flood-the-border-with-agents strategy to deter illegal entries, and many other suggestions are being debated in Congress. These proposals generally add funds to the Border Patrol, step up penalties for alien smugglers, and at least experiment with a more secure system of work-authorisation cards.

The weak link in the current effort to prevent illegal aliens from working inside the USA is widely acknowledged to be the widespread availability of false documents. Under US law, a worker must present, and an employer must see, work authorisation documents 'that appear to be genuine' for all new hires. If an employer has a copy of the worker's documentation on file – most employers copy the driver's license and green card immigrant visa presented by most falsely documented aliens – then the employer has satisfied the law and is not subject to employer sanctions if the workers turn out to be illegal aliens.

Because of fears of discrimination against Hispanic and Asian workers, US employers are prohibited from asking for work authorisation documents until a worker is hired, and then prohibited from questioning too closely the authenticity of the documents presented. There are currently twenty-six work authorisation documents that can be presented, ranging from birth certificates issued by over 3100 counties to tribal identity documents.

Under proposals pending in Congress, the number of work documents would be reduced to six: resident alien or 'green' cards, employment authorisation issued to other work-authorised aliens, a social security card, a US passport, a driver's license, or a state-issued identification card – and there would be at least experimental efforts to develop a secure work-authorisation card. Most proposals centre on making the social security card counterfeit resistant, and then having employers check the card number against a computer data base.

The USA is likely to adopt new measures to prevent illegal entries and employment. But there are many technical as well as political obstacles to adopting and implementing these measures. For these reasons, two other approaches may be tried: guest workers and conditional assistance to emigration countries.

Guest workers

Illegal Mexicans seeking US jobs could become legal Mexican workers under a guest-worker program. The purpose of guest-worker programs is to add workers to the labour force but not permanent residents to the population.

The legacy of guest-worker programs is universal – around the world it is clear that there is nothing more permanent than temporary workers. Guest-worker programs tend to produce immediate economic benefits to migrants and their families and to the employers who hire them, but everywhere they leave a legacy of distortion and dependence.

Distortion refers to the fact that flexible economies and labour markets soon become accustomed to the ready availability of unskilled workers, and that the availability of such workers is soon incorporated into business planning. Investment and other business decisions are made on the premise that labour costs will continue to be held down by immigration.

Distortion soon takes concrete form, as when citrus or avocado trees – that will produce fruit for ten to twenty years and can be picked only by hand – are planted in areas where all new harvesters are Mexican immigrants who pick for ten years or less. It should come as no surprise that the owners of assets whose value has been increased by immigration are willing to spend considerable funds and efforts to keep the border gates open to their immigrant workers.

Dependence or settlement is a reminder that guest workers are mostly young men and, even if most do return, there is invariably some settlement and family unification, setting in motion migration streams that expand over time.

Although they agreed on little else regarding immigration, both Mexican President Salinas and Governor Wilson in November 1994 called for a US–Mexican guest-worker program. The push for guest workers has since picked up steam. California growers, whose power is widely respected after they succeeded in winning immigration exceptions in IRCA in 1986, have developed a proposal to substitute attestation for certification to determine whether foreign workers are needed.

Instead of requesting permission to import foreign workers from the DOL, as is currently required, and then waiting for DOL to certify that the grower tried to recruit US workers at prevailing wages and with offers of free housing, transportation, and contracts for work, the growers would simply assert that they had taken these steps, and DOL would be required to approve their applications unless the applications were incomplete or inaccurate.

The chances of such a radical change in US foreign-worker policy being adopted in an era of tough talk about immigration seem remote. However, if three events happen in sequence, there could be a serious effort to launch a guest-worker program with Mexico, despite the negative halo of the 1942–64 Bracero program and Congressional rejection of the growers' guest-worker concept in the early 1980s:

- if credible farm labour shortages develop;
- if it is concluded that INS border controls have reduced illegal immigration at the border significantly; or
- if Mexico makes a push for a guest-worker program to legitimise and better manage 'inevitable' migration then a program could be approved.

During the early 1980s, disputes centred on how to certify that guest workers were truly needed. Today, the focus of attention is on how to encourage guest workers to return to their countries of origin. Both liberal Frank del Olmo of the *Los Angeles Times* and conservative Attorney General Dan Lundgren, for example, have called for a guest-worker program that withholds 20 to 30 per cent of the guest worker's US earnings to encourage return migration.

Mexican co-operation

Around the world, rich countries that provide assistance to poorer neighbours are conditioning aid on recipients' willingness to follow free-trade policies, to guarantee that foreign investments will not be confiscated, and to give assurance that it will not violate the basic human rights of its own citizens. In Western Europe, countries such as Germany have gone further, making their aid to Poland and other Eastern European countries contingent on recipients helping to deter illegal immigration.

The USA does not provide much formal aid to Mexico, but Mexico was the major beneficiary of NAFTA. NAFTA's labour and environmental side-agreements demonstrated that the USA was willing to make NAFTA's approval contingent on requiring Mexico to adopt and enforce policies that protected basic labour and environmental standards. There was no migration side-agreement.

What might a migration side-agreement to NAFTA have looked like? The USA could have conditioned trade and investment benefits on three types of Mexican policies.

First, Mexican policies could be implemented to reduce the inequality of income and wealth that permits a relative handful of people to capture most of the benefits of faster growth. The Asian economic miracle was based on export-led manufacturing growth shared broadly throughout society. In Asia, rural–urban earnings differences did not get too large; Mexico has allowed them to widen to 1:5 or 1:6, thereby encouraging rural–urban migration and emigration. These disparities create both absolute and relative income incentives for more migration.

Second, Mexico and the USA should co-operate to avoid too much border development. The border area is asymmetric – it encompasses some of the richest parts of Mexico and some of the poorest parts of the USA. If economic and job growth is disproportionately concentrated in the border areas of Mexico, internal migrants will inevitably be drawn there, and some will spill over the border into the USA. The USA and Mexico could discourage such a result by taxing development at the border while subsidising development in the interior.

Third, Mexico could co-operate with the USA to reduce illegal immigration. In no other part of the world do citizens of one nation mass openly awaiting their chance to enter authorised ports, so Mexican citizens attempting illegal entry into the USA are breaking Mexican as well as US law.

Notes

1   Many of the young 'drybacks' in Mexico taught English and otherwise participated in Mexico's boom economy in 1994. Most have returned to the USA in 1995.

2   One condition of the US-led $50 billion bailout of Mexico in March 1995 is that Mexico publish money supply data on a regular basis.

3   Mexicans who managed to convert their pesos into dollars before the devaluation are richer than before, and sales of some luxury goods, such as $50 000 Mercedes, were up 25 per cent in the first quarter of 1995. Expensive restaurants are reportedly full, while medium-priced establishments are struggling. This has reportedly fuelled resentment against rich Mexicans – the top 10 per cent of earners received 38 per cent of the Mexico's income in 1992.

4   In many cases, the border crossing is financed by family members in the USA rather than by the migrants themselves, making the devaluation a less significant barrier to finding the funds to pay smugglers.

5   In rural Mexico, where annual incomes average $1000, the cost of being smuggled into the USA is $300–500. The wages that a newly arrived illegal Mexican worker can expect to earn in the USA depend on his or her network contacts. In agriculture, 1000 hours of work at an average wage of $5 is typical for a worker in the USA 8 to 10 months of the year.

6   In addition, Mexican and Canadian professionals can enter the USA to work for up to six years with H-1B visas, which are granted to foreign workers after a US employer 'attests' that they are needed to fill vacant jobs for which US workers cannot be found.

   DOL must approve US employer requests for temporary foreign workers unless it is 'obviously inaccurate'.

   The H-1B program permits up to 65 000 foreign workers to enter the USA each year and, since each can stay in the USA for six years, there can be a maximum 390 000 H-1B workers in the USA. It is estimated that 40 per cent of the new H-1B visa approvals are for high-tech jobs such as programmers.

Both employer and worker representatives agree that the H-1B program has been abused by so-called 'body shops' or contractors in what one witness called a 'techo Bracero program'. Syntel, a Michigan computer programming firm whose labour force is 80 per cent H-1B workers from India, supplied programmers for insurance company AIG after AIG laid off its US programmers. Mastech, the company that maintains the White House's computerised correspondence tracking system, is under investigation for misusing the H1-B program to import over 1000 of its 1200 workers.

7

Trans-Tasman Migration and Closer Economic Relations

Ganesh Nana and Jacques Poot

I Introduction

Australia and New Zealand have much in common due to their relative geographic proximity and shared colonial past.[1] In 1901, the opportunity was there for New Zealand to join the Commonwealth along with the states of Australia. This opportunity was declined, but nonetheless an agreement to permit free movement of citizens between the two has, in one form or another, been in place since the early 1920s and is a clear expression of the close historical, economic and cultural ties between the two countries. Under the current Trans-Tasman Travel Agreement (TTTA), citizens of either country may freely settle in the other country. New Zealand extends this right effectively also to other permanent residents of Australia.

In contrast, this closeness did not guide external trade policies in the same way. The two self-governing countries became rather protectionist, especially after the Great Depression. But in the 1960s the two governments acknowledged that a reduction of trans-Tasman trade barriers would help develop stronger and more competitive manufacturing sectors and this led to the New Zealand–Australia Free Trade Agreement (the 'original' NAFTA) in 1965. However, NAFTA was not a free-trade area, but rather a vague agreement to gradually remove trans-Tasman trade barriers within an unspecified time frame. Eventually, though, lack of progress with NAFTA provided the impetus for the Australia–New Zealand Closer Economic Relations Trade Agreement (ANCERTA, or CER for short) of 1983. The original CER provided for the achievement of free trade by 1995, but a 1988 review led to a speeding up of the implementation and by July 1990 virtually free trade in goods between the two countries had been achieved (Holmes 1991). Although some barriers to trade in services have also been removed, and further moves towards a true single market are still on the agenda, some obstacles remain at present (for example in aviation and telecommunications). This is primarily due to a more cautious approach to liberalisation by Australia. The difference in attitudes towards completion of the single market is undoubtedly related to the slower pace of deregulation in the Australian economy and the observation that the benefits of CER have to date been reaped disproportionately by New Zealand.

This paper focuses on the impact of the TTTA and trade liberalisation on trans-Tasman migration and the Australasian labour market. The next section briefly summarises earlier empirical work on trans-Tasman migration and the possible linkages with CER.

An interesting question is what the impact of further removal of trade barriers at the common Australasian border might be – both for trans-Tasman trade and for the labour markets of both countries. Section III describes a Computable General Equilibrium (CGE) model which can be used to address this question. This model has already been successfully used to investigate the macroeconomic and sectoral implications of CER (Nana & Philpott 1988, Nana et al. forthcoming).

In Section IV we report the results of additional simulations which show that the effects of extending CER to the bilateral removal of protection against imports from other countries are also beneficial. However, our main concern is with the impact of such policies towards trade liberalisation on factor mobility. Various simulations are considered which differ in assumption about rigidities in factor prices or factor mobility. A direction for further research is suggested.

II Trans-Tasman migration and trade

Since the colonial days of the last century, the movement of people between Australia and New Zealand has been an indicator of the relative economic performance of the two countries. The net movement has tended to be in the direction of the country with the higher growth of real GDP per head (Poot 1993, p. 288).

From the post-Second World War period until the mid-1960s, the fluctuations in net trans-Tasman migration were relatively small and in most years the net movement was in the direction of New Zealand. Commencing with the 1967 recession and until about 1991, trans-Tasman migration started to exhibit large fluctuations and the net movement was predominantly in the direction of Australia. Since 1991, emigration from New Zealand to Australia has been at fairly low levels – similar to those observed during the economic boom years of the early 1970s. Nonetheless, it is estimated that there continued to be net outflows from New Zealand in recent years – for example, of about 3000 persons in the year to March 1994 (see James et al. 1995).

The changes in the flows obviously impacted on the stocks of residents from across the Tasman. The New Zealand-born population in Australia increased from about 47 000 in 1961 to 264 000 in 1991. The Australia-born population in New Zealand increased from about 35 000 in 1961 to 61 000 in 1976, but then declined to 47 000 in 1986 followed by a small increase to 49 000 in 1991. Since 1991 these numbers would not have changed much. Given that the Australian population is about five times the New Zealand population, the long-run 'drift west' has of course been far more significant from the New Zealand point of view.

The net outflow from New Zealand in the late 1970s led to growing political and scientific interest. A workshop was held on the trans-Tasman movement, resulting in a report with an emphasis on demographic aspects (Pool 1980). The migration wave of the late 1980s also spurred research. A project to which academics on both sides of the Tasman again contributed resulted in a voluminous report on the characteristics, causes and consequences of trans-Tasman migration (Carmichael 1993). This report highlighted that the aggregate arrival and departure statistics hide much of the complexity of the population flows between the two countries. However, there are some powerful economic and demographic forces which shape the overall pattern of movement.

Brosnan and Poot (1987) estimated an econometric model of 1950–85 trans-Tasman migration which identified these main determinants. First, overall mobility increased as the cost of trans-Tasman airfares declined in real terms. Second, given the age selectivity of migration, with mobility rates being much higher among young adults, the post-Second World War baby boom also contributed to the large volume of movement, particularly in the 1970s. Third, waves of migration have tended to lead to waves of return migration, since migrants are more mobile (i.e., more likely to move again) than non-migrants.

However, as noted earlier, changing relative economic conditions have been the primary force responsible for changes in the volume of gross migration and direction of net migration. The econometric model identified inflation, unemployment, real earnings and employment growth as significant factors. More recently, this model performed remarkably well at forecasting the wave of migration from New Zealand to Australia in the late 1980s, although the volume of movement was overestimated (Poot 1993, p. 296).

The rate of economic growth in Australia in the post-Second World War period has generally been higher than that of New Zealand, and the ratio of New Zealand's GDP per capita over Australia's GDP per capita (in purchasing power terms) has been on a long-run downward trend. Both countries also found their standard of living slide relative to the OECD average. In purchasing power parity (PPP) terms, New Zealand's GDP per capita ranked sixth among OECD countries in the 1950s, compared with Australia's eighth place. By 1976, the two countries switched relative positions and by the late 1980s, these ranks had become nineteenth and sixteenth for New Zealand and Australia respectively.[2] Nonetheless, from a global perspective, both countries are clearly among the highly developed nations and perform similarly in terms of many welfare indicators. The 'gap' between the two may again be closing as New Zealand has outperformed Australia in recent years in terms of economic indicators such as unemployment, the government budget balance and GDP growth.

The process of trans-Tasman migration is therefore better interpreted as inter-regional population redistribution. An econometric model of a matrix of gross inter-regional migration in Australasia 1981–86 (with New Zealand being one of the regions) showed that there is a common labour market in that all flows responded to inter-regional differences in income and employment opportunities (Poot 1995). However, trans-Tasman migration is not exactly internal migration. There are statistically significant differences in coefficients of migration determinants in this model between intra-Australian flows and trans-Tasman flows. Among the factors responsible for this are the differences between the two countries in tax and public expenditure policies, a different treatment of domestic *vis-à-vis* foreign qualifications, and the gap between the nominal exchange rate and the PPP one.

In terms of merchandise trade, the image of trans-Tasman flows as inter-regional trade rather than international trade is also not entirely appropriate, despite the fact that free merchandise trade was achieved by 1990. The export ratio of New Zealand is about 28 per cent of GDP, undoubtedly lower than the ratio for the states of Australia when inter-state trade is included. Trade flows in the post-Second World War period have also been rather unbalanced, at least until recently. Trans-Tasman exports in the 1950s were only about 2.8 per cent of New Zealand's exports, while imports from Australia accounted for 14.2 per cent of New Zealand's imports (Edwards & Holmes 1994, pp. 130–1). Both export and import shares increased, with exports at a faster rate, so that roughly balanced merchandise trade resulted in recent years. Australia now accounts for one-fifth of New Zealand's trade, while New Zealand accounts for 5 per cent of Australian trade.

Migration and trade in Australasia do not represent flows within a single economy. The migration flows are probably more similar to internal migration than, for example, intra-European migration of European Union (EU) citizens, but we noted that they are behaviourally different from inter-state migration within Australia. Moreover, in terms of trade in services, investment and tax policy, the EU may be considered closer to a true single market than is CER (Lloyd 1991, p. 24).

Nonetheless, in terms of both migration and trade, the trans-Tasman flows have increased in importance during much of the post-Second World War period. This can be seen from Figure 7.1. For comparison, data from before the Second World War have also been included. The relative importance of trans-Tasman trade in this figure has been measured by the sum of exports to Australia and imports from Australia as a percentage of New Zealand's total commodity trade volume (i.e., the sum of exports FOB and imports CIF in New Zealand dollars).[3] Similarly, the importance of trans-Tasman migration is measured by the sum of Permanent and Long-Term (PLT) arrivals from Australia and PLT departures to Australia as a percentage of the sum of total New Zealand immigration and emigration.[4]

Figure 7.1 shows that trans-Tasman labour mobility has always been more important for New Zealand, at least numerically, than the commodity flows. However, the importance of trans-Tasman trade has been increasing quite steadily throughout the post-Second World War period. The ratio has been primarily

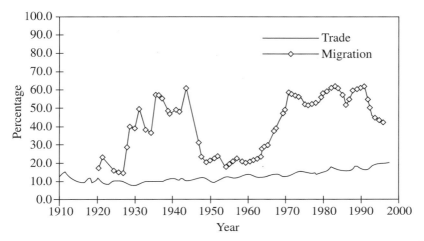

Figure 7.1   The share of the trans-Tasman flows in New Zealand's international trade and migration. **Sources:** see note 4.

driven by the increasing share of New Zealand exports going to Australia, as the import share has grown at a much slower rate. Interestingly, the CER agreement reinforced a continuation of the trend rather than generating an acceleration. It is also noteworthy that the trans-Tasman share of New Zealand trade was relatively higher at the beginning of the century, before protectionist measures were introduced.

In the years leading up to the Second World War, trans-Tasman migration accounted for a large share of New Zealand's migration flows, but became far less significant in the early post-Second World War years. However, trans-Tasman migration became increasingly important again during the post-Second World War period, at least until recent years. At times in which the New Zealand economy experienced relatively buoyant conditions, such as in the mid-1970s and the mid-1980s, a shift in the migration composition took place, resulting in less emigration to Australia and relatively more immigration (and return migration) into New Zealand from the rest of the world. The migration graph is primarily driven by the New Zealand outflow (emigration) in the same way as the trade graph is driven by exports. The sharp drop in the migration graph in the 1990s is due to a combination of a more active encouragement of controlled immigration (primarily from Europe and Asia) by the New Zealand government and, again, a relatively smaller number of people moving to Australia. PLT departures from New Zealand to Australia averaged 36 000 for the years 1987–90, compared with 16 000 for the years 1991–94.

Since trans-Tasman migration and trans-Tasman trade shared a common upward trend for much of the post-Second World War period, it may be tempting to suggest some causal link. There are many unrelated factors influencing one or the other, but one common factor has been the impact of major policy events in the United Kingdom. Australia became the predominant destination of PLT departures from New Zealand after the United Kingdom introduced controls on Commonwealth immigration in the 1960s (Farmer & Buetow 1993). At the same time, the Common Market's share of British trade increased significantly (an increase which preceded formal entry into the Market in 1973) and this had a strong impact on the direction of New Zealand exports.

The implementation of CER in the 1980s has had a positive impact on the New Zealand economy. At the same time, emigration levels from New Zealand to Australia increased after the early 1980s to a peak in 1988. Subsequently, emigration declined to levels experienced in the early 1980s. Consequently, the recent slowdown in net migration in the direction of Australia is consistent with the view that trade and migration are substitutes in the long run. However, one possible explanation for the New Zealand-to-Australia migration wave of the late 1980s is in the presence of a 'migration hump' resulting from trade liberalisation, as explained in the chapter by Martin. The phasing in of CER and other measures of trade liberalisation and economic reforms did lead to significant economic restructuring and rising unemployment in New Zealand during the late 1980s.

A growing trade in services, such as professional consultancy services and tourism, and trans-Tasman investment may also have led to increased labour mobility. There is little information on this. However, business and commerce professionals are over-represented among New Zealand migrants to Australia aged 35 and over (Carmichael 1993, p. 124). There is also some evidence that a disproportionate share of Australian migrants to New Zealand in recent years are 'contract migrants'. These are people who are transferees of Australian firms or hired on short-term contracts by New Zealand firms. For example, in the early 1980s some contract migrants were employed on the government's capital-intensive energy projects (the 'Think Big' projects) and later there was a growing demand for professional workers in the business, finance and technology sectors created by extensive economic reforms and private and public sector restructuring (see also Poot 1993, p. 298).

The stylised facts of long-run post-Second World War economic growth in Australia and New Zealand are consistent with the conventional neo-classical models of migration. The average annual rate of real growth in GDP in New Zealand over the period 1950–93 was 2.7 per cent and in Australia 4.0 per cent. Given population growth of 1.4 per cent in New Zealand and 1.9 per cent in Australia, real income per head grew by approximately 1.3 per cent and 2.1 per cent respectively. As expected, net migration took place in the direction of the country with the higher rate of growth in real income per head.

We note also that part of the faster growth in Australia was due to a faster growth in capital per head, as more of GDP was devoted to investment in that country (except for 1973–77). The data base of the *Joani* model described in the next section suggests that, in PPP terms, the 1986–87 capital–labour ratio in Australia was about 38 per cent higher than in New Zealand.[5] The lower capital–labour ratio in New Zealand indeed corresponded to a higher average rate of return to capital: 7.9 per cent versus 5.6 per cent respectively. Comparable data on earnings suggest that in PPP terms earnings per worker in 1986–87 were 17.5 per cent higher in Australia.

With these stylised facts, the observed trans-Tasman flows make sense. As the Heckscher–Ohlin theory would suggest, Australia allocated relatively more resources to the more capital-intensive manufacturing and mining sectors. Manufactured goods do in fact account for a larger share of trade from Australia to New Zealand than vice versa (Edwards & Holmes 1994, p. 152).

Given the restrictions on trade, until CER, in some commodities where New Zealand would have had the comparative advantage, labour migration from the relatively labour-abundant country can substitute for commodity trade. It could therefore be argued that the Australian trade barriers contributed to net migration from New Zealand to Australia. Similarly, although notoriously harder to measure reliably, the net flow of capital would have been in the direction of New Zealand, the country with the higher rate of return. Bollard (1987) noted that the levels of Australian investment in New Zealand were much larger during the 1970s and 1980s than vice versa. However, capital flows have been restricted. Even at present, despite liberal policies on foreign investment in both countries, New Zealanders cannot invest in Australia on the same terms as Australians.

Despite the large influx of New Zealanders into the Australian labour market over the period 1965–90, there is no evidence to suggest that this movement depressed Australian wages. Indeed, the purchasing power-corrected earnings gap increased throughout this period, after having been virtually zero for the previous two decades.[6]

This observation is not surprising, for two reasons. First, there is little empirical evidence that migrants impact on nominal wages at the macro level (see for example Junankar & Pope 1990). Second, regional trade appears more effective than factor migration in equalising factor prices (Horiba & Kirkpatrick 1981).

Beyond the standard two-good two-factor models which one can invoke to compare with the stylised facts, it is better to use a CGE model to assess the impact of trade policies on the macro economy, on industries and on factor markets. The next section describes such a model, while the subsequent section considers the potential impact of CER on factor mobility.

III The *Joani* model

A CGE model is an effective tool to assess the microeconomic impact of trade policy changes. Both Australian and New Zealand researchers developed such

CGE models in the 1970s, called *Orani* and *Joanna* respectively (see Dixon et al. 1982; Nana & Philpott 1983). Both these models are multi-sectoral, input–output based, oriented towards comparative-static analysis, linear in their growth rates and have common roots in Johansen's pioneering multi-sectoral model of economic growth (Johansen 1960). They could therefore be combined into a two-country model referred to as *Joani*. The *Joani* model was first used to simulate the impact of full implementation of the CER agreement, based on the status quo in 1984–85 (Philpott & Nana 1988). It was found that CER led to GDP and consumption gains for both countries. The gains to New Zealand were noticeably larger than those to Australia and led in New Zealand to some trade diversion in favour of trans-Tasman trade. The differential was due, first, to the greater importance of trans-Tasman trade in New Zealand's total trade and, second, to the initially higher levels of protection in New Zealand which meant that CER induced a greater cost reduction (competitive gain) in that country. The actual outcomes have borne out the model predictions.

Subsequently, a new *Joani* model was generated with 1986–87 input–output data and 1990–91 trade and protection data. This model showed that, starting from a 1990–91 position, further intra-CER tariff reductions had no significant impact, as free trans-Tasman trade had already nearly been achieved (Nana et al. forthcoming). However, the removal of tariffs *vis-à-vis* third countries resulted, as expected, in significant long-run consumption and employment benefits to both countries. Before discussing these results and the possible implications for factor mobility in the next section, we first provide an outline of the characteristics of the *Joani* model.[7]

The *Joani* model identifies three sources and destinations for each country's products, namely home, the trans-Tasman partner, and the rest of the world. The model is purely neo-classical in nature: assumptions of cost minimisation for producers and utility maximisation for consumers form the basis of the simulation of agents' behaviour. Hence, relative price movements between the three sources trigger substitution towards the relatively cheaper source(s). Such a response, however, is limited by substitution elasticities which reflect either differing tastes and qualities of the goods, or technological constraints.[8]

The model identifies twenty-two production sectors in each country, each producing a single commodity. Inter-country links are modelled explicitly at this disaggregated level, with relationships ensuring consistency in trans-Tasman trade volumes and prices for both countries.[9] Furthermore, equality of demand and supply of each domestically produced commodity is imposed via a 'market-clearing' condition.

Household consumption expenditure in each country is determined as a function of household income, which is principally derived from wages and profits. In addition to the substitution towards relatively cheaper source(s) of supply, described above, price and income elasticities of demand ensure that the allocation of consumption expenditure between the various commodities is responsive to changes in relative prices and incomes in each country. Real government consumption and aggregate investment expenditure are assumed exogenous in both countries.

Output in each sector is produced by means of five different types of labour input (occupational categories) and capital. Each sector's demand for labour and capital depends on the sector's level of activity and the relative factor prices. Relative price-induced substitution between the six primary factors in each sector is based on the CRESH functional form.[10] The total primary factor requirement is constrained by the gross output of each sector. The pairwise CRESH substitution elasticities were adapted from Higgs et al. (1981).

Aggregate real investment is allocated across sectors such that expected sectoral rates of return on this new investment are equalised in each country. These expected rates of return are positively related to the current profit rate and inversely related to the price of new capital goods and the rate of growth in the capital stock. Investment expenditure in electricity, gas and water infrastructure, government social services and new house construction is set exogenously in both countries, as such rate-of-return criteria are considered inappropriate in these cases.[11]

Consistent with the neo-classical nature of the model, prices of domestically produced commodities are determined by the costs of production along with a 'zero pure profits' criterion. Prices of items imported (CIF value) into each country are therefore dependent on production costs in the country of origin, inter-country transport costs and the exchange rate. Allowing for tariffs (and tariff-equivalents of other protection measures) imposed by each country, the purchaser's prices of the imports result.

Following the standard Walrasian general equilibrium property that only n–1 of n market-clearing equations are independent, a numeraire (exogenous price) must be chosen. World prices of traded goods (*vis-à-vis* Australian and New Zealand prices) act as the numeraire in the *Joani* model. Since the model does not have a monetary sector, nominal exchange rates are also exogenous.

The model provides a picture of the state of the economy after it has reached a new general equilibrium following a particular exogenous shock, as compared with the status quo. Hence the model does not generate forecasts of the economy, but instead permits a short-run or long-run comparative static analysis.

IV Trade liberalisation and factor mobility

In this section we shall consider the possible impact on the factor markets of Australia and New Zealand of an extension of CER to a jointly agreed reduction of tariffs on imports from the rest of the world to zero. Crucial in this type of modelling is the choice of exogenous variables. Some of these represent the quantitative policy shocks which are under investigation, others are assumed unaffected by the policy shock under consideration and are therefore set equal to zero ('no change').

In this study the trade policy shock is explored under various alternative assumptions about the price and/or quantity adjustment in the factor markets. However, these have all in common an assumed exogeneity of nominal exchange rates, world prices, real world income, real government consumption expenditure and real trans-Tasman transport margins. All simulations are concerned with the long run in which individual sectors can adjust their capital stock such that sectoral rates of return relativities remain as they were before the introduction of the trade policy shock.

In this paper, the *Joani* CGE model is run under six different sets of assumptions. The associated macroeconomic implications from the model are reported in Table 7.1. Run 1 assumes independent (i.e., country-specific) factor markets, as well as the absence of labour shortages. Run 2 assumes no change in available inputs, which leaves only effects attributable to relative price movements. In Run 3, aggregate labour employment and capital stock are kept fixed in both countries. By contrast, a general equilibrium solution subject to a single overall constraint on aggregate employment in Australasia, allocated such that the change in real wage rates is equalised between the two countries, is assumed in Run 4. In parallel to Run 4, Run 5 starts with the assumption of unchanged real wage rates in each country. However, the change in rates of return to capital across the two economies is equalised, given a single overall constraint on the available aggregate Australasian physical capital resources. Run 6 permits a free allocation of both labour and capital across Australasia.

Table 7.1 shows that, as expected, all runs have in common a welfare gain in both countries in terms of growth in real private consumption following the removal of external trade barriers. In all but one case real GDP also grows, while employment grows or stays the same. Another result common to all but two simulations is that trade liberalisation generates a slight divergence in income per worker between the two countries in terms of the change in real GDP per worker, with Australia benefiting more than New Zealand. Furthermore, in all simulations both countries increase their trade with the rest of the world, as expected. Moreover, all simulations show that the trade flow from New Zealand to Australia declines. However, the sign of the change in the trade flow from Australia to New Zealand depends on the choice of model assumptions. More detailed results from each model run are now discussed.

In Run 1 the removal of protection results in increased employment of all occupations, as reported in Table 7.2. The overall strong Australasian expansion follows from the improvement in price competitiveness in both countries *vis-à-vis* the rest of the world as imported inputs become cheaper. The expansion is therefore most pronounced in the export-oriented sectors. Domestic consumption benefits from the increase in household incomes following increased employment.

Table 7.1   Macroeconomic aggregates

(% changes, except trade BOP which is the absolute change as % of GDP)

		Run 1	Run 2	Run 3	Run 4	Run 5	Run 6
NEW ZEALAND							
Real GDP		2.0	0.3	0.3	0.7	0.6	−0.2
Real private consumption		3.3	2.0	2.1	2.3	2.1	1.6
Labour employment		3.1	0	0	0.7	2.0	0.0
Capital stock		0	0	0	0	−1.4	−0.9
Export volumes	to Aus	−1.7	−2.5	−2.6	−2.3	−2.2	−2.6
	to RoW	8.2	3.8	3.7	4.7	6.1	3.4
	Total	6.4	2.6	2.6	3.4	4.6	2.3
Import volumes	from Aus	3.5	−0.2	0.1	−0.0	2.7	−0.5
	from RoW	7.2	7.4	7.5	7.6	5.8	6.8
	Total	6.4	5.9	6.0	6.1	5.2	5.3
Trade BOP	with Aus	−0.2	−0.1	−0.1	−0.1	−0.1	−0.1
	with RoW	−0.5	−1.1	−1.2	−1.0	−0.5	−1.0
Price of imports	from Aus	−6.1	−4.2	−4.3	−4.2	−6.2	−4.3
	from RoW	−8.1	−8.0	−8.1	−8.1	−8.1	−8.0
Consumer prices		−3.6	−2.3	−2.3	−2.5	−3.2	−2.3
Output prices		−2.9	−1.5	−1.4	−1.7	−2.4	−1.4
Rate of return on K		5.3	4.0	3.8	4.1	6.9	5.1
Real wage rates		0	1.8	1.9	1.5	0	1.5
AUSTRALIA							
Real GDP		1.9	0.3	0.3	0.2	2.1	0.3
Real private consumption		2.7	1.6	1.6	1.5	2.8	1.6
Labour employment		2.3	0	0	−0.1	2.4	−0.0
Capital stock ·		0	0	0	0	0.3	0.2
Export volumes	to NZ	3.5	−0.2	0.1	0.0	2.7	−0.5
	to RoW	11.7	5.8	5.9	5.5	12.1	5.8
	Total	11.2	5.4	5.5	5.2	11.5	5.5
Import volumes	from NZ	−2.1	−2.8	−2.9	−2.5	−2.8	−3.0
	from RoW	8.5	9.4	9.4	9.5	8.6	9.6
	Total	8.0	8.9	8.9	8.9	8.1	9.0
Trade BOP	with NZ	0.0	0.0	0.0	0.0	0.0	0.0
	with RoW	−0.2	−0.8	−0.8	−0.9	−0.2	−0.9
Price of imports	from NZ	−5.6	−4.4	−4.3	−4.5	−5.1	−4.2
	from RoW	−10.8	−10.8	−10.8	−10.8	−10.8	−10.8
Consumer prices		−4.8	−2.6	−2.8	−2.7	−4.9	−2.8
Output prices		−4.5	−2.1	−2.3	−2.2	−4.6	−2.3
Rate of return on K		7.3	6.3	5.4	5.3	6.9	5.1
Real wage rates		0	1.3	1.4	1.5	0	1.5

Note: The entry of 0% (no change) for exogenous variables is indicated in bold type.

Table 7.2 Output and factor markets

(% changes)

		Run 1	Run 2		Run 3	Run 4	Run 5	Run 6
NEW ZEALAND								
Gross output		1.6	−0.2		−0.2	0.2	0.1	−0.7
				Price labr				
Employment	PRF	1.8	**0**	−1.0	−0.2	0.3	0.8	−0.3
	SKW	4.3	**0**	−0.3	0.1	1.1	3.5	0.6
	SKB	2.1	**0**	−1.7	−0.8	−0.2	0.9	−0.9
	USW	4.0	**0**	0.7	0.7	1.4	2.9	0.8
	USB	2.5	**0**	−0.5	0.0	0.6	1.1	−0.3
Total employment		3.1	**0**		**0**	0.7	2.0	0.0
Capital		**0**	**0**		**0**	**0**	−1.4	−0.9
Price of gross output		−2.9	−1.5		−1.4	−1.7	−2.4	−1.4
Price of labour		−3.6	−0.5		−0.4	−1.0	−3.2	−0.8
Price of capital		0.1	−0.2		−0.2	−0.1	1.0	0.5
AUSTRALIA								
Gross output		1.5	−0.3		−0.3	−0.4	1.7	−0.3
				Price labr				
Employment	PRF	1.9	**0**	−0.3	0.3	0.2	2.0	0.3
	SKW	2.9	**0**	−0.3	0.4	0.2	3.0	0.3
	SKB	1.8	**0**	−2.2	−0.8	−1.0	2.0	−0.8
	USW	3.0	**0**	0.6	0.7	0.6	3.1	0.7
	USB	1.5	**0**	−4.5	−0.8	−1.0	1.7	−0.8
Total employment		2.3	**0**		**0**	−0.1	2.4	−0.0
Capital		**0**	**0**		**0**	**0**	0.3	0.2
Price of gross output		−4.5	−2.1		−2.3	−2.2	−4.6	−2.3
Price of labour		−4.8	−1.3		−1.4	−1.2	−4.9	−1.4
Price of capital		−2.0	−0.7		−1.2	−1.2	−2.2	−1.3

Note: The entry of 0% (no change) for exogenous variables is indicated in bold-type.

Abbreviations for the Occupational Classification:
PRF: professional workers
SKW: skilled white-collar workers (managers, administrators and para-professionals)
SKB: skilled blue-collar workers (persons in metal, electrical, building and others trades)
USW: semi-skilled and unskilled white-collar workers (clerks, salespersons and personal services providers)
USB: semi-skilled and unskilled blue-collar workers (plant and machine operators, drivers, labourers and rural workers).

Although sectoral results show that, as expected, the move to free trade reduces employment in previously protected sectors, this does not outweigh the expansionary effects resulting from the improvement of competitiveness. Resources are reallocated to the primary sector and to trade, transportation and communication services. The growth in such services is partly induced by the growth in international trade. The textiles and fabricated metal product sectors undergo sharp contractions in activity (the latter includes the motor vehicle assembly industry in both countries).

Comparing the effects in the factor markets in the two countries, Table 7.2 shows that employment in Run 1 increases a little more in New Zealand, while the demand for capital rises more in Australia (where the rate of return on capital increases more, see Table 7.1). These outcomes reflect, in part, the relative factor intensities and differences in the sectoral structure between the two countries. For example, the labour intensity of the agricultural sector in New Zealand is greater than that in Australia (with a labour share in value added of 68 per cent compared with 54 per cent respectively). Furthermore, the agricultural sector accounts for over 8 per cent of total employment in New Zealand, but only 2 per cent in Australia. This helps slant New Zealand's increase in the demand for production factors more towards labour compared with its CER partner. On the other hand, the contraction in the textiles sector is much greater in Australia and this sector is more labour intensive compared with its New Zealand counterpart. This contributes to the lower increase in employment in Australia.

Run 2 only allows effects attributable to relative price movements. Note that aggregate employment and employment by occupation have been assumed unchanged. The consequent shifts in occupational wage relativities (listed in the special column in Table 7.2) provide a further indication of the differences in the impact across sectors of the removal of tariffs.

For example, the reduced demand for semi- and unskilled blue-collar (USB) workers as reflected in the reduction in their wage rate (Table 7.2) can be traced, in large part, to the contraction of the textiles sector. Similarly, the result for the skilled blue-collar (SKB) category is primarily related to the contraction of the fabricated metal products sector. In contrast, the positive outcome for the semi-skilled and unskilled white-collar (USW) category can be associated with the expanding trade services sector in response to growing international trade and rising domestic consumption expenditure fuelled by rising real wages.[12]

The main employers of professional (PRF) labour are the private and public service sectors in both countries. While these sectors are largely driven by similar influences in each country, PRF relative wages decline more in New Zealand than in Australia. This difference is due to shifts in the commodity composition of the consumption basket. Consumer spending in New Zealand shifts away from relatively labour-intensive services as their price relative to goods increases, so reflecting, in turn, the increase in the real price of labour. In contrast, there is in

Australia a relatively larger shift to capital (as noted earlier) and, consequently, a smaller movement in the real price of labour. Hence the consumption basket in Australia does not shift against service commodities and the demand for PRF does not experience as great a decline as in New Zealand.

Relaxing the assumption of fixed employment by occupation in Run 3 captures the effects of substitution between primary factors given unchanged occupational wage relativities and an unchanged total 'pool' of resources in each country. The substitution effects result from the movement in the relative price of capital *vis-à-vis* the skill types in combination with the CRESH substitution elasticities.

These elasticities are such that of the five types of labour, the SKW category is most substitutable for capital while, at the other end of the spectrum, PRF and USB are the least interchangeable with capital. Table 7.2 shows that the demand for SKW rises in both countries, while the relatively high substitutability of SKB is insufficient to offset the effect of the contraction in the fabricated metals sector. Moreover, the outcome for USB is consistent with its low substitutability, compounded by influences in the textiles sector. The results for PRF in New Zealand reflect, in part, its low substitutability, although the distinction with the result for Australia remains due to the consumption effects described above. Despite its low substitutability, the USW category still benefits from expansion in the trade services sector of both countries.

Differences between fixed country versus fixed overall factors are brought out by comparing the results of Runs 3 and 4. In Run 4, with fixed overall factors, the increase in employment in New Zealand is 0.7 per cent and, consequently (employment in Australia being 4.7 times that in New Zealand), Australian employment decreases by 0.1 per cent.

Note that it is here assumed that labour will move freely, so offsetting any potential change in the real wage relativity between the two countries. No behavioural equation for migration is specified. Also, the absorption of the migrants in the trans-Tasman economy is assumed to be immediate: no behavioural differences between migrants and the locally born are incorporated in the model. The latter assumption is not unrealistic given that, among Australian immigrants, the New Zealanders are the closest to the Australians in terms of economic characteristics (e.g., Carmichael 1993, p. 215).

The real wage increases by 1.5 per cent in Run 4 in both countries, where 'real' is defined here relative to consumer prices. The higher level of protection in Australia compared to New Zealand leads to a greater fall in prices when tariffs are removed. This explains the larger decline in the nominal price of labour in Australia shown in Table 7.2.

In parallel to Run 4, Run 5 starts with the assumption of unchanged real wage rates in each country, but changes in the rates of return to capital across the two economies are equalised given a single overall constraint on the available aggregate Australasian physical capital resources. Noting that Run 1 showed that the rate of return in Australia would rise by more than that in New Zealand, this new simulation should *a priori* result in capital increasing in the former (and consequently declining in the latter) in response to the removal of trade barriers.

This is indeed what occurs in Run 5. Table 7.1 shows that the rate of return rises by just under 7 per cent in both countries. As can be seen from both Tables 7.1 and 7.2, nearly 1.4 per cent less capital gets allocated to New Zealand, which is equivalent to an inflow of 0.3 per cent of capital in Australia.[13] Not surprisingly, there is a noticeable reduction from that recorded in Run 1 in the expansion in New Zealand and a slight increase in that across the Tasman. Nevertheless there remains, in both countries, a positive (aggregate) expansion effect from the removal of protection.

Run 6 adopts the most relaxed assumptions on factor movements between Australia and New Zealand. However, assuming fixed overall resources removes the expansionary effect at the aggregate CER level. Thus Run 6 combines the labour market assumption of Run 4 with the capital market assumption of Run 5. Run 6 illustrates the principal gains and losses from the removal of protection arising from the microeconomic reallocation of a fixed 'pool' of Australasian resources.

Such a scenario reinforces the findings of the previous simulations. Namely, the removal of protection is encouraging Australia to become relatively even more capital intensive and New Zealand to become relatively more labour intensive. This is in concordance with the price of capital rising relative to that of labour by 1.3 per cent in New Zealand, but remaining almost unchanged in Australia (Table 7.2). The occupational structure is consistent with previous simulations and shows, as before, employment of skilled and unskilled white-collar workers growing, while the contractions in the fabricated metals and textiles sectors dominate the outcomes for the two blue-collar categories.

The model runs generate outcomes for factor demand and price shifts at the sectoral level which cannot be reported here. Comparing the two countries, the sectoral shifts relative to the change in aggregate output are qualitatively similar in many sectors. However, there are four sectors which become relatively more important in Australia but less important in New Zealand. They are chemicals, petroleum and plastics; non-metallic mineral products; building and construction; and private services. In Australia, the contraction in the textiles and fabricated metals sectors would be equivalent to a loss of nearly 1 per cent in Australia-wide employment.

These *Joani* model experiments indicate that the removal of protection *vis-à-vis* third countries can have both substitution and expansionary effects on the two CER economies, depending on the choice of assumptions for the model with respect to the factor markets. Put another way, the outcome hinges on whether price adjustments or quantity adjustments prevail. Furthermore, the distinction between the factor markets clearing at the individual country level or at the aggregate CER level is also of prime importance.

Thus, constrained by a fixed Australasian 'pool' of labour and capital, the model simulations show the New Zealand economy as becoming more labour intensive and the Australian economy as becoming more capital intensive. Such trade liberalisation may encourage some movement of labour to New Zealand and some movement of capital to Australia.

Among the labour types, the two white-collar categories benefit from the gains to competitiveness *vis-à-vis* the rest of the world and the subsequent rise in household consumption. On the other hand, the two blue-collar categories endure the direct effects of the contraction in the previously protected sectors. One feature arising out of this analysis is the differential impact on the professional labour category between the two countries resulting from the relative shift in the price of labour-intensive consumption commodities.

In terms of magnitudes, however, the positive outcomes for some of the occupational categories are not large in the sense that they would exhaust the available labour supply within each country. It is difficult, therefore, to see the possible microeconomic reallocation gains from protection removal as inducing large net trans-Tasman shifts of labour of a particular occupational type.

One notable exception is the category of professional workers. Run 6 shows a decline of employment of this group in New Zealand and an increase in Australia. Indeed, this is the only category for which employment changes in the two countries have the opposite signs. It is therefore plausible that a further removal of protection at the common external border will lead to trans-Tasman investment in Australia by New Zealand firms (in response to the relatively greater capital requirements there) and a further net movement of professional workers in the same direction.

Further reductions in the real cost of migration with sharply declining costs of transportation, communication and information may well encourage a continuation of the notable gross labour movements between the two countries. Policy shifts towards free trade would also encourage significant intra-country, inter-sectoral and inter-occupational changes. The largest changes in the demand for labour, however, occur in the simulation where the expansion effect has not been 'diluted' (i.e., where abundant labour resources are assumed present). This is demonstrated most clearly by the first simulation presented above (Run 1). Such employment changes may, of course, also encourage trans-Tasman migration. This would reinforce the past experience of the two countries that trans-Tasman migration flows have been predominantly influenced by the relative macroeconomic health of the two economies.

A severe limitation of the analysis carried out in this paper is the focus on long-run comparative statics. Consequently, issues such as increasing returns due to technological change or economies of scale are not taken into account. Nor has capital accumulation been modelled in a way which was consistent with forward-looking behaviour of the entrepreneurs. Both in Australia and New Zealand, new CGE models have been developed which are dynamic and incorporate forward-looking behaviour of consumers and producers (Malakellis 1993, Nana 1995). Such models face considerable technical difficulties, but it may be possible in due course to contemplate a more refined study of the long-run impact of further Australasian trade liberalisation on trans-Tasman trade and factor mobility by means of a dynamic version of *Joani* which takes these issues into account.

Notes

1 A wealth of comparative information about the two countries' economies can be found in Edwards and Holmes (1994).
2 The GDP per capita information is based on Edwards and Holmes (1994, p. 30).
3 These statistics were provided by Dr Tim Beal, Director, Centre for Asia Pacific Law and Business, Victoria University of Wellington. They are based on trade statistics from Statistics New Zealand.
4 The migration statistics are based on arrival and departure card information collected by Statistics New Zealand since 1921. Post-1979 data were obtained by means of the online data base INFOS, while earlier data were found in various official publications.
5 While the data base of the *Joani* model measures employment in both countries on a full-time equivalent basis, we believe that the employment numbers are not fully comparable and that the gap in the capital–labour ratio quoted in the text may be an overestimate.
6 This statement is based on earnings data described in Poot (1993).
7 See Nana et al. (forthcoming) for more detail.
8 The elasticity of substitution between goods from the three sources was set at 2.0 for New Zealand and at the weighted average of those in the constituent *Orani* sectors for Australia.
9 Discrepancies in trade data between the two countries accompanied by differing weight vectors for aggregation may lead to small differences in the results for aggregate trade flows between the Australian-based measures and the New Zealand-based measures.
10 CRESH stands for Constant Ratios of Elasticities of Substitution and Homothetic (Hanoch 1971).
11 In addition, it is conventional in New Zealand CGE modelling to also set mining investment exogenously.
12 This sector incorporates wholesale and retail trade, restaurants and hotels.
13 It should be noted that the model implicitly assumes that the income flowing from this foreign-sourced capital is not repatriated. Instead, part of it will be spent in the local economy.

8

Sub-Regional Economic Zones in East Asia

Chia Siow Yue

I Introduction

East Asian economies have not formed a continental trading bloc of the EC and NAFTA genre, reflecting diversities in historical experience, political–social–economic systems, resource endowment, and stage of economic development. Instead, the region has seen the emergence of the sub-regional economic zone (SREZ) since the early 1980s. The SREZ is a transnational phenomenon, encompassing geographically contiguous parts of countries in an economic integration process that involves flows of goods, services, investments, and people. The rationale is to exploit the economies of scale and agglomeration and of economic complementarity, so as to improve international competitiveness and minimise transaction costs. The driving force is the private sector. Governments act as facilitators, by removing political and policy barriers to economic exchange and providing physical infrastructure and investment incentives. SREZs focus on resource pooling and investment facilitation; they are distinct from trading blocs which focus on market sharing and trade liberalisation. It can include areas with different political and economic systems.

This paper examines the rise of SREZs in the Asia–Pacific Region, identifying the types and factors in their emergence, and examining their impact on flows of trade, investment and people.

II Typology of Sub-Regional Economic Zones

Table 8.1 shows the SREZs in East Asia. They can be distinguished conceptually into the following categories, which may overlap in reality (Chia and Lee 1993).

A metropolitan spillover into the hinterland

The SREZ is essentially a metropolitan spillover phenomenon in a transnational context, with the core and periphery located in different countries. It is typified by the Indonesia–Malaysia–Singapore growth triangle (IMS-GT) covering the Riau islands of Indonesia, the southern Malaysian state of Johor and Singapore.

Table 8.1   Sub-regional economic zones in East Asia

Name of economic grouping	Date formed	No. of countries	Component countries/areas
South-East Asia:			
IMS Southern ASEAN Growth Triangle	1989	3	Riau (Indonesia), Johor (Malaysia), Singapore
IMT Northern ASEAN Growth Triangle	1994	3	West Indonesia, North Malaysia, South Thailand
BIMP Eastern ASEAN Growth Area	1995	4	Brunei, East Indonesia, East Malaysia, West Philippines
Baht economic zone	–	6	Cambodia, Laos, Myanmar, Northern Thailand, Vietnam, Yunnan (China)
Greater Mekong sub-region	1995	6	Cambodia, Laos, Myanmar, Thailand, Vietnam, Yunnan (China)
North-East Asia:			
Greater South China economic zone	1980	3	Guangdong and Fujian (China), Hong Kong, Taiwan
Yellow Sea Rim economic zone	–	3	Northeast China, South Korea, Japan
Japan Sea Rim economic zone	–	5	Northeast China, Japan, North Korea, South Korea, East Russia
Tumen River area development	concept phase	5	North China, North Korea, South Korea, Mongolia, East Russia

It is also typified by the Greater South China (GSC) economic zone, covering Hong Kong, Taiwan and China's south coastal provinces of Guangdong and Fujian (including the four special economic zones in Shezhen, Zhuhai, Shantou and Xiamen).

Singapore and Hong Kong are East Asia's unique city states with non-replicable metropolitan spillovers. Their economic hinterlands lie outside their political borders and extend over large areas of South-East Asia and North-East Asia respectively. They are major regional entrepots, financial centres, and transportation and telecommunication hubs. The metropolitan cores have abundant capital and skill resources, well-developed infrastructure, and enjoy economies of scale and agglomeration. However, sustained economic growth led to growing land and labour constraints, and the relatively more mobile capital move to the peripheries (Johor and Riau for Singapore and South China for Hong Kong) in search of complementary land, natural resources and labour.

Joint development of infrastructure and common resources

Developing East Asia needs massive foreign funds for development, particularly of infrastructure, but faces severe financial constraints. Co-operation and joint development can improve the viability and efficiency of development projects by exploiting scale and agglomeration economies and improving access to private and public funding. Co-operation and joint development can also minimise disputes over ownership and utilisation of a common resource, such as a major river or marine resource, and improve environmental management. This type of SREZ is typified by the Tumen River area project and the Mekong River basin project as well as some ASEAN growth triangles.

In North-East Asia, political changes and economic imperatives in the 1980s are behind many of the proposals for sub-regional economic co-operation, the most advanced being the Tumen River Area Development Project (TRAD). The project encompasses the riparian areas of the Tumen River and the littoral areas of the Japan Sea which it empties into, that is, the Russian Far East, Mongolia, northeast China (Jilin, Liaoning and Heilongjiang provinces), and the two Koreas. The United Nations Development Programme undertook a feasibility study in 1991 and proposes the massive development of infrastructure and transportation networks in the sub-region to facilitate resource exploitation, trade and industrial development. The TRAD proposal highlights two major benefits. First, it will provide a more efficient land transportation link between Japan and Europe, by-passing the circuitous sea route through South-East Asia, and at the same time promote maritime activities in the sub-region. Second, the abundant natural resources and labour supply of TRAD can complement the abundant capital resources, managerial know-how, advanced technology, and large markets of neighbouring Japan and South Korea. However, the proposal faces serious obstacles. UNDP estimated that TRAD would cost about US$30 billion for ports and other transportation facilities alone. Such enormous investment funding is beyond the resources of the participating countries and extensive external funding is necessary. However, political uncertainties and sensitivities and lukewarm support of some national governments pose a problem. Another challenge is creating the technical and operational mechanism for joint infrastructural development and management.

In South-East Asia, the Mekong River and tributaries are a major water resource for the riparian states. The work of the Mekong Committee established in 1957 by the governments of Thailand, Vietnam, Laos and Cambodia to co-ordinate the development of the lower Mekong Basin was disrupted by the ensuing political developments in Indochina. The return of peace in the 1980s led to renewed interest in sub-regional economic co-operation, this time encompassing all the riparian countries of the Mekong River. The new Greater Mekong Sub-region (GMS) covers parts of Cambodia, Laos, Myanmar, Thailand, Vietnam and Yunnan (southwest China). These areas have common ethnic and cultural links and shared interests in the development of agriculture, forestry, fishery, energy, and water transport and in environmental management. Given the low per capita incomes, poor infrastructure, and severe shortages of financial and technical resources, a co-operative effort is more likely to succeed in eliciting the support of development agencies and donor countries to develop the infrastructure and provide the basic framework for attracting private sector investments.

The Indonesia–Malaysia–Thailand Growth Triangle (IMT-GT) encompasses the contiguous areas of west Indonesia, north Malaysia and south Thailand. The Brunei–Indonesia–Malaysia–Philippines East ASEAN Growth Area (BIMP-EAGA) encompasses Brunei, East Indonesia, East Malaysia and South Philippines. The Asian Development Bank is drawing up master plans and conducting feasibility studies. However, unlike IMS-GT, these new growth triangles lack a strong industrial, financial and transportation hub (equivalent to Singapore) to provide adequate spillover effects and act as an engine of growth, and are handicapped by the low level of economic complementarity and the inadequate infrastructure within and between sub-areas. As such, co-operation will focus on joint development of transportation infrastructure, energy, marine resources, agro-industry and tourism.

Geographically proximate areas with common interests

The end of the Cold War and economic factors have revived the historical economic and cultural exchange arising from geographical proximity and ethnic and cultural affinity among the littoral areas of the Yellow Sea and Japan Sea. China's economic strategy of opening the coastal regions to the outside world coincided with the economic restructuring and outward investment drive of Japan and South Korea. In the Yellow Sea rim, South Korea seems the most interested to establish closer trade and investment ties with the Chinese provinces of Shandong, Liaoning and Heilongjiang across the Yellow Sea where two million ethnic Koreans live. Industrial complementation and joint tourism development appear promising, given the economic complementarity and historical and cultural ties. In the Japan Sea rim, Japan's western prefectures are keen to develop economic relations with the other littoral areas but continuing political tension in the Korean peninsula is hindering economic integration.

In continental South-East Asia, an economic zone is emerging encompassing Thailand and the contiguous border areas of Yunnan, Myanmar, Laos, Cambodia and Vietnam. The term 'baht zone' reflects the widespread use of the baht currency as well as Thailand's foreign policy, enunciated in 1988, to turn Indochina from a 'battleground into a marketplace'. The idea for a Golden Quadrangle, embracing Thailand, Yunnan, Laos, and Myanmar was mooted by Thailand in 1992 (Than 1994). Thai businessmen and investors have been active in the border areas engaged in trading and exploitation of forestry, fishery and mineral resources.

III Factors in the emergence of SREZs

The driving forces in the emergence of East Asia's SREZs are political and policy induced, geographical and economic. To the extent that some SREZs are dependent on the world market, a critical condition for success is the ability to compete in, and to have access to the world market.

Political and policy changes

Dramatic political changes and economic reforms in East Asia in the past two decades have facilitated the emergence of sub-regionalism. The market-oriented ASEAN economies and Asian NIEs embarked on reforms of liberalisation, deregulation and privatisation, including more favourable policies toward trade and foreign investment. For the centrally planned economies in North-East Asia and Indochina, the end of the Cold War and political conflicts and domestic political changes and economic reforms have resulted in more market-oriented and outward-looking economies and greater receptivity towards trade and foreign investments, and sub-regional and regional economic co-operation to improve economic performance and prospects.

IMS-GT represents an early effort at ASEAN economic co-operation. In the 1970s Batam was developed by Indonesia as an export-processing zone but failed to take off. A change in strategy towards co-operation with Singapore in the late 1980s led to Indonesian policy changes liberalising investment regulations in Batam[1] and the Singapore government's agreement to encourage the relocation of industries from Singapore. These led to a surge of investments by Singapore companies and foreign MNCs based in Singapore. Joint investment missions went to Japan, Hong Kong, South Korea and Taiwan to promote Batam and Bintan as investment destinations. Singapore and Indonesia entered into three bilateral agreements in 1990–91, and a Joint Ministerial Committee co-ordinates the development efforts and policies on Riau.

Political and economic reforms in China coincided with economic restructuring in Hong Kong and Taiwan to precipitate the economic integration of Hong Kong and the Pearl River Delta in Guangdong province and, to a lesser extent, that of Taiwan with Guangdong and Fujian provinces. Although market driven, the GSC economic zone emerged from the dramatic policy changes that China launched in 1979 to modernise and open its economy to the outside world, particularly policies providing preferential treatment for foreign capital. Four special economic zones (SEZs) were set up with tax concessions, reduced land-use fees, and simplified procedures and formalities. They were strategically located in the southern coastal provinces of Guangdong and Fujian to tap overseas Chinese capital, particularly from neighbouring Hong Kong and Taiwan, to ensure their success. At the same time, their distance from Beijing would help contain any political and economic fallout should the experiment fail (Chen 1994). The geographical areas of the SEZs were later extended to include entire cities. A fifth SEZ was established in Hainan Island, followed by the opening of fourteen coastal port cities and other coastal areas to foreign investment.

Geographical and cultural proximity

In the absence of barriers, neighbouring areas would tend to do business with each other because of lower transaction costs (transportation, information, etc.) arising from proximity and cultural affinity. However, proximity is an economic advantage only if transportation and telecommunications networks are reasonably well developed. For trade in intermediate goods, proximity reduces not only transport costs but also delivery time, an important consideration when the market is constantly changing and delivery schedules are tight. For investment decisions, proximity reduces information and other transaction costs, particularly for small and medium enterprises having to operate in a different political, bureaucratic and legal environment with unfamiliar, complex and non-transparent rules and regulations, and deal with local business partners with different business practices. Geographically proximate areas often, but not always, share a common ethnicity, culture, language and kinship which reduce information costs and cultural misunderstandings. The ethnic-cultural factor is dominant in the Greater South China economic zone and in the baht zone, but is also present to some extent in the IMS-GT and the Yellow Sea Rim and Japan Sea Rim.

In IMS-GT, the prime factor in Batam's success and a major factor in Johor's success in attracting foreign investments is their strategic location adjacent to Singapore. Singapore provides Batam and Johor with world-class airport, seaport, telecommunications network, and financial and commercial infrastructures. Johor is physically linked to Singapore by a causeway, and Batam is linked by a half-hour ferry ride. Firms with operations in Johor and Batam can economise on managerial and technical resources by commuting from Singapore daily or periodically. Singapore also offers a more comfortable and convenient living (though very much more expensive) for business executives and their families. Strong historical, ethnic, cultural and kinship bonds exist between Singapore and Malaysia, and this has facilitated business and other contacts and exchanges.

In GSC, both geographical and cultural proximity have facilitated linkages between Hong Kong and Taiwan and China's southern coastal provinces of Guangdong and Fujian. Hong Kong is only a half-hour train ride from Guangdong, and Fujian and Taiwan are separated only by the Taiwan Straits. The ethnic-cultural-language factor dominates economic exchanges, and in the case of China–Taiwan, surmounts the political barrier. Communal and kinship ties coupled with geographical proximity have enabled Taiwan and Hong Kong businessmen to have a 'special tolerance' (Chen & Ho 1994) for the various institutional barriers of doing business in China, particularly the bureaucratic delays and lack of a legal framework and transparency in rules and regulations.

Economic complementarity

Economic complementarity arises from differences in factor endowment and stages of economic and technological development which are reflected in differences in factor prices and cost structures. A SREZ emerges when the removal or reduction of border restrictions leads to a surge in economic exchange. Cross-border capital flows take place because land and undeveloped natural resources are immobile, while government policies continue to restrict labour mobility. The core also performs an intermediation function in channelling investment capital from the outside world, and a distribution and marketing function, helping to import machinery and intermediate inputs for the periphery and exporting the latter's products to the outside world.

The IMS-GT as an integrated sub-region is more attractive to investors than its separate parts. Singapore's advantage lies in its managerial and professional expertise and its well-developed financial, transportation and telecommunications infrastructure. Riau and Johor can offer land and labour at lower cost than Singapore. Clustering and specialisation produce a competitive business environment. The unique proximity to Singapore enables investors in Batam and Johor to be more efficient and competitive in production and in distribution. While the economic complementarity in the Singapore–Johor and Singapore–Riau nodes of the Growth Triangle are obvious, that of Johor–Riau is less apparent, and explains why this side of the triangle remains relatively undeveloped despite geographical proximity.

In GSC, Guangdong and Fujian are dominated by investments from Hong Kong and Taiwan. Guangdong and Fujian have massive land areas and their population of over 100 million far outnumbers Hong Kong and Taiwan, providing a large pool of cheap and trainable labour. On the other hand, these two provinces lack capital, technology, management and marketing expertise. The provincial and local governments have been highly successful in improving the investment climate for foreign business, and have rapidly sought to develop the necessary infrastructure and industrial facilities. Sustained rapid economic growth, limited land and small population bases in Hong Kong and Taiwan have, as in Singapore, led to severe land and labour shortages but an abundance of capital, managerial and entrepreneurial resources. Both economies have been engaging in massive outward investments, mostly undertaken by small and medium enterprises (SMEs). Proximity enables these SMEs to reduce transaction costs and economise on managerial resources. It has been estimated that some 80 per cent of Hong Kong manufacturers have some relocated facility in Guangdong, mostly outward processing arrangements. A 1991 survey by the Federation of Hong Kong Industries showed that more than 60 per cent of respondents gave labour scarcity and escalating wages as the key impetus for moving into the Pearl River Delta. Taiwan investments in South China had a later start but have leaped in recent years, notwithstanding continuing political restraints.

Investment competition and emergence of regional investors

With economic development a priority in every East Asian country, the need for financing surged, both for infrastructural development as well as for exploitation of natural resources and development of industries and tourism. At the same time, the global and regional competition for private investments intensified in the 1980s as financing options narrowed. Official development assistance became less readily available as industrialised countries succumbed to aid fatigue for various reasons and the international debt crisis made commercial banks more cautious in their international lending. Even infrastructural projects increasingly have to seek private investment financing. The economic liberalisation sweeping Eastern Europe and Latin America, and the formation of continental trade blocs in Western Europe and North America, intensified the investment competition for East Asian developing countries and raised their fears of investment diversion. Governments in developing East Asia are using the SREZ to enhance investment competitiveness.

Japan emerged as a major investor in East Asia in the 1970s but more particularly after 1985, overtaking flows from North America and Western Europe in many countries. The Asian NIEs (Hong Kong, Singapore, South Korea and Taiwan) also became major regional investors in the post-1987 period. These investment outflows from Japan and the Asian NIEs were in response to a number of factors. First, strong trade performances and current account balances led to currency appreciations and foreign exchange decontrols in Japan, Korea and Taiwan. In particular, the Plaza Accord of September 1985 led to a surge in Japanese outward investment. Second, sustained rapid economic growth and currency appreciations led to labour and land shortages and rising costs, which in turn led to relocation of labour-intensive and land-intensive industries. Similarly, growing environmental concerns in Japan, Korea and Taiwan also led to a relocation of polluting industries. Third, outward investments helped to secure regional market access as Japan and Asian NIEs sought market diversification to reduce trade tensions with the US and EC. Fourth, investors from the Asian NIEs invested in neighbouring countries to avail themselves of the textile quotas under the Multi-Fibre Arrangement and the tariff preferences under the Generalised System of Preferences. Finally, investments from Asian NIEs tend to be dominated by SMEs and such investors are more attracted by the geographic proximity and cultural affinity of SREZs, as they help reduce transaction costs and minimise demand on managerial resources.

IV Trade, investment and labour flows

SREZs have some important implications for the sub-regional movements of labour and capital.

Greater South China economic zone

Policy-wise, China does not grant Hong Kong businesses more favourable treatment than other foreign businesses. In practice, however, language and kinship ties are known to have secured more favourable concessions from the Guangdong local authorities (Sung 1992). Immigration and travel restrictions are one-sided. While Hong Kong residents do not require visas to enter China, the reverse flow is restricted as both the Chinese and Hong Kong governments maintain border controls. Restrictions will continue beyond 1997 under the terms of the Sino-British Agreement, which provides for separate immigration control, customs, and currency area for Hong Kong. Trade restrictions are also one-sided as Hong Kong has a free-trade regime though China does not.

For political reasons China accords preferential treatment on trade with and investments from Taiwan.[2] China's local authorities also tend to give Taiwan investors more favourable treatment, such as speedier approval of investment applications and better support services. Taiwan, however, forbade contacts with China until recent years, when indirect exports and imports were allowed. All trade and investment with China were conducted via third parties, usually in Hong Kong. The rapid growth of indirect trade and investment (and of smuggling) has shown that political and bureaucratic restrictions have not been successful and Hong Kong has provided an efficient intermediation service. In July 1992 Taiwan passed the Statute for Relations across the Taiwan Straits, which provided for the gradual and conditional lifting of the decades-old bans on a wide range of contacts, allowing direct air and shipping links, importation of Chinese workers to ease Taiwan's severe labour shortage, and Taiwanese to visit China for an extended period of up to four years.

Data on Hong Kong–China trade are shown in Table 8.2. Hong Kong resumed its historic role as the entrepot of southern China, leading to a boom in its entrepot trade. By 1985 China had become Hong Kong's largest trade partner and by 1988 Hong Kong's total re-exports exceeded its total domestic exports. The profits generated by the China trade, including outward processing production, is estimated to be over 10 per cent of Hong Kong's GDP (Chen & Ho 1994). Taiwan's indirect trade with China, mainly through Hong Kong, represented just over 6 per cent of Taiwan's total exports and 1.6 per cent of its total imports in 1991.

Table 8.3 shows the dominance of Hong Kong investments in Guangdong. Most Hong Kong manufacturers have some relocated facility in Guangdong in the form of outward processing arrangements. Taiwan investments in Guangdong and Fujian had a later start and have grown by quantum leaps in recent years. Guangdong has become the richest and most dynamic province in China. The Pearl River Delta, which includes the Shenzhen and Zhuhai SEZs, is the engine of growth for the province; it is estimated that real income has been growing at over 20 per cent annually in recent years (Chen & Ho 1994). Millions of jobs

Table 8.2   Hong Kong's trade with China

Year	Value in $million	Annual growth (%)	Hong Kong's imports (%)	Hong Kong's exports (%)	China's imports (%)	China's exports (%)
Imports from China:						
1970	470	–	16.1	–	–	20.8
1979	3038	–	17.7	–	–	22.2
1985	7568	–	25.5	–	–	27.7
1986	10462	38.2	29.5	–	–	33.8
1987	14776	41.2	30.5	–	–	37.4
1988	19406	31.3	30.4	–	–	40.8
1989	25215	29.9	34.9	–	–	48.0
1990	30274	20.1	36.8	–	–	48.8
1991	37610	24.2	37.7	–	–	52.4
Imports from China for re-export:						
1970	97	–	20.2	–	–	3.3
1979	962	–	24.1	–	–	5.6
1985	3778	23.6	28.0	–	–	12.7
1986	5620	48.8	35.8	–	–	15.8
1987	9185	63.4	39.2	–	–	19.0
1988	14322	55.9	40.6	–	–	22.4
1989	20517	43.3	54.3	–	–	28.4
1990	30822	50.2	58.1	–	–	37.4
1991	40473	31.3	59.0	–	–	40.5
Exports to China:						
1970	11	–	–	0.4	0.5	–
1979	383	–	–	2.5	2.5	–
1985	7857	56.1	–	26.0	18.6	–
1986	7550	–3.9	–	21.3	17.6	–
1987	11290	49.5	–	23.3	26.1	–
1988	17030	50.8	–	27.0	30.8	–
1989	18816	10.5	–	25.7	31.8	–
1990	20305	7.9	–	24.8	34.3	–
1991	26631	31.2	–	27.1	49.9	–
Re-exports to China:						
1970	6	–	–	1.2	0.2	–
1979	263	–	–	6.6	1.7	–
1985	5907	64.5	–	43.7	19.5	–
1986	5241	–11.3	–	33.4	14.8	–
1987	7716	47.2	–	32.9	15.9	–
1988	12157	57.6	–	34.5	19.3	–
1989	13268	9.1	–	29.9	18.1	–
1990	14219	7.2	–	26.9	17.3	–
1991	19656	38.2	–	28.7	20.0	–

Source: Edward Chen and Anna Ho, 'Southern China growth triangle: an overview'; citing Government of Hong Kong and State Statistical Bureau (PRC) sources.

Table 8.3 Hong Kong's share of foreign capital
in Guangdong province, 1986–93

Year	Guangdong's total foreign capital utilised US$million	Sources (% distribution)			
		Hong Kong	Japan	US	Others
1986	1459	93.7	1.3	4.7	0.4
1987	1217	84.6	1.7	6.4	7.3
1988	2440	91.0	3.6	1.6	3.7
1989	2399	82.4	3.3	4.5	9.8
1990	2023	69.8	9.1	9.3	11.8
1991	2583	79.5	4.3	5.4	10.8
1992	4861	89.0	0.5	2.0	8.5
1993	9652	90.3	1.4	1.2	7.1

Source: Guangdong Statistical Bureau, Statistical Yearbook of Guangdong (various years).

have been created in what were originally farm villages. A 1991 estimate placed the number of workers employed by Hong Kong firms at three million, much higher than total manufacturing employment in Hong Kong itself. The economic opportunities have spurred large-scale migration from other parts of China.

In south China the initial wave of investments by SMEs from Hong Kong and Taiwan has been followed by investments by Hong Kong and Taiwan conglomerates in a broader range of manufacturing and service industries, including infrastructural and tourism projects, real estate, and high-tech and heavy industries. Investments are also spreading north and inland, where the labour supplies are larger and wage and land costs considerably lower. The success of the Guangdong–Fujian model has encouraged China's political leadership to push forward with economic reforms and to replicate the model to other parts of China.

The massive relocation of production facilities to Guangdong, mostly in the form of outward processing, has enabled Hong Kong to overcome its labour shortages and restructure its economy towards service activities. The share of manufacturing in GDP has shrunk from 22.5 per cent in 1980 to 15.8 per cent by 1990, while manufacturing employment declined from 900 000 to less than 700 000. Productivity improved with the shedding of low-end manufacturing operations. Manufacturing in China has enabled Hong Kong firms to remain competitive in international markets. Likewise, the relocation of manufacturing to China has helped Taiwan's industrial restructuring. There are also export gains as materials, components and spare parts that Taiwanese investors used in processing and production are imported from Taiwan.

Table 8.4 Batam's growth statistics

	1988	1989	1990	1991	1992	1993
Population (thousand)	79.4	90.5	95.8	107.6	123.0	146.2
Workforce (thousand)	9.6	11.2	16.3	23.2	32.1	44.0
Tourists (thousand)	228	359	579	609	648	680
Tourism revenue (US$million)	30.5	48.7	78.5	175.2	238.0	249.8
Sea cargo handled (thousand tons)	752	1277	1853	2528	2623	2255
Tax revenue (billion rupiah)	9.5	14.7	26.6	35.8	45.1	55.9
Exports (US$million)	44	53	152	242	565	926
Cumulative investments (US$million)						4525
Government						743
Private						3782
Domestic						2134
Foreign						1648

Source: Batam Industrial Development Authority, Development Data (various years).

IMS Growth Triangle

Johor is Malaysia's second most important industrial region and foreign invest-ment destination. Bilateral economic relations with Singapore have always been close, with Singapore a major market and entrepot. The causeway linking Johor and Singapore is choked with two-way movement of goods-carrying trucks. There are no data on the volume of Johor–Singapore trade. The FDI surge of recent years is rapidly transforming the physical landscape and the labour and property markets. Between 1989 and March 1994, of 1028 foreign investment projects with approved investments of RM12.7 billion, 471 projects (45.8 per cent) with investments of RM 1.9 billion (15 per cent) were from Singapore. More than 50 per cent of the Singapore manufacturing investments in Malaysia are located in Johor. Bilateral co-operation has minimised immigration formali-ties and allows an estimated 25 000 Malaysians to commute daily to work in Singapore. The migration of workers to Singapore in search of higher wages and the rapid economic growth have led to labour shortages in Johor and its depend-ence on in-migration from less-developed parts of Malaysia. During weekends and public holidays, thousands of Singaporeans flock to Johor for food and recreation. The traffic jams caused by movement of goods and people have necessitated the construction of a second causeway linking the two areas.

The impact of IMS-GT is most evident on Batam, where the population grew from a mere 7000 in the early 1970s to over 146 000 by 1993 (Table 8.4). There is no abundant labour in Batam and the supply of labour for infrastructural and industrial development depends on in-migration from populous Java. Ferry crossings every half-hour bring thousands of tourists and commuters from

Singapore to Batam and return daily. Bilateral co-operation on immigration procedures has led to the adoption of computerised processing through smart cards, which has reduced the hassle of commuting and travel between Singapore and Batam. Tourist arrivals (mainly from and through Singapore) grew to 680 000 by 1993, making Batam second only to Bali as a tourist entry point to Indonesia. Free trade exists between Batam and Singapore but not between Batam and the rest of Indonesia. Batam's exports (mainly through Singapore) rose to US$926 million. Investments from Singapore (including MNCs based in Singapore) are the major source of foreign investment in Batam, accounting for over half the foreign companies. Singapore's public and private enterprises are also actively involved in the development of infrastructure in Batam and Bintan. Total cumulative foreign investments in Batam reached US$1.6 billion by 1993.

Participation in the IMS-GT has helped Singapore, *inter alia*, to overcome its labour constraints. There are both physical and social limits to the importation of foreign workers, which already constitute some 15–20 per cent of the labour force. The relocation of labour-intensive industries and processes to Johor and Riau helps to move scarce resources to new areas of comparative advantage in manufacturing and services. In fact, given the limited supply of labour in Johor and Batam, investors from Singapore (both foreign MNCs and Singapore enterprises) are venturing beyond these two areas, extending into the other Malaysian states north of Johor, and into the other Riau islands.

Gains from integration

The SREZ combines the factor resources of geographically contiguous areas, particularly mobile capital with immobile labour, land and natural resources; exploits the differences in comparative advantage and cost structures and the economies of scale and agglomeration; and minimises transaction costs. While integration is a positive sum game for all constituent areas, the benefits and costs are difficult to quantify, as the dynamic effects of growth and structural change outweigh the static allocative effects.

For the SREZ based on the joint resource and infrastructural development model, as with the Mekong and Tumen projects, external economies are strong and alternative development options limited, while the economic benefits to the participating areas are obvious.

For the SREZ based on the metropolitan spillover model, as in the IMS-GT and GSC, the accelerated investments in infrastructural, resource, industrial and commercial developments have a positive effect on economic growth, employment and wages, skill development and technology transfer in the peripheral areas. Guangdong has become the richest and most dynamic province in China and the Pearl River Delta is the engine of growth for the province. In IMS-GT, the development impact is most evident on the Riau islands. It has enabled Indonesia to develop its geographically dispersed peripheral areas (Gandataruna 1994). Batam has become an industrial complex and tourist resort, and Bintan is being extensively developed as a tourist resort. Linkages with Singapore have transformed Batam's economy and landscape. The GDP of Batam has grown at an annual average of 14 per cent in recent years, much higher than the national average. Batam's per capita income and wage levels are higher than other peripheral areas of Indonesia.

For the city-states of Hong Kong and Singapore, the relocation of industries has facilitated industrial restructuring with improvements in resource allocation and productivity. The skill- and technology-intensive and higher value-added functions are retained at home. The structural transformations have reinforced the role of Hong Kong and Singapore as regional service hubs. For Hong Kong in particular, outward processing enabled its enterprises to maintain international competitiveness in labour-intensive industries and earn a higher rate of return on capital and technology than otherwise possible for sunset industries. Outward investments also increased demand for capital goods and intermediate inputs from the home base. But they also raise concern over the possible 'hollowing out' of the home industrial structure. For Singapore, the development of tourism facilities in Batam and Bintan, and of water resources in Bintan, also increased the supply of water and nearby recreational facilities. The impact on Taiwan's economy is less dramatic as the economic linkages have been indirect, started later, and were of smaller magnitude than those between Hong Kong and south China. Industrial restructuring has been facilitated and bilateral trade has expanded. Many Taiwanese manufacturers, after setting up factories in southern China, have transformed their Taiwan operations into headquarters for high-end production, R&D activities, procurement and marketing, provision of technical assistance and personnel training (Tung 1993). Additionally, the bulk of materials, components and spare parts that Taiwanese investors used in processing and production are imported from Taiwan. However, the surge of Taiwanese investment in China in recent years has also raised concern over security implications for Taiwan as well as possible hollowing out of Taiwanese industry.

Problems and issues

The SREZ as a transnational phenomenon involves relations between and within countries, and gives rise to political, distributional and social problems. Not all of these, however, are unique to the SREZ phenomenon, as they are often the by-products of rapid economic growth, industrialisation and urbanisation, and rising foreign investment penetration.

Political relations between Singapore, Indonesia and Malaysia have strengthened under the ASEAN and growth-triangle frameworks. This has encouraged Indonesia and Malaysia and other ASEAN countries to form IMT-GT and BIMP-EAGA. In Greater South China, political relations remain uneasy. China–Taiwan political relations are still constrained by the different positions on Taiwan's political future. And while the Taiwan business community and citizenry are rushing to exploit the economic opportunities and to re-establish community and family ties with southern coastal China, the Taiwan government is concerned over the political and security implications of growing economic interdependence. Economic co-operation and integration between Hong Kong and southern China are to mutual benefit, particularly in the run-up to 1997 when Hong Kong reverts to Chinese sovereignty, with both parties willing to allow Hong Kong to be the engine of growth of southern China and China's window to the world. Still, the dominance of China over Hong Kong's economic fortunes remains unsettling for some of the latter's business community.

Economic relations between the developed and less-developed areas of the SREZs are akin to the core–periphery relations within a country. However, where core and periphery are located in different countries, then the political, social and distributional sensitivities become much greater. In the core areas (Singapore, Hong Kong, Taiwan), adjustment costs have fallen on the workers who lost their jobs with the relocation of industries and on the small and medium enterprises when their corporate customers relocated offshore. Fortunately, these economies continue to be dynamic, so that structural adjustments and job retrenchments have not posed serious political and social problems. For the periphery areas (Riau, Johor, southern coastal China) there are social problems arising from the massive in-migration from other parts of the country. The influx of labour, investors and tourists put pressure on the local infrastructure and supply of goods and services, and contribute to inflation and supply shortages, traffic congestion, environmental pollution, and a rise in crime and vice.

The involvement of FDI creates its own issues. Problems faced by investors, particularly in the transitional economy, include absence of internationally accepted legal, contractual and accounting frameworks, non-transparent and unfamiliar and cumbersome rules and regulations, frequent and unpredictable changes in policies and regulations, restrictive performance requirements and foreign exchange controls, corrupt and inept bureaucracies and unreliable local joint-venture partners. Also, production in Batam and export-processing zones in Johor do not have duty-free access to the rest of Indonesia and Malaysia respectively. Likewise, foreign investors in the SEZs have restricted access to the domestic market. At the same time, host economies worry over the political, security and social implications of extensive foreign ownership, exploitation of local resources and workers, low value-added, limited domestic linkages, inadequate manpower training and transfer of technology, and tax evasion practices.

The SREZ also impacts on intra-national relations with the central government and with other provinces. First, it creates a centrifugal force pulling the periphery area towards a foreign core, possibly undermining central authority and national cohesion. The growing economic clout of the province may lead to demands for greater provincial administrative and financial autonomy, possibly eroding the revenue base of the central government. In IMS-GT, Jakarta–Riau relations appear to be unaffected, particularly as central government ministers are in overall charge of the Indonesian side of the growth triangle. With regard to Kuala Lumpur–Johor relations, the Johor state government has expressed the need for more federal government support. In China, when the Beijing government introduced austerity measures to rein in the overheated economy in 1994, there was some resistance from provincial and local authorities keen to exploit the new economic opportunities.

Second, the SREZ may increase inter-provincial rivalry due to possible investment diversion. The development resources allocated by the central government to the SREZ may be at the expense of other provinces and this raises the issue of equitable resource allocation. In Jakarta, some quarters have questioned the utility and equity of large government infrastructure expenditures on the Riau islands of Batam and Bintan which are perceived to be benefiting only a small elite group of Indonesians, especially when there are strong contending claims for development funds in other parts of Indonesia. Investment diversion also takes place if the SREZ increases its attraction of foreign investment at the expense of other regions of the country. The Indonesian government is keen to promote more investments in the eastern part of the country.

Third, as some parts of the country pull ahead in economic development while other parts are left behind, the issues of widening disparities in development and income and large-scale migration become more serious. In China, the growing disparity between the southern coastal provinces of Guangdong and Fujian and the northern and inland provinces has led China's leader, Deng Xiaoping, to launch an aggressive campaign to open up the interior to foreign trade and foreign investment, and to exhort the southern coastal provinces to act as models of development and engines of growth for the rest of China. The central authorities are also encouraging peripheral areas of the vast country to form SREZs with foreign border areas, so as to spread the impulses of development more evenly and to reduce the disruptive social effects of mass migration. Market-integration processes are emerging in the southwest, linking Yunnan province with the local economies in Thailand, Vietnam and Laos, as well as in the central and northern coastal provinces, linking with the local economies in the Russian Far East, Japan and the Korean peninsula. The Beijing government is also considering removing the special investment incentives accorded to the SEZs and coastal cities.

V Conclusion

Political changes and economic reforms have enabled the underlying forces of geography and economic complementarity to come to the fore and have led to the growth of sub-regionalism in East Asia in the past decade. The SREZs in operation integrate areas of labour scarcity and capital abundance with those of labour abundance and capital scarcity. As government policies continue to restrict the movement of labour, it is capital that moves, creating employment in the labour-abundant areas and enabling its more efficient use in the labour-scarce areas. To facilitate the movement of managers, professionals and tourists, travel formalities can be simplified, such as the waiver of visa requirements or the use of smart cards for regular commuters. Controlled movement of contract workers also eases the labour shortages. However, large-scale illegal migration poses serious social and political problems.

Success with the first wave of SREZs has led to the deepening of integration in the existing SREZs, their geographical extension, and the emergence of new SREZs in East Asia. In south coastal China, investments from Hong Kong and Taiwan were initially labour intensive and undertaken by SMEs and were export oriented. However, rising labour and other production costs are pushing these labour-intensive activities further inland, while newer investments include heavy and chemical industries, infrastructural projects, resource-based and tourism projects, and property development. Also, while the SREZs started off as export platforms, they and the rest of Guangdong and Fujian are rapidly developing into major markets as well. Investors are expecting further liberalisation measures that will enable them to produce increasingly for the domestic market and enter into joint ventures with state enterprises that are being privatised. Investments are also becoming two-way flows, with Hong Kong increasingly playing host to investments from China. In IMS-GT, Johor and Batam are experiencing labour shortages and the local authorities are pressing for more investments with higher value added, skills and technology. Investments in these areas are already diversifying in response to rising wages. Intra-triangle trade continues to face restrictions in Indonesia and Malaysia, and trade liberalisation will take place only within the framework of the ASEAN Free Trade Area.

Existing SREZs are extending beyond their original geographical boundaries. IMS-GT started off with Singapore, Batam and Johor. Integration has extended to the other Riau islands of Bintan, Bulan, Karimun and Rempang, and includes infrastructure projects, tourism and resource and development projects, as well as industrial projects. And as Johor experiences labour shortages and rising property prices, Singapore investors have moved northwards. Johor itself has become a secondary growth centre, generating spillover effects into the ever-widening contiguous areas of Malaysia. Likewise, the GSC first started with Hong Kong and Shenzhen. As Shenzhen became more developed, investments spilled over into other parts of the Pearl River Delta and the rest of Guangdong and Fujian provinces. Labour-intensive industries have migrated progressively northwards and inland as the SEZs in Guangdong and Fujian became secondary growth centres. Enterprises from other parts of China are also increasingly investing in the SEZs, acting as sourcing and procuring agents, thus speeding the integration of the SEZs with the rest of the Chinese economy.

New SREZs are emerging. In ASEAN, the most advanced is the IMT-GT, followed by BIMP-EAGA. There are also proposals linking parts of the Philippines with Vietnam and with Sabah and Sarawak in Malaysia, and linking different border areas in continental South-East Asia. In China, initial success with the SREZs led to the opening of the coastal cities and coastal areas. Further SREZs could develop, linking southwest China with Thailand and Indochina, and northeast China with the Korean peninsula. In 1992 the Beijing government decided to open up thirteen border cities and capital cities in eighteen provinces. Border cities pursue preferential policies similar to those in the coastal open cities. The SREZ model is spreading but some will be more successful than others, depending on the existence of economic complementarity and economics of scale and agglomeration and availability of financial resources.

Notes

1   Investment regulations in Batam became more favourable than those in the rest of Indonesia. Their provisions include (i) 100 per cent foreign equity ownership allowed for the first five years, 95 per cent after that, with no further divestment for 100 per cent export-oriented projects, unlike the mandatory divestment to minority (49 per cent) ownership within fifteen years elsewhere in Indonesia; (ii) investment applications being processed in Batam itself rather than at the Investment Board (BKPM) in Jakarta; (iii) the private sector being allowed to set up industrial estates in Batam, a relaxation which led to the establishment of the Batam Industrial Park, a joint venture between the Indonesian private sector and a Singapore state-owned organisation.

2   In 1979 China proposed the 'three contacts policy', namely direct mail, direct air and sea links and direct trade with Taiwan, a move rejected by Taiwan. In 1980, China abolished all tariffs on imports from Taiwan of trade items of a domestic rather than external nature, and import controls were less stringent than those imposed on goods from other sources. However, following an influx of goods with fake Taiwan certificates of origin, the policy was modified, with adjustment taxes being levied on Taiwan goods, but at rates lower than prevailing import tariffs. In 1988 Taiwan investors were accorded preferential treatment; this included permission to develop land and a longer duration period before divestment of equity joint ventures.

9

Japan and the Asian NICs as New Countries of Destination*

Gary P. Freeman and Jongryn Mo

I Introduction

Asia, with 60 per cent of the world's population, has traditionally been a major source of emigration, but in recent years rapidly intensifying internal migration has turned certain states in the region into destinations for foreign labour. Some scholars argue that these states have reached a 'turning point' in their development where the combination of economic and demographic forces produces a migration transition that changes them from countries of mass unemployment and labour surplus into increasingly rich societies with tight labour markets in at least some economic sectors. A few states have become net importers of labour. How governments are reacting to these new circumstances is the principal question we investigate.

We concentrate on the substantive content of emerging immigration policies and the goals towards which they are directed. The central element in state responses has to do with openness to foreign labour. States might reasonably adopt three broad strategies. First, a strategy of refusal would resist the pressures for immigration (from both internal demand for labour and the external supply of ready entrants) by seeking to develop alternatives to immigration through economic restructuring, foreign direct investment and other means. Certain states clearly lean towards this approach, but we believe the temptations to resort to migrant workers are too strong to make this alternative viable. A second strategy recognises the necessity of additional manpower, but attempts to control its use by insisting that migrants be carefully targeted to particular sectors and designated skill categories, and be admitted for short-term visits only. We dub this the '3-S strategy' and suggest that it best fits the actual policies of the new receiving states. A third and final option involves a more open stance that would permit both short- and long-term migration as part of a general effort to enhance labour market flexibility and sustain long-term growth. States adopting such a policy may be thought to be embracing the transition and accepting that immigration is a normal and unavoidable accompaniment of increased trade and investment within the region.

A second aspect of emerging policies has to do with means and style rather than ends. Whatever the substantive policy goals, the institutional means by which policy is implemented may vary significantly. Do states intervene into labour markets and management decisions in order to set and achieve immigration policy goals, or are they more passively willing to acquiesce in the private decisions of employers and foreign job-seekers?

A final purpose of this paper is to place the Asian cases in a comparative perspective by asking if their policies will gradually assimilate to those of the West. Asian countries are unlikely to follow the path of the settler societies. European states, on the other hand, have gone through migration transitions themselves only recently or are still in the process of doing so. The countries of Northern and Western Europe became the focus of mass immigration flows during the postwar expansion between the late 1950s and early 1970s. More recently, Southern and Eastern European states have had to grapple with economic migrants and political refugees on a major scale for the first time. The common economic and demographic forces that suggest similarities between the Western and Asian experiences may, nevertheless, be overridden by political or cultural factors, producing a distinctly Asian model of immigration policy.

We have cast our net broadly in the selection of cases. Although Japan is a highly industrialised nation, it has only recently begun to be the recipient of significant numbers of migrants and, therefore, qualifies as a new country of destination. The four Asian Tigers – Korea, Hong Kong, Singapore and Taiwan – are the core cases. In addition, Malaysia and Thailand will figure in the analysis, though they are at earlier stages of development and have arguably only begun their transitions.

II Economic growth, demographic change and migration in Asia

Immigration pressures in Asia are a direct result of economic growth and demographic change. The demand for labour is fuelled by the rapid economic growth in the region and is exacerbated by declining fertility. Table 9.1 provides evidence on both scores.

For our seven cases, average annual growth of GDP from 1980 to 1991 was 5.5 per cent and ranged from a low of 2.9 per cent for Malaysia to a high of 8.7 per cent for South Korea. On the other hand, total fertility rates decline sharply between 1965 and 1992 for all the countries except Japan and Taiwan, where they were already low.

Students of the interaction of these factors speak of demographic and migration transitions, or turning points, that are reached when economic growth and fertility declines produce tight labour markets reflected in historically low unemployment rates (see articles by Abella, Fields, Nayyar, and Alburo in a special

Table 9.1   Economic and demographic indicators for seven Asian nations

Country	Population (millions) 1992	Population growth rate 1990–2000	Total fertility 1965	Total fertility 1992	GDP per capita 1991 (in US$)	Average annual growth rate of GDP 1980–1991
Japan	124.5	0.4	2.0	1.7	26 840	3.6
Taiwan	20.6	1.1	2.8†	1.8††	8 790	6.6
Hong Kong	5.7	0.7	4.7	1.4	13 580	5.6
Singapore	2.6	0.9	4.7	1.7	14 140	5.3
South Korea	44.0	0.8	4.9	1.7	6 350	8.7
Malaysia	16.9	.2.1	6.3	3.7	2 520	2.9
Thailand	54.5	1.1	6.3	2.3	1 650	5.9

Note: †1975; ††1991

Sources: Skeldon, 1992a, 1992b; UNDP *Human Development Report*, 1994; ESCAP, *Economic and Social Survey of Asia and the Pacific*, 1993; ADB, Key Indicators of Developing Asian Nations, 1993.

issue of *Asian and Pacific Migration Journal*, 3/1, 1994). Some time after full employment is reached, or in some cases even before (Fong 1994), countries begin to experience immigration. Migration may be limited to specific sectors that are short of labour even though there is mass unemployment in the country as a whole or while significant out-migration continues. The general shift from exclusively exporting to a mix of exporting and importing labour is undeniably evident in the region as a whole, but we must nevertheless note that there is no necessary or simple relationship between these variables in particular states. Each case must be analysed separately with due attention to its peculiarities (Watanabe 1994; Skeldon 1994a, 1994b; Park 1994; Vasuprasat 1994).

Full employment was achieved in Japan in the early 1960s and the migration turning point was reached by the mid-1960s (Watanabe 1994). Taiwan followed close by in the late 1960s (Pookong 1994). Both Hong Kong and Singapore had achieved full employment by the early 1970s. The migration turning point in Hong Kong is open to dispute (Skeldon 1994c), but it took place in Singapore in the early to mid-1970s. Both Korea and Malaysia underwent the migration transition in the late 1980s in the sense that they began to receive significant numbers of foreign workers. However, in the case of Korea this was a full decade after the arrival at full employment (Park 1994), and in the case of Malaysia immigration took place at the same time that unemployment and emigration continued. The situation of Thailand is even more problematic. Technical full employment was achieved in the early 1990s and the country is arguably entering the migration transition in the mid-1990s insofar as in-migration has commenced (Pookong 1994). Yet Thailand has a large rural sector and must certainly be considered a country of labour surplus. The timing of the turning point from emigration to immigration is not always consistent with the advent of full employment, primarily because states can deal with tight labour markets in a variety of ways and recourse to foreign labour is not necessarily the most popular tactic (Skeldon 1992c).

The transformation of a number of Asian countries into magnets for immigration does not mean that Asia has ceased to be a major source of emigration (see Table 9.2).

In 1985 Asians made up half those admitted legally to the USA and about one-third of those going to Canada and Australia. Lim (1994, p. 127) notes that 'between 1969 and 1989, some 11.824 million Asians worked as migrant labourers in other countries'. Outside Asia the most common destination has been the Middle East. From a peak of about 950 000 in 1983, the numbers stabilised at around 750 000 in the mid-1980s (Lim 1994, p. 130). Significant numbers of clandestine migrants from Asia can be found in Europe as well.

For our purposes, the most interesting Asian migration is that confined to the region, especially that from the poorer countries to their faster growing neighbours. Lim and Abella observe:

Table 9.2   Migration situation in seven Asian nations

Country	Migration turning point	Legal emigration to USA, Australia, Canada, New Zealand 1992	Contract labour departures	Total legal aliens[a] foreign workforce[b] legal immigrants annually[c]	Illegal labour force (estimates of predominant mode)[c]
Japan	mid-1960s	14 997	—	1 218 891[a]	296 751 (overstayers)
Taiwan	late 1960s	27 881	—	177 000[b] or 20 000[c]	40 000 (overstayers)
Hong Kong	early 1970s	67 093	—	95 425[c]	27 000 (clandestine entries annually)
Singapore	early 1970s	2 894	—	150 000–170 000[b]	12 000 (clandestines apprehended in recent year)
South Korea	late 1980s	23 628	83 000 (1988)	33 600–80 000[b]	100 000 (overstayers)
Malaysia	late 1980s	7 003	—	134 000[b]	400 000 (clandestine)
Thailand	mid-1990s	56 130	137 950 (1993)	—	300 000–520 000 (clandestine)

Sources: Lim, 1994; Skeldon, 1992a, 1992b, 1995; Cornelius, 1994; Tsay, 1992; *Migrant News*, February 1995.

As these countries internationalise their economies and become key investors in Asia, they have created, whether knowingly or unknowingly, a transnational space for the circulation of goods, capital and culture, which in turn tends to create conditions for the circulation of people and, in effect, the formation of international labor markets. (1994, p. 225)

The results of these forces are evident in all seven of our cases, a rough summary of which is given in Table 9.2. We should note that we are dealing with a very dynamic situation and data on migration are inconsistent, unsystematic and may be unreliable. Most estimates of clandestine immigration, especially those by governments, probably significantly understate the actual situation. Large discrepancies may reflect timing as, for example, legalisation sharply reduces the size of the undocumented labour force from one month to the next.

Japan is the only fully industrialised country in our sample and, as Ito and Iguchi (1994) note, the only country to have passed through that developmental process without experiencing mass immigration. Nevertheless, migration pressures are growing rapidly. The number of foreigners admitted to Japan each year for all purposes has been rapidly rising. In 1980 there were only 461 000; this figure had grown to 2.1 million in 1991 and 3.8 million in 1992 (Morita & Sassen 1994; Cornelius 1994, p. 390). Apprehensions of illegal immigrants ballooned over the same period from just 2536 to 67 824 (Morita & Sassen 1994, pp. 155–6). In 1991 there were 1.2 million registered aliens in Japan, about 80 per cent of whom were from Asia (Watanabe 1994, p. 136). The estimated number of unauthorised visa-overstayers in November 1993 was 296 751, of which at least 75 per cent were from Asian countries. This figure had roughly tripled since July 1990 (Cornelius 1994, p. 384). Foreigners tend to be concentrated in unskilled, low-paid jobs (Mori 1994).

Korea was a major exporter of labour until recently, mostly in the form of contract labourers. The emigration of Korean workers reached its peak in 1982 when there were about 197 000 Koreans working overseas. Thereafter, a strong trend towards net inflows of labour is evident (Lim 1994, p. 132). Prior to the 1992 amnesty there were about 100 000 illegal foreign workers in Korea; immediately afterwards, probably 30 000. By 1995 this figure had climbed back to the 50 000–100 000 mark (Park 1994; Far Eastern Economic Review, 27 August 1992; Migrant News, February 1995; but see Huguet 1992, p. 259). As of March 1995 there were between 33 600 and 84 000 foreigners legally employed in Korea (Migrant News, March 1995).

A major new destination for migrant labour is Taiwan, although the government formally accepts only skilled and highly skilled foreign workers. Skeldon (1992a, p. 47) estimates that there were about 20 000 skilled foreigners legally in the country in 1990. Kanjanapan, looking specifically at highly skilled white-collar and professional workers, reports that there were about 1000 in 1988–90 (1992, p. 569). These figures do not include a growing number of persons who enter Taiwan legally on tourist or other visas and then overstay. Mostly from Malaysia, the Philippines, Thailand, and Indonesia, these clandestine workers were a negligible presence before 1986 but are rapidly becoming a serious concern for the government. The best estimate of their numbers is that of Tsay (1992). He bases his figures on an analysis of official arrival and departure data and shows that from 1985 to 1988 the former grew by 24 per cent while the latter rose by only 6.5 per cent. This leads him to argue that there were probably about 40 000 visa overstayers in Taiwan in 1990.

Although Hong Kong is experiencing heavy emigration in advance of the Chinese takeover in 1997, it is at the same time a powerful magnet for immigration. Lim estimates that about 27 000 Chinese arrive illegally per year (1994, p. 131). In 1989 11 405 professionals were officially admitted. Under the government's labour importation scheme, 3000 skilled workers entered in 1989 and 14 700 skilled and semi-skilled in 1990. Domestics, who are not subject to quotas, rose from about 880 in 1974 to 70 335 in 1990 (Lim 1994). Skeldon (1994, pp. 112–13) estimates that there were 95 425 legal immigrants to Hong Kong in 1992, including 28 376 legal entrants from China, 40 424 entering with employment visas and 26 634 under residence visas. This represented a near doubling of the 49 492 who entered legally in 1983. He also reports that there were 35 645 illegal Chinese migrants apprehended trying to enter Hong Kong in 1992.

The number of foreign workers in Singapore went from 14 000, or 2 per cent of the labour force, in 1970, to 128 000, or 10 per cent, by 1989 (Lim 1994, p. 132). A more recent estimate says that there are between 170 000 and 200 000 foreign workers in 1992 (*Far Eastern Economic Review*, 2 April 1992). Despite harsh penalties, clandestine migration has been significant: a recent sweep found 10 000 Thais and 2000 Indians working illegally (Lim 1994, p. 132).

Migrant flows to Malaysia are larger than to any country in the region. Malaysia hosts about one-half of all Asia's foreign workers (*Migrant News*, February 1995). It is estimated that there are about 120 000–140 000 Indonesians in Sabah state, another 200 000 in Peninsular Malaysia and 10 000 in Sarawak. Most of these are illegal. There may be 100 000 Filipinos in Sabah as well. In 1991 there were about 134 000 registered foreign workers, skilled and unskilled in the country (Lim 1994, p. 132). A conservative estimate would be that there were 400 000 illegal workers in Malaysia in 1994. In 1995 there were also 340 000 legal foreign workers for whom sending-country information was available (*Migrant News*, February 1995).

Despite its lower standard of living, Thailand is also under increasing pressure from illegal migration. The total number was estimated to be about 300 000 in 1992 (Vasuprasat 1994, p. 192). The government officially admits to about 100 000 illegals, but another source puts the figure at 520 000 (*Migrant News*, February 1995).

III Emerging immigration policy

Throughout East Asia, immigration policy objectives and instruments are strikingly similar. Policy-makers have concluded, grudgingly in some cases, that foreign workers are needed to solve labour shortages, but they are also mindful of the social and economic costs of employing them, especially the unskilled. The emerging foreign labour policies of the region may be summarised as a 3-S strategy: policy-makers want skilled workers to take up short-term employment in specific industrial sectors. Within this broad set of objectives, governments seek to limit the overall numbers to the lowest feasible figure.

Generalising about immigration policies in the region is complicated by the fact that the various governments are still in the early stages of recognising that significant migration is taking place, deciding what they want to do about it, and establishing procedures and institutions to achieve their objectives. States may be said to be in some cases at the pre-policy stage (Thailand and Taiwan), at the initial period of setting up formal regulations and procedures (Korea and Malaysia), or at the point of reformulating earlier policies in light of early experience (Japan, Hong Kong and Singapore). Moreover, some of the policies that are on the books are little more than formalities because they are not enforced, either because of institutional incapacity or deliberate inertia. Attempts to assess the effectiveness of immigration policies are confounded because one cannot assume that governments are bent on enforcing controls. At times it seems evident that they are the willing victims of efforts to circumvent their legislation.

All governments in the region seek to control tightly the number of foreign workers in their countries and their formal policies are impressive. They regularly canvass demand for foreign workers and restrict admissions accordingly. The bias in favour of skilled workers is quite strong. Officially, unskilled foreign workers cannot be employed at all in Japan and Korea, but they can be 'trainees'. Governments as well try to discourage the long-term employment of foreign workers. Hong Kong, Singapore and Taiwan allow contract workers, for example, but limit their employment to no more than two to three years. Those workers who are allowed to enter are allocated to specific sectors that are under special labour-market pressures. The employment of foreigners is typically prohibited in some industries. Violation of the various rules regulating the employment of foreign labour can result in stiff penalties, and these are increasingly vigorously enforced. Deportations of illegal immigrants are common and formally strict employer and employee sanctions are in place in all Asian destination countries.

The accomplishment of the three main objectives of foreign-worker policy is aided by the limitation of the economic and political rights of foreign workers (Noiriel 1993). Even when unskilled workers are legally employed, they usually cannot bring their families and have no opportunity to gain permanent residence or citizenship; only Taiwan allows foreign workers to bring their families. In Singapore, unskilled foreign workers are not encouraged to marry Singaporeans and such marriages do not confer the right to enter or remain in the country (Low 1994). The rights of industrial trainees in Japan and Korea are even more constrained. Since foreign trainees are not considered to be regular workers, they do not have the legal rights of nationals or legal migrants. In Korea, for instance, foreign trainees are not protected by labour standards in the first three months of training.

An important method by which the governments in East Asia minimise the social and cultural tensions often associated with foreign labour is in giving preference to certain ethnic groups. Indeed, from a Western perspective the most striking characteristic of migration in East Asia is that it is overwhelmingly of Asian origin. That is perhaps to be expected; it would be surprising if large numbers of persons from rich Western countries were moving to Asia in search of work. It is worth noting, however, that if they were so inclined, Westerners would not be permitted to enter in search of work and residency. Asian governments, moreover, openly discriminate between different Asian nationality or ethnic groups. Formally or informally, Japan, Korea, Malaysia and Singapore give preference to potential migrants with whom they share ethnic affinity.

Despite the strong overall similarities, there are important policy variations among the Asian states. In this section, we compare policies to assess their relative restrictiveness, the degree to which they exhibit an active and interventionist policy stance, and their effectiveness.

Restrictive versus open immigration policy

Japan and Korea are more restrictive than Hong Kong, Malaysia, Singapore, Taiwan and Thailand. A key indicator is that the former have only training programs for unskilled foreign workers while the latter, except for Thailand, run work permit systems. These give a legal status to foreigners that they cannot obtain in Japan or Korea.

The principles of Japan's current immigration policy, as recently delineated by Cornelius, illustrate its restrictiveness: (1) employing foreign workers should be a last resort after all other solutions for labour shortage (such as increasing domestic labour supply, encouraging firms to move off-shore and/or automate their production processes) are exhausted; (2) no unskilled workers should be imported; and (3) all foreigners, including skilled workers, should have temporary stays (1994, p. 387). To achieve these objectives, the Japanese government passed amendments to its Immigration Control Act which took effect in June 1990. Under the new rules, the number of job categories in which foreigners can work in Japan expanded from eighteen to twenty-eight, but none is open to the unskilled. The measure also prescribed heavy penalties for the employment of illegal immigrants (Japan Immigration Association 1990).

The Japanese government seems intent on solving its long-term labour shortage problem, to the extent it requires foreigner workers, with 'company trainees'. Under the new Practical Trainee program, initiated in April 1993, firms are allowed to employ foreign workers for two years. One-third of the trainee's time in the first year is supposed to be spent on instruction in Japanese language and culture, and the rest of the training period goes basically to 'on-the-job' training.

South Korea's responses to labour shortages have followed the Japanese model. Like Japan, Korea has been a homogeneous society without any significant minority or foreigner population. There appears to be no consensus on the issue of foreign labour within the government. The Ministry of Trade and Industry, which tends to represent business interests, supports the importation of foreigners to ease specific labour shortages. The ministries of Labour and Justice, on the other hand, oppose it, as do the trade unions. Policy has been a cautious compromise between the views of the opposing factions. The formal employment of foreign workers in Korea has been limited. Legal status is offered only to skilled workers involved in reporting, technology transfer, business, capital investment, education and research, and entertainment. The government has been reluctant to allow the importation of unskilled foreigners because it is concerned that such guest workers will slow the process of industrial adjustment and that, once legalised, they will make it more difficult to use foreign workers as a buffer against external shocks. Nevertheless, demand is so strong that a trainee system, along the lines of that in Japan, has been put in place which is the only means, under current law, for the legal entry of unskilled workers.

The trainee system was originally intended to upgrade the skills of the foreign workers employed by Korean firms overseas. As labour shortages at home intensified, however, the government began to use the system as an instrument to accept unskilled foreign labour. Beginning in the latter half of 1993, foreign trainees came to work for small and medium-sized enterprises in the ten manufacturing industries deemed essential for Korea's economic development. Originally, trainees were allowed to stay in Korea for up to one year. In December 1993, the maximum number of foreign trainees was increased to 20 000 and was again raised in 1995 to 60 000. The period of residence was increased to two years.

Although Japan and Korea operate policies that are formally more restrictive than those of the other Asian countries, their enforcement efforts raise considerable doubt as to whether they are sincere about preventing the inflow of unskilled foreign workers. Both countries tolerate so-called back-door or side-door avenues for entry of illegal workers and they do not strictly enforce the laws against hiring them. In the case of Japan, Cornelius (1994, pp. 392–3) observes that the government seems to have ruled out many of the options that would have been effective in curbing illegal migration. While the number of apprehensions has been rising, there has not been any large-scale, systematic round-up and deportation initiative.

The Japanese government has permitted South Americans of Japanese descent and foreign students to work as unskilled workers (Nakagawa 1994). Japanese descendants in Latin America are allowed to live and work in Japan with few restrictions and most of them work in sectors with labour shortages. According to a 1991 survey, there were approximately 148 700 Japanese descendants working in Japan, and 79.7 per cent of them had factory jobs and 87.8 per cent were unskilled or semi-skilled workers (Korean Ministry of Labor 1994). A large portion of foreign workers in South Korea are Korean descendants from China, but unlike their Latin American counterparts in Japan, they do not receive special treatment. The Japanese government also tolerates the illegal employment of foreign students. Foreign students are allowed to work for up to twenty hours a week, but most work considerably more than that and many take up unskilled positions.

Compared with Japan and Korea, the immigration policies of our other cases seem to be more open, as they admit unskilled foreign workers on a permit basis. Singapore and Malaysia have issued work permits to unskilled foreign workers since the 1960s. It was only in the late 1980s that Taiwan and Hong Kong began to allow local employers to recruit unskilled foreign workers in sectors experiencing labour shortages. Before 1989, the only unskilled contract workers admitted to Hong Kong were domestic helpers. There are some important differences among these countries, particularly in the treatment of illegal foreign workers. Singapore is, by far, the most aggressive in preventing and apprehending illegals, while Taiwan and Malaysia's enforcement policies are a good deal more lax.

To combat illegal immigration, the Singaporean government resorts to employer, employee and recruiter sanctions. Since 1989 employers who knowingly hire five or more illegals, and illegal workers themselves, have been subject to caning. Sanctions on employers of illegal foreign workers include fines of up to twenty-four times the monthly levy (S$7200 and S$9600 for S$300 and S$400 per worker levies, respectively) and up to six months in gaol. Singapore seems to enforce its employer sanctions relatively strictly. In 1993, the government collected S$4.3 million in fines from 415 employers, and from January to September 1994, S$4.1 million was paid by 278 employers.

Hong Kong has the most experience with immigration control. Having a border with China and being within easy reach by sea from many parts of the Guangdong coast, Hong Kong has long attracted illegal immigrants from Asia's most populous country. Because there has been strong public sympathy for Chinese migrants, the government has not resorted to strict, Singapore-style policies to deter them. It has been able, nevertheless, to contain the number of illegal immigrants from China through a variety of policies: (1) aggressive border patrols; (2) extensive checks by police on the identity cards residents must carry at all times; (3) co-operation from the Chinese government to reduce the flow; (4) a system of one-way exit visas from China; (5) fines and prison terms for employers who employ persons without documents; (6) economic restructuring through which manufacturers in Hong Kong set up subcontracting or full-production units in China; and (7) the importation of labour in selected areas of severe shortage (Wu & Inglis 1992, p. 610).

Recently, the Taiwanese government has also taken steps to stem illegal migration. On 20 October 1994, it amended the Employment and Service Act to increase fines for hiring undocumented foreign workers. Sanctions include up to three years in jail and a maximum fine of NT$300 000. Taiwan also fines employers whose foreign workers leave the jobs for which they have permits. The maximum penalty imposed on runaway foreign workers themselves is deportation. Taiwan will also punish smugglers of foreign workers with up to three years in prison and fines of up to NT$15 000 000 (about US$575 000). The government has recently tightened monitoring procedures at international points of entry.

These steps sound tough, but it remains to be seen whether the government will follow through with them. Historically, Taiwan has been relatively tolerant of illegal immigration (Tsay 1992). Until 1994 there was no law prosecuting employers who hired illegal foreign workers. Prior to 1994, although foreigners were not generally permitted by law to work in Taiwan, there was no enforcement mechanism; most foreign workers could simply overstay tourist visas.

Malaysia has a large population of illegal foreign workers (see Table 9.2), largely due to the lax enforcement of employer sanctions. One possible explanation is concern over the ethnic composition of the population. Malaysia's population is a mix of Malays, Chinese and Indians. It is commonly believed that Indonesians make up the bulk of illegal entries since the religion, customs and language that they share with Malays makes detection more difficult. One estimate is that illegal migration adds about 1 per cent annually to the total population and that the Malay-dominated government is hesitant to impede such a politically useful flow (Martin 1991, p. 186). While there were officially 75 000 Indonesian workers in Malaysia in 1992, trade union sources estimated the more realistic figure to be as high as 800 000 (*Far Eastern Economic Review*, 2 April 1992).

Thailand has made the least progress towards an effective control of illegal migrants. This seems to be the result of the nation's limited experience with migration pressures. The government has been criticised by the National Congress of Private Employees for its failure to stem the illegal influx, but they do not propose stricter controls. Instead, they want the government to register illegals and set fixed wages and benefits and to permit them to work in sectors shunned by Thais. The fact that Thailand's workforce is still over 60 per cent in agriculture would seem to indicate that there could be no real labour shortages, but Thais prefer industrial employment and seasonal agricultural shortages have been reported since as early as 1970 (Huguet 1992, p. 261).

Active versus passive policy

The migration transition presents a challenge to governments not only to delineate coherent objectives of immigration policies, but to establish institutions to work towards official goals. This takes time. Some governments in the region have so far been significantly more interventionist and hands-on than others in managing the recruitment and placement of foreign workers, controlling their skill levels and sectoral destination, and determining their wages and benefits.

Singapore is a polar example; foreign labour has been perceived as an integral part of national economic strategy and an instrument to preserve the city-state's ethnic balance. Consistent with a growing trend, Singapore carries out a two-tiered policy with regard to foreign workers. Policies towards unskilled foreign workers are restrictive while policies towards skilled or professional workers are more liberal. Unlike other countries, Singapore employs active and elaborate programs to recruit professional and skilled labour. Since August 1989, foreign workers who are skilled and professional, or are college-educated and earning at least S$1500 per month, are eligible for permanent residency (Martin 1991). This policy is designed to attract skilled Hong Kong immigrants and to offset the emigration of Singapore's skilled workers to other countries (Lim & Abella 1994, p. 227). The government also encourages foreign workers to upgrade their skills by offering the incentive of permanent residency status to those who do (Appleyard 1991, p. 38).

Moreover, the Singaporean government uses variable employment levies and ceilings to control the number, skill level and sectoral composition of foreign workers. To protect the working conditions of domestic workers and prevent excess dependence on foreign workers, Singapore has imposed levies on employers of foreign workers since 1982. Raised periodically to curb demand, and imposing a higher rate on employers of unskilled workers than employers of the skilled, the tax has as its main purpose to ensure that wages of foreign workers reflect labour market conditions and not simply the marginal cost of hiring a foreign worker (Low 1994, Martin 1991). By making employers pay this levy, Singapore is one of the few countries to take advantage of wage gaps between receiving and sending countries to increase its revenue.

Singapore is also aggressive in shaping the sectoral distribution of foreign workers. In the beginning, only employers of workers from non-traditional sending countries in the construction industry were subject to a monthly foreign worker levy (S$230). The program was then expanded to manufacturing and to all industries, and levies were raised in 1984. Interestingly, the Singaporean government has imposed relatively low rates on domestic helpers to encourage female labour force participation.

To regulate the number of foreign workers, the government has set ceilings on their share of the total workforce. These vary across sectors and change over time as labour market conditions fluctuate. In manufacturing, the number of foreign workers cannot exceed 45 per cent of all employees. In construction, the ceiling was 66 per cent of the total workforce, but this was raised twice in 1992 to 84 per cent. The ceilings are also high (66 per cent) in shipbuilding and repair, but they are much lower (20 per cent) in the services sector. To ensure the return home of temporary work permit holders from non-traditional countries, the government requires foreign workers to post a security bond. Before 1993, the amount of the bond varied from S$1000 to S$3000, depending on the workers' occupation. Since 1993, every worker pays the same rate of S$5000.

Although Japan and Korea are still hesitant to change their current immigration policy, there is strong support among policy-makers and academics for a Singapore-type work permit system. A study group appointed by Japan's Ministry of Labour recommended a work permit system in 1988 during the policy debate leading up to the revision of the Immigration Control Act that took effect in June 1990. In December 1994, the Foreign Labour Policy Study Group organised by Korea's Ministry of Labour also endorsed the introduction of a work permit system for unskilled foreign workers. At least in Korea, there is a good chance that the trainee program will be phased out in favour of a work permit system in the near future. Taiwan asks employers of foreign workers to pay a tax in the form of employment insurance. The Korean government permits only small and medium-sized firms in manufacturing sectors with a labour shortage rate of at least 5 per cent to host foreign trainees.

Government intervention in the migration market is less explicit and active in other countries. Japan displays a contrasting approach to foreign worker migration. Like Singapore, Japan recognises that foreign workers can bring the skills and technologies that are in short supply in Japan. Amendments to the Immigration Control and Refugee Recognition Act make it easier to recruit skilled foreign workers. Japan also recognises that it needs unskilled foreign workers to fill labour shortages in the construction industry and so-called '3-D' (dirty, dangerous and demanding) jobs. Yet Japan hesitates to formally endorse the systematic importation of foreign labour.

First, foreign labour policy is the responsibility of the Ministry of Justice rather than one of the economic ministries, suggesting that economic objectives such as the management of labour supply do not have as much impact on foreign-worker policies in Japan as in other countries. Second, no incentives (e.g., tax benefits or offers of permanent settlement) are being offered to encourage the importation of skilled workers. Third, policies regulating the entry of skilled workers are not transparent. Nagayama observes that the Immigration Control Act that limits activities of foreign nationals to a narrow range of professional and skilled labour areas does not contain an explicit definition of professional and skilled work. Actual classification is at the discretion of officials and this leads to anomalies. Carpenters are popularly considered skilled workers by ordinary Japanese, but under the Immigration Control Act they are labelled unskilled (Nagayama 1992, p. 627). Finally, there does not seem to be as much effort to control the sectoral distribution of foreign workers as is evident in countries like Singapore.

IV Is there an Asian model?

Our review of the developing policy frameworks of East Asian states suggests that there is a reasonably strong convergence on basic immigration goals. The '3-S' strategy that promotes migration that is skilled, short term and sectorally targeted is officially the dominant approach of all the states. This overall pattern is probably more striking than the divergences of individual cases. Some states react to the possibility of migrants more favourably than others, but all have pursued economic policy alternatives to migration and none is enthusiastic about permanent settlement of any but very small and special categories of migrants. Nevertheless, the two dimensions of policy that we identify produce a spread of the cases. Moreover, the positions of states along the two dimensions do not appear to be strongly correlated. More restrictionist states are not necessarily more activist. Japan and Korea, which tend toward the restrictive pole of the first dimension, are not the most activist states in the sample. Singapore, a country that we rate as being at least modestly open to migration, sets the pace in adopting an aggressive and interventionist management style.

The clustering of Japan and Korea at one end of the restrictive dimension, and the location of Hong Kong, Singapore, Malaysia and Taiwan at the other end, suggests immediately that cultural factors may be at work. These two countries of non-Chinese ethnicity are the least willing to admit foreigners on a temporary or permanent basis. Neither Japan nor Korea have any historical experience with significant numbers of foreigners living inside their countries, having been traditionally extremely ethnically homogeneous. A much more intensive investigation of attitudes and policies, and their sources, would be necessary before anything definitive could be said on this sensitive subject.

The sources of the differentiation of the cases along the active/passive dimension seem to reflect broader political and administrative patterns. They may be a function of a more general government preference for market versus non-market policy instruments or the location of decision-making authority in particular ministries. Singapore is an authoritarian city-state that micro-manages many aspects of its residents' lives. Its response to foreign labour apparently simply mirrors its more general policy regime. More free market-oriented approaches in places like Taiwan and Hong Kong seem consistent with key elements of their economic policies. Korea seems to be moving towards the position of Singapore. Japan certainly has the capacity to employ a more activist stance, but appears ambivalent over which course to take.

We may tentatively conclude that whatever their differences in receptivity to migration and in the manner in which they manage it, the states we have discussed exhibit a common pattern of migration policy. Our final objective, then, is to consider whether this pattern is distinctive to the Asian region or is consistent with the broad processes apparent in other parts of the world. As we noted in the introduction, the Western European countries seem much more pertinent to the Asian immigration experience than do settler societies such as the USA, Australia and Canada. Macura has suggested that the settler societies differ fundamentally from the European and Asian states in their responses to immigration as a result of very different nation-state traditions:

> In Europe, particularly in its western, southern and northern parts, and in Japan, the nation-state has evolved over time around the same dominant language, ethnicity and sometimes religion. This process has produced a high degree of cultural homogeneity that gives the nation-state its coherence and sustains it. (Macura 1994, p. 16)

It is evident that these similar historical traditions have yielded converging contemporary immigration policies in the two regions. Asian states seem to have proceeded a little more cautiously (Japan and Korea remarkably more), but all the states are busy running guest worker programs in one form or the other. The '3-S' strategy is very much in the tradition of the classic guest worker systems that European states operated from the 1950s until the mid-1970s. Unfortunately, the European case (as well as such episodes as the Bracero program in the United States) teach us that the three goals of guest worker systems are unlikely to be achieved. Temporary labour recruitment tends not to remain temporary (Castles 1984, Martin 1995), the exclusive selection of skilled workers cannot be maintained (Freeman 1995), and foreign workers cannot be contained to industries of the government's choosing. As Martin has observed:

> Asian countries so far seem to be making the same mistakes that were made earlier in North America and Europe—opening sectors selectively to foreign workers, and changing migrant worker policies frequently as the relative power of domestic 'Let them in' and 'Keep them out' camps ebbs and flows. (1994, p. 520)

Much of the evidence we have presented is consistent with Martin's warning. The lax attitude in some quarters in the face of illegal entry and work, the plaintive appeals of employers short of workers, the stubborn insistence that the natives simply will not take up the available jobs, all are reminiscent of the European experience.

What are the odds that Asia will find the means to avoid the 'mistakes' of European governments, either by resisting the pressures to import foreign labour or by so strictly enforcing their migrant regimes that such labour remains tightly controlled? If the economic pressures brought on by rapid industrialisation and demographic change are similar in both regions, political and cultural differences are striking. These might make us reconsider the inevitability of the breakdown of guest worker schemes.

We can do no more than mention a few key factors that differentiate the politics of policy-making in the Asian states from that in the liberal democracies of the West (Freeman, forthcoming). First, Asian states appear to have the latitude to operate ethnically discriminatory selection policies of the sort that are unavailable to Western states since they were eliminated in the late 1960s. The 'Asians only' or even more ethnically specific selection policies of the region may serve to limit social tensions and lead to a greater tendency to import foreigners. Resistance to the idea of ethnic heterogeneity and aversion to Western-style 'multiculturalism' may, on the other hand, cause Asian governments to avert the creation of permanently resident guest worker populations of the kind that have emerged in Europe. Second, Asian states take a much more summary attitude towards the rights of workers, migrant or national than is common in the West (Noiriel 1993). Even strongly organised unions were unable to resist mass guest worker programs in Europe. The political weakness of Asian workers may be conducive to more efficient and 'successful' migration programs. Finally, the lingering authoritarian character of a number of Asian political systems suggests that governments may have more flexibility in the management of labour markets, the control of borders and the regulation of foreign workers. Strict enforcement and summary expulsions are likely to be much less politically costly in Asia than in Western democracies.

As the global competition for technology and capital intensifies, the demand for skilled labour will likely increase, especially in middle-income Asian NICs that seek to improve their comparative advantage through the introduction of more technology and knowledge-based industries. In such circumstances Asian countries may not be able to sustain their current restrictive policies; they may believe it necessary to offer more economic and political inducements to skilled and professional foreign workers. Korea is a good example. Recently, the Korean Minister of Trade and Industry called for extending the stay for skilled foreign workers from four to six years, which can be renewed twice, and even suggested granting special 'permanent residence' status to them.

The prospects for more open migration policy towards unskilled foreign workers are also improving. All Asian countries, including Japan, believe that their labour shortage problem cannot be solved without foreign labour. As they make further progress towards democratisation and regional economic integration, they will be under pressure from domestic and international sources to legalise undocumented foreign workers. They are likely to adopt a Singapore model of systematic importation of unskilled workers, but without its authoritarian aspects. But this does not mean that Asian countries will have policies as liberal as those adopted in the USA and Europe. As much as there is a growing, if reluctant, consensus on the need for foreign labour, there is a strong desire across Asia to avoid the problems associated with the permanent settlement of unskilled foreign workers.

Note

*   We would like to acknowledge Nedim Ögelman for his invaluable assistance at every stage of this project. Ronald Skeldon was extremely helpful both with his comments and in providing assistance in collection of some of the data in the tables. Wilawan Kanpanajan generously read an early draft. Finally, we would like to acknowledge John Higley, Director of the Edward A. Clark Center for Australian Studies at the University of Texas, for his financial assistance and intellectual guidance during this project.

PART IV

Trade Liberalisation and Migration: Long-Term Consequences

10

Growth and Convergence in the Asia–Pacific Region: The Role of Openness, Trade and Migration

Alan M. Taylor

Introduction

Following a renaissance in the theory of economic growth in the 1980s, much effort has recently been devoted to the empirical analysis of economic growth and convergence. Empirical work has extended its scope beyond mere growth accounting into ever more refined econometric models of growth determinants – with models designed to confront the endogenous or exogenous behaviour of investment, human capital, population and fertility choices, financial development, foreign investment, even democracy and politics. As each new channel is explored, new mechanisms seem to be unearthed and validated. In this paper I consider the implications of recent findings in empirical growth research, and ask what made for winners and losers in the Asia–Pacific Region, with special reference to open economy forces and factor markets.

Theory and empirics

In its most general formulation possible, a theoretical growth model is simply a dynamic system that describes the evolution of a set of state variables x and a set of control variables u over points in time t.

The state variables follow trajectories x_t and include conventional economic stock variables – endowments such as physical and human capital, population, and 'technology', suitably measured. Conventionally, and since it is a function of these state variables, output is often included as another implicit state variable, as it is the major growth variable of interest. Control variables u_t may be endogenously determined and include the conventional economic flow variables – investment in physical or human capital, fertility and migration choice as it affects population growth, research as it affects technology, and so forth. Control variables affect the rate of change of the state variables through what I will term a 'laws-of-motion' equation

(1) $dx_t/dt = f(u_t; a)$,

where a is a set of environmental parameters, such as economic policies including taxes and institutional structures including property rights.

Often, attention is given to only one element on the left-hand side of (1). When dx_t/dt is just the growth rate of output $d\ln y_t/dt$, and the controls u_t are the growth rates of inputs $d\ln v_t/dt$, essentially (1) reduces to the production function once-differentiated, and its estimation. When that estimation is direct, it is called growth accounting. However, when such estimation is econometric, it leads to what I will term a 'growth accounting' regression

(1a) $d\ln y/dt = \alpha_0 + \alpha_1 \, d\ln v/dt + \alpha_2 \, a + \varepsilon.$

This approach has been used in the recent empirical growth literature.[1] However, it suffers from a potential weakness; as the 'new' growth theory stresses, the controls u_t are probably endogenous variables determined according to some behavioural rule. Thus, equation (1) should be complemented by a 'behavioural' equation, rounding out the description of the dynamic system, of the form

(2) $u_t = g(x_t; b)$

which describes the endogenous control choices u_t as a function of current state x_t and another set of putatively exogenous environmental parameters b.

The dynamic system is fully described by (1–2). Econometrically, it should be viewed as a system of simultaneous equations, and (1a) should be estimated with care for simultaneity bias arising from endogenous controls. In its own right, (2) may be usefully estimated as a 'behavioural' regression

(2a) $u = \beta_0 + \beta_1 \, x + \beta_2 b + \eta$

to provide details of the channels through which state variables and environmental parameters affect controls (e.g., factor accumulation) and hence growth.

Which variables are truly exogenous to the system? Clearly, empirical work can implement some standard tests to address this problem. A popular and convenient, albeit costly, escape route exists: namely, to ignore the challenge of modeling the endogenous processes altogether and retreat to a reduced form specification. Integrating the dynamic system (1–2) forward over time yields a 'trajectory' equation

(3) $x(T) = h(x(0); a, b).$

Such an approach may be applied to the trajectory of output to derive a reduced form 'trajectory' regression where state evolution (in this case, the growth rate of output) depends only on initial conditions $x(0)$ and environmental parameters:

(3a) $d\ln y/dt = \gamma_0 + \gamma_1 \, x(0) + \gamma_2 \, a + \gamma_3 \, b + \xi$

The attraction of the last specification is clear; the initial conditions are prede-termined and the endogeneity problem is finessed since the controls u do not enter. There is a cost: a specification like (3a) cannot reveal the channels through which the environment affects growth. The benefit is that (3a) might suggest some parameters which affect growth, and hence inspire investigation of likely channels through which such effects might operate.

A cursory glance at the empirical growth literature reveals a myriad of formulations of the type (1a–3a). In some cases authors have developed a hybrid approach, including some endogenous variables in a reduced form (3a), or, alternatively, adding some controls to the growth accounting regression (1a) but not others. Estimation of behavioural regressions (2a) is quite scarce in the current literature. A serious problem is that of replication and robustness – one study may find a partial correlation but only when omitting variables found to be important in another study (Levine & Renelt 1992).

My empirical design follows three approaches, corresponding to specifica-tions (1a–3a). I begin by estimating the simplest specification, the reduced form (3a), which may serve to identify important exogenous influences on the growth rate. As a second step, I estimate a structural growth regression of the form (1a), looking first at the obvious flow variables for factor accumulation. In a third step, estimation of the behavioural regression (2a) yields insights into growth mecha-nisms – how economic environment affects growth indirectly through control variables in the structural equations.

Data

I now describe the variables I employ in the various specifications. All data are publicly available in electronic form from three major sources: the *World Data* file from the World Bank (1994), the latest Penn World Table due to Heston et al. (1994), and Barro and Lee's (1994) panel data. The data sets cover a broad cross-section of countries in the postwar period (207 countries for 1950–92 in the World Bank source).[2] For this study, I constructed a pooled cross-country data set as averages for four successive five-year periods 1970–74, 1975–79, 1980–84 and 1985–89.

State variables

- GY: The growth rate (rate of change of natural log) of per capita GDP in purchasing power parity units.
- LNY0: The natural log of initial GDP per capita. Expected to influence growth if convergence forces operate, either directly or indirectly (via accu-mulation).[3]
- PYR+SYR+0: Initial years of primary and secondary schooling per person in the population. A proxy for the initial stock of human capital in the economy.[4]

Endogenous control variables

- *P+S*: The average enrolment rate in primary and secondary schools. A proxy for human capital accumulation, expected to have a positive impact on growth.[5]
- *CI*: The ratio of real gross investment to real GDP at constant international prices. A proxy for capital accumulation, and expected to have a positive impact on growth through capital deepening and embodied new technology.[6]
- *GPOP*: The growth rate (rate of change of natural log) of population, expected to have a negative impact on growth via capital dilution, congestion of fixed factors (diminishing returns in non-accumulable inputs), or congestion externalities.[7]

Environmental variables

- *PNXI*: Primary product net export intensity (ratio of primary product net exports to GDP). In a Heckscher–Ohlin–Vanek sense, the relative abundance of natural resources embodied in primary products in any country relative to the world resource endowment. May affect growth via dynamic comparative advantage.[8]
- *POP15+0, POP65+0*: Initial share of population aged under 15, over 65. A control for the initial demographic structure of the economy. May have dynamic growth effects if demography affects investment or human capital accumulation.[9]
- *G*: The share of government spending in GDP at current domestic prices. A proxy for the size of government, and hence overall tax rates. Both the activity of government and the public finance distortions might have adverse growth effects.[10]
- *PNQ*: Political non-qualifier country in the Sachs–Warner (1995) classification. A country fails the test (*PNQ*=1) if it has a socialist economic structure, suffers from extreme domestic unrest, or is characterised by extreme deprivation of civil or political rights. The variable is time-invariant 1970–89 for each country.[11]
- *LNPIPY*: The relative price of capital goods, calculated as the natural log of the ratio of the PPP for investment to the PPP for GDP. The PPPs are relative to the US. Expected to be lower in more open economies with freely traded capital goods. Expected to have negative impact on investment activity and, hence, on growth.[12]
- *BMPL*: The natural log of one plus the black-market premium on the exchange rate. Likely to have dynamic effects if it lowers investment by raising the price of (imported) capital goods, or if it impairs financial intermediation and the capital market efficiency more generally.[13]

- *OWTI*: Own-weight tariff incidence, a measure of average tariff rates in the economy. Another price distortion that is likely to have dynamic effects should it apply to imported capital goods, raising prices and creating disincentives for investment.[14]
- *ONQ*: Openness non-qualifier country in the Sachs–Warner (1995) classification. A country fails the test (*ONQ*=1) if it has high quota incidence on imports, a high proportion of exports handled by state export monopolies, a socialist economic structure, or has a black-market premium above 20 per cent on average in the 1970s or 1980s. The variable is time-invariant 1970–89 for each country.
- *GXR*: The rate of depreciation, measured as the growth rate (rate of change of the natural log) of the exchange rate in currency units per US dollar. A proxy for monetary instability, which might affect growth negatively through instability and risk costs of financial intermediation felt in the capital market.[15]
- *LLY*: The ratio of liquid liabilities in the financial system to GDP. A proxy for the size of the financial sector, and a measure of financial development. Expected to have positive effects of lower transactions costs and enhanced allocative efficiency in the capital market, and hence to promote accumulation and growth.[16]

Results

Growth determinants and unconditional convergence

The empirical growth literature began with findings on *unconditional* convergence for groups of high-income economies like Maddison's sixteen (Maddison 1982, Abramovitz 1986, Baumol 1986), and Table 10.1 replicates the basic findings. Regression 1 reproduces the standard result that, despite the unconditional convergence seen in the sample of currently high-income countries (a tautology, of course), expanding the sample to middle- and low-income countries reveals a tendency toward divergence in the world economy (in the β-convergence sense).

A recent innovation suggests we think of qualifying criteria for membership in the 'convergence club' based on political conditions and the degree of openness in the economy.[17] Regressions 2 and 3 replicate the Sachs–Warner (1994; 1995) findings. Unconditional convergence is strong in the set of qualifiers (1.5 per cent per annum) and weak in the set of non-qualifiers (0.3 per cent per annum); the divergence result of Regression 1 follows from pooling across these sets. Regression 4 cuts the problem another way, by introducing dummy variables into the unconditional convergence test: the growth penalty is most severe for openness non-qualification (3.2 per cent per annum lost on the growth rate) versus the penalty for political non-qualification (0.8 per cent per annum lost). The patterns also obtain for the Asia–Pacific sample in Regressions 5 and 6.

Table 10.1   Growth determinants and unconditional convergence

Regression no.	1	2	3
Dependent variable	GY	GY	GY
Sample	all	SWqual	SWnonqual
N	494	136	358
R squared	.06	.21	.06
SEE	0.0364	0.0218	0.0377
Constant	−0.0083 (0.66)	0.1674 (7.31)	0.0310 (1.80)
LNY0	0.0028 (1.75)	−0.0154 (5.91)	−0.0033 (1.43)

Regression no.	4	5	6
Dependent variable	GY	GY	GY
Sample	all	Asia–Pacific	Asia–Pacific
N	432	60	48
R squared	.15	.00	.49
SEE	0.0326	0.0315	0.0231
Constant	0.0919 (5.10)	0.0275 (0.69)	0.1959 (4.80)
LNY0	−0.0069 (3.37)	0.0008 (0.17)	−0.0177 (3.69)
ONQ	−0.0318 (6.91)		−0.0779 (5.97)
PNQ	−0.0080 (2.08)		0.0290 (2.04)

Notes: See text.

Table 10.2   Growth determinants and conditional convergence:
reduced-form estimation

Regression no.	7	
Dependent variable	GY	
Sample	all	
N	250	ANOVA
R squared	.31	Sums of
SEE	0.0279	squares
Constant	0.2147 (4.56)	0.0598
LNY0	−0.0156 (3.69)	0.0106
PYR+SYR+0	0.0001 (0.11)	0.0000
POP15+0	−0.0906 (1.55)	0.0019
POP65+0	−0.1455 (1.20)	0.0011
PNQ	−0.0033 (0.66)	0.0003
BMPL	−0.0213 (4.22)	0.0139
OWTI	−0.0063 (0.57)	0.0003
G	−0.0009 (3.01)	0.0070
LNPIPY	−0.0214 (3.56)	0.0099
GXR	−0.0332 (3.89)	0.0118
LLY	0.0035 (0.40)	0.0001
PNXI	−0.0129 (0.78)	0.0005
Residual		0.1847
Total		0.2686

Notes: See text.

Growth determinants and conditional convergence: reduced-form estimation

Illustrative as these results are, they only push back further the quest of the study: if openness and political conditions matter for growth, then *how* do they matter? And through what channel(s) do they inhibit growth – Investment? Human capital accumulation? Technological change? Population growth? All of the above?

If we posit exogenous environmental variables underlying the classification of *ONQ* and *PNQ*, then a natural way to begin is by introducing these underlying variables into a full reduced-form estimation of the type (3a), as in Table 10.2. Note that I retain the *PNQ* variable as an explanator since for the present study I am more concerned to identify the channels through which openness affects growth, not politics. However, openness is no longer a dichotomous variable (*ONQ*), but is construed broadly to include measures of black-market currency premia (*BMPL*), tariffs (*OWTI*), and exchange-rate depreciation (*GXR*). The regression includes other distortion measures like the relative price of capital (*LNPIPY*), and the size of government (*G*); and controls for financial development (*LLY*) and resource abundance (*PNXI*). All the above controls are contemporaneous, and also included are initial conditions for the stocks of human capital (*PYR+SYR+0*) and demographic structure (*POP15+0, POP65+0*).

The results are striking: conditional convergence operates at about 1.6 per cent per annum; and, of the controls, only the set of distortion measures matter in a significant way – and, of those, tariffs have minimal importance. This characterisation is true in terms of statistical significance and in terms of the more important quantitative significance revealed by the ANOVA sums of squares. First order contributions (excluding the residual sum of squares) derive from the conditional convergence effect (*LNY0*) and distortions (*BMPL, G, GXR*), each around 0.010. Other effects are at least an order of magnitude smaller.

Growth determinants and conditional convergence: structural estimation

Taken at face value, the results offer little support for claims that a principal trade distortion like tariffs retards growth, or that financial development enhances growth, or that resource endowments may lead to dynamic comparative disadvantage. Such a perspective, is, I will argue, flawed. The reduced form Regression 7 gets us only marginally closer to an answer to the problem of 'why growth rates differ' than did Regressions 1–6. For although it suggests that distortions matter, we want to know how they matter. That is a structural question – it asks how the environmental and state variables affect evolution: how the behavioural equations shift in response to perturbation.

Table 10.3 presents structural 'growth accounting' regressions, which naïvely estimate (1a) for physical and human capital inputs (*P+S, CI*) and population growth (*GPOP*), with only a catch-up term (*LNY0*). We expect the first two variables to enhance growth, the latter two to repress it. Regressions 8 and 9 are simple benchmarks which suggest a 17 per cent return on capital (for the full sample and the Asia–Pacific group) and a labour share of less than one half (for Asia–Pacific, imprecisely estimated). Human capital accumulation is not significantly associated with growth in the full sample, although it is in the Asia–Pacific sample, which compels us to account for the accumulation of all three factors for the present case study.

Table 10.3   Growth determinants and conditional convergence: structural equation estimation

Regression no.	8	9	10	11	12
Dependent variable	GY	GY	GY	GY	GY
Sample	all	Asia–Pacific	all	SWqual	SWnonqual
N	461	56	413	133	328
R squared	.19	.21	.26	.32	.15
SEE	0.0329	0.0283	0.0305	0.0199	0.035
Constant	0.0961 (5.85)	0.1151 (2.34)	0.1579 (7.63)	0.2177 (8.15)	0.0975 (4.95)
$LNY0$	−0.0117 (4.45)	−0.0178 (2.69)	−0.0188 (6.14)	−0.0272 (6.82)	−0.0114 (3.49)
$P+S$	−0.0020 (0.34)	0.0236 (1.45)	0.0034 (0.56)	0.0221 (2.52)	−0.0083 (1.23)
CI	0.0017 (7.51)	0.0017 (2.37)	0.0015 (6.41)	0.0007 (2.36)	0.0017 (5.97)
$GPOP$	−0.8716 (5.94)	−0.6071 (0.89)	−0.4475 (2.71)	−0.1159 (0.64)	−0.8734 (4.19)
ONQ			−0.0224 (4.73)		
PNQ			−0.0102 (2.74)		

Notes: See text.

Regressions 10–12 reintroduce controls and sample splits to allow for the political and openness qualifying variables to play a role here. The results are broadly supportive of the basic points: investment in physical capital has a return of about 15–17 per cent, though possibly lower in richer (qualifying) countries, as we might expect. Population growth congests resources and has a negative effect of growth – though less in the case of richer countries, suggesting there a more elastic supply of technology, perhaps, to overcome Malthusian pressures. Of the qualifying variables, again ONQ appears to matter more (2 per cent per annum growth cost) than PNQ (1 per cent growth cost). Henceforth, I focus on Regression 9 (confined to the Asia–Pacific sample).

We have a reduced form suggesting that distortions are major environmental determinants of growth. And we know from the structural growth equation that factor accumulation matters for growth. Could that be the channel through which distortions operate? An augmented structural equation is suggestive, as in Table 10.4, Regression 13. In Regression 14, I admit explicit endogeneity, including some of the distortion and environment variables we might expect to be co-determined, e.g., financial development (LLY), black-market premia ($BMPL$) and the price of capital ($LNPIPY$).[18] In the end this mattered little, because a specification test rejects 14 in favour of 13.[19]

Table 10.4   Growth determinants and conditional convergence: augmented
structural equation estimation

Regression no.	13	14	13 v. 14
Dependent variable	GY	GY	
Sample	all	all	
N	244	236	Hausman
R squared	.37	.31	Endogeneity
SEE	0.0269	0.0285	Test
Method	OLS	2SLS	(p value)
Constant	0.1807 (3.76)	−0.3847 (0.69)	
LNY0	−0.0182 (4.06)	0.1107 (1.03)	
PYR+SYR+0	0.0003 (0.24)	0.0060 (0.74)	
POP15+0	0.0003 (0.01)	0.8614 (1.12)	
POP65+0	−0.0859 (0.71)	−1.9065 (1.67)	
PNQ	−0.0027 (0.56)	−0.0585 (1.32)	
BMPL	−0.0190 (3.76)	0.2075 (1.16) †	0.46
OWTI	−0.0005 (0.05)	0.0950 (1.00)	
G	−0.0010 (3.35)	0.0001 (0.11)	
LNPIPY	−0.0096 (1.28)	0.0715 (0.59) †	0.83
GXR	−0.0272 (3.14)	−0.1336 (1.73)	
LLY	0.0021 (0.21)	−0.1418 (1.01)	0.62
PNXI	−0.0184 (1.13)	0.1699 (1.23)	
P+S	0.0024 (0.25)	−0.3172 (1.06) †	0.97
CI	0.0011 (2.76)	0.0062 (0.83) †	0.46
GPOP	−0.5539 (2.15)	−20.6041 (1.31) †	0.62

Notes: See text.

Quantitatively what do the results reveal? Regression 13 contrasts with Regression 7 in that the admitted controls CI and $GPOP$ are significant; and in that $LNPIPY$ is no longer significant. This result suggests that the $LNPIPY$ distortion may indeed act via an endogenous channel, most likely through investment demand. The distortion-investment-growth nexus is again highlighted. The question now remains – how does that channel work? And are there other channels by which the environment affects endogenous variables such as those just considered? And, quantitatively, can they explain performance within and outside the Asia–Pacific Region?

Growth determinants: behavioural equation estimation
Only a structural estimation of growth determinants as in (2a) can hope to answer such questions and Table 10.5 tries to do just that. Regression 15–20 estimate the 'behavioural equations' for the proximate determinants of six endogenous variables in the system (CI, $GPOP$, $P+S$, $BMPL$, LLY, $LNPIPY$). The first three regressions can then be coupled with information on the marginal contribution to growth of the various factor inputs (Regression 8 for Asia–Pacific) to help us identify what made the region such a fast-growth area, and what made the four NICs especially fast growers.[20]

Table 10.5(a)   Growth determinants: behavioural equation estimation

Regression no.	15	16	17
Dependent variable	CI	GPOP	P+S
Sample	all	all	all
N	236	225	230
R squared	.74	.54	.85
SEE	4.562	0.0083	0.1657
Constant	73.7032 (4.84)	0.0334 (3.44)	−1.2867 (4.44)
LNY0	−14.0049 (3.69)	0.0012 (0.77)	0.3001 (9.63)
PYR+SYR+0	−1.0449 (3.26)	−0.0008 (1.65)	0.0402 (4.69)
POP15+0	−100.9020 (4.01)		2.2437 (4.48)
POP65+0	143.7300 (2.35)		−3.6764 (4.26)
PNQ	5.7502 (3.20)	0.0011 (0.74)	0.0039 (0.13)
BMPL	−23.2958 (3.85)		
OWTI	−12.4540 (3.85)		
G	−0.0407 (0.56)	0.0001 (0.74)	0.0070 (3.74)
LNPIPY	−16.1287 (7.07)†		
GXR	9.8495 (2.64)		
LLY	18.5170 (5.38)	−0.0029 (1.09)	−0.2283 (3.12)†
PNXI	−17.8299 (3.06)	0.0234 (4.84)	0.2272 (2.08)
P+S	39.2374 (4.22)†	−0.0186 (3.96)†	
CI		0.0002 (1.45)	0.0090 (4.38)
GPOP	2059.0300 (3.81)†		−38.3005 (7.72)†

Regression no.	18	19	20
Dependent variable	BMPL	LLY	LNPIPY
Sample	all	all	all
N	143	223	236
R squared	.52	.51	.29
SEE	0.1891	0.2029	0.3414
Constant	0.4788 (1.31)	−0.3757 (1.56)	−0.1911 (3.23)
LNY0	−0.0648 (1.44)	0.0701 (2.00)	
PYR+SYR+0	−0.0032 (0.23)	−0.0173 (1.97)	
POP15+0			
POP65+0			
PNQ	0.1816 (3.19)	−0.0124 (0.30)	
BMPL		0.0788 (2.06)	0.1654 (2.16)†
OWTI	−0.0449 (0.33)	−0.2262 (2.80)	0.2772 (2.26)
G	0.0106 (3.17)	0.0022 (0.94)	0.0219 (6.64)
LNPIPY			
GXR	0.4751 (5.99)	−0.2110 (2.97)	
LLY			
PNXI	−0.0124 (0.07)	−0.3661 (3.14)	0.2390 (1.34)
P+S			
CI		0.0189 (4.39)†	
GPOP			

Notes: See text.

Regression 15 pinpoints some key determinants of investment. The coefficient of *LNY0* is negative: richer countries would be expected to have high capital intensity and lower marginal product of capital. A higher initial stock of human capital *PYR+SYR+0* also discourages further accumulation, as might be expected with unbalanced growth paths in the 'two-sector' models. Children constitute a major investments drag, consistent with a labour-supply impact on investment demand via *POP15+0*. The size of government (*G*) *per se* does not lower investment, but all other distortions do, including *BMPL*, *OWTI*, *GXR*, and most emphatically *LNPIPY*, the price of capital, as expected. A poor financial system (small *LLY*) depresses capital accumulation significantly, as expected. A natural resource comparative advantage (*PNXI* high) inhibits investment, as would be the case if primary product manufacture were less capital intense. Physical capital accumulation also rises to complement rapid human capital accumulation (*P+S*) and offset capital dilution via population growth (*GPOP*).

Regression 16 explores the determinants of population growth. The results are consistent with the view that fertility choice may embody elements of a quality–quantity trade-off, in that population growth seems to be negatively correlated with human capital stocks and flows. This is suggestive of possible multiple equilibria consistent with high- and low-human capital development paths. Interestingly, population growth does seem to be positively associated with natural resource endowments (*PNXI*), which would be consistent with theories of agricultural labour supply within the household, and also theories of saving (asset accumulation) via investment in children.

Regression 17 reinforces support for the quality–quantity trade-off, in that *GPOP* is negatively correlated with human capital accumulation measured by enrolments (*P+S*). A large share of children in the population is associated with high enrolments too, as expected. In a rare positive impact, high government spending G does spill over into economic growth to the extent that it promotes human capital accumulation. Human capital accumulation *P+S* complements investment *CI*, just as vice versa (see above).

Regression 18 examines the determinants of the black-market premium (*BMPL*) in an attempt to identify the details of the distortions-growth nexus. In keeping with our characterisation of *BMPL* as not directly tied to commercial policy, tariffs (*OWTI*) have little impact on *BMPL*. However, *BMPL* is associated with big government (*G*) and, most robustly of all, with monetary instability (*GXR*). Both seem highly plausible, to the extent that big government is associated with intervention in the form of currency controls or other distortions in the financial system, and to the extent that exchange risk is driven by expectations of devaluation of the currency.

Regression 19 investigates the determinants of financial depth measured by *LLY*. Financial development is associated with high incomes (*LNY0*). It is also readily apparent that increased investment (*CI*) is strongly associated with increased financial depth. Black-market premia are associated with a greater need for financial services. Trade policy seems to matter, in that tariffs (*OWTI*) are associated with reduced financial depth.[21] There appears to be a negative association between monetary instability (*GXR*) and financial depth, as might be expected given the increased risk in financial markets: this effect offsets the aforementioned influences on *LLY* mediated via *BMPL* possibly due to speculation and arbitrage. Countries with comparative advantage in primary products (*PNXI*) appear to have lower financial depth – much saving and investment in agriculture and other primary sectors is outside the scope of financial intermediaries. In addition, the fertility choice issues noted above imply an asset-accumulation choice in the quality–quantity fertility trade-off: that is, children as assets may substitute for financial assets.

Regression 20, finally, examines the determinants of the relative price of capital. As expected, *LNPIPY* is associated with the presence of distortions at various points in the economy. About one-quarter of any tariff-rate change passes through into relative investment prices, which is unsurprising in that a large share of contemporary investment is in the form of tradeable machinery and equipment. About one-sixth of any change in the black-market premium also passes through to *LNPIPY*. The most robust association, however, is between the broad measure of public finance distortions (G) and the investment price, suggesting that beyond trade and the black-market premium, distortions and government interventions at many levels in the economy are associated with higher investment prices.

Why do growth rates differ?

Table 10.6 tries to confront the question of quantitative, rather than statistical significance. In two exercises I compare the variables involved in the structural regression for three samples: the world beyond the Asia–Pacific Region, the four fast-growing Asia–Pacific NICs (Korea, Taiwan, Singapore and Hong Kong) and the other Asia–Pacific economies. I want to examine the questions: why was the Asia–Pacific Region a fast-growth region relative to the rest of the world? And why, within the Asia–Pacific Region, were the NICs such a fast-growth group relative to the rest of the region? That is, what might explain winners and losers at the international and regional levels?

As noted earlier, it is commonplace to address this question via a reduced-form approach. The merit of a structural approach, however, is that we can dissect the linkages between growth and its determinants more finely. Table 10.6 explores the shifts in the structural equations (Regressions 15–20) for the three samples. To that end, Panel (a) shows the sample means of the variables in each case. The basic finding here is that in almost every dimension, the Asia–Pacific Region enjoys advantages relative to the rest of the world: lower population growth, lower distortions, higher investment rates, a deeper financial structure, higher levels and growth rates of human capital, and so on. Moreover, the NIC

Table 10.6 Sample statistics and growth-rate differences within and outside the Asia–Pacific Region

(a) Sample means of variables

Variables	Non Asia–Pacific	Non-NIC4 Asia–Pacific	NIC4	Non-NIC4 Asia–Pacific minus non Asia–Pacific	NIC4 minus non Asia–Pacific
Asia–Pacific	0	1	1		
NIC4	0	0	1		
GY	0.0121	0.0241	0.0654	0.0121	0.0533
LNY0	6.9727	7.9812	8.3867	1.0084	1.4140
PYR+SYR+0	1.5260	5.5190	5.4259	3.9930	3.8999
POP15+0	0.4598	0.3606	0.3262	−0.0992	−0.1336
POP65+0	0.0331	0.0503	0.0447	0.0172	0.0116
PNQ	0.8000	0.3333	0.0000	−0.8000	−0.4667
BMPL	−0.3971	0.0442	0.0332	−0.3529	−0.3639
OWTI	0.2425	0.1619	0.0565	−0.0806	−0.1860
G	23.3930	16.9702	10.4088	−6.4228	−12.9843
LNPIPY	0.7555	0.2349	0.1406	−0.5206	−0.6149
GXR	0.0155	0.0250	0.0020	0.0095	−0.0135
LLY	0.3652	0.5441	0.5786	0.1790	0.2134
PNXI	0.0320	0.1013	−0.0425	0.0693	−0.0745
P+S	0.7706	1.4550	1.6719	0.6844	0.9013
CI	13.8610	21.9083	27.0525	8.0473	13.1915
GPOP	0.0285	0.0186	0.0157	−0.0099	−0.0128

(b) Growth determinants: non-NIC4 Asia–Pacific versus non-Asia–Pacific

due to:	difference in: CI	GPOP	P+S	BMPL	LLY	LNPIPY
LNY0	−14.1232	0.0012	0.3026	−0.0653	0.0707	
PYR+SYR+0	−4.1722	−0.0030	0.1604	−0.0130	−0.0691	
POP15+0	10.0063		−0.2225			
POP65+0	2.4749		−0.0633			
PNQ	−4.6002	−0.0009	−0.0031	−0.1453	0.0099	
BMPL	8.2208				−0.0278	−0.0584
OWTI	1.0041			0.0036	0.0182	−0.0223
G	0.2616	−0.0004	−0.0452	−0.0681	−0.0143	−0.1405
LNPIPY	8.3962					
GXR	0.0937			0.0045	−0.0020	
LLY	3.3139	−0.0005	−0.0409			
PNXI	−1.2354	0.0016	0.0157	−0.0009	−0.0254	0.0166
P+S	26.8545	−0.0127				
CI		0.0013	0.0723		0.1523	
GPOP	−20.3540		0.3786			
sum explained	16.1411	−0.0135	0.5546	−0.2843	0.1126	−0.2046
actual difference	8.0473	−0.0099	0.6844	−0.3529	0.1790	−0.5206
difference in: GY	0.0276	0.0082	0.0131			

(c) Growth determinants: NIC4 versus non-Asia–Pacific

Variables	CI	GPOP	P+S	BMPL	LLY	LNPIPY
LNY0	−19.8023	0.0017	0.4243	−0.0916	0.0992	
PYR+SYR+0	−4.0749	−0.0029	0.1567	−0.0127	−0.0675	
POP15+0	13.4839		−0.2998			
POP65+0	1.6698		−0.0427			
PNQ	−2.6834	−0.0005	−0.0018	−0.0848	0.0058	
BMPL	8.4778				−0.0287	−0.0602
OWTI	2.3164			0.0084	0.0421	−0.0516
G	0.5289	−0.0009	−0.0913	−0.1376	−0.0289	−0.2840
LNPIPY	9.9179					
GXR	−0.1331			−0.0064	0.0029	
LLY	3.9517	−0.0006	−0.0487			
PNXI	1.3275	−0.0017	−0.0169	0.0009	0.0273	−0.0178
P+S	35.3641	−0.0168				
CI		0.0021	0.1185		0.2497	
GPOP	−26.2901		0.4890			
sum explained	24.0542	−0.0197	0.6871	−0.3237	0.3018	−0.4136
actual difference	13.1915	−0.0128	0.9013	−0.3639	0.2134	−0.6149
difference in:						
GY	0.0411	0.0120	0.0162			

Notes: See text.

group enjoys even more of these advantages than the rest of the Asia–Pacific group, for the most part. Thus, Table 10.6, Panels (b) and (c), employ a natural counterfactual exercise: if we were to impose non-Asia–Pacific characteristics, would all of the growth differentials be eliminated?[22]

Openness, trade and growth

The results for the NICs (Table 10.6, Panel (c)) are quite pleasing. The major sources of high investment in the NICs were labour supply effects (POP15+0), a low dependency rate, distortions (BMPL, OWTI and LNPIPY) and human capital accumulation complementarities, which offset low rates of capital-dilution arising from population growth (GPOP). The major source of low population growth was through endowments; that is, natural resource scarcity (proxied by PNXI). High human capital investment was in turn driven in large part by quality–quantity fertility trade-offs, enough to offset the small cohort of school age. Low black-market premia stemmed principally from small government distortions and a relatively favourable political climate. High financial depth derived mostly from high investment demand. Capital price distortions were driven largely by small government distortions, and a little by black-market and tariff effects.

Overall, the structural shifts (NIC versus non-Asia–Pacific) could explain about a 25 per cent rise in CI, about a 2 per cent drop in $GPOP$ and about a 0.7 rise in $P+S$. In accounting for growth, these effects compound to explain about a 7 per cent difference in growth rates in the two samples, similar in order of magnitude to the actual 5.3 per cent difference. In the final row we see that the major impact on GY is due to investment (CI), accounting for a 4.1 per cent difference in the growth rate; human capital accumulation ($P+S$) accounts for 1.6 per cent and population growth ($GPOP$) 1.2 per cent. Examining the final column (GY) suggests that major sources of fast NIC growth were rapid human capital accumulation ($P+S$) encouraging investment and discouraging population growth, low capital goods prices and black-market premia ($LNPIPY$, $BMPL$) encouraging investment, and low dependency rates ($POP15+0$) also encouraging investment.

Going beyond the reduced form, for the NICs at least, has illuminated something of the workings of the growth mechanism. Openness plays a major role, then, since openness criteria (broadly construed) do matter – distortions in the currency system ($BMPL$), in imported goods ($OWTI$), and especially capital goods ($LNPIPY$) account for many of the difference in growth rates. Unfortunately, this conclusion does not extend so well to the rest of the Asia–Pacific group when it is compared with the world beyond (Table 10.6, Panel (b)). Here the same growth determinants over-explain growth differentials by a large amount.

By this reckoning, the non-NIC parts of the Asia–Pacific Region ought to have been growing almost as fast as the NICs in comparison with the rest of the world, around 5 per cent per annum faster, whereas in reality they only grew about 1.2 per cent per annum faster. This underscores the general measure of our ignorance embedded in so many growth regressions. The unexplained variance remains high – good 'luck' (unexplained residual growth) can matter as much as good policy. We can claim some success in explaining why the Asia–Pacific has been a fast growing region relative to the rest of the world; fathoming what made for winners and losers within the Asia–Pacific Region remains a challenge.

Migration and growth

It remains to be asked whether migration, as a force in population growth, also mattered for economic growth in the region. Table 10.7 sketches an answer to that question, which leans towards rejecting the hypothesis that migration mattered very much for *aggregate* economic growth.[23]

How can we measure the growth impact of migration? A natural counterfactual is to imagine a 'no net migration' scenario in which population growth rates are adjusted by subtracting actual net migration rates. This procedure has been applied in the context of mass migrations in the late-nineteenth century from the Old World to the New to argue that international migration can play a potentially huge role in explaining long-run convergence patterns in the world

Table 10.7   Net migration rates for the Asia–Pacific Region, 1970–90
(% per annum)

	NMRT 1970–90	NMRT/GPOP 1970–90	growth 1970–90	NMRT 1970–75	NMRT 1975–80	NMRT 1980–85	NMRT 1985–90
Australia	0.67	0.43	−0.40	0.53	0.69	0.59	0.85
Hong Kong	0.66	0.36	−0.40	0.74	1.31	0.42	0.18
Indonesia	0.11	0.05	−0.07	0.32	0.11	0.00	0.01
Thailand	0.08	0.04	−0.05	0.34	0.11	0.17	−0.30
Singapore	0.05	0.04	−0.03	0.12	0.09	−0.01	0.00
Japan	0.02	0.02	−0.01	0.07	0.02	0.02	−0.04
Papua New Guinea	0.00	0.00	0.00	−0.01	0.00	0.01	0.00
China	0.00	0.00	0.00	0.01	0.00	0.00	−0.01
New Zealand	−0.02	−0.03	0.02	0.55	−0.71	0.05	0.01
Korea	−0.03	−0.02	0.02	0.01	−0.19	−0.14	0.18
Malaysia	−0.04	−0.01	0.02	−0.15	0.00	0.00	0.01
Solomon Islands	−0.16	−0.05	0.10	−0.42	−0.27	0.05	0.01
Philippines	−0.16	−0.06	0.10	−0.10	−0.21	−0.17	−0.15
Fiji	−0.88	−0.53	0.54	−0.60	−0.83	−0.69	−0.41
Asia–Pacific	0.02	0.01	−0.01	0.10	0.01	0.02	−0.05
NIC3	0.23	0.14	−0.14	0.29	0.40	0.09	0.12

Notes: See text.

economy (Taylor & Williamson 1994). Unfortunately, a similar finding is unlikely to be unearthed in the postwar data, at least here for the Asia–Pacific Region: the net migration rates are simply too low. Only three countries have absolute net migration rates above 2 per thousand – Australia (7 per thousand) and Hong Kong (7) as receivers; Fiji (−4) as a sender (Table 10.7, Column 1). For historical comparison, in the period 1900–10 the following countries all had absolute net migration rates over 2 per thousand – Argentina (25), Australia (14), Brazil (3), Canada (23) and the USA (10) on the receiving side; Belgium (−2), Denmark (−3), Great Britain (−7), Ireland (−8), Italy (−18), the Netherlands (−5), Norway (−7), Portugal (−6), Spain (−7), and Sweden (−4) on the sending side. Furthermore, this was in an era of lower population growth rates.

Thus, post-Second World War experience, in historical perspective, is a period of population growth being driven primarily by natural increase, with migration accounting for a small share. This is certainly the case for the Asia–Pacific Region, with the exception of Australia, Hong Kong and Fiji (Table 10.7, Column 2). Applying the coefficient of Regression 9 to the net migration rates (Table 10.7, Column 3) reveals the weak aggregate growth impact of migration: in absolute size the growth rate impacts are less than 0.06 per cent per annum, with the three exceptions. In the region as a whole, migration had a trivial impact on growth rates (−0.01% per annum).

Overall, integration in international labour markets appears to have mattered much less than integration in other markets – financial and money markets, traded goods markets, capital goods markets, and so on. Yet several concerns and caveats should be aired. First, the migration counterfactual is a partial equilibrium exercise. As Taylor and Williamson (1994) argued, when capital is free to chase labour, then the impact of immigration on growth is muted. This would serve to downplay the impact of migration even more. Second, the counterfactual assumes no change in population growth rates: any Walker effect or similar feedback mechanism could also diminish the impact of migration on growth, another bias in the downward direction. Third, can we infer that free migration would have scarcely any growth impact? Probably not: the Lucas critique warns that any change in migration policy would certainly entail different migration responses. Fourth, even if migration mattered little for aggregate economic growth, it likely mattered a great deal for income distribution, the relative incomes of different groups, the returns to different skills and the wages in different occupations; such effects can never be captured in the aggregative empirical growth framework adopted here.

Conclusion

This study has attempted to distil the key content of the empirical growth literature relevant to the question of how openness, trade and migration have affected growth and convergence in the Asia–Pacific Region. I surveyed a large body of impressive work, yet found the conventional reduced-form approaches wanting in terms of insight into precise growth mechanisms. Instead I added a structural approach to estimating the components of the dynamic system of economic growth. This shed some light on the mechanics of economic growth in the Asia–Pacific Region. To summarise:

- Relatively high investment rates were the key to high growth rates in the region, contributing several percentage points to the predicted growth rate. Of lesser order were gains due to human capital accumulation and low population growth. These findings complement direct growth accounting analysis.
- The main cause of high investment rates, in turn, appeared to be human capital complementarities, a low dependency rate, and low distortions. The role of distortions underscores the importance of openness for growth, but should be broadly construed to include commercial, financial and monetary policies.
- Much of investment in the developing economies takes the form of imported capital goods, so the high-investment environment might properly be termed 'import-led' growth. Of course trade balance constraints then entail the

export–growth correlation that has received far more, yet possibly misplaced, attention.
- Little support could be found for the hypotheses that financial depth or
natural resource endowments affected growth, though both were statistically
significant as determinants of several structural equations. For example,
Asia–Pacific's financial depth did augment investment rates considerably.
Natural resource scarcity in the region also appeared to reduce investment,
raise population growth and inhibit financial development, but only by
small amounts.
- All the same, good luck seems to matter in addition to good policy. The
NICs appear to have superior growth performance, as predicted. Yet the rest
of the Asia–Pacific Region disappoints in that its actual growth rate is far
below that predicted.

In an era of relatively restricted migration, it is unsurprising that migration
played little part as a determinant of growth and convergence. The postwar era
stands in marked contrast to the pre-First World War period of free, mass
migrations. Despite such caveats, openness and integration in other markets may
be a partial substitute for labour mobility. The results provide no guide to the
possibly rapid convergence that might ensue should a free migration policy be
adopted.

Notes

1 Notable empirical contributions in this vein have come from Dowrick and Nguyen
(1989) and Mankiw, Romer and Weil (1992), two papers firmly in the Solovian
tradition.
2 Data sources and descriptions are available from the author upon request.
3 Such effects can be a manifestation of the advantages of backwardness and a cause of
technological catching-up (Gerschenkron 1962, Abramovitz 1986). A negative coefficient implies mean reversion in the sample, termed β-convergence (Barro & Sala-
i-Martin 1992). The β-convergence is neither a necessary nor sufficient condition for
s-convergence, the tendency of sample dispersion to diminish. The β-convergence
hypothesis is not unproblematic – sample selection bias and errors-in-variables can
encourage false acceptance (Abramovitz 1986, De Long 1988).
4 Several models suggest that transitional dynamics depend critically on the initial
endowments of physical and human capital (Uzawa 1965, Lucas 1988, Caballe
& Santos 1993, Mulligan & Sala-i-Martin 1993, Barro & Sala-i-Martin 1995,
Chapter 5). Controls of this form appear in empirical studies of conditional convergence (Barro 1991, Mankiw, Romer & Weil 1992, Barro & Sala-i-Martin 1995,
Chapter 12). Measurement problems are serious: the international comparison of
schooling is fraught with quality incomparabilities.
5 The caveats applied to the measurement of initial stocks of human capital also apply
here.

6   Investment has repeatedly been found to have a significant positive association with growth (Kormendi & Meguire 1985, Dowrick & Nguyen 1989, Barro 1991, Mankiw, Romer & Weil 1992). This is one of the most robust results in the literature (Levine & Renelt 1992).

7   By definition this variable is the sum of the rates of natural increase and net immigration rate, both of which may be modelled. Models of migration usually posit a positive relation between level of income per capita and the rate of migration. Models of fertility choice may have a non-monotonic relationship depending on the costs of children and their value as 'normal goods' (Barro & Sala-i-Martin 1995, Chapter 9); interactions with human capital may give rise to multiple equilibria, as with a quality–quantity trade-off in family size (Becker & Barro 1988, Becker, Murphy & Tamura 1988).

8   The use of a control for resource abundance is suggested by Sachs and Warner (1994, 1995). Their measure differs in that they use gross exports (not net), and normalise relative to total exports (not GDP). Dynamic comparative advantage suggests that externalities may give growth and welfare advantages to countries which specialise in manufacturing (Ethier 1982b, Krugman 1987, Young 1991, Matsuyama 1992).

9   On the labour supply effect, there is a robust cross-country partial correlation between the 'labour content' of the population (e.g., share aged from 15 to 64) and investment ratios, even after controlling for price distortions and other determinants of investment (Brander & Dowrick 1994, Taylor 1994a).

10 The best known model is that of Barro, which has some empirical support (Barro 1990, 1991). However, the overall association of fiscal variables and growth, both direct and via the investment channel, remains fragile (Levine & Renelt 1992, Easterly & Rebelo 1993).

11 Political variables have been constructed and widely used by Barro and his collaborators (Barro 1991, Barro & Lee 1994, Barro & Sala-i-Martin 1995). However, the significance and robustness of their role as explanators of growth performance remains controversial (Levine & Renelt 1992).

12 The robust negative correlation of investment prices and quantities has been seen as confirmation of a downward-sloping investment demand curve, and as the likely channel through which many price distortions affect growth (Jones 1992, Brander & Dowrick 1994, Taylor 1994a, 1994b). The impact of distortions on economic growth is widely reported (Agarwala 1983, Edwards 1992, Easterly 1993, Edwards 1993).

13 This is an alternative price distortion variable also used in empirical growth analysis (Barro & Sala-i-Martin 1995, Chapter 12). However, it likely has different properties than the relative price of capital, being more linked to monetary distortions.

14 Yet another measure of price distortions, which might plausibly affect the relative price of capital, and hence investment, as noted above (Jones 1992, Barro & Sala-i-Martin 1995, Chapter 12).

15 Other studies have used the rate of domestic inflation as a proxy for monetary instability and financial repression (Kormendi & Meguire 1985, De Gregorio 1992, Roubini & Sala-i-Martin 1992).

16 Various authors have stressed the importance of financial intermediation for growth (Gurley & Shaw 1955, Davis 1963, McKinnon 1973, Shaw 1973). Such insights can be readily incorporated into endogenous growth models (Greenwood & Jovanovic

1990, Bencivenga & Smith 1991). Recent empirical work has sought to capture these effects (King & Levine 1993a, 1993b).

17   Sachs and Warner work with a single cross-section 1970–89. In the present case, I utilise their definitions of qualifying countries (ONQ=1 and PNQ=1) and consider all other countries to be non-qualifiers (Sachs and Warner omit several countries with insufficient data).

18   As instruments I use the lagged initial values (1965–69) of the endogenous variables. These are 'good' instruments to the extent that the explanators have more persistence across time than does the explicandum, the rate of growth itself, which seems to be the case (Easterly et al. 1993).

19   This is no surprise since the fit of 14 is so much worse – the asymptotic gains of the 2SLS estimator are not seen, and the efficient estimator is OLS. Simultaneity bias appears insignificant using the standard Hausman test (Pindyck & Rubinfeld 1981, pp. 303–4). Endogenous variables are denoted with a †.

20   All six of these regressions were estimated with 2SLS, and Hausman simultaneity tests were employed to eliminate all except the significantly endogenous right-hand side variables (denoted †).

21   It is not clear what the mechanism might be, except to say that throughout economic history financial development has almost always flourished first amongst the mercantile and commercial sectors of any economy, so that a dynamic effect of trade on financial development seems plausible.

22   This exercise is done at the level of the structural equations, where the first six columns assess the shift in an endogenous control variable (CI, $GPOP$, $P+S$, $BMPL$, LLY, $LNPIPY$) as a function of its determinants. The final column assess the growth impact using the shifts in factor accumulation given by the first three columns, and using the coefficient estimates of the Asia–Pacific structural growth equation (Regression 9).

23   This table exploits the United Nations data on population growth and natural increase to impute net migration rates (United Nations 1993). Note that data on Taiwan are not included in the UN records, hence we relabel NIC4 as NIC3 in the following discussion.

11

The Impact of Immigration on Incomes in the Destination Country

William Foster

Like other parts of the world, the Asia–Pacific Region has seen increasing movements of people across international boundaries in recent years. The economic implications of such movements are of obvious interest to the countries concerned, and the present chapter explores some of these implications specifically from the perspective of the receiving country. Within the region, the economic effects of immigration have a special relevance for traditional destination countries such as Australia, Canada, New Zealand and the USA, which indeed continue to account for the greater part of the world's permanent immigration. But they are of growing interest too for 'newer' destinations such as Japan, Singapore and Taiwan, which have also experienced significant net population inflows in recent times.

The economics of immigration is a broad and complex field, however, and despite recent advances in international research there remain many gaps in overall understanding of the topic. The complications arise fundamentally from the nature of immigration itself, since in adding to population, it necessarily affects every area of human activity, and thus every aspect of the destination economy. On the demand side, it affects household spending, business investment and government expenditure; on the supply side, it affects the economy's production of goods and services through the labour, skills and capital funds brought by immigrants to their new country. Its overall impact on the destination-country economy follows from the interaction of all these various demand- and supply-side effects. Thus the extent to which the economy expands with immigration, and the impact on particular industries, are determined by all these factors. So too are the outcomes for traditional economic indicators relating to inflation and unemployment, domestic incomes, the domestic budget and the balance of payments.

The present chapter addresses one aspect of immigration's economic impact – its long-term effect on destination-country incomes. To most observers, this perspective indeed provides the best basis for summarising the economic consequences of immigration. Both welfare dimensions of income – its level and its distribution – are considered in the following discussion of issues and research results. The chapter's key questions are thus how immigration might affect the average level of income, or 'living standards' of the destination country, and how it might affect the destination country's distribution of income between groups and across individuals.

The chapter focuses almost entirely on the effects of permanent immigration. This is not to deny the growing importance of temporary movements in the Asia–Pacific Region, but the available research has tended to focus on the economic effects of permanent movement, and the present discussion reflects that emphasis. Nonetheless, some possible implications for temporary movement are considered briefly at the end of the chapter.

The chapter also focuses specifically on the long-term effects of immigration. In general, the economic contribution and impact of a given intake vary according to time since arrival, so that the economic consequences of any change in magnitude or composition of permanent immigration will also vary with time. Intakes are not immediately integrated into the broader economy, and their economic contributions necessarily change with integration. Furthermore the economy itself takes time to adjust as industry and infrastructure investment associated with a given intake proceeds. The longer-term perspective allows these various adjustments to work themselves through, with any income effects reflecting the full interaction of immigration and broader economy.

The discussion of immigration's income effects is punctuated with recent data and research findings from various countries. These relate mainly to Australia – with which the author is most familiar – but immigration and research perspectives from Canada, New Zealand and the USA are also incorporated where appropriate. The discussion is essentially descriptive and does not pretend to be a rigorous or exhaustive survey of all the issues and research; although some individual studies are mentioned, much of the broader research comment is indeed presented without specific reference. This more general level of discussion in fact draws on several major projects and economic research surveys completed recently for each of the above countries. These include Wooden (1994), and Foster and Baker (1991) for Australia; Employment and Immigration Canada (1989) and Swan et al. (1991) for Canada; Poot, Nana and Philpott (1988) for New Zealand; and Papademetriou et al. (1989), Borjas (1994), and Greenwood and McDowell (1994) for the USA. More detailed treatments of issues and research mentioned here can be found in those reports.

The chapter has three parts. Section I focuses on the possible consequences of immigration for average income in the destination country, while Section II considers some distributional aspects of immigration, both between different population sub-groups and across the whole population. Section III draws the discussion together within the Asia–Pacific context, and raises some broad policy implications.

I Immigration and average income

In considering how immigration might influence average destination-country income over the longer term, it is useful to adopt a simple production framework with two inputs – labour and capital – in the spirit of, for example, Lloyd (1982). From this perspective, various possible channels of influence between immigration and the long-term result for output per capita become apparent, and so also between immigration and the latter's national accounting equivalent – average income.

First, immigration might influence output per capita through changing the amounts of labour and capital per head of population entering the production process. These amounts in turn depend on the quantities of labour and capital available for production, the quality of that labour and capital (which governs the 'effective' quantity), and the extent to which available labour and capital inputs are actually utilised for production. Immigration might thus influence average income through each of these channels. Otherwise, immigration might also affect average income through economies or diseconomies of scale in production arising from expanded population and market size, and through any impact immigration might have on the prevailing state of production technology.

These channels of possible influence are considered now in turn. In practice, however, there can be considerable overlap between different aspects. It is not easy to distinguish, for example, between the effect of immigration on the quality of capital and its effect on the prevailing state of technology. The factors can also interact, so that change to prevailing technology might lead to change in the scope and extent of scale effects, while the latter will also depend on the extent to which labour and capital input amounts move together.

Empirical difficulties indeed abound in any attempt to allocate temporal or regional differences in observed per capita output – or average income – among the various factors outlined above. In Australia, for example, Withers (1988) has utilised statistical causality analysis to detect a significant, albeit small, positive association between net immigration and subsequent per capita output for that country. This result, together with findings from other econometric studies, has contributed to a broadly accepted view that immigration has exerted a small but positive influence on Australia's average income. However, research has been unable to satisfactorily resolve the follow-up question – of what the precise roles and relative strengths of the various factors outlined above might be in generating that positive outcome. Separate consideration of each aspect can provide useful insights, nonetheless, both for the Australian case and more generally.

Quantity and quality of labour

Immigration would affect the population-wide quantity of labour per head available for employment if it led to change in the overall labour force participation rate and/or average number of hours offered for work. It would affect the quality of labour input if it led to change in the average skill level of those working within the destination economy.

Two ways should be distinguished in which immigration might influence the population-wide levels of labour force participation, hours offered or skills. One is through the relevant characteristic of the immigrant group differing from that of the non-immigrant population; the other is through immigration itself inducing change in that characteristic among non-immigrants. Without the latter type of interaction, higher aggregate labour force participation, for example, among immigrants (reflecting the combined effects of age profile and age-specific participation rates) or higher levels of hours offered, or higher skills, would tend to have a positive effect on average income. However, if non-immigrant labour force participation, hours offered, or skills, were at the same time pressured downwards by immigration, then the overall effect on average income would be unclear.

Empirical guidance on the effect of immigration on labour availability is partial and inconclusive. For example, while recent data for Australia indicate that intended labour force participation among new immigrants to that country is generally close to prevailing participation levels among non-immigrants, the longer-term effect will still depend on the extent to which these intentions are realised after arrival. Indeed the labour force participation rate of the foreign-born in Australia has for some years been below the national rate, though the foreign-born are also more likely than average to be in full-time employment (aggregate-level observations such as these are also available for other countries, such as Canada and New Zealand). However, ageing and cohort effects, as well as any possible interaction between immigration and non-immigrant labour market behaviour – on which the literature has little to contribute – mean that such aggregate birthplace comparisons should be treated with caution in assessing the long-term effects of immigration on population-wide labour availability. Overall, it is difficult to reach practical conclusions on the income effects of immigration through this channel.

Turning to skills, it should be noted that for present purposes the relevant notion of skill incorporates more than specific educational qualifications and occupational abilities. Importantly in the immigration context, it also includes destination-country language skills; importantly in the trade context, it also includes foreign-language and cultural skills that might assist with export and import activities. As well, less tangible personal characteristics such as leadership, judgement, ingenuity, creativity and communication skills are included, together with what are more generally seen as 'entrepreneurial' skills. It is often suggested that immigrants bring above-average endowments of these less tangible aspects through the self-selection process implicit in the act of migration; however, that very intangibility makes such a proposition difficult to test.

It should also be noted that the relevant skill contribution from immigration is that applying in the longer term, after any short- to medium-term labour market adjustment by immigrants has taken place. This perspective takes account of skill transfer problems, whereby non-recognition of foreign-based qualifications or language difficulties can lead to some newcomers working – even in the longer term – in lower-skilled occupations than their pre-immigration backgrounds would suggest. It also takes account of the possibility that some immigrants upgrade their skills both formally and informally in their early years after arrival.

In Australia, skill indices based on the occupations nominated by immigrants on entry suggest that intake skills steadily increased through the post-war period. Moreover – even allowing for subsequent downgrading, or upgrading, of reported skills – the immigrant skill level would appear to have consistently exceeded that of non-immigrants over the period, though recent indications are that the difference is now very small. Supporting evidence for at least some margin in favour of immigrant skills is provided by a higher proportion of foreign-born adults in Australia having post-school qualifications than for the Australia-born, with recent immigrants having the highest proportion of all. Similar relativities apply in Canada for the proportion of persons with university education. In the USA, however, whose immigration program has not placed the same emphasis on skills as an entry criterion as have programs in Australia and Canada, the evidence suggests that immigrant skill levels have declined over recent decades; the average years of schooling of immigrants, for example, has fallen below the comparable figure for non-immigrants in that country.

In contrast to labour force participation and hours, the possibilities of interaction whereby immigration influences non-immigrant skill levels have been seen as real by many observers. Two main arguments have been put. One is that any tendency by government or employers towards reliance on immigrant skills might inhibit the development of comparable skills among non-immigrants through a reduced commitment to the domestic education and training system. Recent empirical evidence from Australia (Baker and Wooden 1991), however, suggests that the amount of training undertaken by non-immigrants is not significantly affected by the presence of skilled immigrants. Indeed, limited support for the second view – that immigration might in fact raise the skill levels of non-immigrants through both formal and informal training processes that would not occur in the absence of the relevant immigrants – has also been detected (Stromback et al. 1993).

Overall, the evidence suggests that immigrant skills may have had a positive influence on the average level of income in Australia over the postwar period, and perhaps also in Canada. In recent decades in the USA, however, this possibility would appear much less likely; indeed one could speculate from the evidence that the opposite effect might have latterly prevailed.

Quantity and quality of capital

As noted, immigration could also affect average income by changing the amount of capital per person entering into the overall production process, or by changing the 'quality' of that capital. The empirical literature provides little quantitative guidance on the possible long-term effects of immigration on these aspects. However, concerns are sometimes raised in broader debate on the short- to medium-term effects of immigration on both quantity per head and quality of capital, and these arguments are noted here, even though they are of perhaps limited relevance in the present longer-term context.

One concern focuses on the size of investment required to sustain the pre-immigration ratio of capital per person. In considering the amount of extra capital implied by the application of the prevailing ratio to a given intake, however, it should be recognised that the associated investment will take place over time, with the immigrants' own savings, taxes and other economic contributions – together with those of earlier intakes – playing a growing role as they integrate into the broader economy. Thus to the extent that the average amount of funds brought by immigrants does not match the prevailing level of capital per head, the population-wide ratio will fall in the immediate period after a given intake's arrival. But it will rise again as the investment generated by that intake proceeds. Australian research suggests that investment per capita does respond to immigration. The key question for present purposes is whether the long-term outcome for the ratio differs significantly from the level that would have been achieved in the absence of immigration.

This issue is unresolved empirically, though the data for Australia indicate that capital per person has risen steadily in that country through recent decades of generally strong but often fluctuating rates of immigration. The emphasis in Australia has, in fact, tended to be less on concern for the long-term effects on capital per person and rather more for the extent to which the domestic investment required to sustain the ratio is met from foreign sources. The capital funds brought by immigrants will presumably influence the latter outcome, and also the rate at which the ratio adjusts; there is no clear evidence, however, on the extent of any positive effect of immigrant funds on the ratio's final level.

The associated concern on quality of capital has been that, with immigration, available resources for investment are used to provide newcomers with their appropriate 'portion' of industry and infrastructure capital, rather than to increase capital per person for the existing population (capital 'widening' rather than 'deepening'). More specifically, the housing and infrastructure content in immigration-induced investment, of most relevance in the early period after arrival, is regarded as a relatively unproductive use of resources. But any such apparent lowering in quality of overall capital is, again, a temporary phenomenon. As investment proceeds, a return to the pre-immigration balance between housing and infrastructure capital on the one hand, and industry capital on the other, would be expected. There is again little empirical evidence on how immigration might affect the ratio between these two types of capital over the longer term; aggregate Australian data, however, indicate that the ratio has remained broadly steady over recent decades.

But a further point regarding the long-term quality of capital should also be recognised. To the extent that the investment generated by immigration embodies newer technologies than those within the pre-immigration capital stock, the overall quality of both industry and infrastructure capital will be enhanced. This argument is indeed sufficient for many observers to conclude that immigration does have a clearly positive effect on the quality of capital and technology in the destination country.

Utilisation of available inputs

The distinction between the amounts of labour and capital available for the production process, and the amounts actually used, should now be addressed. For present purposes, the combined effect of any change in the degree of utilisation of both labour and capital is taken to be reflected by change in the aggregate unemployment rate. On this basis, immigration's effect on average income would also depend on its effect on the prevailing unemployment rate.

Empirical research from several countries indicates that immigration does not, in fact, have any long-term effect on the aggregate unemployment rate. In Australia, this neutrality conclusion is based on results from a series of recent econometric studies, which find no statistically significant long-term influence of immigration on the national unemployment rate through the post-war period, and indeed earlier. Statistical neutrality is also found in the influence of immigration on wages and inflation. In Canada and New Zealand, econometric tests have led to the same conclusion for immigration's effect on the aggregate unemployment rate.

In the USA, research has focused more on employment and earnings effects for particular industries, regions or groups of workers, rather than for aggregate-level indicators such as the national unemployment rate. This work finds that the effects can indeed run in either direction, but are typically very small. In this context, a recent divergence of opinion on how these disaggregated results might transfer to the aggregate level should be noted. One view has it that because the effects are small and specific to areas and industries of relatively high immigrant presence, the possibility that immigration has significant consequences for earnings or unemployment across the whole economy can be effectively discounted (Papademetriou et al. 1989). The alternative view stresses the sectoral and geographical mobility of non-immigrants; it suggests that the full labour market significance of immigration for non-immigrants is understated due to this mobility, which has the effect of spreading at least some part of any impact to other parts of the economy (Borjas 1994).

Scale effects

The prospect for scale economies or diseconomies with immigration will clearly depend on the size and other characteristics of the economy concerned. The outcome will also depend on the location of the extra population brought about by immigration, and on the extent to which new producers enter particular industries in response to increased market size. Effective scale change can occur without population growth through the natural evolution or policy-induced rationalisation of existing industry patterns, but immigration can act as a catalyst for these processes in its effect on population distribution. And immigration-induced population change can still be relevant to producers of traded goods, for whom export penetration might provide the more obvious potential for market expansion; domestic scale economies, for example, could lower the costs of production of inputs for export goods, and in this and other ways provide a 'launching pad' of locally realised efficiency gains to enhance the effect of subsequent export expansion.

For Australia, there is little rigorous evidence on current direction and extent of scale effects, although recent syntheses of a diverse range of industry-specific estimates suggest that moderate economies do apply across industry in general. Similar syntheses in New Zealand and Canada suggest that mild scale economies currently prevail in those countries too. For the USA, some observers suggest that scale effects may continue to apply to at least some extent for some industries in some regions, but there is also a strong view among economic historians that available economies had in fact been fully exploited in that country by early in the present century.

It can be noted that the corollary of the last point indeed provides some indirect support for the possibility of contemporary scale economies within the other countries mentioned. Even if scale economies did cease to apply by the turn of the century in the USA, the population of that country say 120 years ago – when economies presumably still did have effect – remains considerably larger than, for example, Canada's today. In turn, the Canadian conclusion of small, positive returns to scale might also be seen as support for the same possibility in less populous countries of comparable socio-economic structure and characteristics, such as Australia and New Zealand.

State of technology

Several channels can be identified through which immigration might influence the destination country's technological and managerial sophistication. For example, by increasing the population, immigration increases the number of technologically gifted people, and so the likelihood of important technological breakthroughs. At the same time, a higher population is likely to better support a research and development infrastructure. Immigrants might bring with them a special propensity for technological inventiveness; more directly, they might bring knowledge that can be immediately applied to transform industrial techniques. It is more difficult to see how immigration could realistically inhibit the destination country's rate of technological development, though it is some-times argued that reliance on low-skill, low-wage immigrant labour could retard the adoption of more technically advanced capital-intensive methods of produc-tion. Again, however, there is a lack of empirical evidence, one way or the other.

II Distributional issues

Immigration's effect on average income in the destination country summarises a range of potentially very different individual experiences, and how the overall effect is distributed between groups and across the whole population raises interesting and important questions. However, given that a great many distribu-tional outcomes can be consistent with a given average income result, the distributional effects of immigration bring further levels of complexity to research and empirical analysis, though guiding principles do apply on some issues. Several distributional aspects are considered briefly now, starting with the special dichotomy of immigrants and non-immigrants. The key issue here con-cerns the manner in which immigration's overall income effect is accounted for between the two groups, and in particular how income within the non-immigrant sub-population is affected by immigration. Other issues touched on in this section include the distribution of overall effects between labour and capital, the distributional implications for different skill and industry groups, and the effect of immigration on the population-wide income distribution.

Immigrants and non-immigrants

The way in which the overall income effect is distributed between immigrant and non-immigrant sub-groups will vary across the different channels of influ-ence of immigration. For example, to the extent that skills are reflected in individual incomes – as the international evidence suggests is very often the case – then any effect of immigrant skills on the overall income average would be confined to the immigrants themselves, with correspondingly less of an impact on non-immigrants. On the other hand, income effects realised through scale change would tend not to distinguish between immigrants and non-immigrants in the same way; if immigration raised the overall average income through scale economies, non-immigrants would share in that benefit with immigrants. Ele-ments of both perspectives are likely to apply to the possible effects of immigra-tion on the state of technology. An immigrant directly contributing to some technological advance might be rewarded with at least part of the associated income gain, but the benefits would also be more widely shared to the extent that the advance is adopted throughout the broader economy.

The overall distribution of any income effect between the two groups would then depend upon the relative strengths of these various factors. Thus if immi-gration's income effect was due essentially to scale change, the effect should be more broadly distributed between immigrants and non-immigrants than if it was mainly attributable to skill differences between the two groups. The issue would be complicated if, for example, immigration affected the skill level of non-immigrants and thus their incomes. If immigration had a dampening effect on domestic skills development, it would pressure non-immigrant incomes below the levels they might otherwise achieve; if it tended to raise non-immigrant skills, perhaps through workplace skill transfers, it would have a positive effect on non-immigrant incomes. As noted earlier, Australian research can find no strong evidence of such interactions in either direction.

It is clear from the above that, in general, immigration's effect on the average income of the whole population will differ from that for just the non-immigrants. The latter's average might remain unchanged from its pre-immigration level, for example, but the introduction of higher- or lower-skilled immigrants would influence the population-wide average in the corresponding direction. If scale economies or technology effects tended to lift the incomes of non-immigrants, the overall result could still be negative if immigrant skills lay sufficiently below those of non-immigrants. One's judgment of the effect of immigration on destination-country incomes can thus depend on which average – that for the whole population, or that for just the non-immigrants – is chosen as the basis for comparison.

Labour and capital

Under the basic Berry–Soligo (1969) framework for assessing the short-term effects of immigration, an overall gain in destination-country income is realised through a lift in production accompanying a real-wage fall brought about by increased labour supply with immigration. The holders of capital experience a rise in average income under this formulation, in contrast to wage earners, with immigration thereby generating a clear shift in the share of destination-country income from labour to capital.

However, this result is based on a relatively simple short-term model. The issue becomes more complicated – and the outcome less clear for the real wage, for average income, and for any income shift – in the longer-term when capital stock adjustment and the full range of immigration's long-run effects are in play. Taking government and external sectors into account adds further to the uncertainty, with foreign ownership of capital, for example, allowing the possibility of income transfers from domestic wage earners to foreign holders of capital (the latter point also stressing the relevance for empirical analysis of the distinction between different output indicators, such as gross domestic product and gross national product).

There has been little direct empirical research on immigration's distributional effects between labour and capital, though some indirect evidence is available. For example, if immigration has no effect on the real wage but does tend to increase output per capita – as the Australian econometric results suggest

– a transfer of income from wage earners to the holders of capital (and land) could be inferred. This is indeed reflected in results from long-term applications of the ORANI model in Australia (for example, Centre for International Economics 1990). Geary and O'Grada's (1985) long-period analysis for the USA found that the real wage in that country has in fact been pressured downwards by immigration, which would have similar – perhaps stronger – distributional implications as in Australia, depending again on immigration's accompanying effect on overall incomes.

Skill and industry groups

The short-term result noted above can be extended to the situation in which labour is divided into high-skill and low-skill components. It can be shown that immigration weighted towards one or other skill type leads to reduced average earnings for non-immigrants in the same skill category. Predominantly low-skill immigration thus pressures down the average earnings of low-skill non-immigrants, but positively affects the incomes of both high-skill non-immigrants and the holders of capital. Again, the actual result over the longer term is complicated by many other factors – including, for example, the possibilities of skills downgrading or upgrading over time – and the overall outcome inevitably requires empirical investigation.

The effect of low-skill immigration on the earnings and employment of various non-immigrant groups has indeed been a prime focus of empirical research in the USA in recent years. A range of studies has assessed the effects of specifically low-skill immigration on both low-skill and higher-skill non-immigrants, within particular industries and occupations, and more generally. The basic conclusion from this research – that there are often discernible, but invariably small, effects of low-skill immigration on the earnings and employment of non-immigrants, and indeed earlier immigrants – suggests that any localised distributional effects, at least, would also be small.

Overall income distribution

The effect of immigration on the population-wide distribution of individual incomes has its own importance, given the significance accorded income inequality as an indicator of socio-economic welfare. Again, both direct and interactive elements can be distinguished. The direct effect would arise through the pattern of immigrant incomes differing from that for non-immigrants; interactive effects would arise through the non-immigrant pattern itself changing with immigration. To the extent that employment incomes reflect skills, for example, a direct effect would follow from any difference in the pattern of immigrant and non-immigrant skills; an interactive effect would follow, however, if immigration affected the skill levels, and therefore incomes, of non-immigrant workers in some industry sectors more than in others. Beyond this possibility, interactive effects associated with other influences of immigration –

such as those on scale or technology – might also affect the overall income spread across particular industries, or the spread of incomes across asset holders, or indeed the balance between earnings and asset incomes for particular individuals.

The research technique best equipped to take account of and assess the practical significance of such complications in long-term distributional analysis is microsimulation. Under this approach, separate households, families, 'income units' or persons from a large unit-record database are individually processed in ways appropriate to the required analysis so that a 'new' data set is generated, whose distributional and other characteristics can be compared with those corresponding either to the original database or to some other scenario prepared in a similar way. It is an approach that enables structural, behavioural and accumulation processes to be incorporated explicitly and relatively easily into long-term distributional analysis.

A recent assessment of the effects of immigration on one destination country's income distribution using microsimulation was undertaken for Australia by Saunders and King (1994). They effectively constructed the income distribution that would have prevailed in Australia in 1990 had there been no immigration to that country from 1982. Appropriate adjustments were made to individuals in the original database so that its age and labour force profile conformed to results from a preliminary macroeconomic model run undertaken with a zero-immigration scenario; relative income levels of database members were also adjusted on the basis of the macroeconomic results. Despite these adjustments, the degree of inequality within the resulting distribution, for both gross and disposable income, was found to be virtually identical to that for the comparison scenario in which immigration proceeded at its actual levels through the 1980s. The effect of immigration on Australia's income distribution over the period was indeed found to be very much smaller than that of contemporaneous 'non-immigration' factors, such as changes in labour force participation, in demographic and labour force structure, in the dispersion of wage and salary incomes, in the social security system, and in the income tax system.

This finding of effective neutrality in the impact of immigration on Australia's income inequality is echoed in recent data indicating a close similarity between the foreign-born and non-immigrant income distributions within that country. The foreign-born and non-immigrant income distributions are also very close in Canada, but are much less so in the USA.

III Remarks

This chapter has considered a number of issues and findings relevant to immigration's effect on destination-country income. In drawing the discussion together within the Asia–Pacific context, it is useful first to note some implications for other population movements – in particular, emigration and temporary movement. Thus, the obvious parallels between many aspects of immigration and emigration mean that much of the chapter's discussion will be relevant also to the income effects for origin countries, as well as to the effects of permanent departures from essentially 'immigrant' countries; in this sense, the main discussion should indeed be read in terms of the income effects of net – rather than gross – permanent immigration.

The chapter's framework of channels through which permanent immigration might influence destination-country income can then be applied to the longer-term effects of a continuing presence of temporary entrants. For example, to the extent that net temporary movement adds to the number of people in a country at any time, the possibility of scale effects will arise. Any consequent industry effects would, however, be likely to vary according to the basis of that population change; the effects of, say, tourists on particular product and service markets would not, in general, coincide with those of temporary workers. The demands of temporary entrants in such markets will also generate industry-specific investment, which will have a positive effect on average income of the resident population to the extent that it increases capital per person for that group, while also raising the quality of capital; again, the spending characteristics of different types of temporary entrants will lead to potentially different income effects.

Temporary labour movement will tend to positively influence average income through lifting the ratio of labour per person in the destination country and increasing the utilisation of national resources. Temporary workers will also influence average income through their effect on the population-wide skill level, depending on their particular skill profile. As well as augmenting local skills, higher-skill temporary workers could generate income gains through influencing the state of technology; on the other hand, to the extent that low-skill temporary workers substitute for the introduction of more capital-intensive methods, such movement might retard technological change.

Overall, despite significant gaps in theoretical and empirical understanding of the economic effects of both permanent and temporary movement, it remains possible to draw some useful implications on immigration's practical income effects for Asia–Pacific countries. Most fundamentally, it is clear that the simple – if perhaps dissatisfying – answer to the chapter's key question of immigration's effect on destination-country income is that it depends on the immigration and it depends on the country. Certain points have a general relevance, but the issue can only be satisfactorily resolved – for Asia–Pacific countries, as for others – through considering information and empirical research specific to the country concerned.

Australia, for example, is a country of relatively small population whose immigrants are relatively highly skilled. As noted, econometric analysis indicates that permanent immigration has had a small, positive effect on average income in that country, and a neutral effect on overall income inequality. From the discussion, a number of influences of immigration – including on skills, scale and technology – could realistically contribute to the positive effect on average income, though the available research is unable to adequately assign relative orders of magnitude. The extent to which non-immigrant incomes in Australia are affected by immigration is thus also unclear since it depends on the relative importance of these factors. Similar considerations would apply to comparable small- to medium-population countries which too emphasise intake skills, such as Canada and New Zealand. The likely effect of immigration on population-wide skills, scale and technology in these countries suggests a positive average income effect for them as well.

The situation for other countries can be assessed in similar broad fashion. In the USA, for example, where the likelihood of scale economies is much less, and where relatively low-skill immigration has been more the case, the general outcome would appear less favourable than for the other traditional destination countries. With a conceivably negative impact of immigrant skills on average income, and with little or no contribution from scale, it is possible that the prevailing income effect of immigration in that country could be neutral for non-immigrants, and negative overall. In Singapore, a more recent destination country, in which permanent immigration of skilled and professional workers is encouraged while low-skill immigrant workers are allowed only on a temporary basis, such factors as the skills of the permanent immigrants and the role of the temporary entrants in meeting labour shortages would be positive influences on average income. At the same time, however, differential movements in the earnings of high- and lower-skill workers attributed to the effects of immigration would suggest that income inequality has increased in Singapore over recent years.

Finally, some basic implications for permanent immigration policy can be noted. First, if the policy aim is for such immigration to raise the whole population's average income over the longer term, then it is possible to tailor an immigration policy to increase the chances of doing so. Ideally, such a policy would focus on young immigrants with high skills, high levels of accompanying funds, and high propensities for continuing labour force participation. In practice, the actual composition of a country's intake is the outcome of a range of policy priorities and other factors beyond the policy-maker's control. Nonetheless, any emphasis that can be placed on these characteristics – such as through a points system for entry within particular visa categories, as currently applies in Australia and Canada – would provide benefit.

If the policy concern is with just the non-immigrant average, however, the focus on skills, funds and participation will be less relevant. Non-immigrants will gain from higher immigrant skills only to the extent that spillover effects transmit the benefits of those skills into the broader economy. From the non-immigrant perspective, the emphasis will be more on the wider-spreading effects, such as enhanced quality of capital, technology and scale economies. These effects may still be more likely with a higher-skill policy – through gifted immigrants' contributions to the broader state of technology, for example – but their relevance clearly depends much less on intake composition.

But whichever perspective applies, there are further implications for policy-makers in the magnitudes of the various income effects. The empirical evidence from studies of permanent immigration in the traditional destination countries invariably indicates that these effects are small. Perhaps this should not surprise, given that immigrants tend not to be too different from non-immigrants, overall, in skills and other characteristics, and that immigration typically adds only a very small proportion of extra people to the population in any year. Even if immigrants are 5 per cent more skilled than non-immigrants, the impact of a 1 per cent net annual immigration rate – which is relatively high in contemporary terms – is to increase the population skill level by only around 0.05 per cent in each year. On scale economies, the Canadian conclusion, for example, implies that a 4 per cent increase in population would increase the average income of that country by around 0.1 per cent. When plausible skill margins or scale parameters are used in long-run applications of large-scale econometric models, it is hardly surprising that the income effects of immigration at realistic inflow rates tend, while positive, to be very small in annual terms.

Of course, small annual effects do accumulate over the longer run, and some decades of skilled immigration at historically high annual rates may lead to an average income that is noticeably higher than would have been the case in the absence of such a policy. However, the difference would be slow to come, and the economy would be subject to a host of other influences in the meantime. While the effects of permanent immigration on destination-country income should always be an integral consideration in the framing of immigration policy, the above evidence from the traditional destination countries suggests that the practical impact of any such effects should not be overstated.

12

Brain Drain and Student Movements

Graeme Hugo

In the search for generalisations about how migrants differ from non-migrants, one of the most consistent findings is that there is a positive relationship between the level of education and propensity to move. In terms of the impact of migration on both origin and destination areas, the extent to which that movement is selective of the most skilled, educated, entrepreneurial, risk-taking and leadership-potential individuals is important. Hence, there is a tendency to exacerbate inequalities between areas of origin and destination. This phenomenon has become known as the 'brain drain'. Focusing on the Asian region and Australia, an attempt is made in this chapter to assess the scale and significance of brain drain migration.

The conventional wisdom regarding the brain drain has been expressed by Adams (1969, p. 1):

> What is the brain drain? The term itself is loaded, pejorative, suggestive of loss of a vital resource without compensation. This interpretation is supported by illustrations that seem to show that human capital, as a strategic resource, is flowing out of economies where it can make the greatest contribution to human welfare, and into economies already well-supplied with trained, capable, scientific and administrative personnel.

The extent to which this characterises the contemporary situation in Asia is discussed. The chapter then considers an alternative view of the brain drain which suggests that loss of highly trained personnel in the contemporary context can have beneficial impacts on the sending countries. The following section examines migration of professional and skilled workers to and from Australia in recent years and the implications of that movement. Student movements are an important part of the brain drain since they often are the prelude to longer-term migration and, in such cases, they represent a huge loss to origin countries because the students' prime working years are lost to their home nation. The chapter argues that in the early post-Second World War period student migration and the brain drain were almost synonymous but in the last two decades this nexus has been broken.

Any analysis of international migration in the Asian region faces consider-able constraints imposed by the lack of comprehensive and accurate information systems to monitor those movements. Moreover, since much movement is non-permanent, it is often not detected in conventional data sources while, by definition, no data are available for the high level of illegal, undocumented movements. Hence, by and large, in the Asian region it is difficult to determine accurately the scale of international movements let alone the characteristics of the movers.

I The brain drain in Asia

In the early post-Second World War decades there tended to be low levels of emigration from most Asian countries and what movement there was tended to be highly selective of the most well qualified people. In most cases it involved people moving overseas to a more developed country (MDC), to undertake higher education, then either staying in that country or returning briefly and later going back to their study country to take up or seek work. While the extent and seriousness of the brain drain varied from one nation to another, it was an almost universal feature.

The last two decades in Asia have witnessed a transformation of interna-tional population movements with a massive increase in the scale, complexity and significance of migrations into and out of, as well as between, the nations of the region. It has also seen some massive changes in the brain drain situation. To establish the dimensions of this we will take each of the major 'types' of interna-tional movement currently occurring in the Asian region and attempt to summa-rise the extent to which such movements are selective of more skilled and educated groups.

Refugees

Asia remains the world's major source of refugees with the UNHCR estimating that two-thirds of the world's 17 million refugees are in Asia. While some refugee movements tend to be selective of a highly educated intelligentsia, this does not appear to be the case with most refugee outflows in Asia. For example, Figure 12.1 shows that at the 1991 census in Australia the proportions of Vietnam- and Cambodia-born with university or other post-secondary education are much lower not only than those among the Australia-born but also when compared with other Asia-born communities. On the other hand, it is also apparent that the refugee movement out of Vietnam, especially in the late 1970s, was highly selective of more entrepreneurial groups who were seen as not being amenable to life in a socialist state (Hugo 1987, p. 241). For example, the outflow from Vietnam increased dramatically after the government shut down 3000 businesses in Cholon, the Chinese business quarter of Ho Chi Minh City in 1978. Moreo-ver, it was suggested that the government of Vietnam encouraged this

Figure 12.1   Proportion of population with university qualifications by birthplace, 1991 (population aged 15+ years)

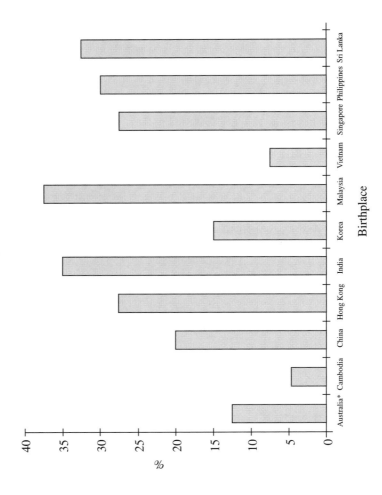

Source: BIMPR Community Profiles; ABS, Queensland Office, 1994.
* 1992 data for population aged 15–69 years only.

outmovement (Das and Sacerdoti 1978). The success of many Vietnamese business people in North America and Australia bears testimony to this.

Permanent migration to more developed countries

It is clear that permanent legal immigration from Asia to the world's MDCs has increased greatly in the last two decades. This has been facilitated by the removal of racist restrictions on the immigration intake in the traditional immigration nations and the acceptance of family reunion as a basis for immigration in those nations. Figure 12.1 shows that, in the Australian case, this type of movement (exemplified by migrants from China, Hong Kong, India, Malaysia, Singapore, Philippines and Sri Lanka) is much more educationally selective than refugee movements. However, it is important here to distinguish between the different categories of entry of permanent migrants leaving Asian countries. Hence, Table 12.1 shows that the proportions of different birthplace groups in managerial, professional and para-professional occupational categories in Australia varies greatly. It is quite low among groups in which refugees are an important component (e.g., Vietnamese, Cambodians and Laotians) while 'economic' categories of immigrants have high proportions in occupations which demand high levels of qualification. The groups in which economic categories predominate include those from Japan, Korea, Taiwan, Singapore, Malaysia, Hong Kong and India.

In groups in which family migrants predominate (e.g., the Philippines) there is a low representation of managerial and professional occupation groups. Hence, whereas in the past the intake of Asian settlers in MDCs was overwhelmingly of a brain drain nature, the contemporary situation is made more complex by family and refugee migration which tends to be of less-skilled, less qualified immigrants. Nevertheless, 'economic' immigrants now tend to be even more explicitly selected on the basis of education and this is institutionalised in the points systems used by several nations to select migrants. Another important feature of immigration to MDCs in the last decade is the introduction of a 'business' migrant category whereby Canada, the USA, Australia, New Zealand, Fiji and other nations have offered virtual automatic settler entry to people with a minimum amount of money to invest and/or a proven record of entrepreneurial and business achievement.

Contract labour migration

The largest international flows currently affecting Asia are those of contract labour from one nation to another. The destinations of contract workers have become diversified over the last decade with intra-Asian movements from labour-surplus nations to labour-shortage nations like Japan, Hong Kong, South Korea, Singapore, Brunei and Malaysia being of increasing significance. It is difficult to generalise about the education and skill profiles of contract labourers, but there is little evidence that these movements are having a retarding effect on

Table 12.1   Australia: occupation distribution by birthplace group, 1991 (%)

Birthplace	Occupation			
	Manager/ Adminis- trative	Professional/ Para- Professional	Trades/ Clerks/ Sales	Plant/ Machine/ Labourers
Australia	12.6	19.3	43.5	18.2
MES*	12.1	22.7	42.3	17.3
NES**	9.7	16.1	37.2	28.2
Asia				
Bangladesh	5.2	28.8	29.1	30.0
Burma	7.4	21.6	37.1	27.1
Cambodia	4.1	5.9	25.5	53.1
China	6.8	12.4	33.4	36.8
Hong Kong	9.6	31.2	40.6	11.1
India	10.3	28.5	39.7	14.8
Indonesia	7.5	16.8	31.8	35.7
Japan	21.2	21.9	43.2	4.0
Korea	10.1	12.2	34.9	30.9
Laos	3.0	8.7	29.3	48.8
Malaysia	9.1	40.2	33.7	10.9
Pakistan	8.7	22.9	34.2	27.1
Philippines	3.6	17.3	40.7	30.8
Singapore	10.1	30.9	40.9	11.7
Sri Lanka	3.3	27.7	40.9	16.2
Taiwan	19.7	19.0	33.7	11.6
Thailand	7.2	10.8	40.0	32.9
Vietnam	4.3	10.8	31.2	43.4

*   Mainly English-speaking origin overseas-born.
**   Non-English-speaking origin overseas-born.
Source: Hugo and Maher 1995

economic and social development in the home countries. In most cases the movement involves workers with limited skills, though there is evidence that the movement of more skilled contract labourers is increasing.

Illegal migration

An important growing trend in recent years has been the increase of undocumented migration (especially of workers) within Asia. It is especially strong in Japan and the Four Tigers, where strict immigration regulations have combined with substantial labour shortages in unskilled areas to encourage illegal movement from labour surplus areas. One of the most substantial movements is from Indonesia to Malaysia (Hugo 1993a) involving up to 1 million workers, who make up more than 10 per cent of the Malaysian workforce and substantially more than 1 per cent of the Indonesian workforce. In recent years China has become a significant source of illegal migrants. While data are, for obvious reasons, lacking, there is little reason to believe that the education profile of these workers is any different to that of the contract workers moving through official channels.

Student migrations

Much of the brain drain out of Asia in the first three post-Second World War decades was associated with the movement of students to MDCs. The scale of this student migration has undoubtedly increased greatly over the last decade. Over the 1987–94 period the number of full fee paying overseas students from Asia studying in Australia increased from 6624 to 59 587 (DEET 1995). In the USA the number of foreign students enrolled in universities increased from 82 709 in 1965 to 438 618 in 1992, while the equivalent figures for Canada were 11 284, and 37 478 (Kritz and Caces 1989; UNESCO 1994).

In the USA it is reported that the number of Americans earning advanced degrees has been declining in recent years, especially in science and technology, and foreigners are making up an increasing proportion of graduate students. Since 1980 more than half of the doctorates in engineering in the USA have been earned by foreigners and in 1990, 57 per cent of all mathematics doctorates were awarded to foreigners. Asians are predominant among the overseas graduates (Tran 1990). Similarly, there is an increasing flow of Asian students to Japan. For example, in 1990 there were around 60 000 researchers from less-developed countries (LDCs) based in Japan (Cross 1990, p. 66). It would thus appear that the opportunities for the student-led brain drain observed in the 1960s and 1970s have multiplied many times in the 1980s and 1990s.

There is a strong connection between student migration and eventual settlement of Asian-origin groups in MDCs. It may occur through students:

- overstaying their education visas;
- gaining a change of status to a resident;
- returning to their home country on completion of their studies and subsequently immigrating officially to the country where they studied.

Unfortunately, there are few data available to establish the extent to which these three processes are occurring in MDCs. In Australia, the overstay rate among students is reported to have declined from 12.2 per cent in May 1989 to 0.5 per cent in December 1993, and at the latter date there were 13 687 student overstayers making up one-fifth of all overstayers (DIEA 1994b). With respect to students who sought to officially change their resident status to become permanent residents, no recent data are available in Australia. Nonetheless, the numbers applying increased rapidly between 1987–88 and 1988–89 from 1530 to 2520, although the number approved fell from 1073 to 1072 (BIR 1990, p. 24). The funding sources for Asian students studying in Australia (including AusAID, the

Australian Development Assistance Agency) have very strict rules about the necessity of funded scholars returning to their home nation.

However, since 1985 the Australian government's international student policy changed from an emphasis on subsidised and sponsored students to recruitment of full fee paying students. This has not only seen a considerable upturn in student numbers but also increased the proportion who are not compelled to return to their home country. In Australia research has shown that there is a connection between flows of students and flows of immigrants, with the substantial recent migration from Malaysia and Singapore being associated with linkages established by previous student movements (Dawkins et al. 1991, p. 21; Lewis 1994). The connection between student migration and eventual emigration from Singapore has also been recognised in research by Singaporean academics (Low, Toh and Soon 1991).

A recent study (Nesdale et al. 1995) interviewed samples of international students at Australian tertiary and secondary education institutions to establish their possible subsequent migration to Australia. Around half the students interviewed considered Australia a good place to immigrate to and 47 per cent of the university sample indicated they had intentions to migrate to Australia after completing their study. While the highest incidence of students intending to attempt to immigrate to Australia was from China, Hong Kong, the Philippines and the Pacific, in all cases except Thailand, around one-third or more intended staying in Australia if they could. However, the proportion of students who are actually able to migrate will of course be smaller due to the application of strict selection criteria. This suggests a very strong connection between student movements and educationally selective migration in Australia.

One country in the Asian region which has major concerns about a student-led brain drain is China where it is estimated that of 220 000 Chinese students who have gone abroad since 1979 only 75 000 have returned (Plafker 1995). This student loss was obviously exacerbated by the Tienanmen Square uprising in 1989 (Goldstein 1994): many students overseas at that time subsequently applied for residence in their country of study. In Australia alone there were 27 162 such applications. Nevertheless, it does represent a significant loss of talent. The State Education Commission in China has strict rules about return but only 40 000 of the 220 000 Chinese students going abroad were state funded (Plafker 1995).

There are also new forms of student migration now occurring in the Asian region. These include the movement of 'trainees' to work in companies in Japan ostensibly to gain experience and upgrade their skills but frequently to overcome serious labour shortages in some sectors of the economy. Official data on foreign trainees being admitted to Japan show that their numbers quadrupled between 1982 and 1992, but Furuya (1995, p. 8) suggests that the 43 627 registered trainees accepted in 1992 (88.1 per cent from Asia) represent a significant understatement of the actual number. This practice is also being increasingly used in South Korea where labour shortages are also significant. The Korean Ministry of Labour has a quota of 20 000 foreign 'technical trainees' permitted in low-end manufacturing.

The burgeoning of the five major types of movements from Asian countries has had an uneven impact in brain drain terms. Refugee movements, family migration, contract labour migration, and illegal migration have generally had limited impacts in depriving Asian nations of scarce talent crucial to their economic and social progress. However, losses of skilled nationals through 'economic' and business migration to MDCs and 'leakage' of students remaining overseas after completing their courses undoubtedly represents a brain drain to some nations.

In the Philippines there is concern that a substantial proportion of the best quality science graduates emigrate (*Manila Chronicle*, 24 March 1994). The USA accounts for three-quarters of all Filipino emigrants, and about 12 per cent of total migrants to the USA from the Philippines in 1992 were in the professional-managerial-technical-administrative category.

In Hong Kong, despite the influx of expatriate workers (Kwong 1992; Do Rosario 1995), the brain drain, along with skilled labour shortages and increasing concern about the competitiveness of the Hong Kong economy (Fong 1993, p. 77), has become an important issue. Moreover, in 1990 Hong Kong emigrants and investors are estimated to have transferred about US$4 billion to Australia and Canada (Ho, Liu & Lam 1991, p. 38).

Similarly, in Singapore the overall labour shortages have been exacerbated by a significant outflow of highly educated people. For example, the number of Singapore-born people resident in Australia has increased from 12 400 in 1981 to 32 700 in 1994. Beng (1990) shows that there was an increase in the number of emigrants leaving Singapore from 5040 in 1986 to 11 770 in 1988 and shows why this is of concern to the government. In addition, around 30 000 Singapore citizens were living abroad in 1990 – mainly students, professionals and managers (Fong 1993, p. 78).

In Malaysia there has been a significant outflow of highly educated and business migrants. This has, for example, seen the Malaysia-born population of Australia increase from 32 580 in 1981 to 88 000 in 1994, and prompted groups such as the Malaysian International Chamber of Commerce and Industry to voice concern as follows:

> . . . there is talk of capital flight. There are signs of increasing emigration by senior management and skilled labour (Seaward 1988, p. 55).

Capital flight from Malaysia, much of it associated with emigration, was estimated by Bank Negara in 1987 to be M$1.2 billion (Seaward 1988, p. 55).

II The impact of the brain drain in Asia: an assessment and some new interpretations

Conventional views of the brain drain see it as both a cause and effect of underdevelopment (Adams 1969). Many have argued with good cause that the outflow of highly educated groups from LDCs to MDCs constitutes a significant loss of resources which will reduce the country's productive capacity and 'represents lost educational investment in that the sending country bears the cost of educating the highly skilled labour but does not directly benefit from it' (Carino 1987, p. 316). While such negative brain drain effects are evident in some contexts in Asia, there are many contexts where the export of highly educated and skilled people is actually resulting in net economic benefits to the origin country.

'Brain overflow'

Some researchers are referring to there being a 'brain overflow' rather than a brain drain (e.g., Adams 1969; Carino 1987; Pernia 1976; Minocha 1987) and argue that the brain drain reflects the basic inability of the origin country's 'economy to absorb the going supply of certain high level skills' (Pernia 1976, p. 71).

Support for such a view can be gathered in several countries in Asia where there appears to be some mismatch between the skills of the graduates of the educational and training system and those required by the local economy. Indonesia is a case in point. Indonesia has a rapidly growing economy but is emphatically a labour surplus nation with estimated 40 per cent underemployment (Hugo 1993b). Only 2 per cent of the labour force had a diploma or degree in 1990. Although overall unemployment levels are relatively low, rates are highest among the more educated groups. Notwithstanding this, Indonesia has been unable to fill vacancies in many of the more skilled categories because of a mismatch between the demand for highly skilled or educated labour and the mix of skills and education currently being taught in tertiary education institutions. Hence, Indonesia has had to import in excess of 50 000 foreign workers in areas such as management, accounting, engineering etc. (Hugo 1994).

While there is a mismatch between skills available and those demanded by the economy, it could be argued that it may be to the origin country's net benefit to export their 'excess' skilled workers. Indeed there is a growing body of evidence from around the region that the emigration of educated workers can result in feedback effects on origin nations which are beneficial to the economic and social development of that country.

Remittances

There has been considerable debate in the literature about the scale of remittances sent back by migrants and the economic and social significance of those remittances. Whereas in the past there has been a tendency to downplay the impact of remittances, more recently opinion has generally shifted to accept that they can and do play a significant role in regional and national economies in LDCs. In the past there has been a tendency to underestimate remittances grossly and to ignore their important multiplier second- and third -round effects. Remittances are now a major element in international financial flows. The role of remittances in the economic policies of LDCs in particular are discussed in full in Chapter 5 of this volume.

Return migration

A common phrase used in Asian countries with fast-growing economies in recent years is 'reverse brain drain'. It refers to the phenomenon of a repatriation of nationals and former nationals who have spent a considerable period living and working overseas in a MDC. This movement has been gathering momentum throughout the late 1980s and 1990s, and is partly associated with the burgeoning opportunities in the rapidly growing, restructuring and labour-short economies of the nationals' home countries. Moreover, the dynamism of these economies has contrasted with the low growth and economic downturns experienced by MDCs in the early 1990s. In addition, in several countries in the region, there has been a deliberate policy to attract back former emigrants who have particular technical, professional and business skills. South Korea represents an important example of such government intervention. Yoon (1992, p. 5) has characterised the reverse brain drain process in South Korea as having the following distinguishing features:

- it has been a concerted state activity, vigorously pursued since the mid-1960s;
- state involvement goes beyond a promotional role to be strongly directive in initiation of organised repatriation in selected social sectors and setting up procedures to achieve objectives;
- the government's efforts have been concentrated in the recruitment of high-level scientists and engineers particularly in public research and development institutes; and
- the state-led reverse brain drain model has been aggressively pursued by the private sector since the early 1980s.

The Ministry of Science and Technology organised professional associations of Korean scientists and engineers in the USA in 1971 (1990 membership 6300), in Europe in 1973 (1500), in Japan in 1983 (815); and in Canada in 1986 (812) to develop a 'reservoir brain pool' for future 'reverse brain drain'. The government scheme alone repatriated 1707 Koreans between 1969 and 1989; almost all had PhDs and were placed in Public Research and Development Institutes and Universities.

The pattern of return migration of Asian migrants from Australia over the last decade is depicted in Table 12.2. This shows the origins of the 429 371 immigrants from Asia settling in Australia between 1984 and 1994, and the number of emigrants from Australia flowing in the opposite direction. The latter group are divided between the overseas-born and Australia-born. In most cases the majority of the overseas-born emigrants moving to an Asian country are returnees. Commentators in Asia (e.g., Fong 1993) have suggested that the return flow of migrants to Asia has increased substantially in recent years. Table 12.2, however, suggests that the backflow from Australia has been quite limited although there is considerable variation from one country to another. The highest rate of return from Australia is among Japanese settlers, suggesting that many Japanese moving to Australia do so on transfer with a Japanese company and after a few years' service in Australia they return to Japan. This may also be the case with Singapore and Thailand. However, for the bulk of Asian birthplaces the backflow is very small indeed.

Only some 5.7 per cent of migrants from Hong Kong to Australia have returned to their home country. However, it is clear that many Hong Kong migrants to Australia, Canada and elsewhere, once they have obtained their foreign passports or permanent residence status in another country, have re-turned to Hong Kong to continue their business activities (Fong 1993, p. 77).

In Canada, there has been some concern that a substantial number of business migrants from Hong Kong have established their citizenship as a form of insurance and then returned to Hong Kong. In the USA, Arnold (1989, pp. 890–91) has referred to similar developments.

The phenomenon of 'astronauting' among Hong Kong immigrants to Canada, USA, Australia and elsewhere has become significant in recent years. This involves Hong Kong people gaining residence or even citizenship in one of the immigration nations and establishing their family there, but with some members of the family becoming bilocal in that they maintain substantial business inter-ests in Hong Kong and spend quite a bit of time there. The significance of this phenomenon in Australia can be seen from results of the prototype Longitudinal Survey of Immigrants to Australia (LSIA). Of the 30 sampled PAs (principal applicants for immigration visa) from Hong Kong who immigrated to Australia between July and September 1991 under the independent visa category, the follow-up survey one year later found that 28 had 'gone to former home country temporarily' (Hugo and Gartner 1993). This phenomenon was found in the LSIA prototype to be not restricted to Hong Kong immigrants, but was also common for independent migrants from Malaysia and Taiwan.

The interpretation of this pattern could take a number of forms:

- one view is that many business migrants (especially those from Hong Kong) are using Australia (and Canada) as 'insurance' and setting up an opportu-nity to leave their home country if political developments make it necessary. The return to China of Hong Kong in 1997 may have negative repercussions for entrepreneurs and others. In Malaysia the New Economic Policy (NEP)

Table 12.2 Australia: immigration from and emigration to
Asian countries, 1984–85 to 1993–94

Country of origin/ destination	Immigrants to Australia	Overseas-born emigrants (Number)	As % of immigrants	Australia-born emigrants	Ratio of overseas to Australia-born emigrants
South-East Asia					
Indonesia	11 719	1103	9.4	977	1.13
Malaysia	40 697	1276	3.1	1027	1.24
Philippines	59 742	885	1.6	545	1.62
Singapore	11 867	1476	12.4	1809	0.82
Thailand	8218	1376	16.7	425	3.24
Vietnam	81 324	403	0.5	68	5.93
Other	14 551	295	2.0	339	0.87
Total	228 118	6232	2.7	5190	1.20
North-East Asia					
China	31 591	449	1.4	170	2.64
Hong Kong	67 056	3817	5.7	3441	1.11
Japan	4959	1164	23.5	627	1.86
Korea	12 090	629	5.2	215	2.93
Taiwan	16 609	669	4.0	151	4.43
Other	1563	45	2.9	19	2.37
Total	133 868	6773	5.1	4623	1.47
South Asia					
India	32 686	344	1.1	127	2.71
Pakistan	3536	85	2.4	46	1.85
Sri Lanka	23 900	133	0.6	45	2.96
Other	7263	41	0.6	49	0.84
Total	67 385	603	0.9	267	2.25
Total	429 371	13 608	3.2	10 080	1.35

Source: Calculated from Bureau of Immigration, Multicultural and Population Research sources.

and possible extensions of it tend to act in a similar way to 1997 for Hong
Kong as an incentive for the non-Bumiputera population to seek a form of
'insurance'. Perhaps there is also some uncertainty in Taiwan about it being
reunited with China;

- an alternative view, is that business migrants take a considerable amount of
  time to transfer their business activities from Asia to Australia. Transferring
  of the often complex web of purchasing, manufacturing and selling activities
  associated with business is more difficult than transferring people. This is
  particularly true during a period of economic downturn in Australia compared to the very rapid economic growth occurring in Malaysia, Hong Kong

and Taiwan. Hence, this temporary return is part of the new mobility (*transilience*) whereby professionals move easily and frequently between nations (Hugo 1992).

Almost certainly both of these explanations have some credibility. Indeed they may represent a new form of settlement. Whereas in the 1950s immigrants from Europe settled definitively in Australia and perhaps could only make a return visit to their home country once each decade, the settlers of the 1990s can interact with their home area much more frequently – not only because Asia is much closer than Europe but because international travel is cheaper and faster and because their Australian-based business activities are strongly integrated with their home countries.

In Taiwan there are indications of a reversal of the brain drain. The rate of return of students who complete their studies in the USA has increased from 8.6 per cent in 1952–61 to 38.8 per cent in 1988 (Selya 1992, p. 788). For the last 20 years Taiwan has offered a no-strings-attached 'Travelling Grant' to nationals wishing to return to Taiwan and the numbers returning doubled between 1990 and 1993. Most of the '*rencai huiliu*' (return flow of human talent) accept pay cuts of 30–40 per cent in exchange for being closer to ageing parents and relatives and what they see as better prospects for upward mobility' (*New York Times*, 21 February 1995, p. A1). Due partly to these activities, but also to the decline in the US job market and the improvement in opportunities in Taiwan, there have been over 1000 Taiwanese experts returning home each year since 1982.

There is evidence of a more significant flow back to India from North America (Yatsko 1995). In China, too, there is some evidence of a small reverse flow of the 120 000 students and scholars who left for the USA between 1987 and 1994. Cities and provinces throughout China have opened returnee centres to lure back business and professional people (Rubin 1995, p. 74). In Shanghai, for example, the Shanghai Returned Students Centre has provided assistance for almost 200 foreign-educated Chinese to return and set up businesses. However, it seems that it is easier to lure back business people than researchers because of the meagre salaries paid in universities (Rubin 1995, p. 75). The Philippines Balikbayan program is a long-standing one which facilitates the return of migrants and assists them in readjusting to life in the Philippines (*Manila Chronicle*, 23 October 1994). The experience with refugee migrations is of very limited return migration but there are signs of an increase in the flow of Vietnamese back to their homeland since the *doi moi* policy change of recent years which has opened up the Vietnamese economy (Zielenziger and Rees 1995). In Cambodia, emigres have returned in substantial numbers since 1992 and now are prominent in the government and bureaucracy (Thayer 1995).

In sum, return migration of highly educated people to their Asian home countries is occurring in the region although not on anything like the scale of the emigration over the last two decades.

Obviously the extent to which emigrants return to their home country lessens the impact of their loss. Indeed, to the extent that they return with enhanced skills, experience, overseas economic networks and economic assets they may have greater positive impact than if they had remained at home.

In Australia, two patterns of return migration are occurring:

- return migration of the conventional type whereby migrants return to settle in their country of origin; and
- 'astronauting' whereby migrants shuttle between their origin and destination countries, often keeping business interests in both countries.

Movements of expatriates into Asian nations

A newly developing dimension to the 'reverse brain drain' is the movement on a long-term basis of professionals and business people who are natives of First World countries into many countries of Asia.

Some examples of the phenomenon are:

- Hong Kong's expatriate population grew from 168 400 in 1986, to 227 600 in 1990, to 382 900 in 1994 (*Hong Kong Standard*, 4 December 1994).
- Singapore has between 150 000 and 200 000 expatriate workers (Vatikiotis, Clifford & McBeth 1994, p. 32).
- In Malaysia there are over 61 000 professionals and other skilled foreign workers who earn at least US$5000 per month (*Business Times* [Malaysia], 28 December 1994).
- In Taiwan there are some 20 000 US citizens who are resident (Baum 1995).

Many expatriates who enter Asian nations under tourist visas engage in some work. The media in the region are increasingly containing stories opposing the impact of foreign skilled workers for individual projects (e.g., *Economic and Business Review Indonesia*, 24 September 1994). However, in a survey of 3000 *Far Eastern Economic Review* readers in April–June 1994 only in Malaysia was there a predominantly positive response to the statement 'There are too many foreigners in my country'.

Other positive roles of emigrants

Some Asian countries are finding it advantageous to have substantial communities of nationals or former nationals resident in MDCs. In addition to the remittance flows discussed earlier, there is growing evidence that these communities can function as beach-heads for the penetration of goods and services supplied by their home country. It is clear, for example, that the substantial Korean communities in North America were crucial in the establishment and expansion of Korean electronic, motor vehicle and electrical appliance sales in that huge market. Overseas-based nationals can be instrumental in encouraging MDC companies to invest in particular Asian countries. For example, 'ethnic

Indian executives who have worked their way up the ranks of American hi-tech firms are often at the forefront of their companies' India efforts, (Yatsko 1995, p. 51).

III Australia: brain drain or brain gain?

Australian data on persons entering and leaving the country are more complete than most nations. Information is collected on the occupations of all persons entering or leaving the country although no information is collected on education or qualifications. Arrivals and departures are divided into three categories:

- permanent departures or arrivals;
- long-term departures or arrivals involving an international absence from or presence in Australia of more than a year but where there is an intention of returning home;
- short-term visits.

In practice there is category jumping between the various categories, especially the first two. Hence, in much of our discussion of the 'brain drain-gain' we will combine permanent and long-term movements.

Data on the long-term movement into and out of Australia by occupation over the 1981–94 period show:

- Australia is experiencing a brain gain, with the numbers in the technical, professional, highly educated occupational categories who settle in the country being almost twice as numerous as those leaving; and
- there is a net gain in all occupational categories, but the net migration gain in relation to the total numbers settling tends to be highest among lower-skilled groups.

If we focus on the population exchanges with Asian countries in Tables 12.3 and 12.4, a similar pattern is apparent to the overall flows, but the ratios of net gain to long-term and permanent settlers is greater than for the total. In other words, the brain gain that Australia receives from Asia is more efficient in that its movement per unit of net gain is less than is the case for other regions of the world.

A significant trend in recent years has been the increase in the numbers of Australia-born persons leaving the country on a more or less permanent basis. The number of such departures reached a record level of 9927 in 1993–94 (BIMPR 1995b). Moreover, until recently the numbers of long term departures of Australian residents were also increasing rapidly reaching a record level of 67 191 in 1991–92 (BIMPR 1995b). Also, in the period 1988–92 there was a substantial excess of resident long-term departures over resident long-term arrivals.

Table 12.3 Australia: permanent and long-term arrivals from and departures to Asia by occupational category, 1981–82 to 1989–90

Occupation Category	Arrivals movements as %	Departures of in- movement	Net movement	Net
Professional/medical	8383	3551	4832	57.64
Other Professional	49 554	20 431	29 123	58.77
Technical	1257	370	888	70.56
Clerical/sales	40 842	7713	33 129	81.12
Skilled workers	10 646	2974	7672	72.06
Semi-skilled workers	30 431	1816	28 615	94.03
Unskilled workers	19 381	1186	18 195	93.88
Services	9331	2563	6768	72.53
Retired	17 817	4571	13 246	74.34
Home duties	68 676	20 869	47 807	69.61
Non-working, children	139 611	46 211	93 400	66.90
Not previously employed	6568	3602	2966	45.16
Unemployed	40 941	5163	35 778	87.39
Not stated	44 601	7870	36 731	82.35
Total	488 039	128 890	358 149	73.59

Source: BIMPR Movements Database 1995a.

Table 12.4 Australia: permanent and long-term arrivals from and departures to Asia by occupational category, 1990–91 to 1992–93

Occupation Category	Arrivals movements as %	Departures of in- movement	Net movement	Net
Managers/Administrators	16 335	4534	11 801	72.24
Professionals	31 678	10 835	20 843	65.80
Para-professionals	5116	1434	3682	71.97
Trades	8453	2509	5944	70.32
Clerks	9905	3087	6818	68.83
Sales/Personal service workers	5063	2358	2 705	53.43
Plant/Machine operators and drivers	2359	571	1788	75.79
Labourers & related workers	3957	1839	2118	53.53
Total	82 866	27 167	55 699	67.22

Source: BIMPR Movements Database.

There is a very substantial net gain in the professional and skilled occupational groups. Furthermore, there has been a large increase in the proportion of immigrants in these occupational groups over the last decade, especially since the CAAIP Inquiry's (FitzGerald 1988) recommendations for a sharpening of the immigration program's economic focus. Indeed the creation of more policy categories placing emphasis on skill, advanced education and entrepreneurial ability have made Australian immigration even more selective of talent, although some would argue that the specific skills of immigrants have not matched the actual skill shortages. (This has also occurred in the other major immigration nations. Even in the USA, where in the past the emphasis in the immigration program has been on national quotas and queuing principles, the government in 1990 tripled the number of visas given to top professionals to 140 000 and instituted a business migration program (Tran 1990).) Hence, the 'brain drain' is being institutionalised in specific elements within the immigration program.

The occupation profile of Australia-born departures is different to that of overseas-born former settlers leaving Australia on a more or less permanent basis. The Australia-born departures are more likely to be in the workforce and also have a higher skill profile than their overseas-born counterparts.

Is there a brain drain among the Australia-born? It was demonstrated earlier that, when only permanent settler arrivals and permanent departures are considered, there has been a substantial net loss of Australia-born persons through emigration over the last decade. Table 12.5 shows that over the 1982–94 period there were 64 166 Australia-born permanent departures but only 4496 Australia-born settlers.

As the NPC (1990, p. 2) correctly points out:

> Australian-born loss is more complex (than settler loss), mainly because many Australian-born, though saying they are leaving permanently, in fact return later on.

Hence, Table 12.5 shows that if we examine long-term arrivals and departures there is a small net loss due to the leakage across categories. Hence, if we take both categories into account the overall *net* loss of Australia-born over the 12 years was greater than the net loss by permanent movement: 91 762 compared with 85 849.

From the perspective of our examination of the brain drain it is important to disaggregate Table 12.5 to see the extent to which skilled and highly trained people are participating in the various flows. Hence, Table 12.6 presents the permanent and long-term arrivals and departures of Australia-born people with professional occupations. It shows that there was a significant net loss of professionals over the fourteen years; totalling some 24 292 professionals persons. To what extent is this counterbalanced by professionals arriving back in Australia after a long-term absence? Table 12.6 shows that over the 14 years there was an

Table 12.5 Australia: Australia-born permanent and long-term departures and arrivals, 1982–94

Year	Permanent			Long-term			Net Total
	In	Out	Net	In	Out	Net	
1982–83	466	5984	−5518	29 868	27 796	+2072	−3446
1983–84	294	6492	−6198	29 917	28 835	+1082	−5116
1984–85	308	6051	−5743	31 680	30 769	+911	−4832
1985–86	281	5600	−5319	32 346	30 080	+2266	−3053
1986–87	381	6099	−5718	30 710	29 162	+1548	−4170
1987–88	435	6792	−6327	31 525	29 688	+1837	−4490
1988–89	542	6560	−6018	31 162	33 985	−2823	−8841
1989–90	352	8399	−8047	31 143	37 162	−6019	−14 036
1990–91	381	9490	−9109	34 972	39 375	−4403	−13 512
1991–92	336	9178	−8842	35 666	38 484	−2798	−11 640
1992–93	384	9803	−9419	38 521	38 817	−296	−9715
1993–94	336	9927	−9591	39 399	38 699	+710	−8881

Source: Data supplied by BIMPR

Table 12.6 Australia-born persons, permanent and long-term departures and arrivals by professional occupation, 1981–95

Year	Permanent departures	In	Long-term Out	Net	Total net
1981–82	−987	9369	8283	+1086	+99
1982–83	−951	8923	8260	+663	−288
1983–84	−889	8466	7654	+812	−77
1984–85	−1009	9548	9197	+351	−658
1985–86	−1047	9650	9252	+398	−649
1986–87	−1300	9528	9260	+268	−1032
1987–88	−1478	10 255	10 364	−109	−1587
1988–89	−1515	10 569	12 007	−1438	−2953
1989–90	−1836	10 964	12 449	−1485	−3321
1990–91	−2628	13 482	15 387	−1905	−4533
1991–92	−2422	13 496	14 689	−1193	−3615
1992–93	−2878	16 204	16 068	+136	−2742
1993–94	−3004	16 187	16 151	+36	−2968
1994–Mar. 95	−2348	13 972	12 867	+1105	−1243
Total	−24 292	160 613	161 888	−1275	−25 567

Source: BIMPR Movements Database.

overall net loss of 1275 professionals through long-term movement so the total net loss through emigration was 25 567 between 1981 and 1995.

There can be no doubt that the global international migration system with respect to highly skilled labour has been transformed since the 1960s when the early brain drain research was undertaken.

Whereas in the 1960s the dominant form of professional international migration tended to involve permanent migration from less developed to more developed nations, the current situation tends to be one characterised by *transilience* of such groups – i.e., that is, hypermobility involving remigration and return (Richmond 1991, p. 4). In the Australian context, the increasing tempo of emigration of Australia-born professionals may to some extent be due to Australia's increasing incorporation of transilients into these international migration systems. Equally it may be a function of economic conditions within Australia.

Much is said and written about Australians' need to 'become part of Asia'. Surely nothing will forge such links so much as the networks created by Asians settling in Australia and by Australians living for at least three or four years in Asia. In this respect it is clear that the 1990s is seeing some significant changes in the destination of highly qualified Australians moving overseas on a long-term basis. Traditionally such movements have been directed toward North America and Europe (especially the United Kingdom–Ireland) but there are some indications that Asian destinations are becoming of great significance in the 1990s. Some of the world's most dynamic economies are located in the Asian region and in several countries there are shortages of skilled labour of certain kinds. Hence, in Hong Kong there has been an increase in movement of Australian expatriate professionals (Sharma 1991). Even in a labour surplus nation like Indonesia, economic growth is outpacing the capacity to supply professionals in areas such as engineering and management.

Conclusion

International migration of students and highly qualified individuals are increasing rapidly in the Asia–Pacific region. Unfortunately our understanding of the impacts of such movements on the individuals involved, their origin and destination communities and countries is very limited. If policies are to be developed which minimise the negative effects of such movement and maximise the benefits accruing from them, it is necessary that the research effort in this area be accelerated.

13

Trade and Migration: The Effects of Economic Transformation in China

Ronald Skeldon

Introduction

Trade, the territorial expansion of states, and the movements of peoples have been inextricably linked for centuries and form a central theme of global history. States expand to trade and the trading networks of merchants pave the way for State and imperial expansion. This was as true for the first great Chinese dynasty, the Han, as it was for nineteenth-century Britain, and it is virtually impossible to separate cause from effect. Not all trade inevitably led to state expansion. In pre-modern times, trade across cultures was carried out by specialist communities of traders who established settlements in foreign areas to trade with the 'home' economy. These trade diasporas were found wherever there was a need for cross-cultural brokers (Curtin 1984) through which were created regions articulated by the circulation of goods and peoples.

The Chinese established trading diasporas throughout South-East Asia that go back almost two thousand years. However, in China, unlike Europe, the merchants occupied lowly positions on the social hierarchy and were discriminated against, which meant that it was mainly peripheral groups from the Han core with access to the sea that participated in these diasporas (Wang 1991). These included the Fujianese, particularly the Hokkien, but also the Hakka and others from south China, a basic pattern that is reflected in Chinese migration even today. Southern China was historically a marginal part of the nation but today it has emerged as the economic powerhouse, a transformation that is clearly associated with its traditions of trade and migration.

Trade and migration in China: the historical legacy

A discussion of virtually any aspect of China has to take into account certain unique characteristics of that nation: first, the sheer physical size of the country and, second, the length of time that the vast heartland has held together as a coherent political and cultural entity. A third characteristic is that, until recently, China was essentially inward-looking, centred around its self-perception as the 'middle kingdom', with scarcely a glance outside. Nevertheless, throughout its history, China has been a major trading nation. A greater tonnage passed through the port of Shanghai in any year in the mid-nineteenth century than through London, the principal city in industrialising Western nations at that time (Fairbank 1986, p. 49). Yet, Chinese trade was essentially internal and, vast and diverse though China was, that trade was primarily within a single political and cultural milieu.

The history of modern China is in many ways a history of trade and dealings with outsiders. Initial contacts had been made by the Portuguese in the early sixteenth century but, for over three hundred years, outsiders were restricted to a very marginal position. The trade with foreigners was often illegal or was tightly controlled by the late Ming and Ching authorities to a limited number of sites and to certain times of the year. Macau, established from 1564, was one of the few centres where foreign traders could settle permanently, and it grew wealthy not simply by trading between China and Europe but by acting as a broker in the lucrative China–Japan trade. However, it was Canton (Guangzhou) that emerged as the most important centre for trade between Chinese and foreign merchants, although these could only deal exclusively with licensed and monopolistic Chinese merchants during the October to March 'trading season', and permanent residence was forbidden (see Spence 1990). It was from the late eighteenth century that the British began to trade opium for Chinese goods, particularly tea. Attempts by Qing authorities to restrict further foreign trade caused the British and the French to force open the Chinese market through the so-called 'opium wars' of 1839–42 and 1856–60, through which the Chinese were compelled to recognise outside powers as equal trading partners rather than as tributary nations. For the first time in its long history China had to deal from an inferior position with peoples who had come by sea to trade. So began the long economic transformation of the economy of China, a transformation that continues to this day.

Foreign merchants were initially restricted to the treaty ports (Canton, Amoy, Foochow, Ningpo and Shanghai) and to those parts of China annexed as colonies, Hong Kong and Macau, and they rarely had an opportunity to travel inland or gain an insight into the degree of commercialisation and sophistication of the Chinese economy of the time (Fairbank 1986, p. 96). It would be incorrect to see the Chinese economy as backward and just waiting for external stimulus; China had, after all, the world's biggest economy until the mid-nineteenth century and accounted for 30 per cent of world manufacturing output in 1830 (*The Economist*, 1 October 1994). China had, if anything, been too successful in its economic development in producing a highly stable and effective system within its boundaries, and the foreign intrusion commenced a restructuring and reorientation of economy and society, a story that is too complex to summarise here (see Fairbank 1986).

The importance of the historical legacy for an understanding of the present-day patterns of trade and migration is not simply to emphasise the long tradition of trade in China but also to draw attention to population movements out of the treaty ports last century that provided the foundation for networks of trade and migration that are still of importance today. Not only was China perceived as a vast market for foreign produce and a source of goods but its population could supply that most critical of commodities to an expanding capitalist system: cheap labour. It has been estimated that there were over 6 million person moves through Hong Kong between the 1850s and 1939, with the migration in the 1850s dominated by movements to the USA and Australia, and that from the 1870s to the Second World War Hong Kong's human flow was dominated by movement to Singapore and the Malay States (Sinn 1995). Macau and Amoy in Fujian (later replaced by Shantou (Swatow) in eastern Guangdong) were the other major ports through which the brokers controlled the flow of labourers and other migrants seeking their fortunes on more or less independent means. In the latter part of the nineteenth century, around 80 000 people a year left both Hong Kong and Amoy, and this figure increased to over 100 000 a year in the early part of this century. Although Shanghai did participate in this labour trade, the numbers leaving from that port were always small.

From the 1880s, North American and Australasian destinations gradually closed their borders to Chinese immigration through a series of exclusion acts. South-East Asian destinations had also essentially been closed by the end of the 1930s. Estimates of the numbers of Chinese outside China vary but there were probably somewhere between 8 and 9 million in the 1920s, the majority in South-East Asia, but by this time Chinese had been transported or had established themselves in virtually every part of the world from islands in the Pacific, such as Papua New Guinea, Fiji, and Samoa, to several countries in Latin America, particularly Peru, Panama, and Cuba, the British and Dutch West Indies, to South Africa, Mauritius and India, as well as the major destinations in North America and Australasia. Before China cut itself off from the international community following the triumph of the Communist Party in 1949 and the foundation of the People's Republic of China, there was in place a global network of Chinese communities, more intensive in some areas to be sure, but global nevertheless. This established network is fundamental to an understanding of subsequent patterns of population movement and of trade.

Migration and the People's Republic of China up to 1978

The period from 1949 up to the end of 1978 was characterised by the centrality of state power and control. There was relatively little migration out of China and movements within the country were strongly influenced by state direction. Certainly, there were periods of 'blind' or uncontrolled movement, particularly to cities during the early part of this period, and also associated with the chaos following the Great Leap Forward (1958), but the significant features of internal migration revolved around government campaigns and control. The 'sending down' of millions of students and workers from cities to the countryside (Kirkby 1985, p. 38) in various programs in the 1950s and 1960s is perhaps the best known, but there were also programs to move people from the populous east to the western provinces, and in fact any movement required official permission. Enforcement was through the household registration system, which ensured that people could only obtain their grain rations in the place in which they were registered. In a socialist economy where almost all grain production was controlled by the state, this system was a powerful force to restrict mobility. With the emergence of free markets after the 1978 reform, this control, was eroded. Chinese government estimates show that, in 1978, less than 10 per cent of total agricultural output was sold through the market, whereas this had risen to 40 per cent in 1991 (cited in Lardy 1994, p. 8). This is an important explanatory factor in the increase in population movements within China since 1978.

Migration for Chinese peoples in general was difficult in the post-Second World War period as few countries would accept them as settlers. One of the few was Britain which, until 1962, accepted all residents from colonies and the Commonwealth and allowed several tens of thousands from Hong Kong to settle during the 1950s and 1960s. That avenue was restricted from 1962 and essentially closed by the end of that decade. However, from the second half of the 1960s, momentous changes were being implemented in the immigration policies of the main settler countries of the USA and Canada, and later Australia and New Zealand. These changes would ultimately transform the global international migration system. They finally swept away the last barriers of discriminatory immigration policies, and non-Europeans began to move to those destinations – in relatively small numbers at first but they came to dominate these international flows over a 25-year period. In the late 1950s, Europeans accounted for around 56 per cent of migrants to the USA and over 80 per cent of migrants to Canada and Australia. By the early 1990s, Europeans accounted for fewer than 20 per cent of migrants to the USA and Canada and fewer than 30 per cent of migrants to Australia. Asians had come to dominate the movements to Australia and Canada, and Latin Americans and Asians the movement to the USA.

By far the most populous country in the world, let alone in Asia, China has been a relatively late participant in these new flows. As discussed above, it had essentially cut its ties with Western market economies after the foundation of the People's Republic of China in 1949 and, following the split within the Soviet socialist camp in mid-1960, had been very much isolated from the world. Chinese peoples from Taiwan and from Hong Kong, though, were able to take advantage of the changed immigration legislation and, by the late 1970s, were moving in quite large numbers. For example, only around 16 000 people moved from Hong Kong to the USA in the decade of the 1950s, but numbers rose to 75 000 in the 1960s and to over 113 000 in the 1970s. Data on migration from Taiwan and China were not recorded separately for the USA until 1982, but we can be fairly certain that the vast majority of the 9657 people moving from China to the US in the 1950s, and of the 34 764 in the 1960s, were from Taiwan. This distinction is not particularly meaningful, as it is likely that the majority of those leaving Hong Kong and Taiwan for North America at these times had been born in China. For example, 75 007 immigrants to the USA admitted between 1961 and 1970 had a last place of permanent residence Hong Kong, while only 22 191 of the immigrants admitted to USA between 1960 and 1969 had been born in Hong Kong. In any discussion dealing with both migration and trade in East Asia, distinctions between China, Hong Kong and Taiwan become blurred.

Migration and trade post-1978

China officially ended its isolation with the West upon Nixon's visit in February 1972 although, in practical terms of migration and trade, little was to change until after the accession to power of Deng Xiaoping in 1977 and the major policy shifts to introduce internal reforms and open China to the outside world taken by the National People's Congress in late 1978. In the late 1970s, China's share of world trade was only one-third to one-quarter of what it had been in the late 1920s, with a total turnover of less than $US15 billion, and China was 'an insignificant participant in international markets for goods and capital' (Lardy 1994, p. 1). There were few students from China in the USA or other major destinations in the late 1970s, and the numbers of others going overseas were still small. Within fifteen years, China has emerged as a major player in international markets and is seen by some to be on its way to becoming an economic super-power and the largest economy in the world by the mid-twenty-first century (*The Economist*, 1 October 1994; *Fortune*, 31 October 1994; Kristof 1993). If these assessments are true, China will have regained its historical economic position, with the major difference that, instead of being simply the largest economy in a segregated world, it will be the largest economy in an interdependent world.

The value of China's trade in 1993 had increased to $US19 572 billion and, in 1992, China was the world's tenth largest export nation (Lardy 1994, p. 2). By the 1990s, China had also started to be a major participant in global migration flows, the repercussions of which are as yet little appreciated. Hence, trade and migration appear to be complementary: as China becomes integrated into the global community, both trade and migration are increasing. It would be strange if it were otherwise. Both trade and migration are the fundamental economic and human linkages through which this integration is coming about and, unless a radical shift in the direction of China's policies takes place, this trend is almost certain to continue.

As argued elsewhere (Skeldon 1992b), migration is an integral part of the development process and trade is one of the key ways through which economic development is realised – as is demonstrated by the experience of the Newly Industrialised Economies (NIEs). Yet, the pattern of migration has changed through the course of the development experiences of these countries. Whereas, in the past, pressures were mostly towards emigration from Korea and Taiwan, these have recently changed towards immigration in what has been termed a 'migration transition' or 'migration turnaround' (Abella 1994). Through an analysis of the Hong Kong experience Skeldon (1994a, b and c) demonstrates that there is no simple transition from one-way emigration to one-way immigration based on economic conditions, but a complex interplay of the two flows influenced by political as well as economic factors. Trade has unquestionably been a powerful factor in the transition of the NIEs to labour-deficit economies and primary targets for, rather than primary sources of, migration. China is at a much earlier stage of development and, because of its sheer size, is unlikely to follow a neat and similar path to that of the NIEs.

Since 1978, migration from China has consisted of four separate types: students, legal emigrants, contract workers and illegal migrants. Students and emigrants are considered together as the distinction between the two in the case of China is not clear-cut.

Emigration after 1978: students and emigrants

The training of students overseas is an important flow that can have profound implications for development. Many of the early revolutionary leaders of China, including Sun Yat Sen, the father of the Revolution (a student in Hong Kong and in Hawaii), Zhou Enlai and Deng Xiaoping (students in Paris), and Yang Shangkun (a student in Moscow), absorbed revolutionary ideas in environments free from the restrictions of the dying Qing dynasty or the subsequent warlord period (Wang 1966). In more recent times, a generation of the present technocrats and leaders was trained in the Soviet Union. In 1978–79, there were only 28 students from China registered in the USA. Taiwan was the second most important source of foreign students (after Iran) at that time, with 17 560 students in degree-granting institutions; Hong Kong was the sixth most important source, with 9900 students in 1978–79. By 1993–94, China was the leading source of foreign students in the US with 44 360, Taiwan added another 37 581, and Hong Kong 13 752. China had also become a leading source of students to Canada, with 4096 in that country in 1992, a long way behind Hong Kong, the leading source with 12 818 students. However, China and Canada have a different definition of 'student', with Canada including elementary and secondary school children in its totals. If we consider only postgraduate students, China is

Table 13.1 Numbers of students at main destinations (latest year)

	Total	Undergraduate	Graduate	Other
United States (1993–94)				
China	44 381	6287	36 370	1724
Taiwan	37 581	11 067	24 623	1891
Hong Kong	13 752	10 427	2832	493
Japan	43 770	31 960	7555	4055
Korea	31 076	12 521	15 785	2770
Canada (1992)				
China	4096	448	2519	1129
Taiwan	3894	305	87	3502
Hong Kong	12 818	187	6589	6229
Japan	5826	517	255	4854
Australia (1994)				
China	4534	3864	670	
Taiwan	3228	1357	1871	
Hong Kong	11 932	8927	3005	
Singapore	7739	7116	623	
Malaysia	9706	8147	1559	
Japan	3887	1290	2597	
Korea	4581	1716	2865	

Sources:
USA: *Open Doors: Report on International Educational Exchange, 1993–1994*, New York, Institute of International Education, 1994.
Canada: *International Student Participation in Canadian Education*, Ottawa, Statistics Canada, 1992.
Australia: *Selected Higher Education Student Statistics 1994*, Higher Education Division, Department of Employment, Education and Training.
Note: The figures are not directly comparable because of differences in the definition of 'student'. The figures for the USA, for example, only incorporate those enrolled in accredited colleges and universities; those for Canada and Australia include primary and secondary school children and vocational students, while those for Australia also include those on English Language Intensive Courses for Overseas Students (ELICOS).

by far the leading source of students to Canada in this category. For the USA, too, the breakdown of China's students is heavily in favour of post-graduate, while the Hong Kong students are more biased towards junior levels (Table 13.1). The pattern for Australia is similar. There were few students from China in Australia in 1978 but, by the end of March 1994, there were some 4534 students paying full fees, a long way behind Hong Kong, Malaysia and Singapore. Again, the vast majority were in the highest levels of education. In 1991 there were also 12 609 students from China in Japan at post-secondary educational institutions.

The experience of the Asian NIEs has shown that large numbers of the students do return home and that the proportion of returnees increases over time (Skeldon 1992a). Official Chinese sources indicate that about one-third of the 220 000 students who have gone abroad to study since 1979 have returned to China, with only one-fifth returning from the USA (*Migration News*, May 1995). While there are always concerns about a 'brain drain', the students who do return have a profound role to play in the economic, social and political transformation of their homeland. Of the twenty-six members of the cabinet of the government in Taiwan, 70 per cent were trained in the West and twelve of the fifteen with doctoral degrees graduated from US universities (Lin 1994, p. 14). The trends towards a more democratic system in Taiwan and the increasing rates of return of students and others from overseas are surely not simply coincidental. As Lin (1994) speculates, if students currently overseas return to China like their revolutionary predecessors, they are likely to support a transformation of China as radical as that wrought by a previous generation of returned students. Although Chinese students today have sought to become permanent residents in Western countries, this does not necessarily imply a permanent exile. Many are waiting to see the direction taken in post-Deng China.

The numbers leaving China permanently on one-way exit permits have increased markedly over the last ten to fifteen years, although totals are still generally small by the standards of the late nineteenth and early twentieth centuries (Table 13.2). The most important destination has been Hong Kong. There was a net addition of some 400 000 migrants from China between 1976 and 1981, most of whom arrived during 1979 and 1980. In these two years, 125 000 legal entrants from China entered Hong Kong, 160 000 entered illegally but reached the urban areas to claim right of residence ('touch base'), and some 200 000 others were caught and sent back to China (Skeldon 1986, p. 7). With the abolition of the reach base policy from October 1980, migration from China was tightly controlled to 75 a day up to early 1994 when it was raised to 105 a day. This controlled migration is made up mainly of the dependants of men who are already Hong Kong residents. This migration could, in some way, be seen as internal to China as Hong Kong, from China's viewpoint, has always been an integral part of the country and it certainly will be after 30 June 1997.

The movements to Australia and to Canada have more than doubled since 1980 but are still relatively small. The principal overseas destination by far has been the USA, where numbers almost doubled from 15 919 in 1981–82 to 29 461 in 1991–92. The dramatic rise to 57 761 in 1992–93 was, almost certainly, exceptional and reflects numbers of students adjusting their status in that year rather than a surge in new migrants. The figures for the USA do not necessarily reflect entrants in any fiscal year, but rather those admitted as immigrants, which includes those who entered in earlier years as students, tourists, company transferees, temporary workers, and so on. Information on such adjustments is not published by 'place of last permanent residence' but only

Table 13.2   Legal immigration to main destinations from China,
1980–1981 to 1993–1994

	Australia	Canada	United States	Hong Kong
1980–81	799	4936	–	–
1981–82	843	6551	–	–
1982–83	375	3572	15 919	–
1983–84	369	2217	14 335	26 701
1984–85	1439	2214	14 425	27 475
1985–86	1663	1883	15 578	27 285
1986–87	1041	1902	16 458	27 111
1987–88	1014	2625	18 589	27 268
1988–89	1570	2778	21 924	28 137
1989–90	1005	4430	20 672	27 263
1990–91	1128	7989	20 879	27 976
1991–92	1525	13 915	23 121	26 782
1992–93	1665	10 429	29 461	28 367
1993–94	1915	9447	57 761	32 909

Sources:
United States: *Statistical Yearbook of the Immigration and Naturalization Service*, United States Department of Justice, Washington, D.C., United States Government Printing Office, various years.
Canada: Immigration Statistics, Ottawa, Employment and Immigration Canada, various years.
Australia: *Australian Immigration: Consolidated Statistics No. 18, 1993–94*, Bureau of Immigration, Multicultural and Population Research, Canberra, Australian Government Publishing Service, 1995.
Hong Kong: Unpublished tabulations, Immigration Department, Hong Kong government, various years.

by 'place of birth' which deals with a somewhat different population. Many of those with place of birth 'China' will have place of last permanent residence 'Taiwan' or 'Hong Kong'. Nevertheless, these figures are used in the following paragraph to illustrate aspects of the current migration from China.

The total number of immigrants accepted into the US in 1992–93 with place of birth China was 65 578, only 24 014 of whom had arrived during that fiscal year: 41 564 had thus adjusted their status, with 9448 of those having arrived in 1989 and 6421 in 1990 (Table 13.3). Of the 41 564 who adjusted their status, almost half, 19 513, had entered as students and 7939 as temporary workers. Hence, a significant factor in the 1992–93 intake and, to a lesser extent, in the 1991–92 intake, was the granting of immigrant status to students who had entered shortly after the Tiananmen Square massacre on 4 June 1989. The large number of student adjustments during 1992–93 was directly the result of the Chinese Student Protection Act of 1992, which allowed almost 27 000 students who had been living continuously in the USA since April 1990 to adjust to permanent status. The numbers of students from China in the USA rose from

Table 13.3   Immigrants with place of birth China admitted to the USA by year of admission and year of arrival, fiscal years 1987/88 to 1993/94

Fiscal year	Total	New arrivals	Adjustments by year of arrival								
			Before 1992	1991	1990	1989	1988	1987	1986	Before 1986	Unknown
1987–88	25 841	22 219	–	–	–	–	–	–	1299	2283	40
1988–89	28 717	24 864	–	–	–	–	–	1367	754	1974	15
1989–90	32 272	23 374	–	–	–	–	1552	710	490	6133	13
1990–91	31 815	23 605	–	–	–	1770	788	566	582	4480	24
1991–92	33 025	26 169	–	–	1837	803	665	542	639	2282	88
1992–93	38 907	24 818	–	3031	1929	1845	1710	1610	1601	1996	317
1993–94	65 578	24 014	5,813	4543	6421	9448	5622	3716	2640	2199	1162

Source: Statistical Yearbook of the Immigration and Naturalization Service, United States Department of Justice, Washington, D.C., United States Government Printing Office, various years.

25 170 in 1987–88 to 45 126 in 1992–93 before dropping slightly to 44 381 in 1993–94. It is likely that the numbers adjusting in subsequent years will be lower, although this will obviously depend primarily on conditions within China.

A similar situation has occurred in Australia, with large numbers of students being allowed to change their status to that of permanent resident following the Tiananmen Square massacre. Some 19 000 students from China were in Australia in mid-1989 but, after it became apparent that the Australian government was willing to allow students to settle following the then Prime Minister Hawke's speech in 1989, some 25 000 others either fled from China or were allowed to leave by their government. The numbers coming from China, however, sharply decreased from January 1990 when Australia brought in revised procedures for the entry of students undertaking non-formal, full-fee studies. The majority (some 40 000) of the students and their accompanying dependants are likely to obtain residence status in Australia following the 1 November 1993 decision of the federal government to allow many of those in Australia to apply for permanent residence. These people will eventually be eligible to apply for Australian citizenship once they meet the residential and other qualifications. The data in Table 13.4 show several different ways of measuring the movement of Chinese to Australia: 'settlers by last place of permanent residence China' (as in Table 13.2), 'settlers by place of birth China', which includes some who have moved through other places of residence, particularly Taiwan and Hong Kong, 'permanent and long-term arrivals by place of birth China', which includes student arrivals but also those who have come through Hong Kong and Taiwan, and 'those with former country of citizenship China who have been granted citizenship'. The data in columns 1 and 2 show that about half of those born in China had been living permanently somewhere else before coming to Australia. A comparison of columns 2 and 3 shows the very large numbers who must have come in as students after 1989, particularly in 1991–92, and the figures in column 4 show the steady rise in the number of those from China gaining Australian citizenship.

No information is recorded on place of origin within China, either of students or of other immigrants to the USA, Canada or Australia. In the historical migration, both to South-East Asia and to North America and Australasia, the two southern provinces of Guangdong and Fujian dominated the flows out of China as ships and brokers operated out of the southern treaty ports. Within these provinces, areas of emigration were also quite localised and centred on coastal districts to the east of Hong Kong in the Chaozhou and Hokkien regions and around the Pearl River Delta region to the north and west of Hong Kong, particularly in an area known as the 'Four Districts' in the western delta (Figure 13.1). The historical pattern of migration to the USA came primarily from the Pearl River Delta and particularly the Siyi, Sanyi and Zhongshan districts. It is likely that the more recent migration from China, while still dominated by southern Chinese people, comes from somewhat more diverse

Table 13.4   Four different measures of the impact of migration from China to Australia, 1984–85 to 1993–94

	1 Settler arrivals with last place of permanent residence China	2 Settler arrivals with place of birth China	3 Permanent and long-term arrivals with place of birth China	4 Persons granted citizenship with former country of citizenship China
1984–85	1439	3163	3888	1422
1985–86	1663	3138	3962	2194
1986–87	1041	2690	3792	2022
1987–88	1014	3282	5000	2384
1988–89	1570	3819	6837	2289
1989–90	1005	3069	7459	3346
1990–91	1128	3256	6658	3795
1991–92	1525	3388	14 272	4850
1992–93	1665	3046	8347	5029
1993–94	1915	2740	6837	5242

Source: *Australian Immigration: Consolidated Statistics No. 18, 1993–94*, Bureau of Immigration, Multicultural and Population Research, Canberra, Australian Government Publishing Service, 1995.

origins. There is no reason why students, self-selected or selected by the central government, should be biased towards the southern provinces; quite the reverse. It would seem more likely that many, and perhaps the majority, would come from the prestige university centres of Beijing and Shanghai.

One analysis of all recent emigration from China suggests that over one-quarter of emigrants originated in Shanghai Province, followed in importance by Beijing, Fujian and Guangdong (Miao 1994). These results were drawn from the numbers recorded in the 1990 population census whose permanent household registration had been suspended because they were abroad at the time of the census. The total number who fell into this category was 237 024 but whether this included students who might be away temporarily as well as the more permanent emigrants, or whether those who had left for Hong Kong were included, is not clear. Despite the difficulties with this approach, the results do suggest that recent emigration does include, for the first time, substantial numbers from areas other than the southern provinces. The Shanghai region had been a major source of students going overseas from pre-Communist China (Wang 1966, pp. 156–64).

There has been a shift in the type of migrant moving to the most important overseas destination, the USA. In fiscal year 1987–88, for example, of the 20 267 who were admitted against the category of China as 'state of chargeability', which is based upon place of birth, all but 1111 were selected under 'relative

Figure 13.1 Main regions of origin of Chinese migrants

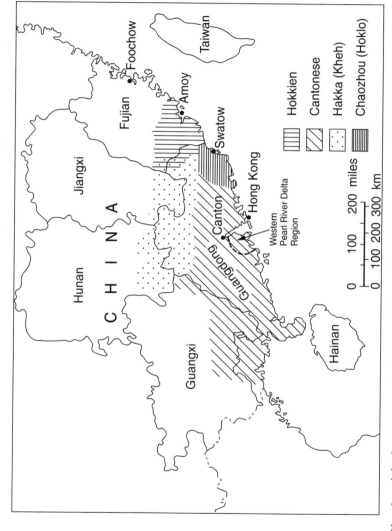

Note: The Hakkas often inhabit the same areas as the Cantonese, Hokkien and other peoples
Source: Modified and simplified from V. Purcell, *The Chinese in Southeast Asia*, Oxford University Press, 1965, second edition, p. 6.

preferences' showing the importance of family linkages in the migration. By 1991–92, the 22 965 admitted by China as state of chargeability were split almost evenly between family-sponsored preferences (11 511) and employment-based preferences (11 454). The 1992–93 intake of 24 726 shows an almost identical split between family and employment preferences. However, rather than indicating an increase in the number of independent migrants, as one might have expected after the 1990 Immigration Act that deliberately sets out to increase the proportion of more highly skilled independent migrants, this change for China was almost certainly due to charging students under the employment third preference in the new act. The students are thus in the vanguard of pushing the migration catchment areas of the USA, and also of Australia, beyond the southern provinces and probably towards the largest cities of the centre and north. These migrants, in their turn, may be expected to generate future family-sponsored members, consolidating these migration fields in the future. It is highly unlikely that the poorer interior provinces are participating to any significant extent in these international flows, which are dominated either by relatives from the traditional areas of migration in the south or by the highly educated – that is, people from the wealthier sectors of Chinese society, from the largest urban areas of the central and northern coastal regions.

Contract migration

In the 1970s China was sending contract migrants to socialist Africa and also at that time there were systems of internal temporary contract labour (Blecher 1984). Since 1979, China's attitude towards its labour force has changed from seeing it simply as a domestic issue to considering it as a factor of trade to obtain foreign exchange (Fang 1991). The numbers engaged in overseas contracts rose from just over 30 000 in 1983 to 173 654 in 1993 (Table 13.5). The numbers rose markedly after 1991 and, although China had contracts in well over one hundred countries, much of the recent increase is due to the huge construction projects in Hong Kong and Macau. Over 40 000 contract labourers from China were working in these two territories in 1991 (Zhang 1995) and numbers have certainly grown since then as the huge Hong Kong airport and associated infrastructure projects have moved into the full construction phases. The vast majority of the labourers going to Hong Kong and Macau are from Guangdong Province, although labourers going to projects overseas, in Japan, Singapore, or the Middle East, are likely to represent more widespread origins. There also appear to be some 15 000 Chinese workers mainly from Heilongjiang province in the far north-east who are working in the Russian Far East (Kakazu 1994, p. 249). This directly reflects the growing trade between Russia and China, most of it informal, following the collapse of the Soviet Union between 1989 and 1996. Chinese merchants have also been quick to establish joint ventures in the opening

Table 13.5 Chinese workers engaged in overseas construction contracts

	Contracted projects		Labour co-operation		Other personnel	Total personnel
	Personnel	Value (US$ million)	Personnel	Value (US$ million)		
1982	8470	346	23 158	161	143	31 771
1983	13 056	799	17 663	125	252	30 971
1984	21 910	1538	27 557	199	508	49 975
1985	30 640	1116	24 895	149	729	56 264
1986	27 403	1189	18 991	170	668	47 062
1987	31 300	1648	31 949	241	896	64 145
1988	30 024	1813	39 810	359	1050	70 884
1989	23 951	1781	41 867	431	1248	67 066
1990	21 823	2125	36 116	478	–	57 939
1991	21 523	2524	68 314	1085	–	89 837
1992	25 420	5251	105 564	1335	–	130 984
1993	34 223	5189	139 431	1661	–	173 654

Source: *China Yearbook of Foreign Relations and Trade*, Beijing, various years.

Siberian economy. There have been claims that there are as many as one million Chinese living illegally in Siberia's border regions (*Asia Yearbook* 1994, p. 199).

Illegal migration

The main problem in dealing with illegal migration clearly relates to data; there are no reliable figures. It is known that in recent years there have been very significant flows indeed from China, primarily from southern China and mainly the coastal areas of Fujian, to the USA. These have variously been estimated at around 100 000 persons a year in the early 1990s, although there may have been some slowing since then. Chinese sources have estimated that there were up to half a million Chinese waiting for transit to the West, to cities in Russia, Eastern Europe, South-East Asia and Latin America. Most appeared to be heading towards the USA, although Australia and western European cities were also destinations (*Migration News*, November 1994; Myers 1993). Some of the mechanics and implications of this movement have been discussed elsewhere (Skeldon 1994a). Suffice it to say here that its significance lies as much in its linkage to international criminal syndicates as in pure numbers. The global outreach and financial resources of these syndicates makes them a powerful force for illegal trafficking in drugs, as well as in people, that almost certainly will have a profound impact on origin and destination economies and societies as these criminal groups are major multinational corporations of global outreach.

Trade development and Greater China

China's trade increased markedly throughout the 1980s from $US38.14 billion in 1980 to $US115.41 billion in 1990 to $US195.72 billion in 1993 (Lardy 1994, p. 2). At the same time as the value of trade has increased, so its direction has changed. The relative importance of Hong Kong has increased both as a source of imports and as a destination for exports. For example, in 1983, Hong Kong accounted for 8 per cent of imports and 26 per cent of exports, whereas by 1992 Hong Kong generated 25.5 per cent of imports and accounted for 44.2 per cent of exports. Clearly, Hong Kong itself is not the origin or destination, it is simply the port through which an increasing proportion of China's trade flows. Hong Kong's re-exports to China increased almost tenfold during the period 1984–1993, and its re-exports from China increased almost seventeenfold over the same period (calculated from data in Hong Kong 1994, p. 98). While Hong Kong could be seen as a conduit for China's production and consumption, the reality is more complex: so much of the increase in China's trade is due to the expansion of Hong Kong and, to a lesser extent Taiwan, into southern China. Labour shortages and escalating wages, rent, and the cost of utilities are pushing labour-intensive industries out of Hong Kong and Taiwan into China. The numbers employed in manufacturing in Hong Kong have declined from a high of 905 899 in 1981 to 483 628 in 1993. Annual indices of industrial production for plastic products, fabricated metal products, and consumer electrical and electronic products have almost invariably been negative since 1988 and, even by the late 1980s, it was estimated that between 70–80 per cent of the electronics and plastics industries had been moved to China (Feng 1991, p. 499). By 1991, there were some 3 million employees in Hong Kong manufacturing based in China itself (*Hsueh and Woo* 1994, p. 708). The data for Taiwan are not so complete as there is still officially little contact between the two societies. However, the numbers employed in manufacturing, in Taiwan declined: from a peak of 2 810 000 in 1987 to 2 587 000 in 1992.

Hong Kong also plays a critical role as a conduit for capital to China. Estimates of total foreign investment to China vary and there is a big difference between the amounts approved (contracted) and those actually utilised. Dealing only with amounts approved, Lardy (1994, p. 63), citing official Chinese statistics, observed an increase from almost $US7 billion in 1990, to $US12.4 billion in 1991, to $US58.7 billion in 1992, to $US110 850 in 1993. Unpublished figures from the Hongkong Bank indicate that the amounts of approved investment flowing from Hong Kong to China in those years were $US4 billion, $US7 billion, $US40 billion and $US75 billion, respectively. Even though the figures are from different sources, the data suggest that the proportion of capital moving to China from Hong Kong is very significant indeed. Of course, the Hong Kong figures say nothing about their provenance but all were funnelled through Hong Kong-based companies and institutions. Much of the investment in China, if not most, comes through overseas Chinese networks and, by the end of 1992, it was estimated that 80 per cent of direct foreign investment in China was from overseas Chinese sources (Ch'ng 1993). These sources include capital generated *in the two economic powerhouses*, of Hong Kong and Taiwan. For a review of the role of Hong Kong in the development of southern China, see Skeldon (1995).

Thus, any discussion of trade and migration in China immediately runs into the question of whose trade and which migration. A significant part of the rapidly increasing trade from China is generated in Hong Kong (and to some extent Taiwan) and it is generated from the *de facto* greater Hong Kong urban and industrial region that includes the Special Economic Zone of Shenzhen but also stretches well beyond towards Guangzhou and around the Pearl River Delta. The Hong Kong and Pearl River Delta region, plus Taiwan and parts of Fujian, is the core of a 'Greater China' which, in the next century, may be the world's leading trader and a powerful economic and political force (Shambaugh 1993). It is the linkages between this region and the communities of Chinese overseas that both augment and project the power and influence of a Greater China. Thus, the international migration from Hong Kong and Taiwan should also perhaps be considered in this respect, but space precludes any meaningful assessment here (see Skeldon 1992a, and 1994b). That migration, heavily weighted towards the educated, skilled, entrepreneurial, and administrative population of Hong Kong is fundamental in establishing and reinforcing the overseas Chinese linkages. That migration, too, has been increasing markedly since the mid-1980s, and is due as much to new opportunities in North America and Australasia and the booming Hong Kong and south China economy as it is to political uncertainties over the return of Hong Kong to Chinese sovereignty in 1997. In terms of its economy and as a functionally integrated urban region, Hong Kong is already part of China.

The export-oriented industrialisation of southern China has had a profound impact on the pattern of internal migration. The emergence of free markets and the erosion of government control over household registration has resulted in the loosening of the Chinese population from their home places. The opening of China to the outside world after 1978 and the establishment of centres of foreign investment and export-oriented industrialisation at points along the eastern seaboard have given direction to this migration. Tens of millions of Chinese are now on the move searching for opportunities, and Guangdong province, together with the Shanghai and Beijing urban regions, have emerged as the principal targets for long-term and short-term population movements. Migration to Guangdong from other provinces accounted for fully 10 per cent of all interprovincial moves between 1985 and 1990 compared with only 4 per cent of moves between 1982 and 1987, with the absolute number of migrants increasing from 260 000 during the earlier period to 1.16 million during the five years before the 1990 census (Li and Siu 1994, pp. 378–9). The census and the preceding survey captured only a relatively small proportion of total mobility and more than one million job-seekers are estimated to have arrived in the Pearl River Delta after Chinese New Year in 1993 (Taubmann 1993, pp. 9–10). Chinese government estimates of the total number of short-term travellers after Chinese New Year in 1994 were in the region of 160 million. The migration to Guangdong is female dominant, with only 86 males per 100 females in the flow measured by the census, reflecting the demand for a cheap, easily manipulated labour force in the newly established labour-intensive activities in the Greater Hong Kong urban area.

Given the difficulties of obtaining a foreign passport in China, it is unlikely that many of these migrants will be able to move on overseas in a sequence similar to that described by Sassen (1988) for countries in the Caribbean. There, the build-up of urban labour forces through internal migration and the periodic turnover of employment creates a pool of the unemployed ready to try their luck overseas. The state in China still tightly controls emigration but, if these controls are eroded, or are allowed to erode, like the internal controls, then we may see this type of effect developing. Already, tens of thousands have left China illegally and the potential for future movement is vast, with implications not only for the USA and other distant countries which already have substantial ethnic Chinese populations but also, and more likely, for prosperous labour-deficit economies much closer to China such as Japan, Korea, Taiwan and the Russian Far East.

Conclusion

China's opening to the world has a long history, from a few tenuous contacts from the early sixteenth century through to the mid-nineteenth century, through a forced participation from the second half of that century to a greater willingness to participate in the global economy in the late twentieth century. There have been clear fluctuations in this development, with periods of self-imposed re-isolation. Nevertheless, Western ideas have been crucial in the transformation of the economy and society throughout this long period, and migration and trade have been equally important in diffusing these ideas. The early role of labour recruiters and brokers was fundamental to the establishment of global linkages, and the later pioneering role of Chinese students in going overseas, learning new ideas, and returning to implement them was clearly of fundamental importance to the directions taken at particular times. There were, circa 1990, around 36.8 million Chinese outside China and Taiwan (Poston, Mao & Yu 1994). Even excluding Hong Kong and Macau, this leaves over 30 million overseas, the majority in Asia, but with the most rapidly growing communities in the Americas and Australasia.

Trade and increasing migration have been complementary and it is unlikely that this will change, assuming that the direction of China's policies remains basically unchanged in a post-Deng era. Should there be a shift towards a more conservative and isolationist regime, trade might slow, but migration would almost certainly persist as many of the newly emerged middle-income group sought to flee. To date, the numbers leaving China have been modest relative to the huge population of China itself. Yet, their importance is not primarily in terms of numbers but of quality and of financial resources. A minority of dynamic entrepreneurs moving within a global network of communities has the potential to create powerful new trading relations. When these migrants originate in what, potentially, may soon be the world's largest economy – and from the early part of this chapter we have seen that China has been the largest economy throughout much of human history – then the implications of these networks for international relations are profound indeed. It is these factors that make the current Chinese diaspora unique and which give it its significance, now and in the future.

References

Abramovitz, M. 1986, 'Catching Up, Forging Ahead, and Falling Behind', *Journal of Economic History*, no. 46, pp. 385–406.

Abella, M. 1992, 'Contemporary Labour Migration from Asia: Policies and Perspectives of Sending Countries', in L. L. Lim & H. Zlotnik (eds), *International Migration Systems: A Global Approach*, Oxford University Press, Oxford.

_____ 1994, 'Introduction', *Asian and Pacific Migration Journal*, vol. 3, no. 1, pp. 1–6.

Adams, W. 1969, *The Brain Drain*, Macmillan, New York.

Agarwala, R. 1983, 'Price Distortions and Growth in Developing Countries', World Bank Staff Working Paper no. 575, Washington, DC.

Alburo, F. 1994, 'Trade and Turning Points in Labor Migration', *Asian and Pacific Migration Journal*, vol. 3, no. 1, pp. 49–80.

Anderson, K. & Norheim, H. 1993, 'Is World Trade Becoming More Regionalised?', *Review of International Economics*, vol. 1, no. 2, pp. 91–109.

Appleyard, R. 1991, *International Migration: The Challenge of the Nineties*, International Organization for Migration, Geneva.

Arnold, F. 1989, 'Unanswered Questions About the Immigration Multiplier', *International Migration Review*, vol. 23, pp. 889–92.

Asian Development Bank 1992, *Asian Development Outlook 1992*, Asian Development Bank, Manila.

Asian Migrant 1993, 'Trends in Asian Labor Migration, 1992', vol. 6, no. 1, pp. 4–16.

Athukorala, P. 1993, 'International Labor Migration in the Asia–Pacific Region: Patterns, Policies and Economic Implications', *Asian–Pacific Economic Literature*, no. 7, pp. 28–57.

Australian Bureau of Statistics (ABS) 1990a, *Foreign Ownership and Control of the Manufacturing Industry Australia 1986–87*, Australian Government Printer, Canberra.

_____ 1990b, *Foreign Ownership and Control of the Mining Industry Australia 1986–87*, Australian Government Printer, Canberra.

_____ 1994, *The Social Characteristics of Immigrants in Australia*, Australian Government Publishing Service (AGPS), Canberra.

Baker, M. & Wooden, M. 1991, *Immigration and Training*, AGPS, Canberra.

Baldwin, R. 1984, 'Trade Policies in Developed Countries', in R. W. Jones & P. B. Kenen (eds), *Handbook of International Economics*, vol. 1, North Holland, Amsterdam.

Barro, R. J. 1990, 'Government Spending in a Simple Model of Endogenous Growth', *Journal of Political Economy*, no. 98, pp. 103–25.

_____ 1991, 'Economic Growth in a Cross Section of Countries', *Quarterly Journal of Economics*, no. 106, pp. 407–43.

Barro, R. J. & Lee, J. W. 1994, 'Data Set for a Panel of 138 Countries', National Bureau of Economic Research, Cambridge, Mass., January. Internet <http://nber.harvard.edu>.

Barro, R. J. & Sala-i-Martin, X. 1992, 'Convergence', *Journal of Political Economy*, no. 100, pp. 223–52.

_____ 1995, *Economic Growth*, New York, McGraw-Hill.

Batam Industrial Development Authority (various years), *Development Data*.

Baum, J. 1995, 'Toil and trouble?', *Far Eastern Economic Review*, 25 May, pp. 56–8.

_____ 1995, 'Passport Politics', *Far Eastern Economic Review*, 18 May, p. 28.

Baumol, W. 1986, 'Productivity Growth, Convergence and Welfare: What the Long-Run Data Show', *American Economic Review*, no. 76, pp. 1072–85.

Becker, G. S. & Barro, R. J. 1988, 'A Reformulation of the Economic Theory of Fertility', *Quarterly Journal of Economics*, no. 103, pp. 1–25.

Becker, G. S., Murphy, K. M. & Tamura, R. 1988, 'Human Capital, Fertility, and Economic Growth', *Journal of Political Economy*, no. 98, pp. 12–37.

Bell, M. & Carr, R. 1994, *Japanese Temporary Residents in Cairns Tourism Industry*, AGPS, Canberra.

Bencivenga, V .R. & Smith, B. D. 1991, 'Financial Intermediation and Endogenous Growth', *Review of Economic Studies*, no. 58, pp. 195–209.

Beng, C. S. 1990, 'Brain Drain in Singapore: Issues and Prospects', *Singapore Economic Review*, vol. 35, no. 2, pp. 55–77.

Berry, A. R. & Soligo, R. 1969, 'Some Welfare Aspects of International Migration', *Journal of Political Economy*, vol. 77, pp. 778–94.

Bhagwati, J. N. 1971, 'The Generalized Theory of Distortions and Welfare', in J. N. Bhagwati et al. (ed.), *Trade, Balance of Payments and Growth: Essays in Honor of Charles P. Kindleberger*, North Holland, Amsterdam.

_____ 1984, 'Why Are Services Cheaper in the Poorer Countries', *Economic Journal*, no. 94, pp. 279–86.

Bhagwati, J. N. & Rodriguez, C. 1986, 'Welfare-Theoretical Analyses of the Brain Drain', *Journal of Development Economics*, no. 2, pp. 195–221.

Blecher, M. 1984, 'Peasant Labour for Urban Industry: Temporary Contract Labour, Urban–Rural Balance and Class Relations in a Chinese County', in N. Maxwell & B. McFarlane (eds), *China's Changed Road to Development*, Oxford, Pergamon Press, pp. 109–23.

Bollard, A. E. 1987, 'Trans-Tasman Investment', in A. E. Bollard & M. A.Thompson (eds), *Trans-Tasman Trade and Investment*, Research Monograph 38, NZIER, Wellington.

Bora, B. 1992, 'The Effects of NAFTA on Australian FDI', Working Paper 92–10, Centre for International Economics, Adelaide.

_____ 1995, 'Import and Export Propensities for APEC Members', mimeo, Flinders University.

_____ 1996a, 'Foreign Direct Investment', in B. Bora & C. Findlay (eds), *Regional Integration and the Asia Pacific*, Oxford University Press, Melbourne.

_____ 1996b, 'North American Free Trade Agreement', in B. Bora & C. Findlay (eds), Regional Integration and the Asia Pacific, Oxford University Press, Melbourne.

Borjas, G. J. 1994, 'The Economics of Immigration', *Journal of Economic Literature*, vol. XXXII, December, pp. 1667–717.

Borrmann, A. & Jungnickel, R. 1992, 'Foreign Investment as a Factor in Asian Integration', *Intereconomics*, November/December, pp. 282–8.

Braga, C. & Bannister, G. 1994, 'East Asian Prospects for Growing Regionalisation in the 1990s', *Transnational Corporations*, vol. 3, no. 1, pp. 97–137.

Brander, J. A. & Dowrick, S. 1994, 'The Role of Fertility and Population in Economic Growth: Empirical Results from Aggregate Cross-National Data', *Journal of Population Economics*, no. 7, pp. 1–25.

Brooks, C., Murphy, J. & Williams, L. 1994, *The Role of Skilled Temporary Residents in the Australian Labour Market*, Bureau of Immigration and Population Research, Melbourne.

Brosnan, P. & Poot, J. 1987, 'Modelling the Determinants of Trans-Tasman Migration after World War II', *The Economic Record*, vol. 63, December, pp. 313–29.

Bureau of Immigration and Population Research (BIPR) 1994, *Immigration Update*, June Quarter, AGPS, Canberra.

Bureau of Immigration Research (BIR) 1990, *Immigration Update December 1989*, AGPS, Canberra.

_____ 1990, *Settler Arrivals 1988–89*, Statistical Report no. 2, AGPS, Canberra.

Bureau of Immigration, Multicultural and Population Research (BIMPR), *Community Profiles*, various issues, AGPS, Canberra.

_____ 1995a, *Emigration 1993–94*, AGPS, Canberra.

_____ 1995b, *Immigration Update*, AGPS, Canberra.

_____ 1995c, *Settler Arrivals 1993–94*, Statistical Report no. 13, AGPS, Canberra.

Bureau of Industry Economics 1993, *Globalisation: Implications for Australian Information Technology Industries*, AGPS, Canberra.

Caballe, J. & Santos, M. S. 1993, 'On Endogenous Growth with Physical and Human Capital', *Journal of Political Economy*, no. 101, pp. 1042–67.

Cantwell, J. 1994, 'The Relationship between International Trade and International Production', in D. Greenaway & L. A. Winters (eds), *Surveys in International Trade*, Blackwell, Oxford.

Carino, B. V. 1987, 'The Philippines and Southeast Asia: Historical Roots and Contemporary Linkages', in J. T. Fawcett & B. V. Carino (eds), *Pacific Bridges: The New Immigration from Asia and the Pacific Islands*, Center for Migration Studies, Staten Island, New York, pp. 305–26.

Carmichael, G. A. (ed.) 1993, *Trans-Tasman Migration: Trends, Causes and Consequences*, AGPS, Canberra.

Castles, S. 1984, *Here for Good*, Pluto Press, London.

Castles, S. & Miller, M. J. 1993, *The Age of Migration: International Population Movements in the Modern World*, The Macmillan Press, London.

Centre for International Economics 1990, *Immigration, Trade and Capital Flows*, AGPS, Canberra.

Ch'ng, D. C. L. 1993, *The Overseas Chinese Entrepreneurs in East Asia: Background, Business Practices and International Networks*, Committee for Economic Development of Australia (CEDA), Melbourne.

Chen, D. 1994, 'Chinese Public Policy and the Southern China Growth Triangle', in M. Thant, M. Tang & H. Kakazu (eds), *Growth Triangles in Asia, A New Approach to Regional Economic Cooperation*, Oxford University Press for the Asian Development Bank, Hong Kong.

Chen, E. & Ho, A. 1994, 'Southern China Growth Triangle: An Overview', in M. Thant, M. Tang & H. Kakazu (eds), *Growth Triangles in Asia, A New Approach to Regional Economic Cooperation*, Oxford University Press for the Asian Development Bank, Hong Kong.

Chia, Siow-Yue & Lee Tsao Yuan 1993, 'Subregional Economic Zones: A New Motive Force in Asia-Pacific Development', in C. Bergsten & M. Noland (eds), *Pacific*

Dynamism and the International Economic System, Institute of International Economics, Washington, DC.

Chia, Siow-Yue 1995, 'The International Procurement and Sales Behaviour of Multinational Enterprises', in E. Y. Chen & P. Drysdale (eds), *Corporate Links and Foreign Direct Investment in Asia and the Pacific*, Harper Educational, Sydney.

Choo, W. 1995, Talent Resource and Singapore's Development, Paper presented at The Third National Immigration and Population Outlook Conference, 22–24 February, Adelaide.

Citizenship and Immigration Canada (CIC) 1994a, *Facts and Figures: Overview of Immigration, 1993*, Strategic Research, Analysis and Information Branch, Policy Sector, Citizenship and Immigration Canada, Ottawa.

_____ 1994b, *Annual Report to Parliament: Immigration Plan 1994*, Citizenship and Immigration Canada, Ottawa.

Clarke, H. & Smith, L. 1994, 'Labour Immigration and Capital Flows: Long-term Australian, Canadian and United States Experience', *International Migration Review* (forthcoming).

Cornelius, W. 1994, 'Japan: The Illusion of Immigration Control', in W. Cornelius., P. Martin, & J. Hollifield (eds), *Controlling Immigration: A Global Perspective*, Stanford University Press, Stanford, CA.

Cross, M. 1990, 'A Magnet in Asia', *Far Eastern Economic Review*, 6 December, p. 66.

Curtin, P. D. 1984, *Cross-Cultural Trade in World History*, Cambridge University Press, Cambridge.

Das, K. & Sacerdoti, G. 1978, 'Economics of Human Cargo', *Far Eastern Economic Review*, 22 December, pp. 10–12.

Davis, L. E. 1963, 'Capital Immobilities and Finance Capitalism: A Study of Economic Evolution in the United States', *Explorations in Economic History*, no. 1, pp. 88–105.

Dawkins, P., Kemp, S. & Cabalu, H. 1995, *Trade and Investment with East Asia in Selected Service Industries*, AGPS, Canberra.

Dawkins, P., Lewis, P., Noris, K., Baker, M., Robertson, F., Groenewold, N. & Hagger, A. 1991, *Flows of Immigrants to South Australia, Tasmania and Western Australia*, AGPS, Canberra.

De Gregorio, J. 1992, 'Economic Growth in Latin America', *Journal of Development Economics*, no. 39, pp. 59–84.

De Long, J. B. 1988, 'Productivity Growth, Convergence and Welfare: Comment', *American Economic Review*, no. 78, pp. 1138–54.

Department of Employment, Education and Training (DEET) 1995, *Overseas Student Statistics 1994*, DEET, International Division, Canberra.

Department of Immigration and Ethnic Affairs (DIEA) 1994a, 'People in Australia Unlawfully', Fact Sheet no. 6, DIEA, Canberra.

_____ 1994b, 'Overseas Students in Australia', Fact Sheet no. 18, DIEA, Canberra.

_____ 1994c, 'Skilled Migration to Australia', Fact Sheet no. 22, DIEA, Canberra.

_____ 1995a, 'Boat People', Fact Sheet no. 4, DIEA, Canberra.

_____ 1995b, 'Boat Arrivals since 1989', Fact Sheet no. 5, DIEA, Canberra.

_____ 1995c, 'Temporary Residence in Australia', Fact Sheet no. 7, DIEA, Canberra.

Dixon, P., Parmenter, B., Sutton, J. & Vincent, D. 1982, *ORANI: A Multi-Sectoral Model of the Australian Economy*, North-Holland, Amsterdam.

Djajic, S. 1986, 'International Migration, Remittances and Welfare in a Dependent Economy', *Journal of Development Economics*, no. 21, pp. 229–34.

Do Rosario, L. 1995, 'Futures and Options', *Far Eastern Economic Review*, 15 June.

Dowrick, S. & Nguyen, D. T. 1989, 'OECD Comparative Economic Growth 1950–85: Catch-Up and Convergence', *American Economic Review*, no. 79, pp. 1010–30.

Drysdale, P. & Garnaut, R. 1993, 'The Pacific: An Application of a General Theory of Economic Integration', in F. Bergsten & M. Noland (eds), *Pacific Dynamism and the International Economic System*, Institute for International Economics, Washington, DC.

Dunning, J. H. 1981, *International Production and the Multinational Enterprise*, George Allen & Unwin, London.

Easterly, W. 1993, 'How Much Do Distortions Affect Growth?', *Journal of Monetary Economics*, no. 32, pp. 187–212.

_____ 1993, 'Good Policy or Good Luck? Country Growth Performance and Temporary Shocks', Working Paper Series no. 4474, National Bureau of Economic Research, September.

Easterly, W. & Rebelo, S. 1993, 'Fiscal Policy and Economic Growth: An Empirical Investigation', *Journal of Monetary Economics*, no. 32, pp. 417–58.

Edwards, S. 1992, 'Trade Orientation, Distortions and Growth in Developing Countries', *Journal of Development Economics*, no. 39, pp. 31–57.

_____ 1993, 'Openness, Trade Liberalization and Growth in Developing Countries', *Journal of Economic Literature*, no. 31, pp. 1358–93.

Edwards, S. & Holmes, Sir Frank 1994, *CER: Economic Trends and Linkages*, The National Bank of New Zealand and Institute of Policy Studies, Wellington.

Elek, A. 1996, 'The Open Economic Association of APEC', in B. Bora & C. Findlay (eds), *Regional Integration and the Asia Pacific*, Oxford University Press, Melbourne.

Employment and Immigration Canada 1989, *Immigration to Canada: Economic Impacts*, Hull, Ottawa.

Ethier, W. J. 1979, 'Internationally Decreasing Costs and World Trade', *Journal of International Economics*, no. 9, pp. 1–24.

_____ 1982a, 'Decreasing Costs in International Trade and Frank Graham's Argument for Protection', *Econometrica*, no. 50, pp. 1243–68.

_____ 1982b, 'National and International Returns to Scale in the Modern Theory of International Trade', *American Economic Review*, no. 72, pp. 389–404.

_____ 1984, 'Higher Dimensional Issues in Trade Theory', in P. B. Kenen & R. W. Jones (eds), *Handbook of International Economics*, North-Holland, Amsterdam, pp. 131–84.

_____ 1986, 'International Trade Theory and International Migration', in O. Stark (ed.), *Migration Theory, Human Capital and Development*, JAI Press, Greenwich, pp. 27–74.

_____ 1987, 'The Theory of International Trade', in L. Officer (ed.), *International Economics*, North-Holland, Amsterdam, pp. 1–57.

Ethier, W. J. & Svensson, L. E. O. 1986, 'The Theorems of International Trade with Factor Mobility', *Journal of International Economics*, no. 20, pp. 21–42.

Fairbank, J. K. 1986, *The Great Chinese Revolution 1800–1985*, Harper and Row, New York.

Fairclough, G. 1995, 'Seeking Fortune', *Far Eastern Economic Review*, 25 May, pp. 58–9.

Fang, S. 1991, 'Mainland China's Overseas Construction Contracts and Export of Labor', *Issues and Studies*, vol. 27, no. 2, pp. 65–75.

Farmer, R. & Buetow, S. 1993, 'Aspects of Trans-Tasman Migration in the 1980s: Insights from New Zealand Data', in G. A. Carmichael (ed.), *Trans-Tasman Migration: Trends, Causes and Consequences*, AGPS, Canberra.

Feng, B. Y. 1991, 'The Role of Hong Kong in China's Modernization', in E. K. Y. Chen, M.K. Nyaw & T. Y. C. Wong (eds), *Industrial and Trade Development in Hong Kong*, The University of Hong Kong, Centre of Asian Studies, pp. 497–509.

Fields, G. 1994, 'The Migration Transition in Asia', *Asian and Pacific Migration Journal*, no. 3, vol. 1, pp. 7–30.

FitzGerald, S. (Chairman) 1988, *Immigration: A Commitment to Australia*, The Report of the Committee to Advise on Australia's Immigration Policies, AGPS, Canberra.

Foster, W. & Baker, L. 1991, *Immigration and the Australian Economy*, AGPS, Canberra.

Frankel, J. 1993, 'Is Japan Creating a Yen Block in East Asia and the Pacific?', in J. Frankel & M. Kahler (eds), *Regionalism and Rivalry: Japan and the United States in the Asia Pacific*, University of Chicago Press, Chicago.

Freeman, G. (forthcoming), 'Modes of Immigration Politics in the Liberal Democracies', *International Migration Review*.

———— 1995, The Quest for Skill: A Comparative Analysis, presented at the Conference on Migration and Migration Policies: The International Experience at MIT, Cambridge, Mass.

Fukasaku, K. 1992, 'Economic Regionalisation and Intra-Industry Trade: Pacific Asian Perspectives', OECD Technical Paper no. 53, Paris.

Furuya, K. 1995, 'Labor Migration and Skill Development: Japan's Trainee Program', *Asian Migrant*, vol. 8, no. 1, pp. 4–13.

Gandataruna, K. 1994, Indonesia–Malaysia–Thailand Growth Triangle Development Project: Indonesian Perspective, Paper presented at the Fourth Southeast Asia Roundtable on Economic Development: Growth Triangles in Southeast Asia, organised by the Institute of Strategic and International Studies, Kuala Lumpur, 27–28 June.

Garrett, A. 1992, The Factor Market Consequences of Foreign Investment in Australia, Honours Research Paper, University of Melbourne, Melbourne.

GATT, 1992, *International Trade 1990–1991*, vol. II, General Agreement on Tariffs and Trade, Geneva.

Geary, P. & O'Grada, C. 1985, Immigration and the Real Wage: Time Series Evidence from the United States, 1820–1977, Paper presented at joint CEPR–RIIA Workshop on International Labour Migration.

Gerschenkron, A. 1962, *Economic Backwardness in Historical Perspective*, Harvard University Press, Cambridge, Mass.

Goldstein, C. 1994, 'Innocents Abroad', *Far Eastern Economic Review*, 15 September, pp. 22–7.

Gould, D.M. 1994, 'Immigrant Links to the Home Country: Empirical Implications for U.S. Bilateral Trade Flows', *Review of Economics and Statistics*, no. 76, pp. 302–16.

Greenwood, J. & Jovanovic, B. 1990, 'Financial Development, Growth, and the Distribution of Income', *Journal of Political Economy*, no. 98, pp. 1076–107.

Greenwood, M. J. & McDowell, J. M. 1994, 'The National Labour Market Consequences of U.S. Immigration', in H. Giersch (ed.), *Economic Aspects of International Migration*, Springer-Verlag, Berlin, pp. 155–94.

Guangdong Statistical Bureau various years, *Statistical Yearbook of Guangdong*, Guangdong, People's Republic of China.

Gurley, J. G. & Shaw, E. S. 1995, 'Financial Aspects of Economic Development', *American Economic Review*, no. 45, pp. 515–38.

Hanoch, G. 1971, 'CRESH Production Functions', *Econometrica*, vol. 39, no. 5.

Hargraves, C. 1994, 'Trade in Services in the Asia Pacific', mimeo, Economic Modelling Bureau of Australia, Australian National University.

Helpman, E. 1981, 'International Trade in the Presence of Product Differentiation, Economies of Scale and Monopolistic Competition', *Journal of International Economics*, no. 11, pp. 305–40.

Helpman, E. & Krugman P. 1985, *Market Structure and Foreign Trade*, MIT Press, Boston.

Heston, A., Summers, R., Nuxoll, D. A. & Aten, B. 1994, 'The Penn World Table, Version 5.6', National Bureau of Economic Research, Cambridge, Mass., November. Internet <http://nber.harvard.edu>.

Hiebert, M. 1995, 'Give and Take', *Far Eastern Economic Review*, 25 May, pp. 54–6.

Higgs, J. P., Parham, D. & Parmenter, B. R. 1981, 'Occupational Wage Relativities and Labour–Labour Substitution in the Australian Economy: Applications of the ORANI Model', Preliminary Working Paper OP-30, IMPACT Project Research Centre, Melbourne.

Holmes, Sir F. 1991, CER, The Free Movement of People and Immigration Policies, Paper presented at the BIR National Immigration Outlook Conference, November 14–16.

Hong Kong 1994, *Annual Digest of Statistics*, 1994 edition, Census and Statistics Department.

Horiba, Y. & Kirkpatrick, R. C. 1981, 'Factor Endowments, Factor Proportions and the Allocative Efficiency of US Interregional Trade', *Review of Economics and Statistics*, vol. 63, no. 2, pp. 178–87.

Hsueh, T. T. & Woo, T. O. 1994, 'The Development of Hong Kong–China Economic Relationship' in B. K. P. Leung & T. C. Wong (eds) 1994, *25 Years of Social Development in Hong Kong*, The University of Hong Kong, Centre of Asian Studies, pp. 469–96.

Hufbauer, G. & Schott, J. 1992, *North American Free Trade: Issues and Recommendations*, Institute for International Economics, Washington, DC.

Hugo, G. J. 1987, 'Postwar Refugee Migration in Southeast Asia: Patterns, Problems and Policies', pp. 237–52, in J. R. Rogge (ed.), *Refugees: A Third World Dilemma*, Rowman and Littlefield, New Jersey.

———— 1991, 'Recent International Migration Trends in Asia: Some Implications for Australia', in J. N. Smith (ed.), *Immigration, Population and Sustainable Environments: The Limits to Australia's Growth*, The Flinders Press, Adelaide.

———— 1992, Indonesian Labour Migration to Malaysia: Trends and Policy Implications, Paper presented to International Colloquium on Migration, Development and Gender in Southeast Asia, organised by the Population Studies Unit of the University of Malaya, Kuantan, Malaysia, 28–31 October.

———— 1993a, 'Indonesian Labour Migration to Malaysia: Trends and Policy Implications', *Southeast Asian Journal of Social Science*, vol. 21, no. 1, pp. 36–70.

———— 1993b, 'International Labour Migration', in C. Manning & J. Hardjono (eds), *Indonesia Assessment 1993 Labour: Sharing in the Benefits of Growth*, Department of Political and Social Change, Research School of Pacific Studies, Canberra, pp. 108–23.

_____ 1994, *The Economic Implications of Emigration from Australia*, AGPS, Canberra.

Hugo, G. J. forthcoming, 'Labour Export from Indonesia: An Overview', *ASEAN Economic Bulletin.*

Hugo, G. J. & Gartner, M. 1993, 'Evaluation of the Prototype Survey First Wave and Some Recommendations for the Full Survey, Bureau of Immigration Research Prototype Survey for a Longitudinal Survey of Immigrants to Australia (LSIA)', Working Paper Series, Working Paper no. 7, April.

Hugo, G. J. & Maher, C. A. 1995, *Atlas of the Australian People–1991 Census*, BIMPR, Canberra.

Huguet, J. 1992, 'The Future of International Migration Within Asia', *Asian and Pacific Migration Journal*, no. 1/2, pp. 250–77.

Immigration and Naturalization Service (INS) 1991, *1990 Statistical Yearbook of the Immigration and Naturalization Service*, US Department of Justice, Washington, DC.

_____ 1993, *1992 Statistical Yearbook of the Immigration and Naturalization Service*, US Department of Justice, Washington, DC.

_____ 1994, *1993 Statistical Yearbook of the Immigration and Naturalization Service*, US Department of Justice, Washington, DC.

International Monetary Fund, various years, *Balance of Payments Statistics Yearbook*, Washington, DC.

Ito, S. & Iguchi, Y. 1993, 'Japanese Direct Investment in Selected ASEAN Countries and its Impact on Migration', Asia–Pacific Migration Affecting Australia Conference Papers, BIPR, Darwin.

_____ 1994, 'Japanese Direct Investment and Its Impact on Migration in the ASEAN 4', *Asian and Pacific Migration Journal*, no. 3/2–3, pp. 265–94.

James, D., Gorbey, S. & Poot, J. 1995, 'Population Forecasting', Working Paper 94/20, NZ Institute of Economic Research, Wellington.

Japan Immigration Association 1990, 'A Guide to Entry, Residence and Registration Procedures in Japan for Foreign Nationals', Tokyo.

Johansen, L. 1960, *A Multi-Sectoral Model of Economic Growth*, North-Holland, Amsterdam.

Jones, C. I. 1992, *Economic Growth and the Relative Price of Capital*, MIT.

Jones, R. W. 1971, 'A Three-factor Model in Theory, Trade and History', in J. N. Bhagwati et al. (ed.), *Trade, Balance of Payments and Growth*, North-Holland, Amsterdam.

Junankar, P. N. & Pope, D. 1990, *Immigration, Wages and Price Stability*, Bureau of Immigration Research, AGPS, Canberra.

Kakazu, H. 1994, 'Northeast Asian Regional Economic Cooperation', in M. Thant, M. Tang & H. Kakazu (eds), *Growth Triangles in Asia: A New Approach to Regional Economic Cooperation*, Oxford University Press, Hong Kong, pp. 243–76.

Kanjanapan, W. 1992, 'White-Collar Foreign Workers in Taiwan', *Asian and Pacific Migration Journal*, no. 1/3–4, pp. 569–84.

Kenen, P. B. 1971, 'Migration, the Terms of Trade and Economic Welfare in the Source Country', in J. N. Bhagwati et al. (ed.), *Trade, Balance of Payments and Growth*, North-Holland, Amsterdam.

King, R. G. & Levine, R. 1993a, 'Finance and Growth: Schumpeter Might Be Right', *Quarterly Journal of Economics*, no. 108, pp. 717–38.

_____ 1993b, 'Finance, Entrepreneurship, and Growth', *Journal of Monetary Economics*, no. 32, pp. 513–42.

Kirkby, R. J. R. 1985, *Urbanization in China: Town and Country in a Developing Economy 1949–2000 AD*, Columbia University Press, New York.

Komiya, R. 1967, 'Non-Traded Goods and the Price Theory of International Trade', *International Economic Review*, no. 8, pp. 132–52.

Korean Ministry of Labor 1994, 'White Paper on Employment of Unskilled Foreign Workers', Seoul, December.

Kormendi, R. C. & Meguire, P. G. 1985, 'Macroeconomic Determinants of Growth: Cross-Country Evidence', *Journal of Monetary Economics*, no. 16, pp. 141–63.

Krauss, M. B. 1976, 'The Economics of the "Guest Worker" Problem: A Neo-Heckscher–Ohlin Approach', *Scandinavian Journal of Economics*, no. 78, pp. 470–6.

Kristof, N. D. 1993, 'The Rise of China', *Foreign Affairs*, vol. 72, no. 5, pp. 59–74.

Kritz, M. M. & Caces, C. 1989, 'Science and Technology Transfers and Migration Flows, Population and Development Program 1989', Working Paper Series 1.02, Cornell University, Ithaca.

Krugman, P. 1979, 'Increasing Returns, Monopolistic Competition and International Trade', *Journal of International Economics*, no. 9, pp. 469–79.

_____ 1987, 'The Narrow Moving Band, The Dutch Disease, and the Competitive Consequences of Mrs Thatcher', *Journal of Development Economics*, no. 27, pp. 41–55.

_____ 1991a, 'Is Bilateralism Bad?', in E. Helpman & A. Razin, 1993, *International Trade and Trade Policy*, MIT Press, Cambridge, Mass.

_____ 1991b, 'The Move to Free Trade Zones', *Federal Reserve Bank of Kansas Review*, December.

Kwong, K. 1992, 'Study Shows Brain Drain on Rise Again', *Sunday Morning Post*, Hong Kong, June.

Lancaster, K. J. 1979, *Variety, Equity and Efficiency*, Columbia University Press, New York.

Lardy, N. R. 1994, *China in the World Economy*, Institute for International Economics, Washington, DC.

Lawrence, R. 1987, 'Imports in Japan: Closed Markets or Closed Minds?', *Brookings Papers on Economic Activity*, Brookings Institution, Washington.

Levine, R. & Renelt, D. 1992, 'A Sensitivity Analysis of Cross-Country Growth Regressions', *American Economic Review*, no. 82, pp. 942–63.

Lewis, P. E. T. 1994, 'Singaporean Entrepreneurs–The Australian Connection', *Journal of Enterprising Culture*, vol. 2, no. 2, pp. 709–33.

Li, S. M. & Siu, Y. M. 1994, 'Population Mobility', in Y. M. Yeung & D. K. Y. Chu (eds), *Guangdong: Survey of a Province Undergoing Rapid Change*, The Chinese University Press, Hong Kong, pp. 373–400.

Lim, L. 1994, 'International Labour Migration in Asia: Patterns, Implications, and Policies', in M. Macura & D. Coleman (eds), *International Migration: Regional Processes and Responses*, Economic Studies no. 7, United Nations, New York.

Lim, L. & Abella, M. 1994, 'The Movement of People in Asia: Internal, Intra-Regional and International Migration', *Asian and Pacific Migration Journal*, vol. 3, nos 2–3, pp. 209–50.

Lin, C. P. 1994, 'China's Students Abroad: Rates of Return', *The American Enterprise*, vol. 5, no. 6, pp. 12–14.

Lloyd, P. J. 1982, 'The Effects of Immigration on Economic Growth via Technological Change and Economies of Scale', in D. Douglas (ed.), *The Economics of Australian Immigration*, Proceedings of the Conference on the Economics of Immigration, 8–9 February 1982, Sydney University Extension Programme, Sydney.

_____ 1991, *The Future of CER: A Single Market for Australia and New Zealand*, Victoria University Press for the Institute of Policy Studies, Wellington.

Low, L. 1994, 'Migration and Singapore: Implications for the Asia Pacific', *Asian and Pacific Migration Journal*, vol. 3, nos 2–3, pp. 251–63.

Low, L., Toh, M. H. & Soon, T. W. 1991, *Economics of Education and Manpower Developments, Issues and Policies in Singapore*, McGraw-Hill, Singapore.

Lucas, R.E. 1988, 'On the Mechanics of Economic Development', *Journal of Monetary Economics*, no. 22, pp. 3–42.

Macura, M. 1994, 'Overview', in M. Macura & D. Coleman (eds), *International Migration: Regional Processes and Responses*, Economic Studies no. 7, United Nations, New York, pp. 1–20.

Maddison, A. 1982, *Phases of Capitalist Development*, Oxford University Press, Oxford.

Malakellis, M. 1993, 'Illustrative Results from ORANI-INT: An Intertemporal GCE Model of the Australian Economy', Impact Project Preliminary Working Paper OP-77, Monash University, Melbourne.

Mankiw, N. G., Romer, D. & Weil, D. N. 1992, 'A Contribution to the Empirics of Economic Growth', *Quarterly Journal of Economics*, no. 107, pp. 407–37.

Markusen, J. R. 1983, 'Factor Movements and Commodity Trade as Complements', *Journal of International Economics*, no. 14, pp. 341–56.

_____ 1995, 'The Boundaries of Multinational Enterprises and the Theory of International Trade', *Journal of Economic Perspectives*, no. 9, Spring, 169–89.

Markusen, J. R. & Melvin, J. R. 1981, 'Trade, Factor Prices, and the Gains from Trade with Increasing Returns to Scale', *Canadian Journal of Economics*, no. 14, pp. 450–69.

Martin, P. 1991, 'Labor Migration in Asia', *International Migration Review*, no. 25/1, pp. 176–93.

_____ 1993, *Trade and Migration: NAFTA and Agriculture*, Institute for International Economics, Washington, DC.

_____ 1994, 'Development, Employment and Migration', *Asian and Pacific Migration Journal*, no. 3/2–3, pp. 511–20.

_____ 1995, Temporary Worker Programs, Paper presented at Conference on Migration and Migration Policy, The International Experience at MIT, Cambridge, Mass.

Martin, P., Wallace, H., Emerson, R., Taylor, J.E. & Rochen, R. (eds) 1995, *Immigration Reform and US Agriculture*, Division of Agriculture and Natural Resources, Berkeley, California.

Marwah, K. & Klein, L. 1995, 'The Possibility of Nesting South Asia in Asia Pacific Integration', *Journal of Asian Economics*, vol. 6, no. 1, pp. 1–27.

Massey, D. 1995, Remarks at a State Department Meeting.

Matsuyama, K. 1992, 'Agricultural Productivity, Comparative Advantage and Economic Growth', *Journal of Economic Theory*, no. 58, pp. 317–34.

McDougall, R. 1993, 'Incorporating International Capital Mobility into Salter', Salter Working Paper no. 21, Industry Commission, Canberra.

McKinnon, R. I. 1973, *Money and Capital in Economic Development*, Brookings Institution, Washington, DC.

Meade, J. E. 1955, *Trade and Welfare*, Oxford University Press, London.

Melvin, J. R. 1969, 'Increasing Returns to Scale as a Determinant of Trade', *Canadian Journal of Economics*, no. 2, pp. 389–402.

Miao, J. H. 1994, 'International Migration in China: A Survey of Emigrants from Shanghai', *Asia and Pacific Migration Journal*, vol. 3, nos 2–3, pp. 445–63.

Minocha, U. 1987, 'South Asian Immigrants: Trends and Impacts on the Sending and Receiving Societies', in J. T. Fawcett & B. V. Carino (eds), *Pacific Bridges: The New Immigration from Asia and the Pacific Islands*, Center for Migration Studies, Staten Island, New York, pp. 347–74.

Mori, H. 1994, 'Migrant Workers and Labor Market Segmentation in Japan', *Asian and Pacific Migration Journal*, no. 3/4, pp. 619–38.

Morita, K. & Sassen, S. 1994, 'The New Illegal Immigration to Japan, 1980–1992', *International Migration Review*, no. 28/1, pp. 153–63.

M. S. J. Keys Young Planners 1990, *Expectations and Experiences: A Survey of Business Migrants*, AGPS, Canberra.

Mulligan, C. B. & Sala-i-Martin, X. 1993, 'Transitional Dynamics in Two-Sector Models of Endogenous Growth', *Quarterly Journal of Economics*, no. 108, pp. 737–73.

Mundell, R. A. 1957, 'International Trade and Factor Mobility', *American Economic Review*, no. 47, pp. 321–37.

Myers, W. H. 1993, 'Statement to the Subcommittee on International Security, International Organizations and Human Rights', mimeo, Committee on Foreign Affairs, House of Representatives, 4 November, The Centre for the Study of Asian Organized Crime, Philadelphia.

Nagayama, T. 1992, 'Clandestine Migrant Workers in Japan', *Asian and Pacific Migration Journal*, no. 1/3–4, pp. 623–36.

Nakagawa, S. 1994, Dekassegui Migration: Immigration Policy and Brazilian Migrants in Japan, MA Thesis, Department of Sociology, University of Texas at Austin.

Nana, G. 1995, 'Developing a Dynamic Multi-Sectoral CGE Model of the New Zealand Economy', Working Paper 12/95, Graduate School of Business and Government Management, Victoria University of Wellington.

Nana, G., Hall, V., & Philpott, B. forthcoming, 'Trans-Tasman CGE Modelling: Some Results from the Joani Model', *Economic Modelling*.

Nana, G. & Philpott, B. 1983, 'The 38-sector Joanna Model', RPEP Occasional Paper no. 73, Victoria University of Wellington.

———— 1988, 'The JOANI Two Country General Equilibrium Model: Data Base and Equations', RPEP Occasional Paper no. 92, Victoria University of Wellington.

National Population Council (NPC) 1990, 'Emigration', Population Report no. 9, AGPS, Canberra.

Nayyar, D. 1994, 'International Labor Movements, Trade Flows and Migration Transitions: A Theoretical Perspective', *Asian and Pacific Migration Journal*, no. 3/1, pp. 31–47.

Neary, P. 1988, 'Determinants of the Equilibrium Real Exchange Rate', *American Economic Review*, no. 78, pp. 210–15.

Nerlove, M., Razin, A. & Sadka, E. 1982, 'Population Size and the Social Welfare Functions of Bentham and Mill', *Economics Letters*, no. 10, pp. 61–4.

Nesdale, D., Simkin, K., Sang, D., Burke, B. & Fraser, S. 1995, *International Students and Immigration*, AGPS, Canberra.

New Zealand Immigration Service (NZIS) 1994, *Immigration Fact Pack*, Issue 1, December, Department of Labour, Wellington.

—— 1995, *Immigration Fact Pack*, Issue 2, February, Department of Labour, Wellington.

Noiriel, C. 1993, 'Labor Rights in Selected Asian Countries', *Asian and Pacific Migration Journal*, no. 2/2, pp. 147–60.

Ohlin, B. 1933, *Interregional and International Trade*, Harvard University Press, Cambridge, Mass.

Organisation for Economic Co-operation and Development (OECD) 1994, *Migration and Development: New Partnerships for Co-operation*, OECD, Paris.

Pacific Economic Cooperation Council (PECC) 1993, *Human Resource Development Outlook 1993–94: Migration and Labour Flows in Selected Pacific Economies*, Times Academic Press, Singapore.

—— 1994, *Human Resource Development Outlook 1994–95: Investment and Labour Flows in Selected Pacific Economies*, Times Academic Press, Singapore.

Pang Eng Fong 1993a, Labour Migration, Economic Development and Regionalisation in Pacific Asia, Paper presented at the OECD Conference on Migration and International Co-operation, Challenges for OECD Countries, held in Madrid 29–31 March.

—— 1993b, *Regionalisation and Labour Flows in Pacific Asia*, OECD, Paris.

—— 1994, 'An Eclectic Approach to Turning Points in Migration', *Asian and Pacific Migration Journal*, no. 3, vol. 1, pp. 81–91.

Pangestu, M. & Stephenson, S. 1995, 'Implementing the Uruguay Round in APEC', in B. Bora & M. Pangestu. (eds), *Priority Issues in Trade Liberalisation: Implications for the Asia Pacific Region*, Pacific Economic Cooperation Council, Singapore.

Papademetriou, D., Bach, R., Johnson, K., Kramer, R., Lowell, B. & Smith, S. 1989, 'The Effects of Immigration on the US. Economy and Labour Market', Immigration Policy and Research Report 1, US Department of Labour, Washington.

Park, Y. 1994, 'The Turning Point in International Migration and Economic Development in Korea', *Asian and Pacific Migration Journal*, no. 3/1, pp. 149–74.

Pearson, C. 1994, 'The Asian Export Ladder' in S. Yang (ed.), *Manufactured Exports of East Asian Industrialising Economies*, M. E. Sharpe, Armonk, New York.

Petri, P. 1993, 'The East Asian Trading Bloc: An Analytical History', in J. Frankel & M. Kahler (eds), *Regionalism and Rivalry: Japan and the United States in the Asia Pacific*, University of Chicago Press, Chicago.

—— 1995, 'The Interdependence of Trade and Investment in the Pacific', in E. Y. Chen & P. Drysdale (eds), *Corporate Links and Foreign Direct Investment in Asia and the Pacific*, Harper Educational, Sydney.

Philpott, B. & Nana, G. 1988, 'Quantitative Implications of Australia–New Zealand Free Trade: A Two Country General Equilibrium Model Analysis', RPEP Occasional Paper no. 93, Victoria University of Wellington.

Pindyck, R. S. & Rubinfeld, D. L. 1981, *Econometric Models and Economic Forecasts*, McGraw-Hill, New York.

Plafker, T. 1995, 'China Fights Brain Drain', *International Herald Tribune*, 24 April.

Pookong, K. 1994, 'Introduction', *Asian and Pacific Migration Journal*, no. 3/2–3, pp. 203–7.

Pool, I. (ed.) 1980, *Trans-Tasman Migration: Proceedings of a Workshop on Population Flow Between Australia and New Zealand and Vice-Versa*, Population Studies Centre, University of Waikato.

Poot, J. 1993 'Trans-Tasman Migration and Economic Growth in Australasia', in G. A. Carmichael (ed.), *Trans-Tasman Migration: Trends, Causes and Consequences*, AGPS, Canberra.

_____ 1995, 'Do Borders Matter? A Model of Interregional Migration in Australasia', Discussion Paper no. 622, Institute of Socio-Economic Planning, University of Tsukuba.

Poot, J., Nana, G. & Philpott, B. 1988, *International Migration and the New Zealand Economy: A Long-Run Perspective*, Institute of Policy Studies, Wellington.

Poston, D. L., Mao, M. X. X. & Yu, M. Y. 1994, 'The Global Distribution of the Overseas Chinese Around 1990', *Population and Development Review*, vol. 20, no. 3, pp. 631–45.

Quibria, M. G. 1986, 'Migrant Workers and Remittances: Issues for Asian Developing Countries', *Asian Development Review*, no. 4, pp. 78–99.

_____ 1988a, 'A Note on International Migration, Non-Traded Goods and Economic Welfare in the Source Country', *Journal of Development Economics*, no. 30, pp. 377–87.

_____ 1988b, 'On Generalizing the Economic Analysis of International Migration: A Note', *Canadian Journal of Economics*, no. 31, pp. 177–83.

_____ 1989a, 'Neoclassical Political Economy: An Application to Trade Policy', *Journal of Economic Surveys*, no. 3, pp. 107–36.

_____ 1989b, 'International Migration and Real Wages: Is There Any Neo-classical Ambiguity?', *Journal of Development Economics*, no. 31, pp. 874–83.

_____ 1990a, 'A Note on International Migration and the Social Welfare Function', *Bulletin of Economic Research*, no. 42, 141–53.

_____ 1990b, 'Note on International Differences in Service Prices and Some Related Empirical Phenomena', *Journal of Development Economics*, no. 33, pp. 357–70.

_____ 1993, 'International Migration, Increasing Returns and Real Wages', *Canadian Journal of Economics*, no. 26, pp. 457–68.

_____ 1994, 'International Migration in Asia: Facts, Issues and Policies', *Journal of Behavioral and Social Sciences*, no. 4, pp. 1–20.

_____ 1995, 'International Migration, Remittances and Income Distribution in the Source-Country: A Synthesis', *Bulletin of Economic Research*.

Quibria, M. G. & Rivera-Batiz, F. 1989, 'International Migration and Real Wages: A Resolution Note', *Journal of Development Economics*, no. 31, pp. 193–4.

Quibria, M. G. & Thant, M. 1988, 'International Migration, Emigrants' Remittances and Asian Developing Countries: Economic Analysis and Policy Issues', in J. Dutta (ed.), *Asian Industrialization and Changing Economic Structures*, Jai Press, Greenwich.

Razin, A. & Sadka, E. 1993, 'Interactions Between International Migration and International Trade: Positive and Normative Aspects', Working Paper no. 4–93, Foerder Institute of Economic Research, Tel Aviv University.

Richards, A. 1993, 'Does Trade Liberalisation Influence Migration? Some Evidence from Developing Countries', Paper delivered to a conference entitled Migration and

International Co-operation: Challenges for OECD Countries, organised by the OECD, Canada and Spain, Madrid @9–31 March 1993.

Richmond, A. H. 1991, International Migration and Global Change, Paper presented at International Conference on Migration, Centre for Advanced Studies, Faculty of Arts and Social Sciences, National University of Singapore, February.

Rivera-Batiz, F. L. 1982, 'International Labor Migration, Non-Traded Goods and Economic Welfare in the Source Country', *Journal of Development Economics*, no. 11, pp. 81–90.

Rod, T. & Webster, E. 1995, *Immigration and Trade with East Asia in the Food Industry*, AGPS, Canberra.

Romer, P. M. 1994, 'The Origins of Endogenous Growth', *Journal of Economic Perspectives*, no. 8, pp. 3–22.

Roubini, N. & Sala-i-Martin, X. 1992, 'Financial Repression and Economic Growth', *Journal of Development Economics*, no. 39, pp. 5–30.

Rubin, K. 1995, 'Homeward Bound', *Far Eastern Economic Review*, 18 May, p. 74.

Ruffin, R. J. 1984, 'International Factor Movements', in R. W. Jones & P. B. Kenen (eds), *Handbook of International Economics*, vol. II, North-Holland, Amsterdam.

Russell, S. S. & Teitelbaum, M. S. 1992, 'International Migration and International Trade', World Bank Discussion Paper no. 160.

_____ 1992, 'Migrant Remittances and Development', *International Migration Review*, vol. XXX, no. 3/4, pp. 267–87.

Sachs, J. D. & Warner, A. M. 1994, *Natural Resources and Economic Growth*, Harvard University Press, Cambridge, Mass.

_____ 1995, 'Economic Convergence and Economic Policies', Working Paper series no. 5039, National Bureau of Economic Research, February.

Saith, A. 1987, 'Macroeconomic Issues in International Migration: A Review', mimeo, International Labor Organization, New Delhi.

Salt, J. 1994, International Movements of Highly Skilled Labour, Paper prepared for the Secretariat, Working Party on Migration, Organisation for Economic Co-operation and Development/Directorate for Education, Employment, Labour and Social Affairs/Employment, Labour and Social Affairs Committee.

Samuel, T. J. 1993, 'Asian and Pacific Migration: the Canadian Experience', *Asia-Pacific Migration Affecting Australia Conference Proceedings*, BIPR, Darwin.

Sassen, S. 1988, *The Mobility of Labour and Capital: A Study of International Investment and Labor Flow*, Cambridge University Press, New York.

Saunders, P. & King, A. 1994, *Immigration and the Distribution of Income*, AGPS, Canberra.

Schiff, M. 1994, 'How Trade, Aid and Remittances Affect International Migration', World Bank Policy Research Working Paper 1376.

Seaward, N. 1988, 'High Stakes Investment in the Private Sector', *Far Eastern Economic Review*, 1 September, pp. 54–5.

Segal, A. 1993, *An Atlas of International Migration*, Hans Zell Publishers, London.

Selya, R. M. 1992, 'Illegal Migration in Taiwan: A Preliminary Overview', *International Migration Review*, vol. XXVI, no. 3, pp. 787–805.

Shah, N. 1993, Migration Between Asian Countries and Its Likely Future, Paper presented in Expert Group Meeting on Population Distribution and Migration, Bolivia, 18–22 January.

Shambaugh, D. 1993, 'Introduction: The Emergence of "Greater China"', *The China Quarterly*, no. 136, pp. 653–8.

Sharma, Y. 1991, 'Brain Gain as Recession Hits Western Countries', *Business Times* (Hong Kong), 1 April, p. 606.

Shaw, E.S. 1973, *Financial Deepening in Economic Development*, Oxford University Press, Oxford.

Shu, J., Khoo, S. E., Struik, A. & McKenzie, F. 1995, *Australia's Population Trends and Prospects 1994*, AGPS, Canberra.

Sinn, E. 1995, 'Emigration from Hong Kong before 1941: General Trends', in R. Skeldon (ed.), *Emigration from Hong Kong: Tendencies and Impacts*, Chinese University Press, Hong Kong, pp. 11–34.

Skeldon, R. 1986, 'Hong Kong and its Hinterland: A Case of International Rural-to-Urban Migration', *Asian Geographer*, vol. 5, no. 1, pp. 1–24.

_____ 1992a, 'International Migration Within and From the East and Southeast Asian Region: A Review Essay', *Asian and Pacific Migration Review*, vol. 1, no. 1, pp. 19–63.

_____ 1992b, 'The Relationship Between Migration and Development in the ESCAP Region', *Migration and Urbanization in Asia and the Pacific*, Asian Population Studies Series no. 111, Economic and Social Commission for Asia and the Pacific, New York, United Nations, pp. 45–62.

_____ 1992c, 'On Mobility and Fertility Transitions in East and Southeast Asia', *Asian and Pacific Migration Journal*, no. 1/2, pp. 220–49.

_____ 1994a, 'East Asian Migration and the Changing World Order', in W. T. S. Gould & A. M. Findlay (eds), *Population Migration and the Changing World Order*, Belhaven, London, pp. 173–93.

_____ 1994b, 'Hong Kong in an International Migration System', in R. Skeldon (ed.), *Reluctant Exiles? Migration from Hong Kong and the New Overseas Chinese*, M. E. Sharpe, New York, and Hong Kong University Press, Hong Kong, pp. 21–51.

_____ 1994c, 'Turning Points in Labor Migration: The Case of Hong Kong', *Asian and Pacific Migration Journal*, vol. 3, no. 1, pp. 93–118.

_____ 1995, Hong Kong and South China Growth Linkages, Paper presented at the Forum on Regionalization and Labour Market Interdependence in East and South-East Asia, International Institute for Labour Studies, Bangkok, 23–26 January.

_____ 1995, 'Emigration from Hong Kong 1945–94: The Demographic Lead-up to 1997', in R. Skeldon (ed.), *Emigration from Hong Kong: Tendencies and Impacts*, Chinese University Press, Hong Kong, pp. 51–77.

SOPEMI 1994, *Trends in International Migration: Annual Report 1993*, OECD, Paris.

Spence, J. D. 1990, *The Search for Modern China*, Hutchinson, London.

Stahl, C. W., Ball, R., Inglis, C. & Gutman, P. 1993, *Global Population Movements and their Implications for Australia*, Australian Government Printer, Canberra.

Stalker, P. 1994, *The Work of Strangers: A Survey of International Labour Migration*, ILO, Geneva.

Stark, O. 1991, *The Migration of Labor*, Basil Blackwell, Cambridge, Mass.

Stolper, W. F. & Samuelson, P. A. 1941, 'Protection and Real Wages', *Review of Economic Studies IX*, November 1941. Reprinted in Readings in H. S. Ellis & L. A. Metzler (eds) 1950, *Theory of International Trade*, Blakiston, Philadelphia.

Stromback, T., Biffl, G., Bushe-Jones, S., Clarke, J., Dawkins, P., Nicholls, S. & Preston, A. 1993, *Immigration, Skill Transfer and Restructuring in Western Australia*, AGPS, Canberra.

Struik, A. & Ward, D. 1992, 'The extent and consequences of emigration from Australia', *Second National Outlook Conference Proceedings*, BIR, Melbourne, pp. 227–43.

Sung, Yun-Wing 1992, Non-Institutional Economic Integration via Cultural Affinity: The Case of Mainland China, Taiwan and Hong Kong, Paper presented at the International Symposium on the Coordination of Chinese Economic Systems, organised by the Hong Kong Society of Asia and Pacific 21 Ltd, the Democracy Foundation (Taiwan), and the Centre for East West Studies in Hong Kong, Hong Kong, January.

Swamy, G. 1981, 'International Migrant Workers' Remittances: Issues and Prospects', World Bank Staff Working Paper no. 481.

Swan, N., Auer, L., Chenard, D., de Plaa, A., de Silva, A., Palmer, D. & Serjak, J. 1991, *Economic and Social Impacts of Immigration*, Economic Council of Canada, Ottawa.

Taubman, W. 1993, 'Socio-Economic Development and Rural–Urban Migration in China since the Beginning of the 1980s', University of Macau, China Economic Research Centre, Discussion Paper Series.

Taylor, A. M. 1994a, 'Domestic Saving and International Capital Flows Reconsidered', Working Paper Series no. 4892, National Bureau of Economic Research, October.

———— 1994b, 'Tres fases del crecimiento económico argentino', *Revista de Historia Económica*, no. 12, pp. 649–83.

Taylor, A. M. & Williamson, J. G. 1994, 'Convergence in the Age of Mass Migration', Working Paper Series no. 4711, National Bureau of Economic Research.

Taylor, J. E. 1987, 'Undocumented Mexico–US Migration and the Returns to Households in Rural Mexico', *American Journal of Agricultural Economics*, no. 69, pp. 626–38.

Than, M. 1994, The Growth Quadrangle of the Mainland Southeast Asia, Paper presented at the Fourth Southeast Asia Roundtable on Economic Development: Growth Triangles in Southeast Asia, organised by the Institute of Strategic and International Studies, Kuala Lumpur, 27–28 June.

Thayer, N. 1995, 'Saints and Sinners', *Far Eastern Economic Review*, 23 March, p. 29.

The Economist 1994a, 'Canada: Less Welcome', 5 November, p. 42.

———— 1994b, 'Japan: No Surrender', 10 December, pp. 24–5.

———— 1995, 'Immigration: Tucson or Bust', 20 May, p. 35.

The World Bank 1994, *World Data 1994: World Bank Indicators on CD-ROM*, The World Bank, Washington, DC.

The World Bank, *The World Bank Atlas*, Washington, DC.

Thompson, H. 1984, 'International Migration, Non-traded Goods and Economic Welfare in the Source Country: A Comment', *Journal of Development Economics*, no. 16, pp. 321–24.

Thornton, E. 1995, 'What Shortage?', *Far Eastern Economic Review*, 25 May 1995, p. 59.

Tran, M. 1990, 'Brains Behind the US—Brought from Abroad', *Guardian Weekly*, 30 December.

Tsay, C. 1992, 'Clandestine Labor Migration to Taiwan', *Asian and Pacific Migration Journal*, no. 1, pp. 637–55.

———— 1992, 'Clandestine Labor Migration to Taiwan', *Asian and Pacific Migration Journal*, no. 1/3–4, pp. 637–55.

Tung, R. 1988, *The New Expatriates: Managing Human Resources Abroad*, Ballinger Publishing Company, Cambridge, Mass.

_____ 1993, Taiwan and Southern China's Fukien and Kwangtung Provinces, Paper presented at the Conference on Taiwan in the Asia–Pacific in the 1990s at Australian National University, Canberra.

UNESCO 1994, *Statistical Yearbook 1994*, UNESCO, Paris.

United Nations Conference on Trade and Development (UNCTAD) 1993, *World Investment Report 1993: Transnational Corporations and Integrated International Production*, United Nations, New York and Geneva.

_____ 1994a, *Liberalising International Transactions in Services*, United Nations, New York.

_____ 1994b, *World Investment Report 1994: Transnational Corporations, Employment and the Workplace*, United Nations, New York.

United Nations 1993, *World Population Prospects: The 1992 Revision*, United Nations, New York.

US Commission for the Study of International Migration and Cooperative Economic Development 1990, *Unauthorized Migration: An Economic Development Response*, US Government Printing Office, Washington, DC.

Uzawa, H. 1965, 'Optimum Technical Change in an Aggregative Model of Economic Growth', *International Economic Review*, no. 6 , pp. 18–31.

Vasuprasat, P. 1994, 'Turning Points in International Migration: A Case Study of Thailand', *Asian and Pacific Migration Journal*, no. 3/1, pp. 175–202.

Vatikiotis, M., Clifford, M. & McBeth, J. 1994, 'The Lure of Asia', *Far Eastern Economic Review*, 3 February, pp. 32–4.

Vines, D. 1995, 'Unfinished Business: Australian Protectionism, Australian Trade Liberalisation, and APEC', *Australian Economic Review*, First Quarter, 35–58.

Wang, G. 1991, 'Merchants Without Empires: The Hokkien Sojourning Communities', in Wang Gungwu, *China and the Overseas Chinese*, Times Academic Press, Singapore, pp. 79–101.

Wang, Y.C. 1966, *Chinese Intellectuals and the West*, University of North Carolina Press, Chapel Hill.

Warren, R. 1994, 'Estimates of Unauthorised Immigrant Population Residing in the United States, by Country of Origin and State of Residence: October 1992', INS Statistical Division, Washington, DC, 29 April.

Watanabe, S. 1994, 'The Lewisian Turning Point and International Migration: The Case of Japan', *Asian and Pacific Migration Journal*, no. 3/1, pp. 119–48.

Widgren, J. 1987, International Migration: New Challenges to Europe, Report prepared for the Third Conference of European Ministers Responsible for Migration, organized by the Council of Europe, Portugal, 13–15 May.

Withers, G. 1988, 'Immigration and Australian Economic Growth', in L. Baker & P. Miller (eds), *The Economics of Immigration: Proceedings of a Conference at the Australian National University 22–23 April 1987*, AGPS, Canberra.

Wong, K. Y. 1986a, 'The Economic Analysis of International Migration: A Generalization', *Canadian Journal of Economics*, no. 19, pp. 357–62.

_____ 1986b, 'Are International Trade and Factor Mobility Substitutes?', *Journal of International Economics*, no. 21, pp. 25–43.

_____ 1988, 'International Factor Mobility and the Volume of Trade: An Empirical Study', in R. Feenstra (ed.), *Empirical Methods for International Trade*, MIT Press, Cambridge, Mass., pp. 231–50.

_____ 1994, 'International Trade in Goods and Factor Mobility', unpublished manuscript.

Wooden, M. 1994, 'The Economic Impact of Immigration', in M. Wooden, R. Holton, G. Hugo & J. Sloan (eds), *Australian Immigration: A Survey of the Issues*, second edition, AGPS, Canberra, pp. 111–57.

World Bank 1993, *East Asian Miracle*, World Bank, Washington.

_____ 1994, *East Asia's Trade and Investment: Regional and Global Gains from Liberalisation*, World Bank, Washington.

Wu, C. & Inglis, C. 1992, 'Illegal Immigration to Hong Kong', *Asian and Pacific Migration Journal*, no. 1/3–4, pp. 601–21.

Yatsko, P. 1995, 'Call Home', *Far Eastern Economic Review*, 26 January, pp. 50–2.

Yoon, B. L. 1992, 'Reverse Brain Drain in South Korea: State-Led Model', *Studies in Comparative International Development*, vol. 27, no. 1, pp. 4–26.

Young, A. 1991, 'Learning By Doing and the Dynamic Effects of International Trade', *Quarterly Journal of Economics*, no. 106, pp. 369–406.

Yukowa, J. 1994, 'Asian Migration in the Media', *Asian Migrant*, vol. 7, no. 4, pp. 121–30.

Zhang, J. X. 1995, The Chinese Labour Export Market, Paper presented at the Technical Seminar: Migration and the Labour Market in Asia in the Year 2000, OECD and Japan Institute of Labour, Tokyo, 19–20 January.

Zielenziger, M. & Rees, J. 1995, 'Back from the Diaspora', *Far Eastern Economic Review*, 18 May, p. 38.

Index